The Comparative History of Public Policy

Europe and the International Order

Series Editor: Joel Krieger

Published

Abram de Swaan, *In Care of the State*
Peter A. Hall, *Governing the Economy*
Judith Adler Hellman, *Journeys Among Women*
Jane Jensen, Elisabeth Hagen and Ceallaigh
Reddy (eds), *Feminization of the Labor Force*
Joel Krieger, *Reagan, Thatcher and the Politics of Decline*
George Ross, Stanley Hoffmann and Sylvia
Malzacher (eds), *The Mitterrand Experiment*

Forthcoming

Russell Dalton, Manfred Kuechler (eds), *Challenging the Political Order:*
New Social and Political Movements in Western Democracies
Mark Kesselman, *Socialism without the Workers:*
A Critical Appraisal of the Mitterrand Presidency
Andrei Markovits, *The West German Left:*
Red, Green and Beyond
David Stark, *Politics and Work in a Socialist Society*

The Comparative History of Public Policy

Edited by

FRANCIS G. CASTLES

Oxford University Press · New York
1989

Oxford University Press

Oxford New York Toronto
Delhi Bombay Calcutta Madras Karachi
Petaling Jaya Singapore Hong Kong Tokyo
Nairobi Dar es Salaam Cape Town
Melbourne Auckland
and associated companies in
Berlin Ibadan

First published 1989 by Polity Press in association with Basil Blackwell.

First published 1989 in North America by Oxford University Press, Inc.,
200 Madison Avenue, New York, New York 10016.

Library of Congress Cataloging-in-Publication Data

The comparative history of public policy / edited by Francis G.
Castles.
    p. cm.
    "First published 1989 by Polity Press in association with Basil
Blackwell"—T.p. verso.
    Bibliography: p.
    Includes index.
    ISBN 0-19-520794-7
    1. Policy sciences. 2. Political planning. 3. Comparative
government. I. Castles, Francis Geoffrey.
    H97.C63   1989
320'.6—dc20   89-3385
                                                           CIP
    ISBN 0-19-520794-7

Typeset in 10½ on 12 pt Ehrhardt
by Hope Services, Abingdon
Printed in Great Britain by T. J. Press (Padstow) Ltd

Contents

Notes on Contributors

Edwin Amenta is Assistant Professor of Sociology at New York University. He is author of numerous articles on the politics of public policy and is currently undertaking research on taxation and social spending policies in depression and war.

Francis G. Castles is Senior Research Fellow in Political Science in the Research School of Social Sciences at the Australian National University and was formerly Professor of Comparative Politics at the Open University. He was amongst the pioneers of the 'politics matters' school of quantitive, comparative public policy analysis and is the author of books on public policy development in both Scandinavia and Australasia. He was the editor of *The Impact of Parties*, an earlier collaborative research endeavour in the comparative public policy field.

Patrick Dunleavy is Reader in Government at the London School of Economics and Political Science. His books include *The Politics of Mass Housing in Britain, 1945–75*, *Urban Political Analysis*, *British Democracy at the Crossroads* and a recent text on *Theories of the State*. He is co-editor of the series *Developments in British Politics*.

T.J. Pempel has been a member of the faculty of the Cornell University Government Department since 1972 and between 1980 and 1985 was Director of the University's China–Japan Programme. He is author or editor of seven books, the most recent of which are *Policy and Politics in Japan – Creative Conservatism*, *Japan: Dilemmas of Success and Democratic Oddities* and *One Party Dominant Regimes*.

Manfred G. Schmidt is Professor of Political Science at the University of Heidelberg. He has published extensively on comparative public policy in both German and English. His books include *CDU und SPD an der Regierung, Wohlfahrtstaatliche Politik unter bürgerlichen* and *Sozialdemokratischen Regierungen* (for which he received the Stein Rokkan prize), *Der Schweizerische Weg zur Vollbeschäftigung* and *Socialpolitik: Historische Entwicklung und internationaler Vergleich*.

Michael Shalev is Senior Lecturer in Sociology and Political Science at the Hebrew University of Jerusalem. He has written on the comparative political economy of advanced capitalist democracies with special reference to labour relations and public policy. Dr Shalev's research on the labour movement in Isarel and its relationship to wider political-economic developments is the subject of a forthcoming book entitled *Labour and the Political Economy in Israel*.

Theda Skocpol is Professor of Sociology at Harvard and was previously Professor of Sociology and Political Science at the University of Chicago. Her books include *States and Social Revolutions, Bringing the State Back In* and *The Politics of Social Policy in the United States*. She is currently completing a book on US social policies in historical and comparative perspective.

Göran Therborn is Professor of Sociology at the University of Gothenburg in Sweden and was formerly Professor of Political Science at the Catholic University of Nijmegen in the Netherlands. His books include *Science, Class and Society, What Does the Ruling Class Do When It Rules?, The Ideology of Power* and *Why Some Peoples Are More Unemployed Than Others*.

Acknowledgements

The research group on The Comparative History of Public Policy has a long history as an idea and a short one as an actual project. The value of examining the origins of national public policy distinctiveness in comparative perspective arose in the late 1970s in the context of the earlier European Consortium for Political Research project on Party Differences and Public Policy. At that time, however, the mapping of the cross-national determinants of a wide variety of policy outcomes in democratic capitalist states appeared a greater priority, and the comparative history approach did not feature in the volume of findings published by the Party Differences research group in 1982.

Thereafter the idea of a subsequent research volume on the origins of national public policy distinctiveness was frequently rehearsed in discussions between Professor Schmidt and the Editor, both members of the original ECPR project, but failed to come to fruition due to the pressure of other commitments and to problems of research funding. Both bottlenecks were resolved early in 1986. The Editor took up the post of Senior Research Fellow in Political Science in the Research School of Social Sciences at the Australian National University, which permitted him the luxury of a fulltime commitment to research as well as conditions of service ideal for organizing a substantial international collaborative research project. In this day and age, such institutions are rare and becoming rarer, and the Editor wishes to acknowledge his indebtedness to the ANU for making this project possible.

To no less a degree, all members of the project wish to acknowledge the intellectual encouragement and financial support of the Research Unit for Societal Developments (RSD) of the University of Mannheim in West Germany. This new policy research unit was founded by

Professor Rudolf Wildenmann, and it was when he took the Comparative History project under the RSD's protective wing that the second bottleneck was overcome. Good collaborative work involves intensive exchange of views and when the scholars engaged in a project come from four continents that involves great expense. Moreover, it is expense that is not readily met by national funding bodies, which, irrespective of the pay-offs, are reluctant to fund travel and living expenses for 'foreign' scholars. Rudolf Wildenmann, as all who know him are aware, has a less parochial conception of the needs of comparative research. He obtained funding from the *Deutsche Forschungsgemeinschaft* (DFG) for a week-long conference in Mannheim in September 1987, made a major contribution to its deliberations, and provided the staff support (most conspicuously, Heinz Gerhard, to whom the group owes particular thanks) which made the meeting such a great success. He is as much a contributor to this research project as any of its authors.

Finally, the Editor wishes to acknowledge his gratitude to the secretarial staff of the Political Science Department of the Research School of Social Sciences of the ANU for their untiring and meticulous work in preparing the manuscript for publication. He further wishes to thank Gillian O'Loghlin for editorial assistance of the very highest standard.

1

Introduction
Puzzles of Political Economy

Francis G. Castles

This book starts from the premise that, despite great promise and very considerable achievement, comparative public policy analysis or the political economy of policy outcomes in advanced capitalist societies is currently characterized by a serious decline in marginal utility. After more than a decade of strong progress, the rate of increase in new knowledge has markedly slowed. The aim is to find a way forward which both builds on the existing findings of comparative research and provides an impetus for its further development. This volume seeks to achieve that goal by focusing on a number of puzzles or paradoxes that seem to emerge when a particular nation's public policy profile is viewed in the context of our present understanding of the determinants of public policy development and diversity. The hope is that by exploring particular anomalies or critical cases located by comparative analysis – by examining what is distinctive about particular countries' policy development – it will prove possible to begin a process through which may be derived more finely grained and historically grounded hypotheses for future comparative research. This introduction briefly sets out the research design for the volume and the intellectual rationale for such an approach.

The Research Design

Comparative public policy analysis has seen its programmatic objective as understanding the main determinants of contemporary public policy outcomes in advanced capitalist states. At first glance, it might therefore appear that the adoption of a historical perspective grounded in national distinctiveness represents less a new way forward towards a desired destination and more an abrupt change in analytical direction forced upon us by methodological constraints. That is not what we intend. Not least amongst the evidence that this volume represents no turning away from the achievements of cross-national public policy research is its authorship. The majority of the contributors have been actively involved in cross-national outcomes research for much of the past decade. Indeed, Professor Schmidt and I were the co-convenors of a major collaborative international research group on 'Party Differences and Public Policy' which was set up under the auspices of the European Consortium for Political Research in 1978. In 1982 that group published a volume of researches entitled *The Impact of Parties: Politics and Policies in Democratic Capitalist States* (Castles, 1982). This project was very much in the cross-national aggregate data analysis mode, utilizing regression techniques to locate the structural and political variables associated with social and defence expenditure, macroeconomic outcomes, incomes policy outcomes and income distribution in capitalist democracies. Already in the introduction to that volume, the notion was foreshadowed that the next obvious stage for such research was the analysis of critical or anomalous cases. The present volume may be seen, and was quite deliberately conceived, as the second stage of a research project begun a decade previously and with objectives substantially unchanged in the interim period.

Moving to that next stage was by no means simple. It demanded contributions from scholars who were more or less equally at home in the literature of cross-national public policy analysis and of the history and politics of a particular nation. Only at the confluence of those two kinds of highly specialized knowledge could the distinctiveness of public policy profiles be located and their puzzling character in light of comparative findings be identified and subsequently analysed. Moreover, the availability of scholars with such qualities necessarily had implications for the range of countries and the range of issues that could fall within the ambit of the research. Ideally, it would have been desirable to cover as many of the major advanced, industrial states as possible, some instances of ostensibly obvious divergence from the OECD norm, and a number of exemplars of extreme variation along dimensions which have been at the heart of comparative outcomes analysis – high and low social security spenders, high and low inflation and unemployment, open and closed economies, right and left hegemonic regimes, and so on. The final selection of countries – Australia, Germany, Israel, Japan, the Netherlands, Sweden, the United Kingdom and the United States – achieves most of these objectives.

It follows from the intention to explore the anomalous and the distinctive that no tight structuring of the format of contributions was possible. What needed explaining could only be derived by a country expert matching up a particular nation's policy experience against the findings emerging from cross-national analysis. In other words, the identification of the puzzles was a part of the research endeavour itself. What was specified was a general research question and certain broad guidelines, designed to ensure some comparability across contributions and the maximum possible relevance to the concerns of cross-national public policy research. For each country – or, in one instance, two countries juxtaposed – the question to be addressed was as follows:

What is distinctive and/or puzzling about its public policy profile and why?

The guidelines specified that distinctiveness or puzzles, wherever possible, be grounded by reference not only to cross-national data, but also with regard to at least some of the more important hypotheses in the comparative literature. The specification of the focus of attention was on broad policy issues – a macro rather than a micro approach – and the public policy profile was similarly broadly conceived in terms of outputs, outcomes and the policy instruments utilized to achieve them. Overall, the intention was to encourage contributors to discuss linkages and trade-offs between aspects of policy, which are usually regarded as wholly separate in much present analysis.

Finally, in order to make it possible to demonstrate the relevance of this approach to the ongoing concerns of comparative policy analysis, it was suggested to contributors that they approach the question of the distinctiveness of the public policy profile through matters pertaining to political economy and, insofar as possible, aspects of political economy with a bearing on contemporary public policy debate in a given country. Hence what we have here are puzzles in political economy, the explication of which, it is hoped, will be sufficient to illustrate the value of a critical case/comparative history approach as a means of extending the explanatory scope of comparative public policy analysis and of demonstrating that an historical approach can add to, rather than divert attention from, the programmatic objective of such analysis. Certainly, the fact that seven enthusiastic comparativists, when asked the question what is distinctive or puzzling about your own country in light of present comparative findings, found no difficulty at all in answering (indeed, in several instances, had to be restrained from writing at much greater length) strongly suggests that some new approach is urgently needed.

Comparison as a Means of Explanation

With only a few conspicuous exceptions (e.g. Cutright, 1965; Aaron, 1967; Denison, 1967 and Pryor, 1968), the scholarly analysis of public policy outcomes prior to the early 1970s – insofar as it existed at all – took forms which failed to offer anything like valid empirical explanation. First there was the plethora of descriptive studies, which examined the specific features of public intervention in a given country. These studies certainly told us of the emergence of new developments in the realms of public policy – the rise of the welfare state, the creation of the mixed economy and the adoption of Keynesian techniques of macroeconomic management – but tended to regard systematic speculation as to the origins of such developments as being well outside their brief. Second, what attempts there were to explain these phenomena as they were manifested in individual countries generally took the form of historical studies, which tended to be over-particularistic and over-determined. The novel features of public intervention in a given state were seen as *sui generis* and to be explained by a developmental trajectory which encapsulated the totality of the national historical experience. Third, the few studies which, in contrast, sought a more generalized form of explanation tended to dissolve all evidence of national variation in a single-minded attempt to locate the fundamental key to supposedly universal developmental tendencies. Such explanations took the following form: all advanced states are welfare states and have mixed and managed economies because they are, alternatively, industrialized, modern, democratic, capitalist or characterized by political party and interest group competition, and so on through the range of central explanatory variables encompassed by contemporary social sciences theorizing.

What made it possible to transcend this unsatisfactory situation, in which evidence of national diversity was systematically divorced from empirical explanation and theory construction, was the gradual emergence of comparative, quantitative and statistical analysis of public policy outcomes. Comparison made possible a simultaneous focus on both similarity and difference, so that the antinomy of national uniqueness and general trends could be analysed and resolved in terms of variations on a common theme. It allowed not only the singular question of the historian, why is country A like this, and the general question of the 'grand theorist', why are all advanced states like that, but also the intermediate and, perhaps, ultimately more answerable question, why is country A rather like country B and rather less like country C? More answerable, of course, because comparison provided the researcher with a logic of causation – or, at least, association – by which the inductive argument could be asserted that similarity stemmed from prior common factors and difference from prior diversity. The use of comparison as a means of explanation was one of the crucial bases of the emergence in the past decade or so of an academic field – 'discipline' would be the wrong word, because such studies often are, and always should be, interdisciplinary in character – of comparative public policy analysis.

It is no accident, but a structured contingency of the sociology of knowledge, that comparison was conjoined with the qualitative statistical analysis of cross-national aggregate data in the scholarly analysis of the determinants of public policy outcomes. We study what society constructs as valid knowledge and we study it with the tools considered scientifically appropriate. Comparison became more and more possible from the 1960s onwards simply because international agencies – most conspicuously the United Nations and the OECD – progressively provided routine, comparative and largely standardized data on the outputs and, to a much more limited extent, the outcomes of governmental policies. In consequence, the initial thrust of comparative policy analysis had a very strong tendency to be concerned with topics for which comparable, and most specifically, quantitative data were readily available – public expenditures and macroeconomic outcomes in particular. Far less was it concerned with qualitative issues or intrusion into areas in which governments had not seen fit to provide standardized data. In other words,the appropriate domain of comparative analysis was conceptualized in terms of officially defined functions of the modern state, not so much because of the values that social scientists brought to their analysis, but rather because governments were themselves deeply implicated in those aspects of the domestic political economy and considered it useful to gather information on such matters. Until quite recently, it is fair to say that comparative policy analysis followed the primrose path of doing what it was easiest to do on the basis of information gathered by others. Statistical techniques were utilized as the primary means of conducting such analysis because they offered the simplest way of manipulating the masses of standardized data provided by governments. Or, to adopt a somewhat less mundane perspective, such techniques made it possible to cope with the additional complexity that necessarily arose once it was conceded that the analysis of single cases was insufficient and the attribution of broadly defined common trends was misleading.

Comparison has provided the logic, quantitative analysis the data and applied social statistics the method for the very considerable achievements of comparative public policy analysis in the past decade. They have permitted not only a far more detailed mapping of variations in the basic parameters of public policy interventions amongst the countries for which we have reasonably reliable data, but also a far more generally agreed and empirically based inventory of hypotheses for explaining that variation (Castles, 1987, p. 203). There are very few studies now published which assert the causal primacy of a single determinant of policy behaviour. Rather, most contributions to the field now use the range of available hypotheses – the impact of economic growth, the openness of the economy, demographic structure, the role of political parties, forms of interest mediation and so on – in a manner somewhat analogous to the natural scientist subjecting his experimental data to a set of standardized tests. That this shift to comparative hypothesis testing has led to a marked advance in our understanding of the determinants of policy outputs and, to a lesser extent, outcomes in democratic capitalist states is undoubted.

But reflection on the progress of rather more than a decade of comparative public policy analysis prompts the question of how much farther this strategy can take us. The advances we have made have been predicated on the notion of harnessing the logic of comparison as a means of explanation – using it as a test-bed for answering questions about why countries vary in the character and extent of their public intervention. Those answers are framed in terms of covariance, which tells us the degree to which outcomes are systematically associated with other factors. Thus, in general terms applying to whatever sample of countries we are investigating, we may essay statements with the following character: welfare state development is in large part a function of economic development, demographic structure and democratic socialist rule. Much more tentatively, for reasons which will become apparent, we can move from the general to the particular, and make statements about individual nations: that, for instance, amongst the more important reasons why Sweden is a developed welfare state is because it is affluent, has a high proportion of age pensioners and has long enjoyed Social Democratic hegemony.

The trouble with such explanations is not that they are inaccurate, but that, as far as they presently go, they do not tell us many of the things that we wish to know. Moreover, there are few signs that the problems we encounter are merely of a temporary nature – that all we have to do is to go away and devise more studies of a similar kind in order to fill the gaps in our knowledge. Our problems are basically twofold: that the explanations we do dispose of are grossly underdetermined[1] and that, in any case, the questions to which they are, at best, very partial answers frequently seem on reflection to be the wrong questions to be asking.

Underdetermination is not, of course, in itself a problem if we have good reason to believe that we possess that means of filling in the lacunae in our knowledge. But is that the situation which confronts us in contemporary comparative public policy analysis? A decade ago, correlations which indicated the covariance of public expenditure with a range of some half dozen basic independent variables represented a major increment to our understanding, as similar studies in disaggregated areas of expenditure and various aspects of macroeconomic activity did subsequently. But the incremental advance thereafter has, at best, been marginal. Surface correlations proliferate, but largely they only confirm, or perhaps slightly modify, what we already know. Typically what we know is that a given outcome is associated with a few independent variables under most circumstances, leading to a level of 'explained' variation rarely exceeding – and often very markedly below – 50 per cent. That in turn means that our explanations of individual cases are only intellectually persuasive to the degree – quite possibly adventitious – that they happen to nestle close to what is usually conceded to be a much underdetermined regression line. The Swedish welfare state happens to fit a very simple model of social policy development. In terms of the knowledge generated by comparative public policy analysis, that case does not appear to constitute a puzzle or paradox, although as Göran Therborn notes in his chapter on *'Pillarization' and 'Popular Movements'*, the degree of fit between comparative theory and reality is rather less than some have assumed. But what of the Netherlands, which is conspicuous neither for its affluence, its ageing population, nor its historical experience of democratic socialist government, but which, since the mid 1960s, has followed an almost identical trajectory of welfare development as Sweden, at least as indicated by available cross-national data on social expenditure?

The suspicion that we may frequently be asking the wrong questions derives from a number of sources. At a gut level, it stems from the natural tendency of even the most committed practitioner of the comparative method to reaggregate, and make judgements concerning, what he or she has so carefully disaggregated for the sake of scientific analysis. That inclination leads to the question of whether the population of a country characterized by a particular distribution of outputs and outcomes is better or worse off than that of another country with a different configuration. The problem is that, whilst at some extremes we are presumably entitled to suggest an answer, those extremes seem very elastic indeed. Japan and Australia have amongst the smallest welfare states in the OECD, Sweden the largest. Are we, therefore, entitled to conclude that the working class and poor are more disadvantaged in the former than the latter? For Japan the answer appears to be an unequivocal no since, as T.J. Pempel's chapter on *Japan's Creative Conservatism* demonstrates, the Japanese enjoy the highest growth rate of GNP, amongst the lowest unemployment and inflation rates in the OECD, and a relatively egalitarian distribution of income. For Australia, as my own chapter points out, the answer is more time specific, with no evidence of weaker economic performance or lesser inequality prior to the 1970s, but signs of greater poverty and inequality thereafter.

That extremes as wide as the gulf between low social spenders, like Japan and Australia, and welfare state giants, like Sweden, may tell us little of fundamental importance about the societies we are comparing is a conclusion that emerges not merely from making overall contrasts, but

8

FRANCIS G. CASTLES

also from an increasing awareness that the mute data of aggregate, cross-national comparison do not speak for themselves. On the one hand, as Titmuss pointed out forcefully more than a generation ago, a given instrument of policy can be utilized for the achievement of wildly divergent objectives – a given level of welfare spending may be designed to ameliorate the condition of the poor, obtain greater equality, raise the birth rate, improve industrial efficiency and so on (Titmuss, 1968, pp. 64–5). On the other, and the puzzles of the overall impacts of both Australian and Japanese public policy illustrate this, seemingly diverse policies are often aimed at – or, at least, because intentionality is not always obvious, often end up – achieving remarkably similar objectives. In such a perspective, high welfare state spending (the Swedish strategy) and compulsory minimum wages (the Australian strategy) or low unemployment (as in Japan) cease to be separate goals of policy, but may be visualized as alternative means to the same end of greater social protection. To come again full circle, the entire package of socially protective measures, and not merely the separate policy instruments of which it is constituted, may be designed to achieve diverse ends. In Sweden and Australia, where intentionality is reasonably clear in virtue of policy design by powerful labour movements, it may be an end in itself. But in Japan, as Pempel's chapter shows, protection may itself be a side-product of an entrenched elite seeking the goal of national economic strength. Both the multi-purpose nature and functional equivalence of policy behaviour suggest strongly that we need to employ methods which can go beyond the present merely quantitative enumeration of outputs and outcomes to a paradigm of investigation which permits us to comprehend the purposes for which and the strategies by which policy is elaborated.

The feeling that the wrong questions are being asked is also a concomitant of the fact mentioned earlier that much of the data of which we dispose is that which is produced for the convenience of governments rather than the scholarly needs of policy analysts. Until quite recently, the language of comparative public policy analysis has often seemed virtually conterminous with the language of national accounts statistics, just because that is what governments produce in a routine and standardized form. Admittedly, there are an increasing number of exceptions, perhaps most conspicuous in the areas of environmental regulation (see Vogel, 1987) and income distribution (namely the Luxembourg Incomes Study), where the very weakness of official data provision has forced scholars to collect the information which governments are reluctant to provide. Nevertheless, the constraint is real. Governments shy away from producing data on the effectiveness of their pollution control measures, if any, the incidence of poverty and the levels-of-living of specified sub-groups of the population, and even those that occasionally do so feel little compunction to provide information of a kind which could be readily compared with other nations. But it is data of this latter sociological rather than economic kind which truly relates to the final societal consequences, the ultimate outcomes, of the total policy-mix in a given country.

This problem is only a specific instance of the more general phenomenon that our present methods constrain our vision. Focusing exclusively on post-1960 data (which is all the OECD provides) means that we are rarely able to address questions concerning the trajectories of policy development. Emphasizing quantitative indicators means that we are frequently unable to go beyond a shallow and narrow conceptualization of the factors that may be of explanatory relevance. Partly, that is a difficulty of whether categorizations mean the same thing in different contexts. How can one use the conventional measures of political strength when, as in Israel, 'when we say union we don't mean union, when we say left we don't mean left, and when we say labour we don't mean labour' (Shalev, ch. 4 this volume)? Partly, it is a problem of the range and sophistication of the variables that can be encompassed by the analysis. The role of state – variously located in terms of particular institutional arrangements, a specific *locus* of power or characteristic notions concerning the legitimate boundaries of public action – is seen by each of the writers in this volume as vital to the explanation of policy outcomes, yet that role is scarcely one that can be captured by means of quantitative indicators alone. Insisting that the independent variables of our research should be ones immediately reducible to interval level data or, more modestly, dummy variables means that we are forced to neglect causal influences which seem, at first inspection, to be unique to a particular nation. If a distinctive institution makes all the difference in controlling inflation – as Manfred Schmidt argues is the case in respect of the West German Bundesbank – that institution should surely be at the centre of our analytical attention rather than at the merely footnoted periphery. The capacity to ask the right questions is a function of moving beyond the self-imposed methodological constraints of an exclusively quantitative methodology.

Comparison as a Mode of Exploration

The studies comprising this volume offer a strategy which may assist in that endeavour. The rationale for such a strategy rests on the recognition that comparison is not merely a means of explanation or hypothesis testing, but also a mode of locating and exploring a phenomenon as yet insufficiently understood, and that these two functions can and should be iterative in character. The establishment of covariance tells us of a range of factors which are associated with the phenomenon we seek to explain, but the existence of covariance together with the discovery of one or more major exceptions to the regularities otherwise apparent creates a puzzle, paradox or critical case that demands investigation. Przeworski's view that 'we should view cross-national statistical results in a highly Bayesian way, *giving extraordinary weight to observations that happen to bisect a syndrome (of normally associated attributes) but were not untangled previously*' (Przeworski, 1987, p. 39, my emphasis) makes precisely the same point: that we should be most interested in what appears most anomalous in terms of previously established scholarship. In the present state of our knowledge, the development of the Dutch welfare state is more puzzling than that of Sweden and Australia's strategy of social protection more puzzling than those of Western Europe. In other words, comparison can be used to dissolve apparent differences by demonstrating identity of causation or it can be used to pinpoint what remains singular or distinctive, despite our best efforts to reduce the world to a set of empirical regularities.

Since the establishment of such regularities is at the core of the scientific endeavour, it appears to follow that comparison's function of uncovering what is atypical is very much a second-best outcome of scholarly research. We would rather dissolve differences than discover their contours. It is for that reason, presumably, that recent public policy analysis has for the most part tended to concentrate on refining the variables that can be entered into regression equations, even though, as we have noted, the increment of knowledge gained thereby has proved disappointingly small. But to admit that the location of puzzles is a second-best outcome does not mean that it is a second-best strategy of analysis under certain circumstances. What a puzzle offers us is a device by which we may define, and subsequently map in fine detail, the territory in which we may reasonably suppose that an explanation of singularity must lie. Adopting such a close focus approach does not necessarily mean a resort to individual case studies of particular nations contrasted with the more general findings of broader cross-national studies, which is the approach taken by most of the contributions to this volume. It can just as well be effected by the intermediate method of utilizing selective comparative case studies of two or more countries, the distinctiveness or similarity of whose policy outcomes is highlighted by their similarities or differences in other respects (e.g. Heclo, 1974; Esping-Andersen, 1980, and Therborn, ch. 6, this volume). In either instance, the focus on a specific puzzle allows us to concentrate our attention in a way that is quite impossible in studies comprising an entire range of cases, and it permits us to examine a range of variables which goes far beyond anything currently available in the lexicon of quantitative social research.[2] The rationale for proceeding in this manner is that which Skocpol has noted as characteristic of the analytic strategy in historical sociology, in which the identification of a why question serves as the stimulus for a search for 'concrete causal configurations adequate to account for important historical patterns' (Skocpol, 1984, p. 375).

Moreover, the variables (or causal configurations) so opened to investigation are precisely those relegated to the periphery of our attention by aggregate cross-national data analysis. They are the variables of intentionality, purpose and strategy, which are always central to the political and historical analysis of events and developments in individual countries, but are quite impossible to capture from quantitative data. Policy determination is never merely a function of the additive interaction of impersonal forces, but invariably involves some component of 'strategic choice', understanding the term 'strategy' to imply 'an overall understanding, among those who exercise effective power, of a set of decision premises integrating world-views, goals and means' (Scharpf, 1984, p. 260). Strategic choices are, of course, constrained by impersonal forces, but their impact is mediated by the perceptions of political actors and how they interpret the past. *Learning from Catastrophes* is the title of one of the contributions to this volume and, in a broad sense, it is that learning process which becomes visible when we focus our attention on individual and anomalous cases. A comparative policy analysis largely restricted to national accounts variables plus some very simple taxonomies of political and social strucures implies a simultaneity of causation which belies all that we otherwise believe about developmental processes: that individuals, groups and leaders interpret their experience and take purposive action to maintain or modify the world in which they find themselves. It is, perhaps, no wonder that surface correlations tell us only part of the story.

The process of learning from catastrophes or, more generally, from experience is a historical process, which is why the notion of history figures in the title of this volume. A sense of history is what is most missing in contemporary policy analysis, a lacuna which can probably only be properly remedied by a focus on the experience of particular cases. Our present analysis can tell us about contemporary outputs and outcomes and it can lay out the sinews of social and political structures, including an enumeration of institutions and political divisions to the degree that they have some counterparts in other countries in our sample. It cannot tell us of the understandings of political actors, the values to which they attach greatest priority, and the meanings they attach to institutions. We can say that a country such as the United Kingdom has for much of the post-war era been characterized by a degree of statism seemingly unwarranted by political, social and economic trends. But we cannot, using cross-national aggregate data analysis, say how British political elites, responding to the experience of wartime political and economic mobilization and the subsequent loss of empire, understood the nature and tasks of government, and that, as Patrick Dunleavy makes clear, is one of the vital keys to unravelling the paradox of 'ungrounded statism'. Nor can our present analysis readily bring to light the synergy of institutional interaction, most dramatically revealed when institutional presences taken for granted in the comparative literature are almost wholly absent in a particular nation: in Japan, the absence of any real labour movement influence or even voice; in the USA, according to Edwin Amenta and Theda Skocpol's account of American public policy exceptionalism, the absence of state capacities sufficiently developed to implement social policy.,

Moreover, a historical approach is essential not merely in providing analytical leverage on the role of human agency in the public policy equation but, no less important, in making it possible to treat *structural* contexts as a totality, rather than as mere rankings or weights on a series of discrete variables. History reveals the one sense in which it is meaningful to say that the sum is more than its parts: the sense in which human action is embedded in its particular context. In these terms, as Pempel makes clear, the role of the Japanese conservatism has to be located in a very specific totality of structural opportunities and constraints, including late industrialization, US sponsorship of the post-war regime, and so on. Amenta and Skocpol are making a fundamentally similar point when they emphasize that the weakness of the drive towards a national system of age pensions in the USA must be seen in the context of early democratization and the existence of the Civil War veterans pensions scheme. Note too, that a crucial aspect of context is often the timing and sequence of events. Innovators and late-comers do not have the same choices, a fact which is not readily made apparent by examining reality in contemporary cross-sectional slices. Furthermore, as the US pensions case exemplifies, past courses of action constrain present choices. A historical approach permits us to investigate meaningfully, in terms of timing and sequences, what appears in a part of the quantitative literature as the right but trite observation of the ruling power of inertia, that the best predictor of policy outcomes at time t is their value at t_{-1}.

All this may be conceded, but it could be argued that it amounts to a justification of a headlong retreat from comparative analysis. That is not, as already noted, the position taken by the authors of this volume, for at least two major reasons. First, we are very far from wishing to deny or ignore the findings of comparative research. Our investigation of particular cases is not a return to the particularistic over-determination of single nation histories. The national distinctiveness and the puzzles we study are defined by what we still fail to understand once the findings of comparative analysis based on the whole universe of discourse of advanced capitalist states have been taken into account. At a minimum, such studies represent a cumulative extension of comparative endeavour, since the goal is to fill in the gaps in our knowledge when that more generalizing comparative analysis has gone as far as it possibly can given current methodological constraints.

Second, comparison need not and should not cease just because the focus of our attention is directed to particular cases. The logic of comparative explanation does not suddenly disappear when we are treating intentional, institutional and historical variables. Learning from a particular national experience will always take particular forms, but patterns of human action and purposes, especially as moulded by the fact of living in societies constrained by common structural parameters, are likely to manifest certain intrinsic similarities as well as residual differences. If we argue, for instance, that the experience of total war shapes the policy-making agenda of future generations in certain determinate ways – and that is the view of several of the contributors to this volume – we need to test that attribution of causality against the experience of other nations. Similarly, it is perfectly possible that, having once identified particular national patterns of social protection in their historical concreteness, one might proceed upwards along 'the ladder of abstraction' (Sartori, 1970) by developing categorizations of socially protective strategies that have attributes or properties that apply across the whole universe of discourse. In such ways we may contribute to an iterative process by which single case analysis uncovers qualitative variables which may ultimately be refined in such a way that they can be utilized as components of mainstream comparative analysis. Filling in particular gaps in our knowledge may, in other words, lead to reduction in 'unexplained' variance in the universe of discourse as a whole. The promise that the historical analysis of particular puzzles set in a self-consciously comparative framework may serve such a function is the justification for labelling our endeavour *The Comparative History of Public Policy*.

Notes

1 In a recent contribution to the methodological literature, Adam Przeworski has argued that the problem of comparative research in this and other areas is *overdetermination* in the sense that we dispose of too many theories or variables and not enough cases to test them (Przeworski, 1987, pp. 38–9). This is, of course, quite true, but it does not alter the fact that, in most cases, what we profess to understand on the basis of our studies tends to leave a very large residual of unexplained variation. The only exception, where overdetermination in both senses may be applicable, is in the arena of the more complex attempts at econometric modelling.

2 The more sophisticated practitioners of the quantitative method are, of

14　　　　　　　　　　　　　　　NOTES

course, wholly aware that, given the limited universe of discourse on which comparative public policy research is based, beyond a certain point resort to qualitative data is the only way forward. That suggests the value of a 'deviant case' approach, in which particular attention is paid to the analysis of the outliers revealed by quantitative research (see Ness, 1985, pp. 1–13). Given that each of the contributors to this volume locates the puzzle or distinctiveness of a particular nation with regard to the existing generalizations of the comparative literature, it would be perfectly appropriate to regard this volume as an attempt to vindicate the general utility of such an approach.

References

Aaron, Henry J. 1967: Social Security: International Comparisons. In Otto Eckstein (ed.), *Studies in the Economics of Income Maintenance*, Washington, DC: The Brookings Institution.

Castles, Francis G. (ed.) 1982: *The Impact of Parties: Politics and Policies in Democratic Capitalist States*. London: Sage.

Castles, Francis G. 1987: Comparative Public Policy Analysis: Problems, Progress and Prospects. In Francis G. Castles, Franz Lehner and Manfred G. Schmidt (eds), *Managing Mixed Economies*, Berlin: De Gruyter.

Cutright, Phillips 1965: Political Structure, Economic Development and National Social Security Programs. *American Journal of Sociology*, 70 (March), 537–50.

Denison, E.F. 1967: *Why Growth Rates Differ: Postwar Experience in Nine Western Countries*.Washington, DC: The Brookings Institution.

Esping-Andersen, Gösta 1980: *Social Class, Social Democracy and State Policy*. Copenhagen: New Social Science Monographs.

Heclo, Hugh 1974: *Modern Social Politics in Britain and Sweden*. New Haven, Conn.: Yale University Press.

Ness, Gayl 1985: Managing not-so-small Numbers: Between Comparative and Statistical Methods. *International Journal of Comparative Sociology*, XXVI, 1–13.

Pryor, Frederick 1968: *Public Expenditure in Capitalist and Communist Nations*. Homewood, Il: Irwin.

Przeworski, Adam 1987: Methods of Cross-National Research, 1970–83: An Overview. In Meinolf Dierkes, Hans N. Weiler and A.B. Antal (eds), *Comparative Policy Research*, Aldershot, Hants: Gower.

Sartori, Giovanni 1970: Concept misformation in comparative politics. *American Political Science Review*, 54, 1033–53.

Scharpf, Fritz W. 1984: Economic and Institutional Constraints of Full-Employment Strategies: Sweden, Austria, and Western Gemany, 1973–1982. In John H. Goldthorpe (ed.), *Order and Conflict in Contemporary Capitalism*, Oxford: Clarendon Press.

Skocpol, Theda 1984: Emerging Agendas and Recurrent Strategies in Historical Sociology. In Theda Skocpol (ed.), *Vision and Method in Historical Sociology*, Cambridge: Cambridge University Press.

Titmuss, Richard 1968: *Commitment to Welfare*. London: George Allen & Unwin.

Vogel, David 1987: The Comparative Study of Environmental Policy: A Review of the Literature. In Meinolf Dierkes, Hans N. Weiler and A.B. Antal (eds), *Comparative Policy Research*, Aldershot, Hants: Gower.

2

Social Protection by Other Means

Australia's Strategy of Coping With External Vulnerability

Francis G. Castles

We must let Australians know truthfully, honestly, earnestly, just what sort of an international hole Australia is in. It's the price of our commodities – they are as bad in real terms as since the Depression. That's a fact of Australian life now – it's got nothing to do with the Government. It's the price of commodities on world markets, but it means an internal economic adjustment . . . If this Government cannot get the adjustment, get manufacturing going again and keep moderate wage outcomes and a sensible economic policy, then Australia is basically done for. We will just end up being a third-rate economy . . . a banana republic.

Paul Keating, Australian Federal Treasurer, 14 May 1986

For a century the dynamics of modern society was governed by a double movement . . . The one was the principle of economic liberalism, aiming at the establishment of a self-regulating market, relying on the support of the trading classes, and using largely *laissez-faire* and free trade as its methods; the other was the principle of social protection aiming at the conservation of man and nature as well as productive organization, relying on the varying support of those immediately affected by the deleterious action of the market – primarily, but not exclusively, the working and the landed classes – and using protective legislation, restrictive associations, and other instruments of intervention as its methods.

Karl Polanyi, *The Great Transformation*, 1944

Introduction: Puzzles of Australian Public Policy

Intellectual puzzles are an artefact of a contradiction between the way the world is and the way we expect it to be. Those expectations may consist variously of untested assumptions, commonplace observations, hypotheses and more or less well grounded theories. How then might we expect Australian public policy to be, if we were guided by some of the assumptions, observations, hypotheses and theories that have emerged from the comparative public policy literature of the past decade or so?

– Australia is a country with a relatively small population,[1] and economic theory tells us that countries with small populations should have open economies, relying on product specialization and international trade to make up for the disadvantage of a small internal market (see the discussion in the section *Economic Vulnerability in Theory and Practice* below). In fact, Australia has the third most closed economy in the OECD,[2] after the vastly larger American and Japanese economies.

– Australia is a country which, in virtue of its highly unusual system of conciliation and arbitration of industrial disputes and compulsory and centralized wage-fixing, may be regarded as possessing an institutionalized national incomes policy of long standing (see Phelps Brown, 1969, p. 121). It has been hypothesized that policy institutions of such a neo-corporatist type are instrumental in helping countries weather economic crisis (see Bruno and Sachs, 1985). Yet Australia's experience in the crises of the early and late 1970s was as bad as any in the OECD. Indeed, Australia was only one of two countries (the other was Denmark) which in the period 1974–9 fell below the OECD median in respect of economic growth, unemployment and inflation simultaneously (see OECD, 1986).

– Australia is a country in which the labour movement, whether measured in terms of union density or electoral support for a unified party of the left, has been traditionally strong, and theories resting on the primacy of class politics suggest that this should be translated into a strong impetus to welfare state expansion (see Gough, 1979, pp. 64–9). In fact, in terms of social expenditure share, only Switzerland and Japan of the advanced OECD countries spend less than Australia (OECD, 1985, p. 21), and in terms of social security and welfare transfers, whether measured in percentage GDP or US dollars per head, only Japan spends less (Varley, 1986, pp. 10–11).

– Finally, we tend to assume that a weak welfare state is likely to coexist with a final income distribution of an inegalitarian kind. After all, the explicit motivation for the left in pressing for a more expansive welfare state has been the desire for greater equality and the extirpation of poverty. In the modern world, the welfare state is conceived as the primary agency of *social protection*, defined, in Karl Polanyi's sense, as the sum of policies designed to protect the individual from the adverse consequences of living in a capitalist market economy (Polanyi, 1944). Yet, until the early 1970s at least, Australia's low levels of welfare spending were not accompanied by income inequality greater than in the other OECD states. On the contrary, only the Netherlands, Sweden and Norway, arguably the world's three leading welfare states at this time, manifested greater post-tax, post-transfer, income equality than Australia (see van Arnhem and Schotsman, 1982, p. 290). Seemingly, in Australia, social protection is – or was – effected by means other than by welfare provision.

These contradictions between expectations derived from the literature of comparative public policy research and the real world of Australian policy outcomes have been sketched both to demonstrate the distinctiveness of the Australian public policy profile and our difficulties in utilizing conventional explanations to address the nature of that distinctiveness. Admittedly, the puzzles located have been chosen to emphasize the lack of explanatory purchase of present knowledge, but even if hypotheses are adduced which fit the Australian case better, the puzzles usually reappear in new guise. The weakness of the Australian welfare state is compatible with hypotheses which suggest that the expansion of the public economy is a function of the openness of the economy (see Cameron, 1978, pp. 1243–61) and of leftist government incumbency rather than class power (see Castles, 1982, pp. 83–8). However, that still leaves us with the old puzzle that Australia has developed a closed economy despite its population size and provides us with the new one of why the strong Australian labour movement has failed to convert its class power into commensurate political strength.

It is not the contention of this volume that our present incapacity to come up with an exact fit between the public policy experience of individual countries and the theories and hypotheses comprising the comparative public policy literature indicates a need to abandon the findings and methods of quantitative, cross-national, aggregate data research. What such research can offer us is a 'description of varying patterns of policy and the structural relationships which underlie them'; what it cannot come to grips with is the impact of human agency, manifested 'in individual choices, strategies and manoeuvres' which may modify those relationships in specific historical contexts (Castles, 1981, p. 129). In order fully to explain the character of public policy outcomes in particular nations, we need to be able to do both. This chapter, which seeks to explore the historical context of Australian public policy development, attempts to use the methods of comparative and historical political economy to increase the degree of fit between theory and observation and hence to reduce our sense of puzzlement. Our enquiry is premised on the view that cross-national and historical studies are not alternative, but rather complementary, means of gaining greater knowledge of the overall dynamics of public policy development.

Before turning to what history can tell us, it is, however, necessary to provide a somewhat more detailed picture of the Australian public policy profile as it developed in the post-war era and to sketch the beginnings of a schematic account of the interrelationship between the economy and public policy development in the modern state. The first is the task of the next section, *The Australian Public Policy Profile*, the second is undertaken in the following section, *Economic Vulnerability in Theory and Practice*.

The Australian Public Policy Profile

The present Australian public policy profile is in flux and has been so, to varying degrees, since the late 1960s. New problems have emerged and old verities are being challenged. Australia's closed economy was a direct product of a long-standing industrial policy stance which sought to protect the manufacturing sector through the imposition of tariffs. Now Australia wants to compete on world markets for manufactured goods and sees the way to doing that as being through tariff reduction. Australia's institutionalized system of wage regulation fell apart in the late 1960s, but was revitalized in the mid 1970s as a means of holding down inflation. Today, it is the centrepiece of a quite explicitly neo-corporatist agreement between trade unions and government to tradeoff wage restraint against other gains for the working class movement. Australia's weak welfare state remained static throughout the 1960s when most of the other advanced capitalist states were markedly increasing their social policy input. In the early 1970s, under the first Labor administration for 23 years, there was a marked change of direction with substantially increased expenditure and a new 'social democratic' philosophy labelled as a doctrine of 'positive equality'. More straitened economic circumstances in the 1980s have led to a fresh welfare tack. The present Hawke Labor government is simultaneously attempting to economize and to abolish poverty by returning to what we shall see to have been a long-standing Australian welfare strategy of welfare selectivity.

Tariff protection, institutionalized mechanisms of wage control and the welfare state are all manifestations of public policy directed to socially protective ends. Each involves the state in interventions designed to shelter groups of individuals from the deleterious impact of an unfettered market economy. Two questions are immediately posed by the present flux in public policy prescriptions. First, why have Australians seen a need to search around for new policy directions? Second, why were the previous policy directions seemingly so different from those of other advanced states or, to put it more specifically, why did Australia embrace protective tariffs, centralized and compulsory wage-fixation and a residual welfare state in an era elsewhere typified by greater international trade, free collective bargaining and welfare state expansion? Answers to these questions take up the whole of this chapter, but an initial entry into the topic can best be made by focusing on the public policy profile *circa* the early 1960s, its last period of discernible stability, and examining the changes that took place thereafter.

In the early 1960s, the notion that there was any serious need to depart from tried and tested policy instruments was hardly one which was readily persuasive. In 1966, Australia was, in per capita terms, the sixth richest of the major OECD nations and economic performance in the immediate post-war decades had been exceptionally satisfactory. Growth rates were high although, when adjusted for the high rate of population increase promoted by migration, hardly very special by the standards of the time. However, they were a marked improvement on Australia's pre-war performance, which may well have been the worst of any of the advanced capitalist states, with real GDP per capita only rising by some 11 per cent between 1889 and 1939 (see McClean and Pincus, 1983, pp. 193–202). Moreover, the increased economic growth of the post-war era had been accompanied by what was then described as 'brimfull employment' (Karmel and Brunt, 1962, p. 10) and only an extremely modest increase in consumer price levels. If social protection can be afforded by high wages, jobs for all who want them and economic stability, Australian public policy seemed to be an outstanding success. To make the picture still more rosy, Australia in the mid 1960s was entering into a period of large-scale resource development which banished for a decade and a half the once omnipresent fear of balance of payments problems (Gruen, 1986, pp. 2–3). Admittedly, the effects of Australia's high level of tariffs were demonstrated in a less dynamic expansion of international trade than most other countries, but it was only later in the 1960s that this began to be perceived as a threat to continuing Australian prosperity.

If the state of the economy seemed a cause for almost universal celebration, one would have imagined there would be less political consensus about Australia's laggardly welfare performance in the 1960s. The Social Services Minister of the hegemonic Liberal/Country Party government could laud the supposed lack of any absolute poverty and define his government's role as one of raising the threshold of '*acceptable comparative poverty*' (Wentworth, 1969, p. 3), but, surely, the weakness of social welfare expenditure was a topic to exercise the minds of a Labor opposition long excluded from power. However, whilst reform of the health sector was an immediate priority of the Labor Party, the general attitude to welfare provision was deeply ambiguous since Labor was only hesitatingly abandoning its long-held commitment to a selective social policy premised on an economistic strategy of social amelioration through state control of income from employment. Minimum wage levels were set by the Commonwealth Conciliation and Arbitration Commission (before 1956, the Commonwealth Court of Conciliation and Arbitration), Australia's most distinctive state apparatus for the settlement of industrial disputes, and so long as that level was such as to provide for the needs of a wage-earner and his dependants,[3] and so long as there was full employment, it was an arguable proposition that the Australian residual welfare state plus minimum wages system achieved the same degree of social protection as more universalist systems by other means. Even if Australia did not constitute a mature welfare state by European standards, it provided a 'wage-earners' welfare state' for those in the labour market and that, in reality, was the main concern for the labour movement as a whole (see Castles, 1985, pp. 82–8).

The very dramatic changes in Australian public policy since the late 1960s are attributable to the complex interaction of a variety of social, political and economic factors. The growth of affluence and the post-war influx of migrants were amongst influences which contributed to a change in attitudes (see Horne, 1980). At the same time, there was a growing perception that Australia's status as one of the elite group of super-rich nations was in jeopardy. As Australia descended rung by rung down the per capita GNP league table, so that by 1982, according to one estimate, it only ranked sixteenth (Jackson, 1985, p. 231. Cf. Dowrick and Nguyen, 1987), traditional policies like tariff protection came in for systematic reevaluation. Electoral strategy also had a major role in inducing change. Labor, out of office for two decades, was looking around for new policy prescriptions that might at last win it office.

Changes in perceptions and attitudes were not restricted to any particular section of the population, but it was Labor, under the leadership of Gough Whitlam, which sought to mobilize that feeling with the slogan, 'It's Time' in its victorious electoral campaign of December 1972. The last vestiges of Australia's racist migration policy were an immediate victim of that victory and a 25 per cent reduction of tariffs followed soon after. Moreover, the Whitlam government came to office with an ambitious programme of welfare reform, which was now beginning to be seen both as an important source of a renewed electoral appeal and as a moral crusade, given the realization in Australia, as elsewhere in the advanced states, that the growth of affluence had masked rather than abolished the existence of poverty (Henderson et al., 1970).

Between the budget years 1972–73 and 1975–76, social expenditure as a percentage of GDP increased from 12.5 per cent to 17.6 per cent, even so still very close to the bottom of the OECD league table of welfare state spending (OECD, 1985, p. 86). This proportionately massive and rapid increase in welfare provision was partly due to increased generosity of existing schemes, partly to a shift to greater universalism (e.g. the partial abandonment of means testing for age pensions) and wider coverage, and partly to the introduction of new programmes (amongst them a comprehensive national health insurance scheme called Medibank and a supporting mothers' benefit). The change was all the more spectacular given the economic storm clouds which had gathered from the time of the first oil shock in late 1973. In the Whitlam era, the Australian labour movement began, for the first time, to pursue a European-type welfare strategy at just that point when the economic preconditions for such a policy were being called into question.

In the period 1974–9, Australia's macroeconomic performance deteriorated radically. Growth in GDP per capita had been an average of 3.3 per cent in the period 1960–73, but now fell to 1.4 per cent per annum. The 1974–9 period also saw an increase in unemployment from 1.9 to 5.0 per cent and in inflation from 3.7 to 12.1 per cent (OECD, 1986). Overall, this amounted to a decline in performance as bad as any in the OECD. The period of the early 1980s saw a reversal of this trend. Between 1980 and 1984, economic growth increased and unemployment and inflation decreased markedly, and Australia moved to approximately the OECD median position on all these economic measures. Moreover, the Hawke Labor government, which on coming to power early in 1983 had promised to create half a million new jobs in its first three years in office, was, against the better judgement of most professional economists, able to deliver on its promise and with some five months to spare. As in policy stance, the overwhelming impression of economic performance from the 1960s onward is one of flux, a lack of a consistent pattern. That impression is reinforced by a new period of economic crisis beginning in 1985, with a progressively rapid adverse change in Australia's terms of trade leading to a decline in overseas indebtedness, a fall in the exchange rate and a need to cut domestic public expenditure. It was this crisis which in mid 1986 made the Treasurer, Paul Keating, speak out about the dangers of Australia becoming a 'banana republic'.

The economic roller-coaster ride of these years had immediate resonances in the political and policy arenas. In November 1975, the Whitlam government was dismissed by the Governor-General after the refusal of supply by the Upper House, a course of events regarded by many on the left as being wholly unconstitutional (see Horne, 1976). It was succeeded by a rightist Liberal-Country Party coalition, under Malcolm Fraser, which was the first government in the OECD to pursue a consistently monetarist policy, including strenuous attacks on public spending and the abandonment of many of the programmes of its predecessor, not least amongst them Medibank, the Labor health insurance scheme. Australia had its welfare backlash before it had anything like a fully mature welfare state (Stretton, 1980, pp. 43–60)! Both the political tensions leading to the ousting of Labor and the economic policies pursued thereafter owe not a little to the historical conjuncture of drastic economic downturn and an unprecedentedly rapid increase in public expenditure, and to the belief that the spending policies of the Whitlam government had greatly exacerbated the impact of the oil shock. Controlling inflation first was the watchword of the Fraser government right through until 1983 when the coalition was defeated at the polls. In its period of office, inflation had been reduced from 15 to 10 per cent, but at the cost of a rise in unemployment from 4.5 to 9.8 per cent; the composition of the 'misery index' had changed, its extent had not!

The new Labor government, heeding the lessons of the past decade, attempted to combine caution with an innovative search for greater economic efficiency and political control of the economy. Social amelioration remained on the political agenda, as was immediately demonstrated by the restoration of a public health care system under the new name of 'Medicare', but tempered by ostentatious caution about the inflationary effects of increased public expenditure. By 1984, it had donned the self-imposed straitjacket of the so-called 'Trilogy' of fiscal promises, that it would not in the life of the next Parliament increase either total taxation, total government expenditure or the size of the budget deficit as percentages of gross domestic product. In the search for efficiency, there was a switch from the Whitlam government's earlier attempt to reduce protection to an emphasis on the deregulation of financial and currency markets. There was nevertheless an important element of continuity insofar as the retreat from protection and the new emphasis on 'freeing up' markets were at one in implying that Australia must in future face the fact that its economic success was a function of its adaptation to the exigencies imposed by the international economy.

Both the Trilogy and deregulation were potentially at odds with what was, undoubtedly, amongst the more important policy innovations of the Hawke government, an attempt to seek a new social consensus through a formally negotiated agreement – the *Accord* – between the Labor Party and the Australian Council of Trade Unions (ACTU). This was inaugurated in February 1983, before Labor came to office, and, including as it did proposals for prices control, orderly wage-bargaining, the protection of living standards for wage-earners and improvement of the social wage, and active intervention to promote full employment and greater investment, might be regarded as a blueprint for a new corporatist model of economic policy-making in Australia (Stillwell, 1986). The need to renegotiate the substance of the agreement with the employers on coming to office, and deterioration in Australia's external trading conditions from 1985 onwards, gradually led to a downgrading of the social wage and interventionist components of the package, leaving it, in much revised form, as an instrument for controlling both unemployment and inflation through voluntary, but highly manipulated, wage restraint.

In mid-1986, with the prospect of real cuts in social expenditure and the Accord itself in seeming jeopardy from the impact of yet another economic crisis, it was, perhaps, scarcely surprising that parts of the Australian labour movement were themselves starting to think that what was required was a complete revamping of economic and social policy priorities. The ACTU response was to send a delegation to a number of European neo-corporatist nations (including Austria, Norway and Sweden) and to issue a report effectively recommending that the price of trade union support for an economy restructured along internationally competitive lines must be concessions of the kind typical in the smaller European states: social wage enhancement, industrial democracy and what it described as a shift to 'strategic unionism' (ACTU, 1987). After some decades of fluctuating economic and political fortunes, and diverse experimentation with new policy initiatives, the dilemma of the Australian left remained much as it had been in the late 1960s: how simultaneously to combine electoral success, adequate economic performance and progressive reform. The ACTU delegation to Europe was only the latest attempt to find a viable solution to that dilemma.

The notion that European solutions might provide an answer to Australian problems raises in a highly practical form the central question which it is the task of this volume to explore. Our theme is the distinctiveness of national patterns of policy outcomes and policy-making institutions and the way in which such patterns have been shaped by their historical context. Although our initial account of Australia's post-war policy development has dwelt neither on institutions nor historical context, enough has been said to demonstrate the distinctiveness of the Australian pattern of policy outcomes not merely in terms of theoretical puzzles but also of differences with other countries. Throughout the period, Australia was an extreme welfare state laggard measured in expenditure terms. In the latter half of the 1970s, its overall macro-economic performance deteriorated extremely rapidly and was very close to the bottom of the distribution for the OECD member countries, and this poor performance was the more remarkable given that it followed two decades of sustained full employment and low inflation. At the beginning of the period Australia was highly insulated from the direct impact of the world economy; by the end of the period, it was seeking desperately to become a part of the economic mainstream.

An attempt to copy another country's policy initiatives or implant its policy-making institutions and structures of the kind implied by the recommendations of the ACTU delegation to Europe rests on the premise that differences in the character of the existing policy pattern are of insufficient magnitude to prevent the transcendence of policy diversity through conscious political choice and social engineering. An evaluation of the possibility of such a policy transformation requires an understanding of the economic circumstances which have shaped the development of Australian capitalism and the historical conditions which have shaped the responses of individuals, groups and classes to the situation in which they have found themselves. Moreover, the very fact of adopting a particular policy initiative or devising a set of institutional arrangements constrains the alternatives for those who come later. Established policies and institutions are themselves a major part of the historical context of subsequent policy change or inertia. Thus, only through an historically contextualized political economy of public policy development can we suggest an answer to the question of whether Australia can overcome 'its present discontents' by purposive policy change.

Economic Vulnerability in Theory and Practice

In seeking to locate the nature of national distinctiveness, there is a temptation to make a premature shift to a level of specificity at which differences are inherently more salient than possible similarities with other nations. In terms of the logic of comparative analysis, such an analytical move is always illegitimate unless it is preceded by an attempt to exhaust the explanatory potential of higher order similarities between groups of nations. It is always necessary to examine the possibility that the phenomena we observe are the consequences of features nations have in common before attributing them to national singularities.

Arguably, such a tendency to analytical closure is a feature of the theory most frequently offered within the political economy paradigm to explain the divergence of Australian policy development from that of other advanced capitalist states. This explanation is a variant of dependency theory, which suggests that countries such as Argentina, Australia, Canada and New Zealand may be grouped together as 'semi-peripheral' states, highly dependent on the imperatives of international capital and, hence, particularly vulnerable to economic conditions emanating from beyond their borders (see Wallerstein, 1979; Evans,

1979; Crough and Wheelwright, 1983). Such an explanation has the undoubted virtue of highlighting Australia's potentially considerable vulnerability to exogenous shocks in the international economic environment, a characteristic that would, arguably, account for the particular severity of Australia's economic problems in the late 1970s, but at some cost in a prior definitional exclusion of that country from the 'core' states of advanced capitalism. Before concluding that Australian distinctiveness is attributable to the fact that it is not a fully developed capitalist economy, it is worth exploring the possibility that Australian economic vulnerability is the result of factors at least to some degree operative in other advanced capitalist states.

The notion that there may be systematic variation in the degree to which capitalist economies may be vulnerable to external economic forces is well established in the literature of comparative political economy. As Dahl and Tufte argue:

In order to develop and maintain a relatively high standard of living, the small country must necessarily go beyond its own boundaries in search of markets, and often in search of raw materials, labor, and capital investment as well. As a consequence, the small country is highly dependent on the behavior of foreign actors not subject to its authority. (Dahl and Tufte, 1973, p. 130)

As developed by Cameron, this hypothesis focuses particularly on the extent to which external vulnerability is a function of the extent of international trade and the degree to which 'domestic prices of commodities, labor and capital [are] established by supply and demand in the international rather than the domestic market' (Cameron, 1978, p. 1249). Since size of the domestic market is both theoretically and empirically inversely related to trade dependence, the assumption must be that small countries will be potentially more vulnerable to exogenous shocks than larger ones. The smallish Australian domestic market might, therefore, be adduced as a significant factor leading to economic vulnerability and hence fluctuating economic performance *were it not for the fact that, as we noted previously, Australia defies the normal tendency for small economies to be open, trading economies.*

This problem can be resolved once it is realised that, for small countries, a large volume of overseas trade is a sufficient rather than a necessary condition of an incapacity to determine the prices of commodities, labour and capital. At least as important is the structure of trade and investment flows. Even a nation with a vast internal market may be heavily dependent on the import of vital raw materials and may experience serious dislocation if price levels rise. Heavy dependence on a narrow range of exports is likely to have similar consequences where prices on the world market are falling, and such export dependence is, once again, likely to be most pronounced in the smaller economies.

Certainly, it is precisely the situation of countries, like Australia and New Zealand, which depend almost exclusively on resource intensive exports (Krause, 1984, p. 282). Moreover, reliance on resource intensive exports is far from being a new phenomenon: Australia and New Zealand rose to prosperity 'on the sheep's back', and Australia's fortunes have always been tied to cycles of boom and bust in the minerals sector. Australia may not appear particularly economically vulnerable in terms of the extent of her overseas trade; she appears far more so, taking into account her *terms of trade* (that is the relationship of the prices of her imports and exports), which manifest greater fluctuation than any other OECD country in the period 1960 to 1984 (see OECD, 1986).

In a sense, a focus on the structure of trade brings us back to dependency theory, since what distinguishes the economies of the Third World 'periphery' is their total reliance on exporting primary commodities to the capitalist 'centre'. However, what emerges from the above analysis is not a clear-cut distinction between types of economies, but rather a spectrum of degrees of external vulnerability depending on a variety of factors including size of markets, the extent of trade and its structure as well as the need to attract overseas investment and the degree of foreign ownership.

Looked at in these terms, Australia certainly falls somewhere towards the vulnerable end of the spectrum of advanced capitalist states, but not necessarily more so than a country like Denmark with a smaller market than Australia's, a much larger volume of trade, and a considerable reliance on the export of processed primary commodities. Nor, any longer, is Australia the only advanced capitalist state which is highly dependent on the export of a small range of resource intensive commodities. With the exploitation of North Sea gas and oil in the last few decades, that has now also become the lot of the Netherlands, the United Kingdom and Norway. No one would describe Denmark or the Netherlands as 'semi-peripheral' economies for these reasons, just as no one would describe Japan in these terms because of that country's heavy dependence on imports of raw materials. It is just as inappropriate to use that label to describe economies such as Australia and New Zealand. All these countries are advanced capitalist states characterized by greater or lesser *potential* vulnerability to external shock, and the appropriate task for comparative public policy analysis is to locate typical patterns of institutional and policy response to the problems imposed by varying degrees and types of vulnerability.

It would be natural to suppose that a high degree of economic vulnerability would make it very much harder for policy-makers to cope with externally generated shocks. Yet, turning from theory to the empirical record suggests that such an expectation is only very patchily supported by the available evidence. Certainly, both Belgium and the

Netherlands appear to have suffered a continuing deterioration in economic performance since 1973, whilst Australia and Denmark experienced a precipitous decline after the first oil shock, only to recover their lost ground in relative terms in the early 1980s. Otherwise, with the exception of Ireland, the smaller and more vulnerable economies weathered the storm remarkably well. Both Austria and Switzerland maintained the strong performance which was already quite evident in the 1960s, and Finland, New Zealand, Norway and Sweden all improved their macroeconomic performance relative to other OECD nations.

In policy terms, of course, what is important is not macroeconomic policy in the abstract, much less relativities between countries, but rather the extent to which the policies adopted in times of economic crisis serve to provide social protection to individuals faced by personal disaster from the workings of the capitalist economy. The extent of unemployment is, obviously, crucial in this regard, and here the seemingly more vulnerable economies have an outstanding record; of the seven OECD countries which succeeded in preventing average annual unemployment in the early 1980s exceeding 6 per cent, only one was a large state (Japan), and the rest were small (Austria, Finland, New Zealand, Norway, Switzerland and Sweden). Other than preserving full employment, the only policy instrument available to minimize the impact on the individual of economic crisis is an extensive welfare safety-net, and it may not be insignificant that three of the worst performers amongst the smaller states in respect of employment levels, Belgium, Denmark and the Netherlands, are amongst the OECD countries with the highest social expenditures. (*Circa* 1981, the four largest welfare states were, in order of magnitude, Belgium, the Netherlands, Sweden and Denmark (OECD, 1985)). In other words, of the eleven small states mentioned above, nine succeeded either in mitigating the direct employment effects of economic crisis or compensated for them by massive welfare intervention. Only Ireland, much the poorest of these countries, and Australia failed in both respects.

Our initial puzzles of Australian public policy are thus compounded. Consideration of the theoretical link between the size of economies and economic performance suggests that economic vulnerability should be most pronounced in the smallest nations. Yet such is apparently not generally the case. Most small nations succeed in providing adequate social protection despite their vulnerability. Australia is puzzling because it is an exception to that empirical regularity, but the regularity is itself puzzling as a seeming contradiction to expectations drawn from economic theory.

To understand why externally vulnerable states actually manifest as high or a higher degree of social protection, it is necessary to move beyond a purely economic analysis and examine the political and institutional responses of classes, groups and individuals to the economic circumstances in which they find themselves. Such a move follows naturally from interest-based theories of political action, whether of a pluralist or marxist kind. In the pluralist account, individuals respond to economic conditions by seeking to adjust the workings of the market in such a way as to maximize individual satisfactions. In such accounts, individuals who perceive themselves as particularly subject to external shocks may be regarded precisely as those most likely to take collective action to minimize exposure to risk. Looked at in this way, the greater vulnerability of small economies may be seen as a greater spur to socially protective political action. In these terms, there ceases to be a contradiction between the expectation generated of economic theory that small economies will be the most vulnerable and the socially protective record of the smaller European states in the crises of the 1970s and 1980s. Economic theory is not so much mistaken as incomplete, for what it ignores is that rational actors, seeking to maximize their own interests, will attempt to use 'politics against markets' in an attempt to further their economic wellbeing.

The classical marxist account, framed as it is in terms of wholly antithetical (zero-sum) class interests, effectively denies the possibility of collective risk minimization as a political strategy. However, much contemporary marxist theorizing admits of the possibility of class compromises, resting on temporary coincidence of such interests at particular historical junctures and/or locations within the world system. Under such circumstances, otherwise antagonistic classes or class factions may find that they have common (variable-sum) interests, and may create institutional structures and ideological frameworks expressing and seeking to solidify the substance of their precarious agreement. It would seem to be an arguable proposition that awareness by historical actors of national vulnerability to shocks emanating from the external economic environment would be precisely the type of circumstance which might be most conducive to relatively long-lasting class compromise. Dramatic fluctuations in macroeconomic performance caused by exogenous shocks impose economic, social and political costs on otherwise opposed classes which it may be in their common interest to minimize or avoid. The costs to the working class in terms of unemployment and reduced income are obvious, but the potential costs to capitalists are no less. On the one hand, irrespective of the logic of capital that maximum returns to capital as a whole will accrue from riding the swings and roundabouts of economic fluctuation, for many individual capitalists economic crisis around every corner implies a constant threat of imminent extinction. On the other hand, what is an economic and social threat to the working class and poor is simultaneously a political threat to the economic order, since economic dislocation necessarily heightens popular discontent. This latter phenomenon is, of course, a variant of the notion of a legitimization crisis, but what must be noted is that the potential treat to legitimacy is inherently greater where external vulnerability exists. Under the circumstances outlined, class actors, who perceive the immediacy of the threat from their international environment, may have very strong motives indeed to establish class compromises with the intention of insuring themselves against the risks of external vulnerability.

Far from being surprising, then, that small, potentially vulnerable, states have a good record of protecting individuals from economic crisis, it is just what might be expected in terms both of pluralist and contemporary marxist theory. Potential vulnerability may be seen as a stimulus to political and institutional responses of a kind which are consciously designed to diminish the degree and/or impact of economic fluctuation. What may be more surprising is that this analysis is presented as a theoretical prologue to an account of the development of a distinctive Australian policy pattern. Given that Australia was one of the very few smaller countries which failed to offer reasonable protection to its citizens in the crises of the 1970s and 1980s, it may appear strange to focus on the conditions leading to political action which had such protection as its objective. However, as the remainder of this chapter will seek to demonstrate, what is distinctive about the pattern of public policy which developed in Australia this century was not the absence of such political action and class compromise, but the particular institutional and ideological form it took. In the past two decades, the traditional Australian response to economic vulnerability has proved far less adequate than in the past, and it is for precisely this reason that policy has been in as great a state of flux as economic performance.

Institutional and Ideological Responses to Economic Vulnerability

In this section, we shall seek to contrast the Australian pattern of institutional and ideological response to problems of external vulnerability with that characteristic of the smaller countries of Western Europe. It is, however, important to stress that such a contrast is for a variety of reasons ideal typical in character. First, national policy profiles always involve a mix of diverse strategies and a contrast over any appreciable period of time will rarely be able to point to the exclusive use of one set of policy instruments in a given country as compared with the use of an entirely different set in another country or group of countries. For instance, we shall argue that Australia is distinctive in the extent to which it has deliberately set out to protect its manufacturing sector by the use of tariff barriers and import quotas, but this is not to say that other states, small and large, have not occasionally resorted to such a strategy. Second, a contrast between a single country, Australia, and a group of countries, like the smaller European states, inherently involves an underestimation and fudging of the national distinctiveness of the latter. Apart from historical differences between them, a whole range of social, economic, cultural and even locational differences may facilitate or hinder the adoption of particular policy options.

Finally, it is not the case that the countries here contrasted are the only ones which seek to find solutions to problems of external vulnerability. At times of severe international economic dislocation, all countries, large and small, experience such problems and devise policy strategies accordingly. The only distinction that we would stress is that the countries experiencing chronic and enduring vulnerability are those most likely to have the incentive to transform initially temporary policy compromises into institutional arrangements to cope with the high probability of future dislocation. This distinction is, arguably, the vital criterion of difference between the organic historical development of neo-corporatist arrangements, in countries such as Austria and Sweden, and artificial attempts to institute tripartite mechanisms of prices and incomes control, in countries like Britain and the United States. In our terms, the reason the latter tend to fold up after a short period is that the perception of external threat tends to fade more rapidly in the larger states. Seen in this way, neo-corporatist political arrangements may be regarded as an institutionalized response to the economic problems imposed by endemic external vulnerability.

In terms of policy patterns and institutional arrangements, the diverse responses to external vulnerability of the smaller states may be respectively labelled as the *politics of domestic compensation* and *the politics of domestic defence*.[4] The former may be seen as the characteristic response of the smaller European states to the vulnerability forced on them by attempting to compete in world markets. The strategy starts from the premise that for economies without a sizeable domestic market to cushion the impact of external changes in demand and supply, there is no alternative but to respond directly to market forces and adjust production roughly along lines dictated by external requirements. Given that all these countries are dependent on the export of a relatively narrow range of manufactured goods, the prices of which are externally determined, any wage or price developments which threaten external competitiveness can only lead to lost orders, a balance of payments crisis and eventual currency devaluation.

But a strategy of rolling with the punches of economic fluctuation inherently involves massive dislocation costs, and it is these which the politics of domestic compensation sets out to mitigate. A range of policy instruments are utilized for this purpose, with the mix varying quite considerably from country to country, but all have in common an attempt to facilitate, or even speed up, the response to the external environment, whilst compensating for the inevitable costs to individuals and firms of the changes brought about thereby. These policy instruments include: regulatory and fiscal efforts to smooth fluctuations in the business cycle (for example, Sweden's investment reserve), subsidies and other active intervention to promote industrial restructuring, active labour market policies aimed both at shifting the labour force into more productive sectors and protecting individuals from the consequences of such restructuring (for example, by retraining programmes and dislocation allowances), wages and prices controls to prevent export commodities being priced out of the market, generous income maintenance programmes for those directly or indirectly damaged by economic change, and, more generally, a substantial extension of the public sector in both expenditure and employment terms with the aim of enhancing government control of the national income. Each of these policies necessarily involves a set of trade-offs for organized groups within the national collectivity which can only be resolved through institutional arrangements which permit continuous negotiation and monitoring of the balance of advantages and disadvantages accruing to particular groups from the policy pattern as a whole. Such arrangements are, in effect, those usually described in terms of 'neo-corporatism', a phenomenon which developed precisely in the economic crisis of the 1930s and, in its most enduring institutional form, in the smaller countries of Western Europe.[5]

The emergence of neo-corporatist arrangements in some of the smaller states of Europe dates from the 1930s and was consolidated in the post-war period. The politics of domestic defence was an earlier response to the depressed economic conditions which in the last decades of the nineteenth century afflicted the primary commodity exporting countries of Australia and New Zealand with particular severity. Its policy content in outcome terms is rather harder to capture than is the case of the politics of domestic compensation, since its rationale consisted of an attempt to use policy and design institutional structures with the aim of preventing outcomes (that is, major economic changes) from coming about. Rather than rolling with the punches of economic fluctuation, the chosen response was to seek a defensive strategy to block their impact. Basically, the politics of domestic defence consisted, and to a limited extent still does, of three closely interrelated policies: protection of manufacturing industry through tariffs and other trade restrictions, conciliation and arbitration of industrial disputes and control of immigration. Each may be seen as interlocking components of a system of shock-absorbers designed to defend and stabilize the existing structure of economic opportunities and rewards from any rapid or excessive disturbance from exogenous forces. Together, they may be seen as constituting a structure of social protection quite different in form from that later adopted in Western Europe.

How much protection was to be afforded Australian industry was the central issue of political debate and controversy in the years immediately preceding and following Federation in 1901. The high tariff levels which were a characteristic feature of trade policy from the early 1920s onwards were only partly, although always rhetorically, associated with the objectives of building up infant industries and fostering national development, and were at least as much designed *to defend* the existing character of domestic industrial production and urban infrastructure which had experienced periodic structural transformation under the impetus of the natural protection afforded Australia by her distance from overseas suppliers in time of international crisis. A similar motivation applied under circumstances where native industries were threatened by decreases in import prices. Rather than permitting local enterprises to fail or wage levels to decline, tariffs were demanded by both manufacturers and unions, and granted by the institutionalized agency of protection, the Tariff Board. Already by the 1920s, the nature of protection as an instrument of class compromise was quite apparent to perceptive commentators such as Brigden:

The protection of manufacturers and of labour marches in one indissoluble unity, and . . . the two lions of employer and employed lie down at the same feast, with the same 'lamb', consuming the consumer . . . We protect industries against the competition of high wage enterprises in the USA with the same gusto as against low living standards in Asia. (Brigden, 1925, p. 29).

Moreover, the legitimacy of adopting a protective policy was reinforced whenever public policy was directed at enhancing population through migration since the labour intensive character of small-scale manufacturing for the home market provided the basis for labour absorption and the higher wages that could be paid in protected industries were seen as the best possible lure to prospective migrants (Butlin et al., 1982, pp. 60–1; Anderson, 1938, p. 102). Finally, in addition to serving as a defence of existing manufacturing industry and working class incomes and facilitating population growth, protection may be seen, although such an objective was not consciously articulated, as an automatic shock-absorber of external fluctuation in much the same way as high levels of state employment in the contemporary smaller European states slow the impact of changes emanating from the world market. Living entirely off the sheep's back would, in a world of fluctuating commodity prices, have meant both higher peaks of prosperity and lower troughs of depression and unemployment.

Given these considerations, it is scarcely surprising if some economists have seen tariff protection in Australia as a sort of insurance system designed to prevent undue fluctuations in income distribution as a consequence of changes in the external economic environment. Indeed, it has been suggested that tariffs were utilized to achieve what might be called 'a conservative social welfare function', by which any decline in real incomes was minimized, the government provided insurance against income loss and social peace was protected by ensuring that 'no significant group's income shall fall if that of the others is rising' (Corden, 1974, p. 108). That such a policy could be embraced in Australia, and be regarded as an effective means for bringing about a 'fair' distribution between classes, whilst the smaller European economies could see no alternative but free trade in manufactured goods is, of course, largely a function of the diverse character of these countries' respective bases of comparative advantage: in Australia, an overwhelming emphasis on resource intensive exports, and in Europe specialization on a narrow range of manufactured commodities. Tariff protection of manufacturing industry in Australia may have been a long-term source of economic inefficiency, but it did not mean, as it would have in Europe, killing the goose that lays the golden eggs.

The role of tariffs as a defence of working class incomes eventually became an article of faith of the Australian labour movement, but in the debate on the policy directions to be taken by the new Federation it was a concession granted to the manufacturing interest in return for a rather more direct form of wage guarantee. The depression of the 1890s led to a major shift in labour movement strategy. Having previously focused attention on wage struggles with particular employers, the unions, now beset by high levels of unemployment, declining wages and a dramatic decline in the potency of the strike weapon, turned to the political arena in order to protect their interests. Employers at the time were deeply divided both over the issue of tariffs and of 'unfair' competition, and those favouring protection and the abolition of price undercutting through sweated labour could only get their way 'by conceding some of labour's demands for legal wage regulation' (McCarthy, 1970, p. 182). Initially, those concessions were in the form of State boards and tribunals with voluntary or compulsory powers to settle disputes and fix wages, and compulsory powers for the conciliation and arbitration of disputes were written into the new Federal Constitution. In 1906, this latter became the basis for the historic compromise, enunciated in policy terms as the 'New Protection', by which Labor parliamentary support was mobilized behind the tariff in return for a legally guaranteed minimum wage for unskilled labour. In the 1907 Harvester Judgement, the President of the Commonwealth Court of Conciliation and Arbitration, Mr Justice Higgins, declared that he could not think of 'any other standard appropriate' . . . to assess a 'fair and reasonable wage . . . than the normal needs of the average employee regarded as a human being living in a civilized community' and made it clear in a subsequent judgement that '(t)he remuneration of the employee cannot be allowed to depend on the profits of his individual employer' (Higgins, 1922).[6] No clearer articulation of a socially protective goal could possibly be imagined!

Thereafter, the notion of a 'living wage', one sufficient to support a normal-sized family, was a fundamental orthodoxy of the Australian public policy pattern, and it was notionally guaranteed by subsequent indexation on the basis of changes in the consumer price index. But if a more elaborate and regulated system of state intervention in wage-fixing than in any other capitalist nation provided the Australian working class with some defence against world market fluctuation, it necessarily created inflexibilities for employers who could only demand tariff protection and raise prices to the extent that these did not flow on into the costs of resource intensive commodity exports with serious implications for that sector's external competitiveness. In response to the orthodoxy of the living wage, the employers progressively fostered the idea that wage awards must be tempered by the 'capacity of the economy to pay'. It is, at least, an arguable proposition that the fact that in Australia, unlike the corporatist economies of the smaller European states, the apparatus of wage-fixing was ostensibly above the political struggle and in the hands of a seemingly neutral judicial arbiter, armed with conflicting, but highly compelling, 'myths', was a means for squaring this particular circle (see Scherer, 1983, pp. 166–8). In normal times, the arbitration system could serve to establish a market-clearing wage acceptable to labour under circumstances where, otherwise, wage levels would have necessarily reflected the instabilities of the much smaller land and capital resource based sector. In times of massive economic dislocation, as in the 1930s and during the Korean War, the Arbitration Court could step in and use its accumulated legitimacy to impose wage restraint in the name of the twin imperatives of 'capacity to pay' and national economic survival. In these terms, one might regard the functioning of Australia's arbitration system for much of this century as an institutional mechanism analogous to European corporatist wage-bargaining: both were devices to mediate the conflict between labour and capital in a threatening external environment.[7]

Control of immigration, the third component of the politics of domestic defence, may be seen as a response to the dilemmas of national development in a new nation of European settlement. On the one hand, there was a natural 'desire to attain a population of a size sufficient to make effective use of known resources (and a) fear that population might be insufficient to meet a threat of aggression' (Borrie, 1963, p. 2). From the time of early settlement right down to the present, Australian governments have seen it as a primary responsibility of public policy to foster migration to the extent permitted by economic conditions, and where they could to manipulate economic conditions (for example, by tariff protection, wage regulation and organizing the inflow of foreign capital) in such a way as to facilitate population growth through migration. On the other hand, the objective of national development through population growth was simultaneously an arena of aggravated class conflict. The extent and character of permitted migration has been a perennial source of contention between employers and employees, simply because, in an isolated colonial outpost with only a relatively small indigenous population, the nexus between the supply and demand for labour was brutally obvious to all sections of society. In the first hundred or so years after settlement (that is, until around the close of the nineteenth century), employers consistently promoted schemes for increasing the labour force, whether through increased transportation of convicts, more assisted passages for English and Irish settlers, or bringing in Pacific Islanders to work on the sugar plantations of Northern Queensland. Equally consistently, every employer scheme to bring in labour and every influx of migrants was met by working class protest and opposition, based on an admixture of fears of the employment and wages consequences of a looser labour market and an increasing tide of racialist sentiment (see McQueen, 1970, pp. 42–55).

The crucial class compromise came once more with Federation and the adoption of the 'white Australia' policy which was to be an established part of the Australian public policy pattern for the next seventy years.[8] By excluding any further inflow of low-wage, coloured labour, Australia avoided the normal destiny of European colonial settlements of a segmented labour market in which the indigenous population was segregated as the supplier of low wage, labour intensive production (see Duncan and Fogarty, 1984, pp. 40–1). The interlocking character of the various components of the politics of domestic defence is once again demonstrated by the use of protective tariffs to assist the Queensland sugar industry, making it economically viable to do without Pacific Island labour and offer wges comparable to those paid elsewhere in Australia. The link between the 'white Australia' policy and the defence of working class living standards in face of external threat could hardly have been clearer:

It was no accident that racism should be given such stark institutional form during this period of nation building, for the White Australia Policy was New Protection writ large. Whatever prosperity the citizens of the new Commonwealth might share was to be safeguarded by shutting out unwanted competition. (McIntyre, 1985, p. 54)

Given the developmental emphasis on population growth at a rate faster than could be supplied by natural increase, the 'white Australia' policy could hardly be expected to dispose of all conflict over the issue of the extent of immigration. However, it did provide a consensual framework within which government intervention to overcome the natural barriers to migration imposed by distance from Europe could be used as a regulator of labour supply, balancing the needs of employers with the labour movement's demand that existing real wage levels should not be undermined. The belief that the supply of labour was susceptible to such policy manipulation was an underlying premise of the post-Federation historic compromise which sought to tame Australia's potential external vulnerability to the mutual benefit of the industrial working class and employers in the sheltered manufacturing and services sector.

Because they have similar objectives, the policy strategies inherent in the politics of domestic compensation and the politics of domestic defence have many affinities: their pivotal institutions are arrangements to secure greater control of wages (through corporatist wage-bargaining or conciliation and arbitration), both seek to promote high levels of employment through government intervention (through active labour market policy or tariffs), and both seek to protect the individual against economic risk (through high levels of transfers or minimum wage levels). This last similarity is the key to understanding one of our initial puzzles: why Australia has achieved a distribution of incomes not significantly less egalitarian than the advanced welfare states of Western Europe? Social protection, however it is achieved, means altering the distribution of rewards that flows from the unregulated market mechanism. That Australia, no less than Sweden and Norway, has been characterized by distributional outcomes more equal than countries in which political forces have not pressed so effectively to modify the impact of the market offers support for both the view that 'politics matters' and that politics often involves conscious strategic choice.

But, although born of the common dilemma of securing social protection under circumstances of economic vulnerability, the two strategies have substantially different implications for the character of the emergent policy pattern. First, it is immediately apparent that the strategy of domestic compensation has an inherently more dynamic economic growth potential than that based on domestic defence. Grabbing competitive niches in new markets is built into the former, whilst tariffs serve, precisely, to insulate the economy from competition. This difference in strategies is presumably amongst the factors which explain why economic growth rates this century have been so much higher in the smaller countries of Western Europe than in either Australia or New Zealand. Second, whilst, as we shall see subsequently, the Australian state was much stronger than that of most European countries at around the turn of the century, its potential for dynamic growth was more restricted than in these countries. Whereas shelter

from economic vulnerability through domestic compensation could only
be effected by increasing the extent of government employment and
transfers, domestic defence sheltered labour intensive enterprises in the
private sector by keeping out foreign competition. Finally, the two
strategies of social protection had quite different implications for the
development of the welfare state since compensation necessarily led to
the expansion of welfare transfers and services whenever the costs of
economic change imposed new risks to the individual, whereas the
defence of working class living standards through the wages system
meant that, from its very inception, the welfare state would be seen
as a residual safety-net of the last resort. Australia's poor welfare
performance in recent decades is a direct legacy of the institutional form
taken by the historic compromise at the beginning of the century.

The contrast between the strategies, institutional forms and implications of these two, ideal typical responses to external vulnerability also
reveals a fascinating parallel with the two main strategies of social
amelioration advocated by the democratic socialist parties of advanced
capitalism: namely, social democracy and labourism. Social democratic
reformism can readily be seen as an attempt to tame capitalism by
compensating the poor and the weak for the inevitable dislocation caused
by economic competition, whereas labourism stresses the need to defend
the working man by the economistic strategy of protecting or enhancing
the size of his paypacket. From a cynical viewpoint, this coincidence of
responses to economic vulnerability and strategies of social amelioration
might be taken to imply that the dominant ideological forms of
democratic socialism were merely the propaganda facades for the
variants of industrial policy favoured by bourgeois elites in small and
potentially vulnerable economies.

But such an interpretation is far too simplistic. On the one hand, it
ignores the extent to which both responses are genuine class compromises,
serving the interests of a sizeable part of the working class as well as
sections of the capitalist class, and, on the other, it neglects the role of
the labour movement in establishing such compromises in the first place.
With reference to the latter, the ideologies of democratic socialism may
be seen as the set of fighting slogans by which the labour movement
mobilizes support for the establishment of policies and institutions
encapsulating that variant of a compromise most favourable to working
class interests. Quite apart from the fact that such interests are necessarily somewhat different from those of capital, tactical considerations
dictate that labour movement demands are pitched at such a level that
real advances can be presented as negotiated compromise. The
Australian Labor Party was extraordinarily hard-headed about this and
in its fight from the 1890s onward 'to make and unmake social
conditions' it offered its political opponents 'Support in Return for

Concessions' (see Crisp, 1983, p. 191). In the next section, we shall explore the nature of the historical circumstances which made the politics of domestic defence and a labourist strategy appear the most appropriate compromise at the time.

The Origins of Historic Compromises

Adopting a comparative political economy approach, we have located two quite different responses to the problems posed by high degrees of potential economic vulnerability: the politics of domestic compensation and the politics of domestic defence. The obvious question which then arises is why given countries settled for one rather than another of these historic compromises. Was the choice fortuitous, if conscious choice it was, or was it overwhelmingly determined by structural conditions? An answer can only be found by a comparision of the historical circumstances in which these diverse responses emerged. In the very limited space available, all that is possible is the briefest of discussions of the ways in which the situation confronting political actors in these countries differed and of the implications these constraints may have had for the adoption of coherent policy strategies. More than ever, the reader is warned that the summary comparisons are ideal typical in character and, in contrasting the situation of Australia with that of the smaller European states, do considerable violence to the diversity of the developmental experience of the latter.

Economic development Australia had a startlingly modern economic structure at the end of the nineteenth century with only 25 per cent of workers employed in rural industries, some 40 per cent in mining, manufacturing, construction and utilities, and the remainder in the service sector (Butlin and Dowie, 1969). Moreover, it was the rural sector, already predominantly organized on a capitalistic, non-labour intensive basis, which then, even more than now, was the source of virtually all Australia's export earnings. In contrast, many of the smaller countries of Western Europe remained to a greater or lesser degree peasant economies, and the process of industrialization that was to transform them into specialized manufacturing economies had, for the most part, only just begun. In these terms, it would appear that a major structural change in the economy was far less imperative in Australia, a country which had already found its niche of comparative advantage in the world market. Even though the issue of national development loomed large in Australian thinking at the time, and certainly included a wish to promote a larger manufacturing base, the problems that were most emphasized were those of population size and the extent of settlement rather than wholesale change in the established economic structure.

Standards of living Australia, just because she had proceeded a long way down the path of capitalist development, was, *circa* 1890, amongst the very richest countries in the world.[9] One numerical estimate suggests that Australian GDP per capita was at this time nearly 50 per cent higher than that of the USA and three times higher than those of small European countries like Austria, Finland, Norway and Sweden (see Maddison, 1977). Because of a tight labour market and strong demand in the mining and construction sectors, wages were high except in the 'sweated' trades, and working conditions and hours were favourable compared to those in Europe,[10] and there is no reason to doubt that individual workers and their organizations were fully aware of the contrast. After all, a not inconsiderable proportion of the wage-earning class were recent migrants who had the means of direct comparison between Australian conditions and those of their countries of origin. From such a comparative viewpoint, the notion that Australia was, or could easily be made into, 'the workingman's paradise' (the title of a novel written by a leading figure on the Australian Left in the last decade of the nineteenth century) could appear as genuinely persuasive, and a defensive posture by the trade unions is hardly surprising. Even the serious depression of the 1890s, which certainly disturbed the apple-cart of prosperity, with unemployment exceeding 10 per cent and sharply reduced wages, was hardly radicalizing in the normal sense since it promoted a desire to return to the good old days: the Harvester minimum was seen by many as precisely a step in that direction (McCarthy, 1968, pp. 497–502; Hancock, 1979, p. 131). By way of contrast, for the emergent Social Democratic parties of the smaller European states it was only too apparent that capitalist accumulation still had a very long way to go before it could offer anything like a decent standard of life for the working population, much less that surplus required for the establishment of socialism.

Social structure Australia at the turn of the century was amongst the most highly urbanized countries in the world, whilst the smaller European states retained substantial peasant minorities or, in some cases, majorities. Admittedly, the weaker feudal traditions of the smaller states made possible peasant mobilization against ruling elites, and eventually a reformist-democratic alliance of proletariat and peasantry through which Social Democratic rule was eventually established in some of these countries in the 1930s, but none of these smaller nations had anything like the urban base for popular mobilization drawn on by the Australian Labor Party after 1890. Moreover, Australia was extremely modern in class composition, insofar as it lacked an indigenous landed nobility or ruling class hallowed by tradition. There were, of course, large landowners and merchants, whose economic self-interest was opposed to the compromise represented by the New Protection, but, numerically, they were vastly outweighed by small traders and entrepreneurs in the manufacturing and services sector who were exactly those most likely to suffer most in an unregulated economic environment.[11]

Political mobilization The possibility for small traders, urban radicals and workingmen to make their voice heard politically came very early in Australia. In the majority of States, male suffrage was granted in the 1850s and parliamentary sovereignty was conferred at much the same time. By 1891, Labor held the balance of power in the New South Wales Assembly, the world's first Labor government briefly took office in Queensland in 1899, and the first Federal Labor administration took office in 1904. Throughout the first decade of the new century, the Labor Party at the Federal level was in a position to determine which of the contending protectionist and anti-protectionist parties should be in office, and a strategy of 'support in return for concessions' was far from being rhetorical. In 1910, Australia was the first country in the world to be ruled by a majority Labor government. Outside of parliament, trade unionism was also a growing force. Although the unions suffered setbacks in the depression of the 1890s, their growth thereafter was phenomenal and, with the strong impetus provided by the state through the conciliation and arbitration system, 'Australia became the world's most unionized nation in the first decades of this century', with the level of union density somewhere between 40–50 per cent by 1920 (Rawson, 1986, p. 21). Parliamentarianism and male suffrage were, generally, much later in coming in the smaller European states and, even in the countries of Scandinavia, the parties of Social Democracy only achieved a parliamentary position comparable to that attained at the turn of the century by the Australian Labor Party some two or three decades later.

Strategic position The party system which emerged in the years preceding Federation and which continued until 1909 was strategically highly favourable to the assertion of labour movement interests, since the economic division between the rural and urban sectors was reflected in lack of bourgeois unity at just that point where decisions about the shape of policy in the new nation-state had to be made. This is, arguably, a major point of similarity between Australia and the small European states which took the Social Democratic path in the 1930s, and it seems tenable to propose that political disunity on the Right is a necessary condition of establishing an historic compromise with a genuine potential to realise goals of social amelioration (see Castles, 1978). It is also arguable that

Labor, by facilitating the historic compromise of New Protection, and so removing the barrier to bourgeois unity, took advantage of the short-term policy gains on offer at a price of lasting political impotence. Certainly, that is what happened from the 1920s onwards, and is what some commentators at the time expected to happen (La Nauze, 1968, p. 196).

The role of the state   At the turn of the century, the conception of the state held by Australians was substantially different from either the *laissez-faire* notions of contemporray Liberalism or the mercantilism of idealistic authoritarianism. Their perspective was fundamentally Benthamite, seeing the state as essentially an arrangement for the public good, 'an instrument ready to hand to be employed for diffusing among themselves and their neighbours comfort and prosperity, the things they really care for . . .' (Bryce, 1921, p. 355). In the context of colonial settlement, the state had been the creator of civil society and had a degree of leverage at its command unheard of in the larger European states or in America. Indeed, the term 'colonial socialism' has been aptly used to describe late nineteenth-century Australia, in which, between 1860 and 1900, the state had subsidized the inflow of 350,000 migrants, had secured half the flow of total foreign capital imports and accounted for about 40 per cent of domestic capital formation. By 1900, the government owned half the total fixed capital in Australia and employed 5 per cent of the total workforce (Butlin et al., 1982, pp. 16–17). Under these circumstances, it was scarcely surprising that a labour movement with strong political support and a favourable strategic position should turn immediately to the state to achieve its programme and to choose forms for its realization where the state could stand guarantor of their implementation. On the contrary, given the weakness of the industrial arm of the working class movement, demonstrated in the strikes of the early 1890s, it would have been extraordinary had it not done so. This is possibly an area in which the contrast between Australia and, at least, some of the smaller European states may be less great, since the relative weakness of feudalism had given a greater role to the state bureaucracy and late industrialization had mitigated the influence of *laissez-faire* ideology. At the turn of the century, the state was in some of these countries an active participant in the thrust to economic modernization, but nowhere was it armed with the powers that Australians simply took for granted.

Timing   An historic compromise cannot come about before the class to whom concessions are granted is mobilized in such a way as to be able to exert pressure on behalf of its demands. In other words, the democratic socialist parties of the smaller states of Western Europe could not have reached a *modus vivendi* with capitalism until their parliamentary representation enabled them to threaten control of the bourgeois state.

Analogously, parties which operate in the democratic arena cannot afford to wait too long to transform ideology into institutions, lest they be accused of failing to represent the immediate interests of their supporters (cf. Esping-Andersen, 1985, p. 86). But because the time-slot for historic compromise is circumscribed by political constraints, actors are not free to chose from an extensive repertoire of policy solutions: they must grab and adapt what is there and waiting. Hence, the Australian labour movement, whose 'window of opportunity' coincided with the world-wide debate on the merits and demerits of tariff protection as an instrument of national development,[12] was constrained to favour a solution to problems of external vulnerability quite different from that adopted thirty years later by the Social Democratic parties of Western Europe.

Taking all these factors together, the emergence of diverse responses to economic vulnerability and diverse ideological strategies of social amelioration is readily comprehensible. The politics of domestic defence, based on an implicit conservative social welfare function, made sense in the context of an economy in which the need for major structural change was not apparently urgent and which provided for many, if by no means all, the basis of a civilized existence. No wonder, then, that the strongly mobilized party of the urban working class was willing to settle for guarantees provided by a neutral, if not positively friendly, state in the form of arbitration and an indexed real wage, seen as a realized objective which was 'definite and defensible, a rallying point in the class struggle, a trench to man against the attacking forces of capitalism' (Hancock, 1930, p. 157). Moreover, the willingness to see the state as the panacea for all things, not just wages, but protection of manufacturing jobs and a tight labour market, was all the more understandable in the light of the revealed incapacity of the unions to combat the effects of exogenous shocks, as demonstrated by the depression of the 1890s, and the seemingly inexorable march of the political labour movement to state power. Indeed, another appeal of the arbitration system was that it made the growth of trade unions a suitable case for treatment by the healing power of state intervention; the arbitration system nurtured a union movement which, because of craft and federal fragmentation, would have been rather unlikely to flourish otherwise (see Rawson, 1986, p. 21 and Howard, 1977).

The situation in most of the smaller European states was quite different. A defensive response, preserving things as they were, would have meant the acceptance of poverty and exploitation and, in any case, no compromise was possible before the labour movement could bargain as a more or less equal partner in state and economy. For the labour movements in Europe, then, the historical context of the early twentieth century dictated an emphasis on structural economic change which would serve to produce not only the necessary economic surplus for social amelioration, but also the shock troops of political reform. Hence, Social Democracy had a built-in predisposition to favour a response which involved adjusting to economic change, and an imperative to labour movement mobilization which could ultimately wrest control of the bourgeois state. The economic contrast between a defensive posture and slow economic growth on the one side and adjustment and rapid growth on the other, and between a labour movement emasculated by its reliance on the state and a labour movement with the independent strength and solidarity to make a voluntary corporatist compromise with business is inherent in the diverse origins of the social democracy of the smaller European states and Australian labourism.

Between Historic Compromises

The introduction to this chapter sketched a number of puzzles which emerge when we contrast the character of the Australian public policy profile with expectations derived from the literature of comparative public policy analysis. Our historical account of the development of a distinctive Australian strategy of social protection has already gone some way to resolving some of those puzzles. The weakness of the Australian welfare state follows naturally from a strategy of social protection which focused on wage levels rather than social wage benefits, and the seeming paradox of equality in the absence of an advanced welfare state is vindication of the effectiveness of that wage strategy. The remaining puzzles may be resolved by examining the manner in which Australia's distinctive strategy of social protection developed since its emergence at the turn of the century. As we shall see, that course of development is also the key to an understanding of the present flux of the Australian public policy profile.

Before turning to an account of that development which, in effect, supplies the missing historical dimension to our earlier discussion of the character of the Australian public policy profile, it should be emphasized that the picture of Australian policy distinctiveness as a particular political response to the problems of economic vulnerability should not be over-interpreted to imply a *sui generis* development that wholly sets apart that country's pattern of public policy development from all other advanced capitalist states. Australia's institutional arrangements may have been more or less consciously elaborated to insulate her from the winds of economic, and accompanying social, change which have transformed the role of the modern state this century, but neither the influence of changing intellectual ideas nor of economic and social realities could be shut out entirely. What Australia could do, and did do, was to assimilate and moderate such change in the light of her own distinctive institutional pattern and the conventional wisdom that had grown up around it.

Australia's response to the depression of the 1930s was to apply the politics of domestic defence immediately. Raised tariffs and arbitrated wage reductions, arguably, succeeded in shortening the period of economic downturn, but the human misery implied by the long lines of the unemployed taught Australian policy-makers the same lesson that was learnt elsewhere. The 1945 White Paper on 'Full Employment in Australia' was clearly Keynesian in inspiration and promised, with the same vigour as similar policy programmes elsewhere, to make the abolition of unemployment the first priority of post-war public policy. However, in its final form, it relied so heavily on the single instrument of using public capital expenditure to boost demand that it was scarcely distinguishable from policies, dating back at least to the days of 'colonial socialism', of public works as the sovereign remedy for unemployment (Black, 1984). Much the same went for that other public policy innovation characteristic of the twentieth century, the welfare state. Certainly, the wartime Labor government introduced the panoply of 'social services which have become standard in the contemporary social service state' (Greenwood, 1978, p. 391), but it retained the traditional selective emphasis through means testing and a mode of financing through general tax revenue which more or less guaranteed continuing opposition to greater generosity or universalism in welfare provision (see Castles, 1985, pp. 88–102). For a labour movement which continued to believe that the answer to the problem of inequality in capitalist society lay in the regulation of the wages structure, the welfare state remained a second order priority. Australia had equipped herself with the policy instruments required to follow the march of the advanced capitalist economies towards a Keynesian welfare state, but hoped against hope that such a course would not be necessary, and that she could get away with her own tried and trusted solutions.

Those tried and trusted solutions were not the intellectual property of any one party but were diffused across the entire political spectrum. Australia, from the time of the New Protection right up until the early 1970s, displayed much the same syndrome of strong party competition combined with basic policy consensus as has characterized many of the European smaller democracies in the post-war era. In both cases, the reasons are fundamentally the same, for the parties' underlying policy stances, both in Australia and the smaller European democracies, were tied to the historical compromises which represented the common denominator of how classes with diverse interests might best survive the perils of external vulnerability. Within that consensus, there was still much scope for promoting sectional interest, but not to the degree where it might threaten the basic foundations of the established policy edifice.

In Australia this situation was, seemingly, more paradoxical than in the smaller European states, for the historic compromise which expressed so much of the labourist ideology was largely presided over by parties of the right: between 1910 and 1970, the Labor Party, although averaging well over 40 per cent of the vote in Federal elections, was only in office for some sixteen years. As already noted, the capacity of the right to exercise political power was itself partly a function of the historic compromise which permitted fusion of the divided interests of urban and rural capital on the basis of a second-best solution to the vexed issue of Australia's trade policy.[13] Whilst Australia depended for her prosperity on the export of rural (unprotected) commodities, and whilst her manufacturing sector was reliant on high tariff levels, the coalition of interests on the right was always conditional on such a compromise being maintained. Moreover, the continuing electoral strength of Labor made all-out assault on the wage regulation component of the historic compromise just as dangerous to right-wing political fortunes as would have been an attack on the principle of tariff protection. It was tried just once in the late 1920s when the Bruce government threatened to abandon the Federal arbitration system and make industrial relations an exclusive prerogative of the States. The result was the only electoral defeat suffered by the right in the entire inter-war period.

Given the way in which considerations of economic self-interest and political advantage remained tied in with institutional arrangements, it is scarcely surprising that the post-Federation historic compromise retained its hold for so long. Moreover, the fact that this compromise was based on the acceptance of a strategy of social protection that promised some defence of the economic position of the wage-earner in itself goes far to explain why the thrust to Labor political power was blunted in Australia. It is difficult to generate great enthusiasm for political change when one's opponents are already administering a political programme largely of one's own making. Moreover, for the generation of conservative politicians who guided Australia into the post-war era, the fundamentals of the historic compromise were no longer institutional devices to be adopted or discarded as circumstances dictated, but the very fabric of the Australian political culture. Throughout the long reign of Sir Robert Menzies as Prime Minister of a Liberal-Country Party coalition from 1949–66, it was the older pattern of response, rather than the newer Keynesian welfarism, which was the dominant influence shaping public policy.

Indeed, the 1960s may be seen as, at one and the same time, the era of the fullest flowering of the historic compromise sealed at the turn of the century and as the decade that set in motion the weakening of the established institutional fabric, leaving it unable to cope with the exogenous shocks of the 1970s. Australia in the mid 1960s could readily be presented as an economic success story: a rich country with low unemployment and inflation and with high incomes, drawing, literally, millions of post-war migrants to her shores. Who but a cynic or a professional economist could doubt the contribution that tariff protection and the arbitration system had made to such outcomes? The official ideology was that tariffs provided employment, and, given that premise, it did not appear strange that domestic manufacturing relied on an average effective level of tariff assistance of well over 30 per cent (see Industries Assistance Commission, 1976, p. 114), or that, progressively since the 1920s, protection had been demanded and granted to sectors other than manufacturing; most particularly, and with the partially political objective of cementing the coalition with the Country Party, rural industries without any inbuilt comparative advantage in the world market. The notion that tariffs could protect jobs, not just in manufacturing, but throughout the economy, was symbolized in the term 'all-around' protectionism used by John McEwen, Deputy Prime Minister and leader of the Country Party, to describe Australia's trade policies.

Whether or not these policies actually contributed to employment growth, they certainly were a major factor in Australia defying the post-war trend of the leading capitalist nations to increase trade as a percentage of GDP.[14] In these terms, we can see that the puzzle of Australia's exceptionally closed economy is not a puzzle of economic structure, but rather of socially protective policy. For more than five decades, Australian policy-makers chose to shut out the impact of the world economy because they believed that to be a means of achieving a variety of goals they and their constituents valued: full employment, high wages, manufacturing growth and the infrastructural base for mass migration. No clearer example is needed of the way in which institutionalized political choice shapes subsequent policy development.

The arbitration system had similarly been extended in scope since its beginnings in the early part of the century. From a system initially designed to settle individual disputes, it had been transformed into a mechanism of national wage fixing. This operated according to a two-tier arrangement by which the basic, 'living' wage was established through a national wage case and margins for skill were settled in secondary awards. In addition, there was a third informal tier of so-called 'over-award' payments negotiated on the basis of collective bargaining. Until 1953, the basic wage was indexed to changes in the Consumer Price Index on a quarterly basis but, thereafter, increases had to be justified on the basis of a variety of economic indicators, including the likely impact of inflation on the national economy. Before that change, indexed cost of living increases had constituted the crucial component of a wages system acceptable to the labour movement and, arguably, its removal was the first major step in dismantling consensus around the established historic compromise, but the implications of the change were masked for more than a decade by Australia's growing prosperity. In the long term, the removal of indexation might make it more difficult to cope consensually with major dislocation caused by fluctuations in Australia's external environment; in the short term, it made it easier to deal with inflationary tendencies inherent in an economy subject to overheating under conditions of full employment.

Even more than protection, the arbitration system was a living and popular expression of Australia's distinctive policy pattern. The vast majority of Australians were regularly affected by its decisions, not just in respect of wages, but also across a wide range of matters relating to conditions of employment including hours of work, holidays, long-service leave and, in the late 1960s, equal pay for equal work. Moreover, with the benefit of hindsight, it is possible to see the system as it operated for much of the 1950s and 1960s as constituting a highly effective incomes policy of a kind not unlike those which have been evolved in the more corporatist economies of Western Europe. In this respect, its crucial characteristics were its popular legitimacy and its quasi-autonomy. Expressed in the language of the analysis of contemporary corporatism, the former provided an institutional analogue of the 'social partnership' ideology to be found in the smaller European democracies and the latter offered an alternative basis to 'encompassing' sectoral organization of the labour market for making difficult decisions in hard economic times. Looking back at nearly two decades of economic growth and stability in a country which experienced considerable fluctuations in its terms of trade, Australia appeared to have been well served by its unusual institutional arrangements for settling industrial conflict.

But if the 1960s were the heyday of Australia's distinctive response to the problems of economic vulnerability, they were hardly a period in which the traditional labourist ideology of the working class movement was thriving. Both the industrial and the political wings of the movement were separately questioning the validity of long-established conventional wisdom. For the unions, growing rigidities in the wages system and its apparent subordination to goals of macroeconomic management in a period of manifest 'capacity to pay' were an incentive to reconsidering industrial strategy. A union movement nurtured by the conciliation and arbitration system was beginning to wonder if it couldn't do better by abandoning the constraints imposed by arbitration. In particular, the larger and more powerful unions wondered if the more aggressive forms of bargaining practised by the strong trade union movements of Western Europe might not lead to an improved deal for their membership.

For the Labor Party, issues of strategy were closely bound up with the question of how to achieve political office. In the political wilderness since 1949, it was natural enough to think that new policies could be the key to winning the hearts and minds of an electorate transformed by the economic changes wrought in the post-war era. Greater affluence made the existing residual welfare safety-net seem progressively tawdry. It also made a European-style welfare state seem increasingly affordable, and the minerals boom of the late 1960s made such a change in policy stance seem almost painless. But at the same time as Australians were becoming richer in real terms, they were falling behind other countries in relative terms. That made for questioning of traditional economic policies like tariff protection, which were increasingly coming under fire from the professional economics community. Jettisoning the politics of domestic defence for that of domestic compensation looked as if it might be an electoral winner, consolidating Labor's hold on the disadvantaged and, through enhanced economic growth provided by freer trade, securing the political allegiance of middle income earners. Whitlam's accession to the leadership marks the victory of this new line of strategic thinking. Thus, by the end of the 1960s, the Australian labour movement, the co-architect of the historic compromise of the New Protection, was getting ready to try new solutions to the problem of altering the rewards structure of capitalism. A political strategy devised to cope with the external vulnerability of the late nineteenth-century economy had been outmoded by the economic transformation of the post-war era.

The trade unions had the first opportunity to attempt a breakthrough. The abandonment of the two-tier system was accompanied by an effort on the part of the Arbitration Commission to assert greater control of over-award payments by absorbing them into the new total wage. The unions defied the Commission and not only forced it to rescind its decision, but also in the process procured the effective abrogation of the penal provisions of the Conciliation and Arbitration Act. In the following years there was a 'drift from arbitration' towards collective bargaining, leading to wage increases higher than productivity gains and concomitant inflation, itself fuelled by the 'flow-on' effect of attempts by the Commission to regain control by passing on to less productive industries the gains made by those unions best able to exploit their new-found militancy. By the end of 1972, when Labor was at last elected to office, whatever implicit incomes policy Australia had once had had now been abandoned.

But in the mid 1970s an incomes policy was precisely what was most needed. Partly, this was because the new government was intent on making a major shift to public consumption, which, at a time of increasing real wages, could only be financed from dramatic economic growth or a major squeeze on profits. Partly, it was because the two-pronged labour movement attempt to break away from the old policy pattern was made at almost exactly the same time as the post-war boom

ended. Many of the consequences of this unfortunate conjuncture have
been described in earlier sections of this chapter and it is possible to
interpret all the political and policy changes of later years as attempts to
reassert effective political control of an economy which had once again
proved all too vulnerable to external threat. Certainly, this course of
events helps resolve our initial puzzle that a country with an established
incomes policy mechanism should fare so badly in the economic crises of
the 1970s. In that period, for the first time since the inflationary crisis of
the Korean War, Australia had to cope with a massive deterioration of its
external economic position without the shock-absorber provided by a
functioning arbitration system.

The attempt to find new policy solutions, Fraser's monetarism,
Hawke's quasi-corporatist Accord, possible borrowings from European
models, does not mean that the traditional policy pattern has been wholly
superseded. The normal response to adversity is to go back to the old
solutions which worked in the past. That is precisely what the Whitlam
government did in going back to full indexation of wages in order to
prevent wage-costs exceeding inflation, and subsequent governments
went a step further in using the arbitration system to secure partial
indexation (that is, real wage restraint). It is arguable that, in the Hawke
era of negotiated neo-corporatist Accord between government and trade
unions under circumstances of recurrent economic crisis, the Arbitration
Commission has acquired a new and vital role as the buffer between the
labour movement and the unpalatable decisions forced on its leadership.
The Whitlam government similarly reversed its stand on reducing tariff
protection and imposed import quotas in a number of particularly labour
intensive industries. The Fraser government attempted to cut back
public expenditure, although more in step to the drum of monetarist
ideology than with a view to reasserting the old labourist preference for
selectivity. The Hawke government has rediscovered selectivity as a
means of slowing public expenditure growth, and one of its earliest
actions was to legislate a new means (assets) test on old age pensions.
More recently, it has moved to means-test child benefits as part of its
attempt to target welfare resources on those most in need. Certainly, this
legacy of the politics of domestic defence appears to be alive and kicking
in the highest policy-making circles of the Labor Party and continues to
be a significant factor in explaining the puzzling weakness of Australia's
welfare state.

But the partial return to the old pattern and elements of the labourist
tradition equally does not mean that the impetus to new policy
directions has been exhausted. Far from it! Whatever the practical
difficulties in the present economic situation, all major political
groupings have concluded that Australia can no longer insulate herself
from the mainstream of international economic competition. That aspect

of the traditional public policy is now dead. What remains at issue is how, or whether, a shift to economic deregulation can be combined with a measure of social protection. Labor, judged by its actions, seems to believe that wage control through arbitration and the Accord, plus a selective social policy, will provide an adequate solution, drawing on the best components of social democratic and labourist practice. The ACTU, however, takes the position that flexible adjustment in the economy demands domestic compensation in the arena of social protection: that, if Australia is to take the lead of the smaller European economies in competing in world markets, it must also follow their lead in expanding the social wage and forging instruments for more developed collective control of the economic process (see ACTU, 1987). Finally, the experience of the economic turbulence of recent decades seems to have detached large parts of the political Right from its attachment to the historic compromise of the past. They demand not only economic deregulation, but deregulation of the labour market (that is, the abolition of the arbitration system) and a still more vestigial welfare system. As Australia confronts the social and economic challenges of the late 1980s, she is caught between the historic compromises of domestic defence and domestic compensation, with a sizeable and vocal minority opposed to both. Unless the labour movement in its search for new policy directions can fashion some acceptable synthesis of the old and the new, that minority may, by default, become a majority and take Australian public policy into wholly uncharted waters.

Notes

For a book-length treatment of the theme of this chapter, see Castles (1988).

1   As of 1987 the population is just over 16 million, making it the eighth largest of the advanced states in the OECD area in population terms. On the other hand, the gap in population size between it and Canada, the seventh largest with around 25 million, is much greater than between it and the Netherlands, the ninth largest with around 14 million.

2   The discussion in this chapter is restricted to the 18 most advanced OECD nations with more than 1 million in population. They are Australia, Austria, Belgium, Canada, Denmark, Finland, France, Germany, Ireland, Italy, Japan, the Netherlands, New Zealand, Norway, Sweden, Switzerland, the United Kingdom and the United States.

3   Awards made under the Arbitration system between early in the century and the late sixties assumed that male wages should be sufficient to support wife and children, but that female wages need only be such as to provide for a single person. This built-in sexism in the wages system started to disappear in 1969 with a Commission decision to implement equal pay for equal work.

4   The term, 'domestic compensation' is derived from Katzenstein (1985). I should like to take this opportunity of acknowledging that not only is the following discussion of the response to economic vulnerability of the smaller European states based largely on Katzenstein's account, but also that the whole argument of this chapter amounts to an attempt to extend his challenging analysis in such a way as to make sense of the Australian case.

5   It is an arguable proposition that, of all the larger countries, contemporary Germany and Japan are those which have evolved institutions most closely resembling those of the neo-corporatist smaller European states (see chs. 3 and 5 below), and it was, of course, these nations whose collective consciousnesses were most scarred by the demonstration of external vulnerability through military defeat. As Katzenstein points out, a similar explanation may account for Austria's shift from being the most conflictual to being, possibly, the most consensual of the European smaller democracies. ibid. p. 188.

6   Note the similarity with the Swedish trade unions' 'wage policy of solidarity', where capacity to pay is also regarded as secondary to the need to achieve wage levelling for the lower paid. The difference in policy tenor between the small European economies and the Australian strategy comes out clearly in the fact that in Sweden firms unable to pay the stipulated wages are expected to go out of business and workers relocated to more profitable sectors of the economy. In Australia, the traditional response would have been to increase tariffs to such a point that the employers could afford to pay the award wages.

7   In terms of both functions and structures, there are some curious parallels between the role of the arbitration system in Australia and the German Bundesbank (see ch. 3). Both involve the establishment of quasi-autonomous state organs as institutionalized guarantees of economic stability.

8   It was also, significantly, the first stated principle of the Federal Labor Party programme adopted in 1905: 'The cultivation of an Australian sentiment based on the maintenance of racial purity and the development of an enlightened [sic!] and self-reliant community.'

9   This conclusion is derived from the work of Butlin (1962). Butlin's analysis is currently the subject of some revisionism (see McLean, 1987), but doubts as to how rich Australia was at this time are not sufficient to qualify broad contrasts with other countries.

10   McCarthy, 1970; Fry, 1956. These views are also subject to revision by a new generation of economic historians who suggest that increasing differentiation in the colonial labour market prevented many from enjoying the fruits of prosperity (Lee and Fahey, 1986), but again this does not disturb broad contrasts with the European experience.

11   Returning to the point made earlier that economic fluctuations can threaten the imminent extinction of large groups of the capitalist class, it is apparent that this is most likely where enterprises are typically small and that, hence, this particular pressure for class compromise is likely to be

maximized where many small businessmen can exert political influence to defend their interests.

12 Protection was the basis of party realignments in most of the liberal democratic states at around the turn of the century, but in all, other than Australia, the tariff debate preceded the full mobilization of the urban working class.

13 It was also partly a function of the Alternative Vote system for the Lower House of Parliament which allowed the parties representing urban and rural capital to exchange preferences between themselves, and so avoid the usual fate of smaller parties under territorial systems of electoral representation.

14 In 1949–50, imports plus exports as a percentage of GDP amounted to 43.8 per cent of GDP; fifteen years later, the figure was 26.9 per cent (see Norton and Kennedy, 1985, p. 3).

References

ACTU 1987: *Australia Reconstructed*. Canberra: AGPS.

Anderson, Karl 1938: Protection and the Historical Situation: Australia. *The Quarterly Journal of Economics*, LIII, 86–104.

Black, Laurel 1984: Social Democracy and Full Employment: The Australian White Paper. *Labour History*, 46.

Borrie, W.D. 1963: The Peopling of Australia. In H.W. Arndt and W.M. Corden, *The Australian Economy*, Melbourne: F.W. Cheshire.

Brigden, J.B. 1925: The Australian Tariff and the Standard of Living. *Economic Record*, 1.

Bruno, Michael and Sachs, J.D. 1985: *Economics of Worldwide Stagflation*. Cambridge, Mass.: Harvard University Press.

Bryce, James 1921: *Modern Democracies* vol. II. London: Macmillan.

Butlin, N.G. 1962: *Australian Domestic Product: Investment and Foreign Borrowing, 1861–1938/9*. Cambridge: Cambridge University Press.

Butlin, N.G. and Dowie, J.A. 1969: Estimates of Australian Work Force and Employment, 1861–1961. *Australian Economic History Review*, 9.

Butlin, N.G. et al. 1982: *Government and Capitalism*. Sydney: George Allen & Unwin.

Cameron, David 1978: The Expansion of the Public Economy: A Comparative Analysis. *American Political Science Review*, 72, 1243–61.

Castles, Francis G. 1978: *The Social Democratic Image of Society*. London: Routledge & Kegan Paul.

Castles, Francis G. 1981: How does Politics Matter? Structure or Agency in the Determination of Public Policy Outcomes. *European Journal of Political Research*, 9, 119–32.

Castles, Francis G. (ed.) 1982: *The Impact of Parties*. London: Sage.

Castles, Francis G. 1985: *The Working Class and Welfare*. Sydney: George Allen & Unwin Australia.

Castles, Francis G. 1988: *Australian Public Policy and Economic Vulnerability*. Sydney: Allen & Unwin Australia.

Corden, W.M. 1974: *Trade Policy and Economic Welfare*. London: Oxford University Press.

Crisp, L.F. 1983: *Australian National Government*, 5th edn Melbourne: Longman Cheshire.

Crough, J.G. and Wheelwright, E.L. 1983: *Australia: A Client State*. Ringwood: Penguin Books Australia.

Dahl, R.A. and Tufte, E.R. 1973: *Size and Democracy*. Stanford, CA: Stanford University Press.

Dowrick, S. and Nguyen, D. T. 1987: *Australia's Post War Economic Growth: Measurement and International Comparison*. Centre for Economic Policy Research, Canberra: Australian National University.

Duncan, Tim and Fogarty, John 1984: *Australia and Argentina: On Parallel Paths*. Melbourne: Melbourne University Press.

Esping-Andersen, Gösta 1985: *Politics Against Markets*, Princeton, NJ: Princeton University Press.

Evans, P. 1979: *Dependent Development*. Princeton, NJ: Princeton University Press.

Fry, E.C. 1956: *The Condition of the Urban Wage Earning Class in Australia in the 1880s*. Ph.D, Canberra: Australian National University.

Gough, Ian 1979: *The Political Economy of the Welfare State*. London: Macmillan.

Greenwood, G. 1978: *Australia: A Social and Political History*. Sydney: Angus & Robertson.

Gruen, F.H. 1986: Our Present Discontents. *Presidential Address to the Economic Society of Australia*, Discussion paper 149, August 1986. Canberra: Centre for Economic Policy Research, Australian National University.

Hancock, Keith 1979: The First Half-Century of Australian Wage Policy – Part II. *The Journal of Industrial Relations*, 21, 129–60.

Hancock, W.K. 1930: *Australia*. Brisbane: The Jacaranda Press.

Henderson, R.F., Harcourt, A. and Harper, R.J.A. 1970: *People in Poverty*. Melbourne: Cheshire.

Higgins, H.B. 1922: *A New Province for Law and Order*. London: Constable & Company.

Horne, Donald 1976: *Death of the Lucky Country*. Harmondsworth: Penguin.

Horne, Donald 1980: *Time of Hope*. Sydney: Angus & Robertson.

Howard, W.A. 1977: Australian Unions in the Context of Union Theory. *The Journal of Industrial Relations*, 19.

Industries Assistance Commission 1976: *Annual Report 1975–76*. Canberra: AGPS.

Jackson, Gordon 1985: The Australian Economy. In *Australia: The Daedalus Symposium*, 114, 1.

Karmel, P.H. and Brunt, M. 1962: *The Structure of the Australian Economy*. Melbourne: F.W. Cheshire.

Katzenstein, Peter 1985: *Small States in World Markets*. Ithaca, NY: Cornell University Press.

Krause, L.B. 1984: Australia's Comparative Advantage in International Trade. In R.E. Caves and L.B. Krause (eds), *The Australian Economy: A View from the*

North, Washington, DC: The Brookings Institution, 275–311.

La Nauze, J.A. (ed.; 1970: *Federated Australia: Selections from Letters to The Morning Post*. Melbourne: Melbourne University Press.

Lee, Jenny and Fahey, Charles 1986: A Boom for Whom: Some Developments in the Australian Labour Market, 1870–1891. *Labour History*, 1–27.

McCarthy, Peter 1968: *The Harvester Judgement: An Historical Review*. Ph.D. thesis, Canberra: Australian National University.

McCarthy, Peter 1970: Employers, the Tariff, and Legal Wage Determination in Australia – 1890–1910. *Journal of Industrial Relations*, 12, 182–93.

McCarthy, Peter 1970: Wages in Australia 1891–1914. *Economic History Review*, X.

McClean, I.W. and Pincus, J.J. 1983: Did Australian living standards stagnate between 1890 and 1940? *Journal of Economic History*, 43, 193–202.

McClean, I.W. 1987: Economic Wellbeing: Living Standards and Inequality since 1900. In R.R. Maddock and I.W. McClean (eds), *The Australian Economy in the Long Run*, Melbourne: Cambridge University Press.

McIntyre, Stuart 1985: *Winners and Losers: The pursuit of social justice in Australian History*, Sydney: George Allen & Unwin.

McQueen, Humphrey 1970: *A New Britannia*. Ringwood: Penguin.

Maddison, Angus 1977: Phases of Capitalistic Development. *Banca Nazionale del Lavoro Review*, 30.

Norton, W.E. and Kennedy, P.J. 1985: *Australian Economic Statistics 1949–50 to 1984–85: I Tables*. Canberra: Reserve Bank of Australia.

OECD 1985: *Social Expenditure 1960–1990*. Paris: OECD.

OECD 1986: *Historical Statistics: 1960–84*. Paris: OECD.

Phelps Brown, E.H. 1969: Balancing External Payments by Adjusting Domestic Income. *Australian Economic Papers*, 45 (109), 111–21.

Polanyi, Karl 1944: *The Great Transformation*. New York: Rinehart & Company.

Rawson, Don 1986: *Unions and Unionists in Australia*, 2nd edn Sydney: George Allen & Unwin.

Scherer, Peter 1983: Nature of the Australian Industrial Relations System: A Form of State Syndicalism? In Keith Hancock et al., *Japanese and Australian labour markets: A comparative study*, Canberra: Australia-Japan Research Centre, 157–82.

Stillwell, Frank 1986: *The Accord . . . and Beyond*. Sydney: Pluto Press.

Stretton, Hugh 1980: In J. Wilkes (ed.), *The Politics of Taxation*, Sydney: Hodder & Stoughton, 43–60.

Van Arnhem, Corina and Schotsman, G.J. 1982: Do Parties Affect the Distribution of Incomes? The Case of Advanced Capitalist Democracies. In Francis G. Castles (ed.), *The Impact of Parties*, London: Sage, 283–364.

Varley, Rita 1986: *The Government Household Transfer Data Base 1960–1984*. OECD Department of Economics and Statistics Working Papers, 36. OECD: Paris.

Wallerstein, I. 1979: *The Capitalist World Economy*. Cambridge: Cambridge University Press.

Wentworth, W.C. 1969: Social Services and Poverty. In G.C. Masterman, *Poverty in Australia*, Sydney: Australian Institute of Political Science.

3

Learning from Catastrophes
West Germany's Public Policy

Manfred G. Schmidt

The Policy of the Middle Way

What is distinctive about West Germany's public policy profile? My
answer to the research question has two parts: first, that, in terms of
comparison with the post-war experience of other industrial democracies,
West Germany's public policy profile is characterized by a somewhat
unusual mix of policies of conservative-reformist, liberal and social
democratic complexion.[1] What is most striking is the coexistence of a
determined and long-standing policy of price stability which, in extreme
circumstances, has priority in the inflation-unemployment dilemma even
when the Social Democrats are in power, and a strong welfare state, itself
to a large extent the product of rule by hegemonic non-socialist
tendencies. The West German policy-mix falls between the extreme
poles of US market capitalism and Social Democratic welfare capitalism
– it is truly a policy of the middle way!

Despite the unusual nature of the policy mix, being in the middle may
appear a strange claim to distinctiveness. A second aspect or dimension
of the West German experience, which vindicates such a claim, emerges
when we take a historical perspective which juxtaposes contemporary
West German public policy development with what preceded it under
previous regimes. The *Sonderweg* of pre-1945 Germany, that country's
exceptionalism in the process of modernization, came to an end with the
defeat of National Socialism and the post-war establishment of West
German democracy.[2] From *Sonderweg* and exceptionalism, Germany has
taken a path towards relative normalcy. Its public policy profile still
differs somewhat from those of other Western nations, but far less
dramatically than was once the case. To state our puzzle as a deliberate

paradox: *what is distinctive about West Germany's public policy is that it has ceased to be dramatically distinctive.*

The political economy of pre-1945 Germany was notorious for its exceptionalism. Industrialization in nineteenth-century Germany was undoubtedly capitalist in character but, in sharp contrast to the situation in the United Kingdom and the United States, the rise of public bureaucracies preceded capitalist industrialization, and in contrast to many other nations, democratization came late in Germany. Given the relative backwardness of the economy, the relative weakness of the bourgeoisie, the dominant position held by pre-capitalist ruling classes of mainly agrarian origin, and the weakness of democratic institutions, it was the bureaucracy which took the lead in the reforms from above which transformed the larger German states from absolutist regimes to the civil society of the nineteenth and twentieth century. Moreover, although Germany's level of economic wealth was lower than that in many other European countries, reform from above was manifested by the early introduction of comprehensive education for the population aged 6–14 and of compulsory social insurance systems in the 1880s which established Germany as a pioneer nation in social policy (Rimlinger, 1971; Alber, 1982; Schneider, 1982).

While an active role of the state pervaded economic and social policy, militarism and political authoritarianism characterized German political institutions and attitudes in the later nineteenth century and for much of the first half of the twentieth century. The democratic interlude of Weimar proved itself to be the exception rather than the rule. Democracy came late to Germany, it was built on weak pillars and it collapsed after a short period. The establishment of authoritarian presidential regimes in 1930–3 already was indicative of the fundamental weakness of the Weimar Republic, and the assumption of power by the National Socialist Workers Party rang the deathknell of the First Republic.

In an even more dramatic manner, pre-1945 Germany's *Sonderweg* was exemplified by the twelve years of the National Socialist regime from 1933–45. In this period the National Socialist movement established a totalitarian single-party state, and it reorganized the economy along the lines of a highly politicized state-capitalist order. Within its context, the degree of autonomy of industrial enterprises and firms in manpower policy, investment and prices were narrowly circumscribed by political intervention by the government and the Nazi Party. Civil rights fell a victim to the National Socialist 'Behemoth' (Neumann, 1977), and so, too, did the democratic order and freedom of association and coalition. The 'dual state' (Fraenkel, 1949) which characterized the first few years of National Socialist rule (that is, the coexistence of relative predictability in economic affairs and the complete unpredictability which marked the political process) gradually was superseded by a fully fledged totalitarian regime. In terms of policy, the National Socialist regime comprised an apocalyptic mix of welfare, employment and job security for the 'deserving working Germans' ('*die schaffenden Deutschen*' in National Socialist ideology), political inclusion and exclusion (defined in political terms as well as in ethnic and racist ones), reform and repression, a rhetoric of peace and the reality of preparation for war, and the persecution and physical destruction of those who were regarded by the regime as enemies of the new order (Schönbaum, 1967; Bracher, 1983).

In contrast to all other regimes that have ruled Germany, the political order in West Germany in the post-1949 period was much less pervaded by the spirit of exceptionalism. With the defeat of the National Socialist order and the rise of West German democracy, the German *Sonderweg* (in the sense of a radical deviant case) had come to an end. It was replaced by a road to political and economic modernization which was much less spectacular in character. Politics and policy in West Germany evolved in a fashion, and with a substance, which – in contrast to much of the pre-1945 period – were more similar to, and differed more by degree than in kind from, other developed Western nations.

This change can largely be attributed to dramatic changes of the political-institutional apparatus after 1945 and after 1949 and – no less important – to the emergence of a regional and religious cleavage structure which was less complex and less conflict-ridden than previously. The changed cleavage structure was largely attributable to the partition of Germany and, in particular, to the breakdown of Prussia's hegemony among the states of Germany and to the decline and virtual dissolution of the social class of East Elbian *Junker*. However, it also mirrored the emergence of a new interconfessional people's party of Christian Democratic complexion. Furthermore, processes of learning from the political catastrophes of the past strongly influenced the nature of the democratic order which was restored in the western occupation zones of Germany. Four institutional changes were particularly significant: the establishment of a federal state, the creation of two peoples' parties, the strong institutionalization of industrial conflict, the establishment of powerful autonomous institutions such as the central bank (Bank deutscher Länder and since 1957 Deutsche Bundesbank) and the Constitutional Court (Kocka, 1979; Eschenburg, 1983; Katzenstein, 1987; Wildenmann, 1987).

Focusing on the political economy, it can be argued that a policy of the middle way is distinctive of West Germany's public policy. The policy of the middle way comprises a unique combination of market-oriented, liberal policies and policy measures of an etatist complexion. It is marked by a unique combination of responses to political challenges and policy dilemmas, such as the inflation-unemployment dilemma and the trade-off between efficiency and equality (Okun, 1975). A determined non-inflationary stance in monetary policy and low rates of inflation coexist with a high level of state intervention in general and high levels of welfare statism in particular, and an economy of fairly resilient and efficient character. The policy of the middle way marks a third road between the extreme poles of Scandinavian social democratic welfare capitalism (Korpi, 1978) and political economies in which centre-right, or rightist tendencies dominate.

For reasons which will be discussed in detail in later sections, the concern for price stability does not necessarily involve a policy detrimental to employment goals. Indeed, West German politicians, in particular policy-makers of Social Democratic or Christian Democratic complexion, have been deeply and genuinely concerned about unemployment. However, in the long run, the ultimate priority in economic policy has been the maintenance of price stability. This course of action has the full support of the non-socialist parties and, given the preference for full employment, more muted support from the Social Democrats. Most significantly, price stability comes high on the preference ordering of rank and file members of the labour movement. Since the inflation of 1914–23, labour has seen price stability as a crucial goal of economic policy, and indeed as one which can have priority over other goals of trade unions. Thus, the politics of price stability on the part of Germany's labour movement since the mid 1920s, with the exception of the intense distributive struggles of the 1969–74 period, has differed rather markedly from the greater nonchalance displayed by most other European labour movements *vis-à-vis* moderate inflation.

The emphasis that West Germany's policy-makers have given to price stability oriented policy has been remarkably successful. West Germany's average inflation rate in the 1950–85 period was the lowest among the OECD nations. (There were only a few years in which the pace of price increases in Germany exceeded those of other low-inflation countries, such as Switzerland or the United States.) Moreover, in the 1950s relative price stability coexisted with dramatic decreases in the rate of unemployment and dramatic increases in total employment figures. Even more striking was the maintenance of relatively low inflation rates and full employment in the periods 1959/60–1965 and 1967/68–1973. In contrast to many other Western democracies, it was not until the early 1970s that there was an implicit trade-off between the remarkable success of inflation control in West Germany and dramatic employment losses (see table 3.1).

The trade-off between price stability and mass unemployment is commonly regarded as an economic policy of liberal-bourgeois complexion (see Hibbs, 1977). Moreover, one would expect this underlying preference order to pervade all other aspects of economic and social life. However, here again we are confronted with another manifestation of

Table 3.1 Rates of inflation and rates of unemployment, 1950–1985

Country	1950–1959		1960–1973		1974–1985		1950–1985	
	Inflation	Unemployment	Inflation	Unemployment	Inflation	Unemployment	Inflation	Unemployment
Australia	6.5	2.0	3.6	1.8	10.4	6.4	6.7	3.4
Austria	7.9	3.9	4.1	1.7	5.7	2.5	5.9	2.6
Belgium	1.8	4.1	3.6	2.3	7.8	9.1	4.5	5.1
Canada	2.4	4.1	3.3	4.8	8.5	8.6	4.8	5.9
Denmark	3.8	4.5	6.3	1.3	9.8	7.6	6.8	4.3
Finland	6.8	1.3	5.9	2.3	10.9	4.9	7.8	2.9
France	6.6	2.1	4.6	2.2	10.5	6.5	7.1	3.6
Federal Rep. of Germany	1.2	5.0	3.5	0.8	4.4	4.8	3.2	3.3
Ireland	3.9	8.0	11.5	5.2	14.2	9.5	10.3	7.4
Italy	3.1	7.2	4.5	5.5	15.6	7.8	7.8	6.7
Japan	1.3	2.0	6.2	1.2	7.0	2.1	5.1	1.7
New Zealand	5.0	1.6	4.9	0.3	13.4	2.3	7.8	3.7
Netherlands	3.7	2.6	4.8	1.2	5.9	7.9	4.9	3.8
Norway	5.1	2.0	5.0	1.7	9.0	2.1	6.4	1.9
Sweden	4.5	1.8	4.5	2.0	9.8	2.3	6.3	2.0
Switzerland	1.8	0.0	4.2	0.1	4.1	0.4	3.5	0.2
United Kingdom	4.1	2.5	5.2	3.1	12.3	8.3	7.3	4.7
United States	2.1	4.4	3.2	4.4	7.7	7.4	4.4	5.4
Arithmetic mean	4.0	3.3	4.9	2.3	9.3	5.6	6.1	3.8

Source: OECD *Economic Outlook, Historical Statistics, 1960–1984.* Paris, 1986; OECD *Economic Outlook, Historical Statistics, 1960–1986.* Paris, 1988; data for 1950–9 are taken from Maddison, 1982, p. 208 and Schmidt, 1982, p. 206.

distinctiveness of the West German policy-mix. In contrast to other determined price-stability countries, particularly the United States and Switzerland, control of inflationary pressure in Germany has not prevented policy-makers from responding to the efficiency-equality dilemma (Okun, 1985) in a fashion which has been social-reformist in character. Every national government in West Germany has been strongly committed to both the maintenance of economic efficiency, measured by rates of GDP growth or rates of productivity improvement *and* expansive social protection, measured by indicators of social security effort and by attempts to enhance equal opportunity and equality in fields such as education and income maintenance.

Moreover, social policy *and* legal protection of job security *and* a high level of codetermination of labour in enterprises have carried considerable weight on the political agenda over the post-1949 period as a whole. Thus, despite the emphasis that government has given to the promotion of growth and productivity increases, the overall policy was not one of growth at all costs. Conscious efforts to control the economy and the rules of distributional conflict between labour, capital and the state resulted in a mix of a more balanced nature, comprising growth, inclusion of labour and social security (see, for economic policy, Schmidt, 1986 and, for social policy, Alber, 1982 and 1986). Indeed, the level of welfare state provision in West Germany has been high since the early 1950s. The share of social expenditure as a percentage of GDP in West Germany in the 1950s was higher than in all other OECD nations (Alber, 1982), and despite cut-backs in the late 1970s and during the first half of the 1980s it has continued to be high (OECD, 1985; Alber, 1986).

It follows from this that the extent to which the government in West Germany intervenes in the economy, and distributes and redistributes resources, is fairly large by historical and cross-national comparison. However, in contrast to many other big-government countries, a large proportion of the total outlays of government in West Germany consists of transfer expenditure for purposes of social security and, hence, the share of public consumption expenditure in GDP and the share of public employment as a percentage of total employment are only of moderate strength (Kohl, 1985; Rose, 1985; OECD, 1987). Moreover, a substantial proportion of total social spending is financed directly by social insurance contributions from employees and employers, and this, in turn, mirrors the strong degree to which the West German welfare state has been pervaded by a spirit of conservative reformism (Schmidt, 1988a).

In a sense, West Germany's policy of the middle way can be regarded as an 'historical compromise' between political forces of liberal-bourgeois complexion, conservative reformist tendencies, mainly of a Catholic predisposition, and movements of Social Democratic composition.

Hence, the policy of the middle way represents a third road between the extreme poles that are marked by the hegemony of Social Democratic parties, such as in Sweden until 1976, and a mixed-economy approach dominated by bourgeois tendencies, such as in the United States, and, to a lesser extent, in Japan and in Switzerland (see figure 3.1).

The strong emphasis on the simultaneous achievement of stability and social protection distinguishes West Germany from other nations with highly developed welfare states and from other low-inflation countries. In the latter group of nations, the United States and Switzerland deserve first mention because efforts to control inflationary pressure in these countries have been relatively successful, while the authorities in the Benelux states and in Austria[3] were rather less successful in controlling

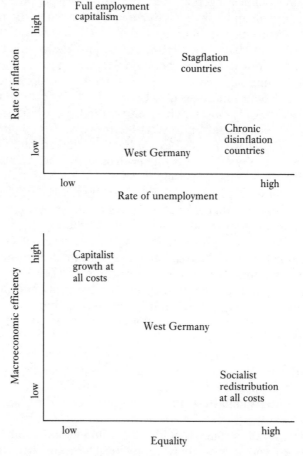

Figure 3.1 The policy of the middle way – a stylized presentation of the distinctive characteristics of West Germany's economic and social policy

inflationary expectations. In contrast to West Germany's policy of the middle way, control of inflationary pressure in the United States and in Switzerland coexists with, and is complemented by, economic and social policies of mainly liberal-bourgeois complexion. In particular, in both the United States and Switzerland the maintenance of relative price stability has been associated with a relatively small size of government and relatively low, and selective, levels of welfare statism[4] (see table 3.2 and table 3.1).

Table 3.2 Social expenditure shares (as a percentage of GDP), 1960 and 1981

Country	1960	1981
Australia	10.2	18.8
Austria	17.9	27.7
Belgium	17.4	37.6[a]
Canada	12.1	21.5
Denmark	—	33.3[b]
Finland	15.4	25.9
France	13.4[c]	29.9
Federal Republic of Germany	20.5	31.5
Ireland	11.7	28.4
Italy	16.8	29.1
Japan	8.0	17.5
Netherlands	16.2	36.1
New Zealand	13.0	19.6
Norway	11.7	27.1
Sweden	15.4	33.4
Switzerland	7.7	14.9[b]
United Kingdom	13.9	23.7
United States	10.9	20.8
Arithmetic mean	13.7	26.5

[a] 1980. [b] 1979. [c] excluding education.
Source: OECD: *Social Expenditure 1960–1990. Problems of growth and control.* Paris: OECD, 1985, p. 21.

West Germany's policy of the middle way differs not only from a policy-mix of a liberal-bourgeois complexion, but also from the policy stances that are adopted in a group of countries in which high levels of state intervention and welfare statism coexist with higher, or high, inflation rates and mass unemployment, such as in Italy or France ('stagflation countries'). Even more striking is the difference between West Germany and nations which are ruled by hegemonic Social Democratic parties, such as Sweden until 1976 and Austria in the 1970s. While politicians and the mass public in these countries tolerated rates of inflation which were somewhat higher than those in West Germany, major emphasis was placed on the maintenance of full employment ('full employment capitalism countries'). Moreover, in Sweden equality tended to be traded off against efficiency. Clearly, the Swedish response to classical policy dilemmas differed fundamentally from that adopted by West Germany's policy-makers.

The pattern of a policy of the middle way which we have discussed with regard to price stability and social security is also typical of many other aspects of the policy process in West Germany, such as the balanced coexistence of macroeconomic efficiency and social equality (in contrast to a policy of capitalist growth at all costs and also in contrast to a strategy of socialist redistribution at all costs), a transfer-intense welfare state (in contrast to more statist patterns of social protection and also in contrast to a *laissez-faire* stance in policy). A position in the middle (or in the upper middle area) of the distribution is also characteristic of many other performance indicators, such as the relationship between invest- ment and consumption, patterns of inequality by social class and by gender and level and rate of expansion of the public debt (for empirical details see OECD, 1986, Schmidt, 1983). In oversimplified terms, it could be argued that Germany's policy of the middle way comprises classical right-wing economic policy and classical left-wing social policy. This differs markedly from a more coherent combination of right-wing oriented economic policy and rightist social policy (such as in the United States) or from the combination of left-wing economic policy and leftist social policy, such as in Sweden. How such an extraordinary policy-mix became established is the puzzle that is examined in the remainder of this chapter.

Historical Determinants of the Policy of the Middle Way

Why is West Germany's policy profile marked by the strange combination of a market-oriented economic policy and a welfare statist social policy and, in particular, by determined efforts to control inflationary pressure and to maintain high levels of social security? It has been pointed out above that the modernization process in Germany has been of an exceptional nature. In this section we shall argue that the conditions which were conducive to the emergence of Germany's exceptionalism in the nineteenth and in the twentieth centuries also had an indirect influence on both the institutional context and the substance of public policy in the post-1945 period. It will further be argued, that the distinctiveness of the post-1945 policy record of West Germany can, at least in part, be traced to the impact of historical trends and historical events, despite the dramatic regime change that resulted from defeat in the Second World War, the division of Germany and the restoration of democracy under the supervision of the occupation powers.

The tradition of state-led economic development

A high degree of state intervention was characteristic of the industrialization process in Germany. As pointed out above, the rise of public bureaucracies preceded capitalist industrialization and strongly influenced the nature of the capitalist process. Thus, for example, bureaucratic structures and bureaucratic norms became the prevailing organizational form in larger firms, with the emergence of the *Angestelltenschaft*, the white-collar class, and its transformation into a distinctive *Privatbeamtenschaft*, a distinctive social class with privileges and codes that were similar to those of the *Beamtenschaft*, the civil servants' class (Kocka 1979, 1981, 1982). Moreover, state interventionist practices pervaded all major aspects of economic life.

Relative to the comparatively low level of economic development, there was hardly another country in the second half of the nineteenth century in which the government role in economic development was more visible and more powerful than in Germany. This can be demonstrated in terms of the active role of public economic policy in organizing, supporting and safeguarding the process of accumulation of capital, the large size of the government's share of capital stock and of the national product, the pioneer role that the German-Prussian government played in comprehensive education and in social insurance policy, the role of businessmen and officials in local reforms, and the response of the public authorities to civil protest (see, for example, Dahrendorf, 1968, ch. 3; Kocka, 1981, 1982; Wehler, 1973; Rose, 1985; Flora et al., 1983; Maier, 1986). In terms of economic resources mobilized, Wilhelmine Germany and the inter-war regimes, together with France, Britain and Italy were clearly among the highest public spenders. In more qualitative terms, it is also apparent that regulatory and judicial developments in Germany were of a kind to ensure a high degree of political control of the economy (Flora et al., 1983; Conze and Lepsius, 1983).

In a sense, a high degree of political control of the economy has remained a characteristic of the German experience, regardless of the nature of the political regimes. Of course, there have been differences in the extent to which the state controlled, organized, distributed and redistributed. Obviously, the apogee of state intervention was the National Socialist era, especially with the impact of war from 1939 onwards. But even after the defeat of the Third Reich, and despite the fact that the occupation powers and the West German political elite sought to dismantle many interventionist features of the Nazi state apparatus and, through denazification, to purge its personnel, the pattern of bureaucratic continuity and long-grounded expertise in managing economy and civil society remained a crucial factor shaping politics and policy.

The tradition of a conservative-reformist welfare state

Among the historical determinants of West Germany's policy of the middle way, the tradition of a powerful authoritarian welfare state had an important role (Dahrendorf, 1968, pp. 44–8). In the late nineteenth century, Germany was the pioneer nation in social protection. Earlier than other countries, and at a lower level of economic wealth than France or Great Britain, the authorities in Germany introduced the pillars of what later became a fully developed welfare state. Compulsory social insurance against the risks of old age, poverty, permanent disablement, sickness and work accidents were established in the 1880s (Alber, 1982; Hentschel, 1983).

The state's ultimate responsibility for the social welfare of its citizens has been a long-standing principle in Germany, sustained over various regimes (Maier, 1986). Undoubtedly, paternalistic motives of responsible leadership guided social policy-makers in Imperial Germany, but it should also be emphasized that considerations of a genuinely political character were of major importance. The activist stance in social policy in the 1880s complemented the policy of repression against the German Social Democratic Party and the trade unions, with the major political objective of alienating the working class from the organized labour movement and winning its allegiance for the monarchy. Furthermore, the social policy measures of Bismarck and his successors comprised a policy of *divide et impera*. The level of social security benefits was made largely contingent upon the socio-economic status of the insured person, and upon the level of income that he or she gained in the market economy. Moreover, social policy was consciously tailored in such a manner that it reproduced, and in fact strengthened, the cleavage between blue-collar workers, the white-collar class and civil servants. Social policy in Germany thus reproduced to a considerable extent market-generated social inequality and also contributed to a type of status differentiation within the dependent labour force which is unique in industrial countries (although, of course, functional equivalents exist in other countries, such as the labour aristocracy in Britain (see Kocka, 1983)).

Selective as the policy of social insurance may have been, the pace of its expansion in the late nineteenth century and in the twentieth century was impressively rapid, with the exception of temporary interruptions, such as during the First World War and during the Depression of the

1930s. Until the early 1920s, Germany ranked first in social insurance coverage ratios, and, as already noted, it retained its leadership status as the biggest social security spender, as measured in terms of GNP share, until well into the 1950s. Only thereafter was it surpassed by the Scandinavian and Benelux states, but even then Germany remained amongst the leading group of welfare states. Moreover, it should be emphasized that the welfare state tradition in Germany has been cultivated by governments of the most diverse political complexion, both pre- and post-war (Hentschel, 1983; Alber, 1982, 1986; Schmidt, 1988).

The progress of state interventionism in Germany probably would have been less pronounced if a pure *laissez-faire* ideology had commanded a strong position in the political history of Germany in the nineteenth and in the first half of the twentieth century. However, liberalism was an influential doctrine in policy-making for only a short period – in the two decades between 1850 and the early 1870s. Even in this period, public administration continued to utilize a large body of legal instruments of a non-liberal, welfare statist and authoritarian complexion (Stolleis, 1980). Moreover, the history of political economy in Germany until the 1940s reveals a comparatively weak role of liberalism in economic thought. Thus, for example, supporters of Adam Smith among German political economists reformulated the theory of government of the *Wealth of Nations* in rather statist terms. Basing their thinking on the notion of the political leadership's responsibility for the well-being of its subjects, German political economists (Adolph Wagner amongst them) opted for an economic order in which the state would play an active role in the economic process. That option, with varying nuances, has been the choice of the vast majority of German political leaders – irrespective of political regime – for the last century.

Learning from economic and political catastrophes

The tradition of pervasive state intervention in the pre-1945 regimes in Germany must be counted as one of the major determinants of the high degree of political control to which West Germany's economy and society are exposed. Moreover, the lessons that were drawn from the agony of the Weimar Republic and, in particular, from the politically disastrous impact on the political and social fabric of Weimar made by the deflationary stance in social and economic policy in the early 1930s generated among the majority of the political elite in post-1945 Germany a widely shared concern for social policy and for active economic intervention on the part of the government (see, for example, Conze and Lepsius, 1983).

The collapse of the Weimar Republic and the experience of National

Socialism also initiated a process of learning after 1945 which resulted in the discovery or rediscovery of political and economic liberalism. Among West German politicians of the immediate post-war years a widely shared consensus on political liberalization emerged rapidly after the breakdown of the National Socialist regime. The concern for political liberalization measures, itself strongly supported by the Anglo-American occupation forces, was complemented by the promotion of economic liberalization and a widely shared concern for sound housekeeping in fiscal and monetary policy (Eschenburg, 1983; Schwarz, 1981, 1983).

Among the factors that have strengthened economic liberalism in general, and sound housekeeping in fiscal and monetary policy in particular, the economic policy and economic philosophy of the Western occupation forces in Germany 1945–9 deserve first mention. However, the traumatic experience of hyperinflation of 1923 and the currency reform of 1948 worked in the same direction. Both these experiences of inflation gave rise to redistributive processes of the most unpredictable kind. The costs that were involved in the redistribution of assets, income and life chances were disproportionately shifted onto the shoulders of small middle-class savers and those entirely dependent on income from wages, and hence, extremely vulnerable to galloping inflation rates (Feldman, 1985). Even decades later, what may be described as the 'policy memory' of the electorate still vibrates to the impact of the inflations of 1923 and 1948. It was for this reason that every policy measure regarded as a potential threat to 'orderly housekeeping' in fiscal and monetary policy has been punished by the majority of the electorate in the post-1949 era. It is also for this reason that the maintenance of price stability or, at least, strict control of inflationary pressure is now commonly regarded by the public as one of the most important public goods. Numerous empirical studies have established the extraordinary importance that the majority of the electorate attaches to the maintenance of price stability (see, for example, Katona, Strümpel and Zahn, 1971, pp. 215–20; Frey, 1978; Whiteley, 1984; Kort-Krieger, 1986). The inflation rate is one of the major yardsticks by which the large majority of voters evaluates the government's economic performance. Control of inflationary pressure is thus part of the political orthodoxy in West Germany and an imperative for every government, regardless of its partisan composition and irrespective of the kind of public policy philosophy which it prefers. Contrary to the assumptions and finding of much comparative public policy analysis that a strong preference for price stability is a feature of bourgeois dominance, the West German public policy profile can only be understood to the degree that it is realized that aversion to inflation is not a source of major partisan division.

However, a full understanding of the politics of price stability in West

Germany requires a perspective in which inflation avoidance is regarded as a part of a larger 'quest for security' (Edinger, 1985, p. 318). Relative price stability in West Germany is a part of a policy of avoiding any significant amount of economic destabilization, itself partly due to prior inflationary traumas, but also to the vast destruction of life and property experienced by Germany in the Second World War. More than 10 per cent of the country's population was killed and millions of citizens were caught up in utter economic and social chaos (Medley, 1982, pp. 127–8).

Under these circumstances, security, predictability and political, social, and economic stability are goals that are uppermost in the voters' minds, in particular among voters who were born before the period of post-war economic prosperity.[5] Hence, any type of government and any type of economic arrangement which fails to provide high levels of security, predictability and stability – in particular, in terms of price stability, economic growth and disposable income – will have great difficulty in surviving politically (Medley, 1982, p. 129; Whiteley, 1984).

This learning from catastrophes that has occurred in the political history of Germany has thus resulted in the coexistence and intermeshing of two distinct, though not mutually exclusive, philosophies of public policy: a philosophy of a social-reformist, interventionist policy-making and another of a liberal, democratic and market-oriented kind. Both philosophies of public policy have been cultivated by the political class of West Germany. The tradition of an interventionist state found its most visible expression in the maintenance and expansion of the welfare state, and in the provision of a wide variety of tax allowances, investment subsidies, export subsidies and other incentives for producers and investors. In contrast to this, the liberal philosophy of policy-making materialized in the restitution of democracy, the reform of industrial relations and the liberalization of the state-capitalist features that the National Socialist regime had implanted in the economy.

The anti-nazi morality which pervaded political life in post-1945 Germany merged with the anti-communist sentiment produced by the creation of a socialist state in East Germany. Anti-nazism and anti-communism were factors that were conducive to the condemnation of planning, nationalization and other policies seen as distinctively socialist, and thus strengthened the liberal features of West Germany's policy of the middle way.

The impact that the combination of liberalism, anti-nazi morality and anti-communism exerted on the timing and substance of institution-building in the Western part of Germany was very strong. Among the institutional reforms that were introduced in the post-1945 period, or in the post-1949 period, three deserve special mention as key factors shaping the West German development of public policy of the middle way:

the high degree of political autonomy that was given to the Deutsche
Bundesbank as the guardian of a stable currency;
the low inflation potential inherent in West Germany's well organized
system of industrial relations; and
the federal structure of the state, which leads to a policy bias in
favour of social policy and price stability, and against – at least in
critical conjunctures such as those of the 1970s and 1980s – full
employment.

It is to the interaction between these institutional changes and the
historical determinants of the policy of the middle way that we now turn.

The German Bundesbank and the Politics of Price Stability

The guardians of the currency

Among the central banks in democratic industrial nations, the Bundesbank enjoys, perhaps, the highest degree of autonomy from government,
parliament and interest groups (von Bonin, 1979; Caesar, 1981; Baum,
1983). The German Bundesbank is a public law institution but, in sharp
contrast to earlier periods in the history of Germany, it has been
distanced from the competitive interest politicking that is commonly
associated with party government (von Bonin, 1979; Dyson, 1979, 1981;
Caesar, 1981; Sturm, 1989). The Bundesbank was explicitly designed as
an institutional safeguard against undisciplined policies of taxation and
spending on the part of government (Wildenmann, 1969). For example,
the Bundesbank Act states that the central bank shall be required to
support the general economic policy of the federal government, but that
it is bound to do so only so long as that policy does not interfere with the
overriding aim of safeguarding the strength of the national currency. To
a considerable extent, this mirrors the lessons that have been drawn from
the hyperinflations of 1923 and 1948, both of which have been
commonly regarded as the result of undisciplined fiscal and monetary
policy. Thus, the relative autonomy of the Deutsche Bundesbank may be
seen as an institutionalization of the political will to maintain price
stability (Sachverständigenrat, 1976, para. 215). Moreover, given the
commitment of the mass public to price stability, the Bundesbank has
become for many voters the foremost symbol of social and economic
stability.

Although the Bundesbank must be counted among the most powerful
central banks in the West, its autonomy is not unconstrained. Politically,
the structure of the central bank and the precise nature of its major goal,
rather loosely defined as safeguarding the currency, are, in principle,

contingent upon an Act of Parliament requiring a majority of votes in the Federal Parliament and the Federal Council.

A further restrictive condition arises from the global and indirect nature of the instruments that are at the disposal of the Bundesbank. Moreover, they are less numerous and less powerful than the policy instruments which are available to the central banks in France and in the United Kingdom (Caesar, 1981). On the other hand it should be added that the Bundesbank, given the inflation aversion on the part of the mass public, commands greater room for manoeuvre in its efforts to control inflationary pressure than do the Bank of England or the Banque de France. It has also been pointed out that the scope for discretionary action that is available to the Bundesbank is constrained by the stance that the federal government adopts in exchange rate policy (which lies in the discretionary power of the government and not of the Bundesbank) (Arndt, 1963; Emminger, 1986). For example, the preference for stable exchange rates of the Deutschmark against the currencies of the major countries of the West in the 1950s and 1960s involved considerable problems for the stabilization policy of the Bundesbank on the domestic front. In particular, in the period following the introduction of full convertibility of the Deutschmark in 1958, stabilization policy efforts on the part of the Bundesbank were often weakened by 'imported inflation' and speculation against the undervalued currency. In this period, success in maintaining relative price stability in domestic markets tended to threaten the preconditions of the price stability strategy. In contrast to this, the breakdown of the regime of fixed exchange rates in the early 1970s and its replacement by 'managed floating' of major European currencies against the dollar considerably enlarged the room for manoeuvre for stabilization policy efforts on the part of the Bundesbank (Emminger, 1986).

A strict division of control over fiscal policy and monetary policy (except exchange rate policy) between government and the central bank *and* the ultimate responsibility of the federal government for exchange rate policy is characteristic of West Germany. This division of labour does not preclude the coincidence of interests on the part of the federal government and the Bundesbank. In fact, a fairly strong consensus on the desirability, if not priority, of price stability has been characteristic of the government and the central bank (Frey, 1978). However, there have also been a number of instances of dramatic conflict between the central bank and the government: for example in 1951 and 1955/56 (when the federal government strongly opposed the drastic stabilization policy of the central bank), in 1965/66 (when the Bundesbank contributed to a major stabilization crisis), in 1968/69 (in a conflict on the appreciation of the currency to which the Christian Democratic Grand Coalition partner, but not the Social Democratic Party, was strongly opposed) and in 1979–82, when the determinedly restrictive stance of the central bank's policy clashed with preferences for full employment oriented policies – or, at least, for more moderate monetary policy – on the part of the governing Social Democratic Party (see Caesar, 1981, pp. 188–90; Emminger, 1986; Sturm, 1989).

In terms of the substance and timing of monetary policy, empirical studies have demonstrated that the Bundesbank ultimately gives the highest priority to safeguarding relative price stability subject to constraints from foreign economic policy and from international economic linkages (Jarchow, 1976; Duwendag et al., 1977, p. 273; Basler, 1979; Caesar, 1981, p. 143; Scharpf, 1987). Premising its policy on the assumption that this course of action in the long run guarantees the maintenance of full employment, stable growth and balanced current accounts, the Bundesbank tends to regard price stability as the major goal of economic policy. On the whole and despite problems of identifying the precise nature of the causal links between policy and outcomes,[6] it can be argued that the Bundesbank has been successful in its effort effectively to implement such a policy.

As already noted, the instruments at the central bank's disposal are mainly of a global and indirect nature. Furthermore, and in particular in the late 1950s and in the 1960s, monetary policy was frequently confronted with adverse conditions in international monetary markets, largely due to restrictions imposed by the regime of fixed exchange rates, and to price stability problems stemming from an unwillingness to appreciate the currency. In the long run, the aim of maintaining price stability and the attempt to maintain constant exchange rates proved to be incompatible goals (Sachverständigenrat Jahresgutachten, 1966, para. 282; Emminger, 1986; Caesar, 1981, p. 485). Given these circumstances, the rate of inflation in West Germany in the long run could not be kept at a level below that of the US inflation rate. Thus, as long as the government chose not to allow the Deutschmark to find its true level, higher inflation was imported. This situation prevailed in the 1950s and – except for a short interlude, due to a small appreciation of the Deutschmark in 1961 – also in the 1960s until the substantial appreciation of the German currency in 1969, shortly after the SPD and the FDP first took office.

So long as the currency was severely undervalued (but also after the onset of the floating exchange rate regime, although then to a much smaller extent), the Bundesbank never managed fully to reach its target, defined in terms of price stability. Some critics have therefore argued that the German central bank has been unsuccessful in its monetary policy (Caesar, 1981). However, this view is derived from evaluative criteria which are too rigid and which, moreover, do not sufficiently take account of the fact that, in the long run, the Bundesbank has done a much better job in controlling inflationary pressure than central banks in other industrialized nations (see Caesar, 1981; Chouraqui and Price, 1984; Pätzold, 1985; Hibbs, 1985). Furthermore, the management of monetary policy in the mid 1960s (Lindner-Narr, 1984) and in the period following the first oil price shock in 1973 demonstrated that the Bundesbank was willing to establish monetary discipline despite high costs. In particular, it did not hesitate to trade off substantial macroeconomic losses, such as reduced levels of economic growth and increases in unemployment, against the maintenance or achievement of price stability (Kloten et al., 1985; Scharpf, 1984, 1987).

The priority accorded to controlling inflationary pressure became even more pronounced after 1973. In this period, the autonomy of the central bank was considerably enlarged. This was mainly due to the breakdown of the Bretton Woods system and, in particular, to the floating exchange rate regime of the post-Bretton Woods era as well as to the creation of the European monetary currency system which, although more restrictive than the pure floating exchange rate regime, involved more latitude on the part of the Bundesbank.

In this period the Bundesbank redefined the theory and the practice of monetary policy. In contrast to the pre-1973 period, in which the Bundesbank premised its anti-cyclical policy on a pragmatic combination of a credit theory of Keynesian complexion and monetarist theory, the monetary policy stance that was adopted thereafter placed greater emphasis on monetarist theory and practice (see, for details, Duwendag et al., 1977; Pätzold, 1985; OECD, 1984). The goals of monetary policy were now targeted to the path of potential production and not to the business cycle and the change in money supply was substituted for the interest rate as one of the major goals of monetary policy (Pätzold, 1985, pp. 106–8). The new policy was complemented by a strong appreciation of the currency. The new policy approach on the part of the central bank involved considerable gains in terms of price stability and credibility of central bank behaviour, but it also involved considerable costs in terms of growth losses and unemployment. In fact, employment losses were larger than in most other countries, except for Switzerland which had a similarly restrictive monetary policy (Prader, 1981; Boltho, 1982; Schmidt, 1985b). However, with respect to price stability, the results have been exceptionally good. By international comparison, the Bundesbank was much more successful in controlling monetary aggregates than most other OECD countries and it was particularly successful in maintaining a low rate of inflation in the period of 'managed floating' of the exchange rate.

Fiscal policy and industrial relations

While the German Bundesbank is rightly praised in the OECD area for its outstanding success in controlling inflationary expectations, the efficiency and effectiveness of the central bank's policy is also much facilitated by the low inflation potential inherent in the preference order of the mass public and in the institutional conditions of West Germany's political economy. The priority accorded to the maintenance of relative price stability by both public and politicians was a potent factor in reducing inflationary expectations. This, in turn, has facilitated the adoption of a determined non-inflationary stance in monetary policy on the part of the central bank.

Furthermore, the maintenance of relative price stability was greatly assisted by the moderate stance adopted in fiscal policy and by the relatively low growth rates of public expenditure until the early 1960s and since the mid 1970s (Schmidt, 1989). Foreign observers of the West German economy of the 1950s and 1960s have generally regarded the high priority accorded to price stability and the relative unimportance of fiscal policy as a tool for demand management as characteristics which distinguish West Germany from other industrial countries (Shonfield, 1969). Despite the fact that the Bundesbank on several occasions vehemently attacked the tax and expenditure policies of the federal government, as in 1960, in 1965/66, and in the 1970s (Duwendag et al., 1977; Emminger, 1986), fiscal policy on the whole remained remarkably cautious, albeit procyclical, in character. With the possible exception of the late 1960s and early 1970s, it did not fundamentally jeopardize the effort to control inflationary pressure (see, for example, McCracken, 1977; Chouraqui and Price, 1984; OECD Economic Surveys: Germany; Knott, 1981; Scharpf, 1987).

The attempt to control inflationary pressure was also much facilitated by the nature of the industrial relations regime in general and the nature of the trade unions in particular. It is widely accepted that the West German brand of trade unionism can be given a considerable share of the credit for the comparative strength of the country's economy. Although the spirit of 'social partnership', which has long been regarded as a central feature of Germany's well organized system of industrial relations, was put under strain by distributional conflicts in the early 1970s and 1980s and by protracted recession, the general willingness of the trade unions to adjust their policy to the fundamental requirements of a stable and resilient economy was of great importance. In particular, the unions' policy of tolerating wage moderation and of accepting productivity increases and concomitant spells of unemployment and sectoral shifts in jobs are factors that have greatly alleviated the adoption and effective implementation of a price stability oriented policy, at least in the 1950s and early 1960s and since the mid 1970s.

Undoubtedly, the policy stance of the trade unions reflects the strong anti-inflation priorities of both the leadership and core membership constituencies stemming from the traumatic learning experiences of the 1920s onwards (see Borchardt, 1985 on the willingness of labour to concede wage cuts for price stability during the stabilization crisis in the early 1930s). Moreover, there cannot be much doubt that the consultation and informal or formal integration of labour in the policy formation process and the high degree to which trade union power is institutionalized in the West German industrial relations regime have contributed to labour quiescence in wage policy.

Consultation, integration and institutionalized codetermination are all arrangements which offer considerable possibilities for the trade unions to trade off wage moderation and other policy restraints against benefits in other areas. These areas include such matters as the quality of the workplace environment, trade union participation and representation and other forms of industrial democracy. The role of works councils in West Germany's economy and the recruitment of trade union officials to ministries are but some examples of the rather considerable success achieved by the German trade unions in such trade-off activity in the post-war period (Streeck, 1981, 1984, 1985; Czada, 1983; Dittrich, 1983; Armingeon, 1988).

It is here that we are confronted with a powerful explanation of the unions' acceptance of the most advanced practices of capitalist modernization and here it is also that we find the key to an understanding of the remarkably moderate strike behaviour of the West German trade unions, itself an important causal factor in the effort to control inflationary pressure. International comparison over the post-1945 period suggests that strike volumes and lockouts in West Germany were much less frequent and much smaller than in most other countries, except Austria and Switzerland (Hibbs, 1978; Armingeon, 1983). While the low level of industrial conflict did not preclude the possibility of single dramatic labour conflicts, such as the struggle over the reduction of working hours in the late 1970s and in the 1980s, the long-run trend in the mode of class conflict resolution in West Germany has been characterized by the notion of social partnership between labour and capital. Due to the low level of industrial conflict, the emergence of wage-price spirals tended to be interrupted or suppressed, so long as wage restraint by trade unions was rewarded with job security, social income, tax concessions and rights and resources for the core constituency of the trade unions.

The low level of strike activity in West Germany is partly attributable to the fact that in developed welfare states the *loci* of distributional conflict have been shifted from the market to parliamentary and bureaucratic arenas (Hibbs, 1978, pp. 169–71) but it also mirrors the joint impact of structural attributes of the trade unions, conscious choices on the part of the trade unions' leadership, and trends inherent in the political history of Germany. For example, it is well known that the reconstruction of industrial relations in West Germany after 1945 established free collective bargaining and politically united trade unions on an industry wide base. Thus, from the outset, West German trade unions avoided the numerous intra-union or inter-unions conflicts that tend to emerge from craft fragmentation. Moreover, the low strike-proneness of West Germany's trade unions can at least partly be attributed to conscious choices that were taken by the leaders of the trade unions. Premising their action on the experience of the breakdown of the Weimar Republic and of the destruction of the trade unions in 1933, and premising their policy on the assumption that large-scale mobilization of union members would fuel the escalation of political conflicts and ultimately result in threats to the trade union movement, the union leaders hesitated to use the strike weapon or other forms of labour unrest.

The low degree of open class conflict in West Germany has led to a greater stability and predictability in the behaviour of labour. Greater stability and predictability, in turn, enhanced the probability of stable and successful economic exchange between labour and capital, and thus fostered the conditions required for sustaining a monetary policy of a stable and credible kind.

The low level of industrial conflict, positive effects on price stability and the low conflict proneness of the unions contributes to a wider pattern of conflict avoidance which is itself a distinctive aspect of the West German political culture. Here, too, an historical hypothesis is of relevance. Conflict avoidance is a part of the emphasis which a large majority of the public places on goals such as stability, security and predictability, which are themselves largely traceable to the experience of instability, insecurity and unpredictability that marked the political history of Germany in the first half of the twentieth century.

Thus, in a sense, the process of learning from the political catastrophes that have haunted Germany in the twentieth century explains much of the institutional and behavioural development of West Germany's system of labour relations, and that development has been among the major determinants of the successful control of inflationary pressure. A large part of Germany's price stability record can thus be attributed to the structure of labour relations, cultural factors, historical trauma and institutions such as the Bundesbank. But how can we account for the *two* faces of West Germany's policy of the middle way? Why is the public policy profile distinguished by the combination of price stability and a strong welfare state? We have already seen that Germany's historical legacy of statism is part of the answer, but there is more to it than this. It is to the latter aspect of the puzzle of the policy of the middle way that the following sections are devoted.

The Impact of West Germany's Federalism on the Policy of the Middle Way

Institutions circumscribe the room to manoeuvre that is open to policy-makers. In terms of the range of options and the type of policy they allow for, institutions are biased. For example, the Bundesbank, for reasons that have already been discussed, is *a priori* biased towards price stability policy and biased against a full employment stance. Similarly, the institutional grammar of West Germany's system of industrial relations is of a kind which facilitates the control of inflationary expectations.

In this section it will be argued that the distinctive features of West Germany's public profile are also shaped by the policy selectivity inherent in the federal structure of the state. In particular, it will be pointed out that the institutional characteristics of West Germany's federalism, at least in a period of economic recession, are also, implicitly, conducive to a further bias towards price stability at the expense of full employment policy. In contrast, the responsiveness of West Germany's federalism to the trade-off between equality and efficiency is of a more balanced nature and allows for the formation and implementation of statist policies in general and welfare statist policies in particular.

The unique character of West Germany's federalism has often been misunderstood. In contrast to the American model, political authority in West Germany is not allocated to either one or the other level of government, but is shared by the federal government and *Länder* governments (see, in particular, Scharpf et al., 1976; Scharpf, 1985). More specifically, the *Länder* governments have a considerable share in administration and in legislation. In practice, all important federal legislation requires majorities in both the Bundestag, the popularly elected lower house, and in the Bundesrat (the Federal Council), made up of delegates of the state governments. Therefore, federal legislation to a large extent depends upon the agreement of the state governments. Moreover, the states in the Federal Republic of Germany have a significant share in the exercise of many of the important functions of the federal government.

The structure of the German federal state and, in particular, the manner in which the federal, *Länder* and local governments are politically intermeshed (*Politikverflechtung*) is conducive to a specific selectivity both in respect of the scope of policy-making action and its timing and substance. For example, the emergence of active, long-term and redistributive policies tends to be impeded, due to differences that exist among the states in terms of levels of economic wealth, economic structure, rates of growth, levels of unemployment, tax revenues ('poor states' versus 'rich states') and differences in interests between the *Länder* and the federal government. Differences in the distribution of power between political parties, and differences in the political composition of governments ('Christian Democratic states' versus 'Social Democratic states') also narrow the range of consensus in policy-making. In addition, the non-synchronization of the electoral calendars for Landtag and Bundestag elections must be counted as a major obstacle to policy development of a co-ordinated and active kind.

Empirical studies of West German federalism have demonstrated that the process of policy formation is rather systematically biased. For example, redistributive policy, such as far-reaching reforms in education, is generally thwarted by the divergence of interests between the *Länder* governments, the federal government, the governing parties and the opposition parties (Lehmbruch, 1976). Moreover, it has been shown that the federal structure of the state impedes or thwarts the pursuit of anti-cyclical fiscal policy (Kock, 1975; Knott, 1981; Scharpf, 1987). Co-operative federalism has proved rather inflexible, and this has been particularly the case in respect of coping with the challenge of policy adjustment in response to the pressures imposed by the economic recessions of the 1970s (Scharpf, 1985).

At a more general level, and basing our judgement on Scharpf's seminal contributions (Scharpf, 1973, 1977, 1985, 1987; Scharpf et al., 1976) and studies of obstacles to reform policy (Lehmbruch, 1976), it can be argued that the cost-benefit calculus of the major participants in the policy-making game in West Germany's federalism makes for systematic policy bias. Its roots are to be found in a variety of techniques of consensus-building and conflict-avoidance on the one hand, and in differences in the level of fiscal resources, ideology and the impact of party competition on the other. The techniques of consensus-building and of conflict-avoidance include a variety of decision-making rules such as segmentation of decision-making, negative co-ordination from bottom up, adjournment of conflict resolution, abstention from intervention and abandonment of redistributive policy, to mention just a few examples. Consequently, certain kinds of policy problems cannot be handled, or solved, in an efficient and effective fashion, and therefore assume the status of non-decisions (Bachrach and Baratz, 1970). These non-decisions include, in particular, problems of a structural-redistributive nature, those which require for solutions drastic changes both in the level and the distribution of activities, and interaction problems, that is, problems that are marked by complex networks of interdependent externalities produced at a decentralized level (Scharpf et al., 1976).

Moreover, and at least partly as a result of differences in political ideology and strategies of party competition, the policy process in West Germany's co-operative federalism tends to impede the formation of policies which are rapidly designed, well co-ordinated, compatible with the interests of state and federal governments, and encompassing and non-egoistic in nature. Thus, it can be argued, the federal structure of the state itself is an impediment to an active and encompassing policy response to processes of rapid structural change. In contrast to this, policy problems of a more simple character, such as those of a distributional nature which require only more or less of a given activity, are often solved in an efficient and effective manner.

Concerning the distinctive features of the policy of the middle way, the implication that can be derived from the logic of policy-making in West Germany's federalism is as follows: federalism tends to impede or thwart the delivery of anti-cyclical policy, and thus acts as an obstacle to the successful management of large cyclical recessions. Moreover, and probably more important, West Germany's federalism also tends to obstruct all policy initiatives that are targeted to the solution of highly complex problems, including mass unemployment stemming from cyclical and structural factors, and which are inherently unamenable to treatment in terms of policy initiatives of a purely distributive nature.

The policy immobilisme that is intrinsic to West German federalism is further complicated by institutional disincentives to full employment policy. This perverse situation mirrors an institutional pathology, itself largely due to the cost-benefit distributions that result from the restoration of full employment policy. Public spending aimed at restoring full employment necessarily gives rise to a systematic incongruence between costs and benefits among the budgets of the federal government, the state governments, local governments, the Federal Office of Labour and the various social insurance funds. For example, the social insurance funds and local governments would benefit greatly from a full employment initiative promoted by the federal government effectively taking on the role of free rider of central government policy costs. For the federal government, of course, the logic is reversed: costs of full employment policy tend to outweigh gains, at least as long as the mass public is willing to tolerate higher levels of unemployment. Thus, in practical terms, the absence of an integrated labour market budget and the high degree of institutional fragmentation in labour market policy must be regarded as a major impediment to a full employment policy (see, in particular, the in-depth study by Bruche and Reissert, 1985).

Regarding the inflation-unemployment trade-off, the implication of the immobilisme characterizing labour market and employment policy is obvious enough. Within the context of West German federalism there is little in the policy process which is conducive to a trade-off between inflation and full employment. On the other hand, there is nothing in this policy process which is incompatible with the goal of price stability. Thus, the priority that economic policy-makers give to the maintenance of price stability is fully encouraged and strengthened by the logic that pervades the policy-making process in West Germany's federalism.

Concerning policy problems of a less complex nature and of a non-redistributive kind, West German federalism allows for interventionist responses. Due to the logic of consensus-building within the context of co-operative federalism, and for reasons which are discussed fully in Scharpf et al. (1976), bargaining between the states and the federal government over distributive problems tends to result in high spending and high levels of state intervention. Illustrative examples can be taken from public expenditure infrastructure, health policy and social policy in general. Thus, West German federalism is paradoxical in its overall impact on the substance of public policy. It encourages price stability – at the expense of full employment – and discourages radical policy initiatives, and yet at the same time it tends to favour the further extension of the interventionist role of the state.

The Role of Political Parties in Shaping the Policy of the Middle Way

The explanation of West Germany's policy of the middle way that has been developed in the preceding sections of this chapter needs to be complemented by an analysis of the extent to which public policy is shaped by the distribution of political power between political tendencies in general and party politics in particular. An analysis in these terms provides the final crucial key to the post-war transformation of the German public policy profile. In theoretical terms, the approach to political forces offered here rests on a novel analytical paradigm combining traditional party political and democratic class struggle perspectives with an interpretation of public policy stemming from Kirchheimer (1965) and Olson (1982).

The distribution of power in West Germany's party system

In the Federal Republic of Germany, an alternating party system of high concentration has replaced the multi-party system of the 1950s (Stöss, 1984). Only a few parties have won parliamentary seats in elections to the Bundestag and only three parties have consistently attained more than 5 per cent of the vote and, hence, have overcome the hurdle which the law on elections to the Bundestag establishes. These are the Christian Democratic Union (CDU) together with its separate Bavarian sister organization, the Christian Social Union (CSU), the Social Democratic Party (SPD) and the Free Democratic Party (FDP).

Measuring the degree of party concentration by the number of parties consistently polling 2 or more per cent of the national vote, the Federal Republic obtains a score which is rivalled only by a few developed industrial nations, such as Austria and the Anglo-American democracies. The West German party system is characterized by a small number of parties and by the existence of two large parties of the people's party type which appeal substantially across political and social cleavages. On the centre-right are the CDU and CSU, organizations of an interconfessional, pragmatic conservative-reformist, if not populist character (Mintzel, 1977; Pridham, 1977; Haungs, 1983) and on the centre-left is the SPD, a reformist, wage-earner-oriented party which more actively than many other Social Democratic parties has attempted to convert itself into a centre-left people's party (Thomas, 1975).

In national elections in the 1970s and 1980s, some 45 per cent of the votes were cast for the Christian Democratic Party, some 40 per cent of the voters supported the SPD, and 10 per cent or less were mobilized by the Free Democratic Party, while the Green Party, which made an entrance on to the parliamentary stage in the late 1970s, won 6 to 8 per cent of the votes. Judging by this distribution of the voters, the non-socialist tendencies have an advantage over the Social Democratic tendency of, on average, 15 percentage points. Thus, the natural centre of gravity of West German politics falls somewhere within the non-socialist camp and not, as in Sweden, within the Social Democratic Party.

The distribution of political power in the economy is similar to that of the party system, insofar as the power of capital clearly outweighs the power resources of organized labour (Cameron, 1984, pp. 165–7). Given these facts, one must conclude that those commentators who have, implicitly or explicitly, regarded the SPD and/or the trade unions as politically dominant or even hegemonic have profoundly misunderstood the character of the German political process (see, for example, the concept of the 'SPD-Staat' in Grube/Richter, 1977). Despite a respectable showing, as indicated by the organizational strength of unions and SPD, the left vote and union density figures, to mention but a few possible measures, the West German labour movement is weaker than that of many other countries, and in particular weaker than labour in countries such as Sweden, Norway and Austria. Indeed, the Social Democratic vote in West Germany only ranks tenth among the Social Democratic parties of the OECD area in the period from 1949 to the mid 1980s.

However, quantitative data on voters and members of political tendencies can be deceptive if taken as the only indicators of power resources. Such a perspective does not capture other major components of the distribution of power, such as the organizational and ideological cohesiveness of political tendencies. From the mid 1950s to the late 1970s the cohesiveness of the left-wing tendency and the incohesiveness of the non-socialist tendencies compensated to a considerable extent for the weakness of the left-wing tendency in West Germany. Concerning centre-left or left-wing parties of non-trivial size, the SPD was the only party of the left in West Germany in this period. Since the late 1970s, however, the SPD's position has been weakened by the rise of the Green Party, which, by mobilizing a not insubstantial share of left-wing voters, has now made serious inroads into SPD support and the cohesion of the left tendency.

The non-socialist tendency has always been organizationally and ideologically incohesive in character. This is partly due to the organizational separation of the Bavarian CSU from the CDU, but it mainly mirrors the fact that the non-socialists are divided into separate Christian Democratic and liberal camps. Moreover, the Free Democratic Party, the institutional expression of the liberal tendency, has entered coalitions not only with other non-socialist parties, but also with the Social Democratic Party, and has thus, at least temporarily, reduced the political weight of the non-socialist tendencies.

Although the Free Democratic Party manages to mobilize just 5 to 10 per cent of the voters, the Liberals command the strategically pivotal position in the party system. The liberal party is the 'Zünglein an der Waage' – the FDP tips the balance between Christian Democracy and Social Democracy. Indeed, the only exceptions were the Grand Coalition period 1966 to 1969 and the one-off situation in 1957 when the CDU/CSU won a parliamentary majority in its own right. Otherwise the Free Democratic Party has been the king-maker, allowing the SPD to take the reins of power in 1969 and the CDU/CSU to resume them in 1982.

The political composition of governments in West Germany

The Free Democratic Party has fully exploited its strategic central position in West Germany's politics. Although the FDP is the smallest of the three established parties, it participated in government in the period from 1949 until the mid 1980s for longer than any other party. At the federal government level, the FDP was in office from 1949 to 1956, from 1961 to 1966, and from 1969 until the time of writing (1988). It has thus participated in government for more than 80 per cent of the total period, while the Christian Democratic Party, although of a strength many times greater than that of the Liberals, spent just 28 years – 65 per cent of the total period – in office (from 1949 until 1969 and from 1982 until the present time). The Social Democratic Party had to content itself with 16 years in office (1966–82), which is equivalent to 40 per cent of the total period since 1949. If there exists anything like a permanent governing party in West Germany, that role belongs to the Free Democratic Party. 'In the Federal Republic of Germany', one of West Germany's leading journalists commented, 'the following proposition is true: it is impossible not to be governed by the FDP' (Zundel, 1986).

Somewhat less extreme has been the distribution of cabinet seats among the parties in the *Länder* of the Federal Republic of Germany, although the extent to which the FDP participated in state governments in the total post-war period is impressively large. Particularly successful were the Free Democrats' efforts to gain portfolios in states which were of centre-left or of centrist complexion, judging by the distribution of votes by the two big parties. For example, in Berlin the FDP held cabinet seats for more than 85 per cent of the total period from 1949 to 1986. The Liberals in Hamburg were also highly successful (some 65 per cent), and those in Schleswig-Holstein, the Rhineland-Palatinate and Bremen only marginally less so (some 50 per cent of the total post-war period). In contrast to this performance, the Free Democrats participated to a much lesser extent in the governments of Hamburg, Lower Saxony, the Saar, Baden-Württemberg and, in particular, Bavaria where the FDP's share of years in office was just 20 per cent.

Of course, the number of months or years which a party spent in government is not a sufficiently valid indicator of the party's role in shaping public policy. For example, the observation that the FDP has participated in national government over a longer period than any other party in West Germany – and also longer than most other liberal parties in the OECD area – is fully compatible with the fact, that the CDU/CSU is West Germany's most influential governing party, measured by the average share of cabinet seats across the 1949–86 period followed, at a considerable distance, by the SPD.

In the Federal Republic of Germany, the political composition of national governments has never been consistent with the partisan make-up of government in the states of West Germany or in the Bundesrat. As a rule, the major opposition party in the Bundestag has played a powerful role in government at the level of the states. The Christian Democratic Party has long been the incumbent party in Bavaria, in Baden-Württemberg, Rhineland-Palatinate, Schleswig-Holstein, until 1984 also in the Saar, and since 1981 in Berlin. In contrast, the Social Democratic Party has dominated governments in the city-states of Hamburg and Bremen, in North Rhine-Westphalia since the 1960s, in Hesse (until 1987) and – until 1981 – also in Berlin. In a third group of states, the distribution of power between the parties, and the political complexion of government, was of a more mixed nature, as in Lower Saxony (which is now governed by a CDU/FDP coalition); and in North Rhine Westphalia (which is now governed by the SPD) until the 1960s.

The most striking discrepancy between the power distribution at national and state level (including state representative institutions) existed in the 1970s. In this period, the SPD/FDP coalition governments found themselves confronted with a majority of states which were governed by the CDU or the CSU and with a majority of CDU/CSU-votes in the Federal Council. Due to the powerful role of the Federal Council in the process of policy formation, the Christian Democratic parties' majority of the seats in the Federal Council virtually resulted in the CDU/CSU's co-determination in policy-making with the social liberal coalition.

Thus, the political composition of governments in West Germany is not sufficiently defined by indicators of the political complexion of national governments. Scholars who take the latter indicators at face value significantly tend to underestimate the importance of the opposition party in the Bundestag and, at the same time, overestimate the room for manoeuvre available to the incumbent party. Moreover, a further caveat should be added. While the distribution of votes in national elections results in a comfortable majority for the non-socialist tendencies, it has by no means universally been the case that the non-socialist majority consistently results in the formation of governments of non-socialist complexion. Despite the dominance of non-socialist parties, the Social Democratic Party has participated in office to an extent which broadly accords with the SPD's historical share of the vote in the post-war period, mainly due to the liberal party's flexibility in coalition policy. The overall political complexion of government in Germany has not been marked by the hegemonic position of a single party. Rather, more typical have been coalitions of a centre-right or the centre-left kind, depending mainly on the coalition partner chosen by the FDP. Over the long haul, it may be argued, the post-war complexion of government has been predominantly centrist, rather than Christian Democratic or Social Democratic in character. The policy of the middle way has been accompanied by the politics of the middle way!

Coalitions are the most normal form of government at the national level, and also at the level of the states (although the states have experienced a trend towards single-party governments in the 1970s and in the 1980s). Regarding the frequency of coalitions, politics in the Federal Republic of Germany thus deviates from the pattern of alternating single governing parties which characterizes the majority of the Anglo-American democracies. However, West German coalition practices are also at variance with those of many other democratic nations. Governments in West Germany have been characterized by a wide variety of types of coalitions. All-inclusive coalitions, ranging from the liberals to the Communist Party, were prevalent in the immediate post-war period. However, as soon as the Cold War began, all-party coalitions were replaced by coalitions which excluded the Communist Party and, later, by minimum-winning coalitions of a variety of political complexions. Although a clear trend towards centre-left or centre-right coalitions had emerged in the 1950s, the Grand Coalition experiment at the federal level of the late 1960s had some precursors at the state level. The recent tendency to single-party governments in the states has not been duplicated federally, where the alternatives have been centre-right and centre-left coalitions.

The frequency of coalition government demonstrates that the major parties of West Germany succeeded rarely, if at all, in mobilizing the majority of the voters. Thus, and in particular at the level of the national government, parties of different ideological orientation and different social constituencies have formed coalitions. The social composition and the ideological make-up of the various coalition governments have varied considerably. Very broadly speaking, and focusing attention on the preferences of the majority of each social and political milieu, voter alignments can be characterized as follows: the Christian Democratic parties are the major representatives of farmers, entrepreneurs, the self-employed, old middle classes and of the upper white-collar class. Both the Christian Democratic Party *and* the Social Democratic Party mobilize voters from the lower white-collar class and from recipients of social policy benefits. Even among working class voters the Christian Democratic Party has a substantial following. In contrast, there are only a few groups of voters in which the Social Democratic Party is the single representative party: these are trade union members and, in particular, organised workers with a low degree of religious affiliation.

While it can be argued that, in comparison with the past, differences between the parties' social constituencies have been reduced, it must be stressed that the social profile of the Social Democratic voter differs from those of the Christian Democratic and liberal voters. So, also, differ the political ideologies propagated by the parties. In ideological terms, the Free Democratic Party is asymmetrically located between the CDU/CSU and the SPD (Dittberner, 1987). Its ideology reflects the interests of a social constituency which is characterized by a middle-class or upper-class ideology, a low degree of religious affiliation, a deep belief in the benign effects of competitive markets and a preference order which puts emphasis on self-reliance in the market rather than social protection organized by the welfare state and/or trade unions. Thus, the Free Democratic Party's position in the cleavage structure of West Germany stands in marked contrast to the positions that are taken by its larger coalition partners. For example, in contrast to the SPD, the FDP is not a party which is ideologically affiliated to the trade unions, and in contrast to the CDU/CSU, the Liberals are strongly secular in character. Moreover, and in contrast to both the Christian Democrats and the Social Democrats, the FDP is only marginally linked to the interests of the welfare state bureaucracy and the interests of the recipients of benefits from social insurance and other types of welfare provision.

The impact of party on public policy

What policy consequences can be derived from the distribution of political power between the parties and the political composition and coalitional status of governments? If one assumes that the parties' ideologies and practice mirror to a considerable extent the interests of their major social constituencies, it follows that the various coalition governments in West Germany are representative of a wide variety of social constituencies. These differences, and differences in ideology and philosophy of policy-making on the part of the government, are reflected in more or less significant differences in the policy profile, such as higher or lower spending, higher or lower taxes, or provision of more or less extensive rights for specific target groups.

However, there are also commonalities between the policies of centre-right and centre-left governments in West Germany. It is arguable that such common themes are exceptionally strong in West Germany because the electoral base of centre-right and centre-left coalitions is of a kind which has the characteristics of Kirchheimer's 'catch-all party' (but note that Kirchheimer talked about single parties, while the proposition here is that catch-all partyness will only be *approximated* by a *coalition*, particularly coalitions in which the Christian Democratic parties participate).[7] For example, both types of coalitions attract the support, and to some degree are interest coalitions, of manual workers, lower white-collar workers and upper white-collar strata, old middle classes and new middle classes, entrepreneurs and recipients of welfare state provision.In both kinds of coalitions, almost all social classes tend to be represented. In this respect, the electoral base of centre-right governments is similar to that of centre-left coalitions and this is why a wider range of similarities characterizes the policies that each pursues (which does not, of course, preclude the possibility of party-specific policy-making). It is precisely in these similarities that we may locate a further key to an understanding of the West German policy of the middle way.

A brief discussion of the mechanisms which link similarities in policies with the catch-all characteristics of centre-right coalitions and centre-left coalitions might be helpful at this stage. Due to their 'catch-all' characteristics, centre-right and centre-left coalitions are driven by similar incentives. Of course, the incentives for the Liberals are markedly different from the incentives for any of the larger parties, but the interaction of all participants in the coalition-opposition game yields similar results. The incentives for the Social Democratic Party and for the Christian Democratic Party work in favour of solving policy dilemmas in a fashion which yields non-trivial and non-particularistic results. This is partly due to the reformist stance of both parties, but it mainly mirrors the logic of incentives to which fairly encompassing organizations find themselves exposed (see Olson, 1982, 1986), and to the preferences for centrist policy on the part of the large majority of the West German wage earners (Lepsius, 1982).

In contrast to this, the Liberal party, being a very small party and a representative of particularistic class interests, at least in economic and social policy areas, opts for a strategy of maximizing the special interests of its major social constituency, subject to the constraints that the goal of safeguarding the survival of a given coalition imposes on the party. As a consequence, the Liberals prefer solutions of policy dilemmas which are more extreme, more biased and more particularistic in character than those favoured by the larger parties. For example, the Liberal's philosophy accords priority to efficiency at the expense of equality, to the market at the expense of statist and welfare statist provision and to price stability at the expense of job security and full employment. At least so far as economic policy and often also social policy issues are concerned, the Free Democratic Party thus acts as a party of a rather pure variety of bourgeois class-politics.

However, the policy stance of the Free Democrats needs to be reconciled with that of its coalition partner. The coalition partners have found it not too difficult to reach agreement on the priority that will ultimately be placed on the maintenance of price stability. Agreement has been greatly facilitated by the fact that price stability is regarded as a major goal and a major success in virtually all social classes and political milieus. However, the limits of consensus are reached as soon as price stability involves persistently high levels of unemployment. Under these circumstances, the coalition governments in which the Liberals participate will reach the upper limit of consensus and policy capability. The Liberals are not willing to go along with efforts to restore full employment at a cost of higher inflation rates.

Moreover the Free Democratic Party is not interested in allowing for a softer mix of lower unemployment rates and moderately high inflation rates for reasons which are perfectly compatible with the class-interest of its social constituency among well-to-do self-employed or among the salary-dependent middle class. However, in principle, the uncompromising stance of the Liberals *vis-à-vis* the unemployment-inflation trade-off can itself be traded with a more flexible stance on social policy. In periods of economic prosperity the Liberals have accepted their larger coalition partner's preference for maintaining and expanding the welfare state, but in periods of recession, such as in 1966, in the 1970s and in the early 1980s, the Liberals uncompromisingly pursue a policy which sacrifices social protection for economic efficiency and full employment for price stability. The Free Democrats' tolerance of a highly developed welfare state is contingent upon high rates of economic growth and conditional upon a particular type of welfare state: one which is characterized by transfer-intensive delivery of public social services, and one in which social policy is mainly financed through contributions from employees and employers and not through tax revenues.

Thus, the logic of consensus-building and policy formation that takes place within the centre-right and the centre-left coalitions that has been characteristic of West German governments has significantly contributed to the policy of the middle way. In particular, that logic has resulted in price-stability oriented policies and in a developed welfare state of the transfer-intensive kind. At the risk of oversimplifying complex relationships, it can be argued that the non-socialist tendency in West Germany is so powerful, and the Liberals, in particular, are so influential that the priority given to price stability and other goals commonly regarded as typical of bourgeois tendencies requires almost no further explanation. However, what requires explanation is the fact that the substance of policy in other areas has been of a rather centrist complexion or even of a centre-left character.

The key to an understanding resides in the relative incohesiveness of the non-socialist tendency, particularly in the split between the Free Democratic Party as the class-interest-party of economic liberalism on the one hand, and the conservative-reformist, pragmatic Christian Democratic Parties on the other. The cleavage within the non-socialist tendency, in conjunction with the pragmatic, conservative-reformist approach to policy on the part of the CDU and the CSU, and the relative strength of the Social Democratic Party are of major relevance in explaining the coexistence of price stability and high degrees of state intervention in general and high levels of social security in particular. West Germany's policy of the middle way rests on a particular type of historical compromise between economic liberalism, pragmatic conservative reformism of a Christian Democratic complexion and Social Democracy.

Conclusion

The focus of this chapter has been on the explanation of what is distinctive about contemporary West German public policy. What we have analysed is an historical and political process by which Germany's traditional policy exceptionalism – its *Sonderweg* – has been dissolved, leaving in its place the relative normalcy of the policy of the middle way. The genesis of that policy, and the keys to the puzzle from which we began, lie in processes of political and institutional learning from historical catastrophes and in a specific compromise between economic liberalism, conservative reformism and Social Democracy.

The historical roots of West Germany's policy of the middle way are to be found in the tradition of a state-led industrialization process as well as in the long-standing tradition of a conservative reformist welfare state. Moreover, the relative weakness of pure *laissez-faire* ideology was a factor that further strengthened German interventionism. However, the process of learning from political catastrophes – in particular, the closely associated legacies of hyperinflation and democratic vulnerability – significantly strengthened the liberal philosophy of policy-making.

The foremost example of the translation of the liberal approach and lessons drawn from past catastrophe is, of course, the priority given to price stability policy. For the public and for the vast majority of politicians, controlling inflation is *the* goal of economic policy *par excellence*. There are institutional and political processes which help to explain the unusual salience of such a policy stance: the role of the Bundesbank as the guardian of the currency, the structure of both industrial relations and federal arrangements as well as the pivotal position in the party system of the FDP. But the crucial backdrop to all these processes is the fact that this is an arena of public policy in which for strong historical reasons division and disagreement are at a minimum.

That is why, despite the somewhat centrist complexion of coalition government over the post-war period as a whole, Germany's performance in respect of price stability has been of a kind that comparative outcomes analysis would assume to be characteristic of an extreme liberal hegemony (see, for example, Hibbs, 1977). That Germany is an outlier in this respect can be understood only in terms of her historical development and its impact on political processes and political institutions.

The impact of history is, as we have already noted, shown just as clearly on the welfare statist side of the public policy profile: in the weakness of *laissez-faire* attitudes, the tradition of state welfare paternalism and the actuality of bureaucratic continuity and incrementalism. But here, too, there are institutional and political factors similarly conducive to particular kinds of statist outcomes. Co-operative federalism may impede dramatic and radical policy changes, but it facilitates distributive incrementalism. Similarly, the logics of policy-making in the centre-right and centre-left catch-all coalitions are inherently favourable to welfare largesse, and particularly so in periods of high economic growth. Price stability plus social security through income transfers are the priority ordering of socially protective goals in contemporary West Germany, and there is much evidence from attitudinal studies that the ordering accurately reflects the views of the majority of the mass public. Thus, in overall terms, the distinctiveness of the German policy of the middle way can largely be explained by the distinctiveness of political demands on the part of the public and by the distinctive features of West Germany's political institutions.[8]

The analysis of the West German case suggests strongly that the structural regularities revealed by comparative public policy analysis are quite insufficient as a means of characterizing and explaining the most significant aspects of a country's public policy profile, unless supplemented and contextualized by a comprehension of the distinctive features of its historical development and contemporary political process. On the other hand, our analysis lends further support to what has, in recent years, become the conventional wisdom of comparative analysis, that politics determines policy.

There are three major ways in which the explanatory model utilized in this essay differs from the conventional mode of analysis in the comparative public policy literature. First is the emphasis that our analysis has placed on the Free Democratic Party in West Germany. It can be argued that the FDP is one of the most influential Liberal parties in the OECD area, not so much in terms of the liberal vote, but much more in terms of the number of years that the Liberal Party has participated in office and in terms of its role in shaping the substance of policy, particularly in respect of economic policy and civil rights issues. Most of the comparative literature on OECD nations has grossly underrated the impact that the liberal parties have on policy. It is precisely here that one of the great virtues of shifting to a more concentrated focus on distinctive or even anomalous cases becomes clearly visible: the new focus highlights the importance of factors which tend to get lost in the manipulation of the gross categories of comparative analysis.

Second, the analysis has documented the pivotal role that has been played by relatively autonomous institutions, such as the West German central bank, and here again it can be argued that the role of the Bundesbank does not generally receive sufficient attention in the work of political scientists (for exceptions see Uusitalo, 1984; Hibbs, 1985; Scharpf, 1984, 1987, 1988).

Third, our analysis has pointed to the importance that traumatic historical experiences and processes of learning from political catastrophes has on the institutional apparatus and on the timing and substance of public policy. Our study has demonstrated that the 'anomalies' of German political development of the nineteenth and twentieth centuries – and, in particular, the collapse of the Weimar Republic, the rise and fall of National Socialism and the traumatic hyperinflationary experiences of 1923 and 1948 – are of vital relevance to a full understanding of the distinctiveness of the contemporary West German public policy profile. Dramatic events, political and economic catastrophes, the process of learning from such catastrophes and the role of pivotal and relatively autonomous institutions are of far greater explanatory importance than has been assumed in the comparative public policy literature. It must be hoped that future research in the genre finds some way to incorporate these factors into its analytical framework.

Notes

1   The focus in this chapter, as of all others in this volume, is exclusively on domestic aspects of the political economy of the nations under study. It follows from this that one major distinctive aspect of public policy in West Germany is not discussed here: the partition of Germany, the 'national question' of a divided nation, and the specificity of West Germany's foreign policy towards Eastern countries in general and of its military policy in particular.

2   See, for example, Rosenberg, 1967; Wehler, 1973; Kocka, 1983; Berghan, 1982; for a critical assessment of the *Sonderweg* literature, in particular as far as the Wilhelmine Reich is concerned, see Blackbourn and Elly (1980). For a critical review of the revisionist view held by Blackbourn, Elly and others see, in particular, Wehler, 1981; Kocka, 1981 and Winkler, 1981; Grebing et al., 1986.

3   However, it should be emphasized that the public policy profiles of Austria and the Benelux states are somewhat more like West Germany than others. Largely due to the openness of the economy and to extensive trade with Germany monetary policy in these countries necessarily tends to follow the lead taken by the Bundesbank. For these reasons, these countries – explicitly or implicitly – have pegged their currency to the Deutschmark with a degree of success which varies from country to country depending on a wider range of factors, such as the trade unions' willingness and capacity to accept a flexible wage policy and differences in the extent to which inflation has been imported via price increases for imports. It follows from this that a substantial proportion of the cross-time variation in inflation rates in Austria, Belgium and the Netherlands can, statistically and theoretically, be attributed to changes in West German price levels and West German monetary policy.

4   However, it can be argued that the political process in the United States and in Switzerland is characterized by policies which are functionally similar, if not functionally equivalent to, the welfare-statist component of West Germany's policy of the middle way. Thus, for example, the priority that the Swiss authorities accord to the maintenance of job security for nationals, including foreign workers with permanent residence permits, and the high

level of take-home pay on the part of wage-earners in Switzerland produce a level of economic security for Swiss labour which fully matches the level of social security for white collar workers and civil servants in West Germany.

In the United States the role of the welfare state in the twentieth century has been more muted than in most other industrial countries of the West. Key national social welfare programmes arrived late or not at all. However, it must be noted that the United States has, in the words of Hugh Heclo, 'historically . . . more than matched its Europeean neighbours in commitment of resources to education . . . In a sense, an implicit trade-off has been made. Americans have emphasized education to provide equal opportunity, and from this commitment any resulting inequalities of social conditions could be justified more readily' (Heclo, 1985, p. 16). It should also be added that the provision of equal opportunity through education has contributed to considerable, though not exceptionally high, social mobility (Erikson and Goldthorpe, 1985), while the lesser emphasis that German policy-makers placed on education policy in general and the strong degree of inequality that is inherent in the structure of West Germany's education system probably have been among the determinants of the relatively low rate of social mobility in the Federal Republic of Germany (Müller, 1986).

5   Studies of value change in Western democracies in general, and in West Germany in particular (Inglehart, 1977), suggest that the social constituency of West Germany's policy of price stability has been weakened. There is strong evidence for the view that a substantial proportion of voters who are young, better educated and critical of materialistic values prefer policies of a post-materialist nature. Conversely, materialist policies, such as measures that are targeted towards economic growth and price stability, to mention just two examples, receive weak support from this group of voters which comprises, at the most, 15 per cent of the electorate (Feist and Leipelt, 1987, p. 295). In the long run, this could result in a threat to future policies of price stability. However, in the short- to medium-term perspective, and other things being equal, it is important to emphasize that a large majority of the electorate continues to support price stability, even if a high proportion of the post-materialists of today remain post-materialistic in later stages of their life.

6   This is not to argue that the economics profession (not to mention political scientists) has identified details and nuances of the impact of monetary policy (or other policies or events or activities) on the inflation rate (see, for example, the critical account of the limits to knowledge in this field in Streit, 1981). However, on the basis of a combination of cross-national and cross-time 'surface-correlations' between policy instruments and outcomes, and on the basis of a political-institutionalist analysis of central banks' behaviour (see, for example, Scharpf, 1987 and 1988) and recent studies from economists (such as Rasche and Johannes, 1987), it can be plausibly argued that the Bundesbank's relatively restrictive stance in monetary policy has been one of the major, if not the major, determinants of relative price stability in Germany (see, for example, Hibbs, 1985; Chouraqui and Price, 1984; Scharpf, 1987, 1988).

7   There is no party in Western Europe which fully conforms to Kirchheimer's

pure 'catch-all' party type. However, the parties that are somewhat closer to the 'catch-all' party type than most others are the West German Christian Democratic parties (for a critical assessment of Kirchheimer's hypothesis, see Schmidt, 1985a). Kirchheimer's hypothesis does not demonstrate a particularly good fit to single parties, but it becomes an extremely powerful analytical device as soon as it is focused on coalitions between parties. 'Catch-all' characteristics tend to be fully realized only in fairly encompassing coalitions.

8 It does not follow from the analysis presented here that the West German policy mix of social protection and price stability has only winners and no losers. There are losers in the West German policy game and there are winners who won more and others who won less. The core group of winners comprises employed persons within the primary labour market segments, old age pensioners with a working life of 35–45 years with few spells of unemployment or no unemployment experience at all and with wages or salaries above average wage levels, and social classes with income from ownership of firms, shares, monetary assets and land. It is important to emphasize that the core groups of the winners are at the same time the core groups in the electorate of each of the established parties of the Federal Republic of Germany.

The losers from the policy of the middle way are mainly to be found among the unemployed, in particular job-seekers with frequent spells of unemployment experience or the long-term unemployed, among groups with short working life careers and low income from work and, hence, low income from social security schemes, and among post-materialists. Using the rule of thumb that the share of post-materialists in the electorate is some 15 per cent (Feist and Leipelt, 1987), and that the unemployed in the mid 1980s constitute some 5–6 per cent of the electorate, and that one-third of old age pensioners have low and insecure income levels, it can be argued that three out of ten voters belong to the core group of the losers. In contrast to this, the core group of winners comprises probably more than 40 per cent of the electorate (assuming that two thirds of the labour force and the majority of the wealthy classes are among the winners). Neither figure takes into account the number of household members. If one were to add household members to the core groups, it is clear that a substantial majority of the electorate finds itself in the position of winners in the West German policy of the middle way game.

References

Alber, J. 1982: Vom Armenhaus zum Wohlfahrtsstaat. Frankfurt and New York: Campus.

Alber, J. 1986: Germany. In P. Flora (ed.), *Growth to Limits*, vol. 2, Berlin: De Gruyter, 1–149.

Armingeon, K. 1983: Streiks. In M.G. Schmidt (ed.) *Westliche Industriegesell-schaften*, 419–28.

Armingeon, K. 1988: *Die Entwicklung der westdeutschen Gewerkschaften 1950–1985*. Frankfurt and New York: Campus.

Arndt, H.-J. 1963: *Politik und Sachverstand im Kreditwährungswesen*. Berlin: Duncker and Humblot.

Bachrach, P. and Baratz, M.S. 1970: *Power and Poverty*. New York: Columbia University Press.

Basler, H.-P. 1979: *Wirtschaftspolitische Zielpräferenzen und theoretische Orientierung in der Geldpolitik der Deutschen Bundesbank*. Tübingen: Mohr (Paul Siebeck).

Baum, T.M. 1983: Empirische Analysen der Bundesbankautonomie, *Konjunkturpolitik*, 29.

Berghan, V. 1982: *Modern Germany*. Cambridge: Cambridge University Press.

Beyme, K. von and Schmidt, M.G. (eds) 1985: *Policy and Politics in the Federal Republic of Germany*. Aldershot, Hants: Gower.

Blackbourn, D. and Elly, G. 1980: *Mythen deutscher Geschichtschreibung*. Berlin: Ullstein.

Boltho, A. (ed.) 1982: *The European Economy*. Oxford: Oxford University Press.

Bonin, K. von 1979: *Zentralbanken zwischen funktioneller Unabhängigkeit und politischer Autonomie*. Baden-Baden: Nomos.

Borchardt, K. 1985: Das Gewicht der Inflationsangst in den wirtschaftspolitischen Entscheidungsprozessen während der Weltwirtschaftskrise. In G.D. Feldman (ed.; *Die Nachwirkungen der Inflation auf die deutsche Geschichte 1924–1933*, 233–60.

Bracher, K.-D. 1983: *Die deutsche Diktatur*. Frankfurt, Berlin and Vienna: Ullstein.

Bruche, G. and Reissert, B. 1985: *Die Finanzierung der Arbeitsmarktpolitik*. Frankfurt and New York: Campus.

Caesar, R. 1981: *Der Handlungsspielraum von Notenbanken*. Baden-Baden: Nomos.

Cameron, D.R. 1984: Social Democracy, Corporatism, Labour Quiescence, and the Representation of Economic Interest in Advanced Capitalist Society. In J.H. Goldthorpe (ed.) *Order and Conflict in Contemporary Capitalism*, 143–78.

Castles, F.G. (ed.) 1982: *The Impact of Parties*. London and Beverly Hills: Sage.

Chouraqui, J.-C. and Price, R.W.R. 1984: Medium-Term Financial Strategy: The Co-ordination of Fiscal and Monetary Policy. *OECD Economic Studies*, 2, 7–50.

Conze, W. and Lepsius, R.M. (eds) 1983: *Sozialgeschichte der Bundesrepublik Deutschland*. Stuttgart: Klett und Cotta.

Czada, R. 1983: Konsensbedingungen und Auswirkungen neokorporatistischer Politikentwicklung. *Journal für Sozialforschung*, 23.

Dahrendorf, R. 1968: *Gesellschaft und Demokratie in Deutschland*. Munich: Piper.

Deutsche Bundesbank (ed.) 1976: *Währung und Wirtschaft in Deutschland*. Frankfurt: Fritz Knapp.

Deutscher Sonderweg – Mythos oder Realität. 1982: Kolloquien des Instituts für Zeitgeschichte. Munich: Oldenbourg.

Dittberner, J. 1987: *FDP – Partei der Zweiten Wahl*. Opladen: Westdeutscher Verlag.

Dittrich, W. 1983: Mitbestimmungspolitik. In M.G. Schmidt (ed.), *Westliche*

Industriegesellschaften.Wirtschaft – Gesellschaft – Politik. Munich and Zurich: Piper, 248–55.

Dörge, F.-W. and Mairose, R. 1969: Die Bundesbank – eine Nebenregierung?. *Gegenwartskunde*, 18.

Duwendag, D. et al. 1977: *Geldtheorie und Geldpolitik*. Cologne: Bund Verlag.

Dyson, K. 1979: The Ambiguous Politics of Western Germany: Politicization in a 'State' Society. *European Journal of Political Research*, 7.

Dyson, K.H.F. 1981: The Politics of Economic Management in West Germany. *West European Politics*, 4.

Edinger, L.J. 1985: *West German Politics*. New York: Columbia University Press.

Emminger, O. 1986: *D-Mark, Dollar, Währungskrisen*. Stuttgart: DVA.

Erikson, R. and Goldthorpe, J.H. 1985: Are American rates of mobility exceptionally high? *European Sociological Review*, 1.

Eschenburg, T. 1983: *Jahre der Besatzung 1945–1949*. Stuttgart and Wiesbaden: DVA and Brockhaus.

Feist, U. and Liepelt, K. 1987: Modernisierung zu Lasten der Großen. *Journal für Sozialforschung*, 27.,

Feldman, G.D. (ed.) 1985: *Die Nachwirkungen der Inflation auf die deutsche Geschichte 1924–1933*. Munich: Oldenbourg.

Flora, P. and Heidenheimer, A.J. (eds) 1981: *The Development of the Welfare State in Europe and America*. New Brunswick and London: Transaction Books.

Flora, P. (ed.) 1983: *State, Economy and Society in Western Europe*, vol. 1, 1815–1975. Frankfurt, New York and London: Campus and Collier Macmillan.

Flora, P. (ed.) 1986: *Growth to Limits*, vol. 2. Berlin and New York: De Gruyter.

Fraenkel, E. 1949: *The Dual State*. New York: Ostagon Books.

Frey, B.S. 1978: Politometrics of Government Behaviour in a Democracy. *Scandinavian Journal of Economics*, 81.

Goldthorpe, J.H. (ed.) 1984: *Order and Conflict in Contemporary Capitalism*. Oxford: Oxford University Press.

Grebing, H. et al. 1986: *Der 'deutsche Sonderweg' in Europa 1806–1945*. Stuttgart: Kohlhammer.

Grube, F. and Richter, G. 1977: *Der SPD-Staat*. Munich: Piper.

Hartwich, H.-H. 1970: *Sozialstaatspostulat und gesellschaftlicher Status quo*. Opladen: Westdeutscher Verlag.

Haungs, P. 1983: Die Christlich Demokratische Union Deutschlands (CDU) und die Christlich Soziale Union in Bayern (CSU). In H.-J. Veen (ed.), *Christlich-demokratische und konservative Parteien in Westeuropa*, vol. 1, Paderborn: UTB, 9–194.

Heclo, H. 1985: *The Welfare State in Hard Times*. Washington, DC: APSA.

Hentschel, V. 1983: *Geschichte der Sozialpolitik in Deutschland 1880–1980*. Frankfurt: Suhrkamp.

Hibbs, D.A. 1977: Macroeconomic Policy and Political Parties. *American Political Science Review*, 71.

Hibbs, D.A. 1978: On the Political Economy of Long-Run Trends in Strike Activity. *British Journal of Political Science*, 8.

Hibbs, D.A. 1985: Inflation, Political Support, and Macroeconomic Policy. In L.N. Lindberg and C.S. Maier (eds), *The Politics of Inflation and Economic Stagnation*, 175–95.

Hockerts, H.-G. 1980: *Sozialpolitische Entscheidungen im Nachkriegsdeutschland*. Stuttgart: Klett Cotta.

Inglehart, Ronald, 1977: *The Silent Revolution*. Princeton, NJ: Princeton University Press.

Jarchow, H.-J. 1976: *Theorie und Politik des Geldes*. Göttingen: Vandenhoek and Ruprecht.

Katona, G., Strümpel, B. and Zahn, E. 1971: *Zwei Wege zur Prosperität*. Düsseldorf and Vienna: Econ.

Katzenstein, P. 1987: *Policy and Politics in West Germany*. Philadelphia, PA: Temple University Press.

Kirchheimer, O. 1965: Der Wandel des westeuropäischen Parteiensystems. *Politische Vierteljahresschrift*, 6.

Kloten, N. and Vollmer, R. (1985): West Germany's Stabilization Performance. In L.N. Lindberg and C.S. Maier (eds), *The Politics of Inflation and Economic Stagnation*, 353–402.

Knott, J.H. 1981: *Managing the German Economy*. Budgetary Politics in a Federal State. Lexington Books.

Kock, H. *Stabilitätspolitik im föderalistischen System der Bundesrepublik Deutschland*. Cologne: Bund Verlag.

Kocka, J. 1979: 1945: Neubeginn oder Restauration?. In C. Stern and H.A. Winkler (eds), *Wende punkte deutscher Geschichte 1848–1945*, Frankfurt: Fischer, 141–68.

Kocka, J. 1981: Capitalism and Bureaucracy in German Industrialization before 1914. *Economic History Review*, 2nd series, 33.

Kocka, J. 1982: Der 'deutsche Sonderweg' in der Diskussion. *German Studies Review*, 5.

Kocka, J. (ed.) 1983: *Angestellte im europäischen Vergleich*. Göttingen: Vandenhoek and Ruprecht.

Kohl, J. 1985: *Staatsfinanzen in Westeuropa*. Frankfurt and New York: Campus.

Korpi, W. 1978: *The Working Class and Welfare Capitalism*. London: Routledge and Kegan Paul.

Kort-Krieger, U. 1986: Der realistische Wähler. *Politische Vierteljahresschrift*, 27.

Lehmbruch, G. 1976: *Parteienwettbewerb im Bundesstaat*. Stuttgart: Kohlhammer.

Lehmbruch, G. 1984: Concertation and the Structure of Corporatist Networks. In J.H. Goldthorpe (ed.), *Order and Conflict in Contemporary Capitalism*. 60–80.

Lepsius, R.M. 1979: Soziale Ungleichheit und Klassenstrukturen in der Bundesrepublik Deutschland. In H.-U. Wehler (ed.), *Klassen in der europäischen Sozialgeschichte*. Göttingen: Vandenhoek and Ruprecht, 166–209.

Lepsius, R.M. 1982: Bundesrepublik Deutschland. In *Nachkriegsgesellschaften im historischen Vergleich*. Munich and Vienna: Oldenbourg, 33–40.

Lindberg, L. and Maier, C.S. (eds) 1985: *The Politics of Inflation and Economic Stagnation*. Washington, DC: The Brookings Institution.

Lindner-Narr, G. 1984: *Grenzen monetärer Steuerung. Die Restriktionspolitik der Bundesbank 1964–1974*. Frankfurt and New York: Campus.

Maddison, Angus 1982: *Phases of Capitalist Development*. Oxford and New York: Oxford University Press.

Maier, H. 1986: *Die ältere deutsche Staats- und Verwaltungslehre*. Munich: DTV (first published in 1966).

McCallum, J. 1983: Inflation and Social Consensus. *The Economic Journal*, 93.

McCracken, P.W. 1977: *Towards Full Employment and Price Stability*. Paris: OECD.

Medley, R. 1982: Inflation Policy in Germany: the Institutional and Political Determinants. In R. Medley (ed.), *The Politics of Inflation: A Comparative Analysis*, New York: Pergamon, 127–53.

Mintzel, A. 1977: *Geschichte der CSU*. Opladen: Westdeutscher Verlag.

Müller, Walter 1986: Soziale Mobilität: Die Bundesrepublik im internationalen Vergleich. In M. Kaase (ed.), *Politische Wissenschaft und politische Praxis*, Opladen: Westdeutscher Verlag, 339–56.

Neumann, F. 1977: *Behemoth. Struktur und Praxis des Nationalsozialismus.* Cologne and Frankfurt: EVA (first published in 1942 and 1944).

Organisation for Economic Co-operation and Development (OECD) 1984: *OECD Economic Outlook, Historical Statistics 1960–1983*. Paris: OECD.

OECD 1985: *Social Expenditure 1960–1990*. Paris: OECD.

OECD 1986: *OECD Economic Outlook, Historical Statistics 1960–1984*. Paris: OECD.

OECD (annually): *Economic Survey: Germany*. Paris: OECD.

Okun, A.M. 1985: *Equality and Efficiency: The Big Tradeoff*. Washington, DC: The Brookings Institution.

Olson, M. 1982: The Rise and Decline of Nations. New Haven, Conn.: Yale University Press.

Pätzold, J. 1985: *Stabilisierungspolitik*. Stuttgart and Bern: Verlag Paul Haupt.

Prader, G. 1981: *50 Jahre schweizerische Stabilisierungspolitik*. Zurich: Schultess Polygraphischer Verlag.

Pridham, G. 1977: *Christian Democracy in Western Germany*. London: Croom Helm.

Rasche, R.H. and Johannes, J.M. 1987: *Controlling the Growth of Monetary Aggregates*. Boston: Kluver Academic Publishers.

Rimlinger, G.V. 1971: *Welfare Policy and Industrialization in Europe, America and Russia*. New York: Wiley.

Rose, R. (ed.) 1985: *Public Employment in Western Nations*. Cambridge: Cambridge University Press.

Rosenberg, H. 1967: *Große Depression und Bismarckzeit*. Frankfurt, Berlin and Vienna: Ullstein (first published in 1967).

Sachverständigenrat zur Begutachtung der gesamtwirtschaftlichen Entwicklung (annually): *Jahresgutachten*. Stuttgart: Kohlhammer.

Scharpf, F.W. 1973: *Planung als politischer Prozess*. Frankfurt: Suhrkamp.

Scharpf, F.W. 1977: *Politischer Immobilismus und öhonomische Krise*. Kronberg: Athenäum.

Scharpf, F.W. 1984: Economic and Institutional Constraints of Full-Employment Strategies: Sweden, Austria and West Germany, 1973–1982. In J.H. Goldthorpe (ed.), *Order and Conflict in Contemporary Capitalism*. 257–90.

Scharpf, F.W. 1985: Die Politikverflechtungs-Falle: Europäische Integration und deutscher Föderalismus im Vergleich. *Politische Vierteljahresschrift*, 26.

Scharpf, F.W. 1987: *Sozialdemokratische Krisenpolitik in Europa.* Frankfurt and New York: Campus.

Scharpf, Fritz W. 1988: Inflation und Arbeitslosigkeit in Westeuropa. *Politische Vierteljahresschrift*, 29.

Scharpf, F.W., Reissert, B. and Schnabel, F. 1976: *Politikverflechtung.* Kronberg: Scriptor.

Schmidt, M.G. 1980: *CDU und SPD an der Regierung.* Frankfurt and New York: Campus.

Schmidt, M.G. 1982a: *Wohlfahrtsstaatliche Politik unter bürgerlichen und sozialdemokratischen Regierungen.* Frankfurt and New York: Campus.

Schmidt, M.G. 1982b: The Role of the Parties in Shaping Macroeconomic Policy. In F.G. Castles (ed.), *The Impact of Parties*, 97–176.

Schmidt, M.G. (ed.) 1983: *Westliche Industriegesellschaften.* Munich and Zurich: Piper.

Schmidt, M.G. 1985a: Allerweltsparteien in Westeuropa? *Leviathan*, 13.

Schmidt, M.G. 1985b: *Der Schweizerische Weg zur Vollbeschäftigung.* Frankfurt and New York: Campus.

Schmidt, M.G. 1986: Politische Bedingungen erfolgreicher Wirtschaftspolitik. *Journal für Sozialforschung*, 26, 251–73.

Schmidt, M.G. 1987: The Politics of Labour Market Policy. In F.G. Castles, F. Lehner and M.G. Schmidt (eds), *Managing Mixed Economies*, Berlin and New York: De Gruyter, 4–53.

Schmidt, M.G. 1988: *Sozialpolitik.* Opladen: Leske.

Schmidt, M.G. 1989, forthcoming: Staatsfinanzen. In K. von Beyme and M.G. Schmidt (eds), *Politik in der Bundesrepublik.* Opladen: Westdeutscher Verlag.

Schneider, R. 1982: Die Bildungsentwicklung in den europäischen Staates. *Zeitschrift für Soziologie*, 11.

Schönbaum, D. 1967: *Hitler's Social Revolution. Class and Status in Nazi Germany 1933–1939.* London: Weidenfeld & Nicolson.

Schwarz, H.-P. 1981: *Die Ära Adenauer. Gründerjahre der Republik. 1949–1957.* Stuttgart and Wiesbaden: DVA and Brockhaus.

Schwarz, H.-P. 1983: *Die Ära Adenauer. Epochenwechsel. 1957–1963.* Stuttgart and Wiesbaden: DVA and Brockhaus.

Shonfield, A. 1969: *Modern Capitalism.* Oxford: Oxford University Press.

Stolleis, M. 1980: Hundert Jahre Sozialversicherung in Deutschland. *Zeitschrift für die gesamte Versicherungswirtschaft*, 69.

Stöss, R. (ed.) 1984: *Parteienhandbuch*, 2 vols. Opladen: Westdeutscher Verlag.

Streeck, W. 1981: *Gewerkschaftliche Organisationsprobleme in der sozialstaatlichen Demokratie.* Königstein: Athenäum.

Streeck, W. 1984: Co-Determination: The Fourth Decade. In A. Sorge and B. Wilpert (eds), *International Perspectives on Industrial Democracy*, London: Macmillan, 391–422.

Streeck, W. 1985: *Industrial Relations in West Germany 1974–1985: An Overview.* Discussion Paper IIM/LMP 85–19, Wissenschaftszentrum Berlin.

Streit, M.E. 1981: Demand Management and Catallaxy – Reflections on a Poor Policy Record. *Ordo*, 32.

Sturm, R. 1989, forthcoming: Die Politik der Bundesbank. In K. von Beyme and

M.G. Schmidt (eds), *Politik in der Bundesrepublik Deutschland*, Opladen: Westdeutscher Verlag.

Thomas, J.C. 1975: The Decline of Ideology in Western Political Parties: A Comparative Analysis of Changing Policy Orientations. *Sage Professional Papers, Contemporary Political Sociology Series*, I.

Uusitalo, P. 1984: Monetarism, Keynesianism and the Institutional Status of Central Banks. *Acta Sociologica*, 27.

Wehler, H.-U. 1973: *Das Deutsche Kaiserreich. 1871–1918*. Göttingen: Vandenhoek and Ruprecht.

Wehler, H.-U. 1981: 'Deutscher Sonderweg' oder allgemeine Probleme des westlichen Kapitalismus? *Merkur*, 3.

Whiteley, P.M. 1984: Inflation, Unemployment and Government Popularity – Dynamic Models for the United States, Britain and West Germany. *Electoral Studies*, 3.

Wildenmann, R. 1969: *Die Rolle des Bundesverfassungsgerichtes und der Deutschen Bundesbank in der politischen Willensbildung*. Stuttgart: Kohlhammer.

Wildenmann, R. 1987: The Party Government of the Federal Republic of Germany: Form and Experience. In R.S. Katz (ed.), *Party Governments: European and American Experiences*, Berlin and New York: De Gruyter, 78–117.

Wilensky, H.L. 1981: Leftism, Catholicism and Democratic Corporatism: The Role of Political Parties in Recent Welfare State Development. In P. Flora and A.J. Heidenheimer (eds) *The Development of the Welfare State in Europe and America*, 345–82.

Winkler, H.A. 1981: Der deutsche Sonderweg: eine Nachlese, *Merkur*.

Woolley, J. T. 1985: Central Banks and Inflation. In J.H. Goldthorpe (ed.), *Order and Conflict in Contemporary Capitalism*, 318–48.

Zöllner, D. 1981: *Ein Jahrhundert Sozialversicherung in Deutschland*. Berlin: Duncker and Humblot.

Zundel, Rolf 1986: Ein Sieg der Machttechniker. *Die Zeit*, 41 (26), 1.

4

Israel's Domestic Policy Regime

Zionism, Dualism, and the Rise of Capital

Michael Shalev

Introduction

A central theme of recent research in comparative political economy has been the scope for, and consequences of, 'political control of the economy' in advanced capitalist societies. A major, although not uncontested, finding of such research has been that a 'neo-corporatist' interleaving of state and economy, mediated by powerful associations of the major classes, makes possible co-ordination, consensus and a sufficiently long time horizon for successful economic stabilization in the face of external shocks. Given that most conceptions of neo-corporatism are premised on the existence of a powerful labour movement, and that a strong argument has also been mounted that the welfare state is substantially a function of the strength of labour organizations and parties, we might reasonably expect that Israel should be an exemplar of economic stability and socially protective public policy. By all normal criteria of comparative measurement, the Israeli labour movement is both very strong and exceptionally closely integrated into the structure of state and society. Until 1977 the labour movement party historically known as Mapai (today's Israel Labour Party) enjoyed a longevity in office matched only by that of the Swedish SAP. And to no small extent, Mapai's hegemony rested on the influence and resources of a peak organization of labour, the Histadrut (General Organization of Workers), which is arguably closer to the corporate model of interest organization than any of its counterparts in the Western world. Accordingly, the paradox we seek to resolve in this chapter is that in neither respect are the public policy expectations derived from comparative research consistent with the Israeli experience. Israel's ostensibly powerful labour movement has coexisted with a weak welfare state and, after 1973, with spiralling hyperinflation and budget deficits.

Policy Outcomes

In order to come to grips with the theoretical incommensurability between Israel's institutional superstructure and its pattern of domestic policy, it will first be necessary to elaborate on the policy profile itself. What have been the main characteristics of public priorities and outcomes in respect of the economy, welfare and distribution?

Economy

Israel's economic performance over the period since 1960 (see Figure 4.1) presents a dramatic contradiction between developments before and after 1973. From the mid fifties until 1973, barring a very sharp recession in the mid sixties Israel enjoyed a more rapid growth rate than any of the 18 core OECD countries except Japan. The puzzle is that after 1973 the growth of per capita product, at little more than a percentage point a year, dropped to the lower reaches of the OECD group. As a result, Israel's historical trajectory in terms of the standard of living (per capita income) started to switch. That trajectory had been upward, moving Israel from a Third World level to a First World level. Since 1973 it has been sinking down again, to the point of being overtaken by some of the newly industrializing countries.

Quite the opposite contradiction characterizes Israel's labour market performance. Compared to the OECD block, Israeli unemployment rates were relatively high throughout the pre-1973 period. That may not be such an unremarkable achievement, given the fact that the labour force doubled over a short period due to mass immigration. Nevertheless, comparatively speaking it was not a particularly impressive record. But in the 1970s, precisely when the economy bogged down in crisis Israel's unemployment performance got better rather than worse. Throughout the period since 1975 it has ranked just below the select group of nations which embrace what Therborn (1986) terms an 'institutionalized commitment to full employment'. Yet for two reasons, the economy's capacity to create jobs should have been in a terrible state after 1973. First, in the course of the 1970s the cost of Israel's oil imports rose from 1 per cent to 12 per cent of GNP – a massive outflow of resources. Secondly, defence spending shot up in the wake of the surprise Yom Kippur War of 1973. Despite stepped-up American aid, the resultant balance of payments problem was very grave, and in the face of a domestic downturn the growth of productivity and output abruptly

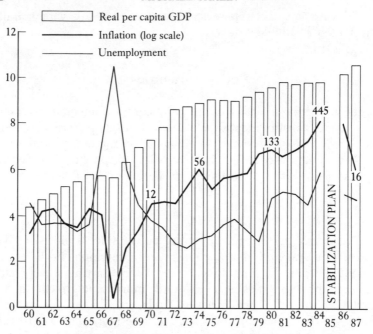

Figure 4.1 Israel: economic performance indicators 1960–1987

ceased. As indicated in Figure 4.1 the stagnation of domestic product persisted over most of the next decade.

Figure 4.1 also reveals that 1973 was a turning-point in terms of inflation. In the preceding decade or so, price increases had barely reached double digits and their fluctuations were 'well behaved' with respect to trends in unemployment. But beginning in 1973 prices soared, to a peak of close to 450 per cent inflation reached in the course of 1984 (simultaneously, unemployment was actually rising, albeit modestly). Since the introduction of an 'Emergency Economic Stabilization Plan' in July 1985 the economy has experienced dramatic disinflation, with very little increase in unemployment and even some resumption of growth. We have chosen not to analyse these more recent trends here, among other reasons because it would be premature to interpret developments since 1985 as a durable volte-face away from economic stagnation.[1]

Figure 4.2 compares Israel with the seven OECD countries surveyed in this volume to highlight the peculiarity of Israel's major economic trends since the October 1973 war and the coincident oil price shock. On the basis of changes between the five-year periods before and after 1973, it emerges that both the slowdown in growth and the increase in inflation were three times the seven-country mean; whereas Israel's success in forestalling rising unemployment was paralleled only in Sweden.

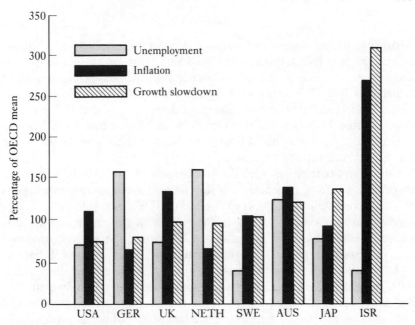

Figure 4.2 Deterioration in economic performance after 1973 – Israel and seven OECD countries (the figure shows the relative rise in unemployment and inflation and the relative decline in growth rate)

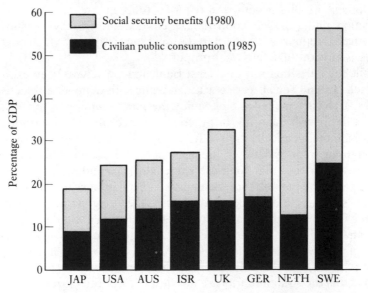

Figure 4.3 The size of the welfare state – public expenditure in Israel and seven OECD countries

Welfare

According to the social-democratic view of things, where a labour movement party has been in power for a long period of time (and there is nowhere in the West other than Sweden where that happened more remarkably than in Israel) you also get a big welfare state which offers a high degree of social protection along solidaristic lines. But as Figure 4.3 demonstrates, Israel's social security spending is such that, in Wilensky's (1975) rather narrow terms, it is a pronounced 'welfare state laggard'. On the other hand, expenditure on direct social services like education and health is not far from the OECD mainstream. A broad indicator of the scope of this kind of state activity is the national accounts category known as 'public consumption'. At 16 per cent of GDP (1985), Israel's *civilian* public consumption is squarely in the middle of the range captured by our seven countries. (Its 22 per cent of GDP devoted to *military* consumption, not shown in figure 4.3, is more than triple even the high US figure.)

As for the underlying rationale or principles governing the welfare state, the qualitative aspects which are no less important than its quantitative dimensions, these seem to fly in the face of the most hallowed principles of the social-democratic welfare state. There is a noticeable degree of non-uniformity (bordering on segregation) of policy provisions for different population groups, particularly so far as Arabs and Jews are concerned. Jews get all the benefits, Arab citizens (15 per cent of the total) get some of the benefits. Arab non-citizens, which means Palestinians in the occupied territories (one quarter of the overall population under Israeli control) are entitled to virtually no income maintenance support and are offered public social services which bear no comparison with those in Israel proper.

While the Palestinians of the West Bank and Gaza have been exposed to Israeli law and social service arrangements with deliberate selectivity, Israel's Arab citizens in principle enjoy the same standing in the welfare state as the Jewish majority. In practice they are strongly discriminated against, although typically indirectly, and to a varying extent – least of all (although far from trivially) in income maintenance and education, and most of all (to the point of near exclusion) in employment creation, housing, and the personal social services. This partial segregation of the welfare state is undoubtedly rooted in the long-standing hostility between Israel and the Arab states and the national conflict with the Palestinians, which has encouraged state agencies to adopt a restrictive policy of rationing benefits of all kinds to the Arab sector in return for 'good behaviour', and has legitimized the opinion held in some Jewish quarters that the Arab minority are not deserving of full citizen rights. As we shall argue below, however, the nationality-based segmentation of social policy has also served concrete material and political interests of the Jewish majority.

However one cares to explain the second-class standing of Arab citizens in Israel's welfare state, given Israel's official self-image as 'the Jewish State', it is much less surprising than the phenomenon of a lesser but still significant discrimination among Jews. This is reflected in the fact that in comparison with other countries' welfare states (and not just the social-democratic ones), Israel's has been strongly permeated by particularism and selectivity. This was particularly so in the period of mass immigration, the fifties and the early sixties, when basically a two tier system of welfare developed for Jews. The upper tier was for the veterans of the period before sovereignty, most of whom were *Ashkenazim* (of European or 'Western' origin). Here social protection depended primarily on the employment relationship. The veterans had access to the best jobs and enjoyed a high degree of job security as a result of strong organization and punitive severance pay agreements. In turn, with employment stability went entitlements to a variety of insurance-based income maintenance schemes, some public and others negotiated with employers. In contrast, recent arrivals naturally lacked job seniority, and a great many were outside of the labour market, unemployed, or in temporary jobs. Instead of the employment-linked system of social protection, they were dealt with harshly by means of a 'residual' system of niggardly means-tested benefits and manipulative forms of so-called treatment and rehabilitation. The ones who suffered the most were those who had the least, mostly the 'Eastern' Jews who emigrated to Israel from North Africa and the Middle East.

In the 1970s there was some movement towards a more 'institutional' welfare state. Compensatory education for the children of Eastern immigrants was greatly expanded. There was also a major jump in income maintenance provision in the form of progressive family allowances, the rationale being that big families are the poorest. The Likud government which entered office after Labour's election defeat in 1977 introduced a universal minimum income guarantee and embarked on an ambitious programme of urban renewal. These elements of change were accompanied however by significant continuities, for instance the exclusion of Arab neighbourhoods from the renewal scheme and the concentration of new educational opportunities for Easterners in 'dead-end' vocational schools.

In addition to the dualist elements consequent on discrimination between citizens on primordial grounds, social protection in Israel is noticeably dualist (in the sense of Goldthorpe, 1984) in relation to the balance between private and public provision. The 'private' (although state-regulated and subsidized) social services operated by the Histadrut are especially significant. The clinics and hospitals of the Histadrut health plan serve some 80 per cent of the population and have traditionally overshadowed the activities of the Ministry of Health. Similarly, while public pension expenditure is noticeably low in Israel compared with OECD countries, this universal form of social insurance coexists with a Histadrut supplementary pension scheme which largely bypasses the secondary labour market. Israel's atypically low concentration of elderly citizens undoubtedly diminishes its pension and health requirements (just as large cohorts of children have invited relatively high spending on family allowances). But Israel's laggard public 'pension effort' also reflects the fact that the state again made space for an employment-based system. Increasingly, this has been true of a broad spectrum of 'occupational welfare', the growth of which has accentuated the split between the sheltered and secondary segments of the labour market.

Distribution

A comprehensive perspective on social welfare cannot ignore the fact that both public and private forms of social protection are supplementary to the outcomes of prior distributional processes in the market arena. Social democracy may be thought of as a particular model of linkage between the economic and political markets, characterized by a 'virtuous circle' of full employment and comprehensive social spending on the one hand, and on the other a high degree of trade union solidarity and self-restraint in the labour market (Castles, 1978). But Israel once again constitutes an exception. The labour movement's historic self-image of its wage policy as ultra-egalitarian was in reality no more than a half truth. More recent evidence regarding both wage differentials and the overall distribution of income shows that inequality has been on a rising secular trend, and is high in Israel in comparison with OECD countries. This is not terribly surprising in view of the well-documented existence of a persistent national and ethnic hierarchy in the division of labour and the distribution of economic rewards in Israeli society – the same hierarchy encountered in our earlier discussion of welfare state segmentation.[2]

In democratic capitalist societies, disputation in the labour relations sphere is the most important quantifiable indicator of how distributional conflicts are pursued and managed. From a cross-national perspective, strike activity in Israel is high. By the measure of relative labour force involvement in conflicts, Israel has been close to the top of the OECD league table since the early 1970s. The 'political' shape of strikes – typically brief but broadly based – also stands out, and is symptomatic of the high concentration of labour disputes in the public sector (including state-owned transport, communication and utilities). In fact over the last two decades Israel has ranked poorly on *all* of the components of what Schmitter (1981) once referred to as 'ruliness' – reflecting not only labour strife, but also extraparliamentary protest and governmental turnover.

To conclude, what we have in the Israeli case is a dominant Labour Party only partially accompanied by a 'full employment welfare state'. We see labour organized in a highly corporate way, but without industrial peace (or very effective wage restraint). Israel's labour market operates with unmistakable dualist tendencies, again posing a paradox because at least according to Goldthorpe, political economies and particularly their labour markets tend to be structured along either corporatist or dualist lines. Yet in Israel a corporate labour organization enters into social contracts with the state, while at the same time members of marginalized social groups form an exposed underclass in the labour market, with clearly inegalitarian consequences.

Peculiarities of Working Class Mobilization

Enough has been said already to make it plain that the Histadrut and Israel's long-dominant Labour Party hold the keys to unlocking many of the mysteries of Israel's domestic policy exceptionalism. But a fundamental problem in discussing the workers' movement in Israel, is that when we say union we don't exactly mean union, when we say left we don't mean left, and even when we say labour we may not really mean labour. The concept of unionization is a good example. For decades, the Histadrut's coverage of Israel's wage-earners has stood at about three-quarters on the basis of membership claims, or two-thirds according to opinion poll data. From an international viewpoint, these are very high figures indeed. But does this mean that once upon a time a union was formed, launched an organizing drive, and won employer recognition? Not at all. For the Jewish newcomers streaming into Israel during the first two decades, it usually meant simply that on entering the country they received a free trial membership in the Histrdrut health plan, which was subsequently renewed by their employers or the institutions which were sheltering them. Even today, some Jews and most Arabs live in localities where no other health service is available.

The role of its Sick Fund is but one symptom of the fact that trade unionism is by no means the Histadrut's only mission, and neither are wage-earners its only constituency. In addition to representing labour, the Histadrut also performs the functions of both the state (today most notably in the social services) and capital (the Histadrut owns or claims the affiliation of institutions responsible for somewhere between a fifth and a quarter of total output and employment). Consequently the Histadrut not only organizes across the entire spectrum of the working class, but also accommodates housewives, the self-employed, and pensioners.

Trade unionism is in principle just another Histadrut service for which members may qualify. As in Austria, national trade unions are subsidiaries of the 'confederal' organization and members cannot join them directly. As in Britain, for many Histadrut members the most relevant trade union bodies are shop or workplace-level Workers' Committees which are often only loosely integrated into the official union structure. One reason for the gulf between central and workplace trade unionism is the extraordinary formal insulation of the Histadrut's local and national trade unions from their rank and file. The labour organization's statutes (which *de facto* apply very loosely to those sections of the workforce with strategic positions in the labour market) require that union officials be appointed by political parties in accordance with their relative standing in nationwide elections. Legitimate authority over union activity is concentrated in the hands of top Histadrut officials and their sponsoring party.

In common with the nationally unique institutions which have shaped public policy profiles elsewhere, the Histadrut (and the broader labour movement of which it is a part) defies understanding unless placed in historical context. Our next task is therefore to specify the most important elements of this context, and to demonstrate its close causal links to Israel's policy puzzles. The discussion is divided between two formative epochs, the first encompassing the era of modern Jewish colonization which began shortly before the turn of the century and reached a climax with Israel's declaration of independence in 1948; and the second comprising the first five to ten years of sovereignty, which laid new or modified foundations for the contemporary political economy.

Zionism and the labour movement

The idea of Zionist colonization of Palestine was one response (primarily of Russian and Eastern European Jewry) to the push of antisemitism and the pull of modern nationalism. It was in fact the choice of only a minority – most *Ashkenazi* Jews either emigrated to other 'new nations', or else stayed on only to perish in the Holocaust. Labour Zionism was a particular branch of European Zionist thought and activity, which arose out of the polarization of the Jewish masses (against the background of the rise of Communism) between an internationalist majority and those who believed socialism could only be realized within an autonomous Jewish 'national home'. In the space of only thirty years a small vanguard of young Labour Zionist settlers in Palestine established a framework which subsequently became the predominant political and economic force in Israeli society. The labour movement which they created rested on three pillars.

The Histadrut was founded in 1920 as the 'General Organization of Jewish Workers in the Land of Israel'. Created and governed by the leading Zionist workers' parties of the period, its function was to direct and co-ordinate the entire gamut of activities hitherto carried out by parties or self-help associations: agricultural settlement, urban co-operatives and contracting gangs, group health care and other forms of collective protection, as well as local labour exchanges and rudimentary trade union activity. The evolution of the Histadrut deviated quite fundamentally from the European model of labour organization: it did not emerge out of the class struggles contingent upon capitalist industrialization and political democratization; it was primarily concerned with the realization of national interests in the rural sector rather than with the class interests of urban wage-earners; and it was founded from the top down rather than crystallizing and aggregating spontaneous processes of working class formation.

The Kibbutzim (agricultural communes) and other forms of co-operative rural settlement represented in concrete form the fusion of Zionist and socialist ideals to which the Jewish labour movement aspired: to extend the territorial and economic frontier of Jewish colonization within collectivist frameworks. However, due to the high price of land and the attractions of the urban milieu to most immigrants, only a small minority of them ended up in workers' settlements.

Mapai was the Palestine Workers Party, founded by merger in 1930. By the mid thirties Mapai was not only the pre-eminent party within the labour movement, but also the controlling factor in the 'national institutions' of the Zionist community in Palestine and world-wide. The party and its successors (the Israel Labour Party, running at election time in 'alignment' with a smaller left party) headed every Israeli government formed until 1977, when Labour lost its voter plurality to the Likud (literally, Unity Party, an alliance of the major nationalist and bourgeois parties).

The Histadrut's founding members were a few thousand propertyless Jewish immigrants. They called themselves workers, but in fact were typically the poorly endowed scions of *petit bourgeois* Russian and Polish families. Most of the leaders were survivors of the first modern waves of Zionist immigration, which entered late-Ottoman Palestine in the hope of building up the Jewish presence there. What they found was an undeveloped economy where virtually the only Jewish employers to whom they could consider applying were small-scale plantation farmers. However, those farmers already had an excellent source of labour: Arab villagers, who first of all were used to farming, and secondly were only semi-proletarianized. Arab labourers could thus be paid very low wages yet were more productive than the Jewish newcomers. The latter turned to various means of dealing with this competitive threat. They tried evicting Arabs from their jobs, but the employers refused to comply. For a time they were protected by subsidies to Jewish farmers furnished by foreign philanthropists. Increasingly, they turned to collectivist economic experiments, supported by the Zionist movement, to bypass the labour market and maximize external subsidy. The formation of the Histadrut can best be understood as embodying the alliance with organized Zionism sought by the Jewish worker-settlers in the context of scarce resources and Arab competition. It represents what may be succinctly described as a long-term political bargain between a workers' movement without work, and a settlement movement without settlers.

The British conquest of Palestine in 1918 for the first time aroused genuine prospects of organized Jewish colonization. But Palestine was not a very attractive destination except to traditional religious Jews, and the small stream of secular Jewish settlers consisted of either idealists or those who really had no alternative. The 'workers' among them were both willing and able to take on the tasks of colonizing Palestine and setting up a Jewish infrastructure there, provided they could be aided by the world Zionist movement. The role of the Histadrut was to organize this political exchange, and to direct Zionist funds to the settlement of outlying areas (where farmers-for-profit would not go) and to the making of a Jewish working class, the necessary cornerstone of an autarkic Jewish community. This in turn placed the Histadrut in a uniquely favourable position to serve the interests of the parties which founded it. On the one hand, the labour movement was critical to the fulfilment of Zionist aspirations, and on the other, only it could provide propertyless newcomers with the essential means of existence. Indeed, many of the immigrants were dependent on the labour movement even to obtain an entry visa. Once in Palestine, those who could not be absorbed by collective settlements found jobs via the Histadrut's labour exchanges or in its construction gangs. Through their membership in the Histadrut they were networked into a primitive but effective system of social protection financed by a combination of membership dues and Zionist subsidy.

This peculiar formation did not pass without challenge. The left of the labour movement opposed class collaboration within the Zionist movement and called for solidarity with Arab workers and greater emphasis on traditional working class struggle. It was however unable to offer concrete solutions to either the seemingly unlimited supply of cheap Arab labour, or the poverty (left to the market alone) of Jewish workers. The labour leaders developed an ideology which glorified the Jewish working class as the vanguard of Jewish nationbuilding. This ideology even portrayed Jewish labour as the motive force for the progress of the Arab masses. It was indeed true that periodic booms in the Jewish sector created demand for the labour and products of the Arab sector. But at the same time, Jewish workers organized themselves almost exclusively on a national basis and never gave up the struggle to reserve jobs with Jewish employers for 'Hebrew labour'. Moreover, those who founded agricultural settlements deprived some Arab peasants of their livelihood as a result of land sales by absentee owners and disregard of traditional property rights. Interlocking with these material frictions over land and labour, and eventually overshadowing them, was the evolving radical nationalism fuelled by Arab reactions to Jewish colonization and Jewish responses to Arab hostility and attack. Some of the protagonists on both sides sought to harness the emergent national cleavage in the service of their class and political interests. On the Zionist side, it was the labour movement which played this role. By becoming the standard-bearer of Jewish exclusivity the organized working class made good its claim both to privileged access to Zionist resources, and to moral (and therefore political) authority within the Zionist community.

During the 1930s this closing of ranks against the Arabs, complemented by successful overtures to middle-class voters and pressure groups, furnished the basis for Mapai's rise to hegemony over the entire Palestinian *Yishuv* (Hebrew for 'settlement'). The party was aided in this respect by the lopsided and fragmented character of the non-labour strata, comprising a swollen petit-bourgeoisie alongside a narrow bourgeoisie divided by conflicting sectoral interests. Moreover, most members of these strata recognized their dependence on labour controlled institutions for settlement, defence and even modest bailouts at times of economic crisis. Inside the labour movement, successful institution-building coupled with judicious use of the 'national capital' (foreign donations) distributed by the Zionist movement, created an effective Mapai machine around the Histadrut which was capable of co-opting or freezing out most rivals and even some major enemies. At the grass roots level the party apparatus skilfully manoeuvred individuals' material dependence on the resources under its control to help inculcate and reinforce political loyalty.

The social policy legacy

It is not difficult to locate the origins of many of the most central features of Israel's social policy regime in the foregoing historical account. One of these is the central role played by political clientelism in Israel's early years. With the addition of some further characteristics of the pre-sovereignty setting, our historical perspective will be fully able to explain three other enduring features of social protection. They are: (1) the labour movement's strong preference for 'voluntarism' over statutory provision of welfare; (2) the pattern of national and ethnic segmentation of social protection; and (3) the labour leadership's preoccupation with employment creation and its aversion to income maintenance entitlements.

1   The historic delegation of social policy tasks to the labour movement was in part a reflection of prevailing state structures. While the post-First World War British regime in Palestine possessed the necessary authority to tax, spend and regulate, its hands were tied by the immense objective material and organizational differences between the condition of the Arab and Jewish working classes, by stringent fiscal restraint imposed from London, and by the virtual stalemate on British initiative caused by the Arab-Jewish conflict. At the same time, within the Yishuv a sectoral social policy operated by and for Jewish labour possessed compelling attractions. From a Zionist point of view it was desirable that only Jews, and only those Jews willing and able to serve the Zionist cause, would benefit. For the labour movement, control over access to its manifold programmes of so-called 'mutual aid' was a potent incentive to rank and file political loyalty. This fusion of political motives is exemplified by two new measures introduced to strengthen the Workers' Sick Fund soon after Mapai's David Ben-Gurion became chairman of the Jewish Agency in 1935. Workers now became obliged to join the Histadrut in order to participate in the Sick Fund; and in addition, the practice was initiated of granting new immigrants free initial membership in the Fund, at Jewish Agency expense.

2   While the Histadrut was in principle open to all Jewish workers, the Arabs were not in fact alone in being left outside the labour movement's subsidized system of 'voluntary' social protection. Those Jewish immigrants (mostly from Arab countries) deemed unfit to participate in land settlement or the organized labour market were also excluded. This exclusion was based on fears of their susceptibility to the influence of anti-labour political trends, and also on a certain reluctance to share Zionist subsidies with 'outsiders'. The result was a tripartite division of welfare. Jobs or help in finding them, health care, some housing, workers' education and even soup kitchens were provided through the Histadrut on a members-only basis. Far less comprehensive services were dispensed to non-members, with the framework dependent on who they were – Arabs were cared for (if at all) by the British authorities, while the unorganized Jewish poor were assisted by local volunteers and social workers supported by foreign philanthropy.

3   Programmatically, the social policy of the labour movement was distinguished by an overriding concern for the absorption of immigrants and a deep distaste for 'handouts'. The debilitating effects of economic

deprivation on the feasibility of Jewish settlement were well known to the long time leaders of the Histadrut and Mapai, most of whose contemporaries had long ago fled Palestine in desperation. Moreover, cash in hand might enable the unemployed to stay on and affirm their attachment to Zionism and the labour movement – but only 'constructive' activity could simultaneously meet the further objective of contributing to the building up of the Jewish enclave.

After Prehistory: The Impact of Nation-statehood

As a result of the British withdrawal from Palestine, Israel's unilateral declaration of independence (ratified by the UN), and its success in repelling the armies of the surrounding Arab states, Israel emerged during 1948–9 as a fragile but fully-fledged nation state. Because of the obvious threads linking the pre- and post-sovereignty eras – in particular, an almost unaltered balance of electoral forces – it is tempting to exaggerate the elements of continuity and to treat sovereignty merely as an incident which facilitated the enlargement and consolidation of the prior social formation. This would be a mistake. Statehood vastly enhanced the overall range of the political elite's activity – its scope for forging interstate alliances, opening or closing the gates to immigration, and modifying the distribution of power and economic resources in civil society. Also, the circumstances attending Israeli sovereignty created a new social map in the Israeli part of Mandatory Palestine, by setting in motion the flight of four-fifths of the Arab population and, immediately afterwards, by inviting a doubling of the Jewish population after just four years of immigration. Taken together, these new parameters had the potential for radically altering the contours of economic structure, state-society relations and mass politics in the 'post-revolutionary' era.

Three specific issues require attention. Firstly, what happened to the Yishuv pattern of social protection? Specifically, why is it that the hallmarks of clientelism, segregation, and the centrality of the Histadrut, persisted without any major overhaul? State, party and class interests in the new circumstances implied by sovereignty all played a part in reproducing the broad features of pre-1948 social protection. Secondly, the focus thus far on social protection has necessarily deferred consideration of economic questions, and in particular the way that public policy led the Israeli economy first along a path of rapid expansion and later on into a quagmire of hyperinflation and stagnation. Building on the institutional background already provided, we shall demonstrate how crystallization of the political economy after 1948 established lasting patterns of economic structure and state-economy relations, and also laid the basis for rapid economic growth. The third and last puzzle sketched in our introductory review of policy outcomes was why it is that in Israel, the combination of long-term social-democratic political pre-eminence and a highly corporate labour centre has failed to bring about industrial peace. It will be shown that 1948 constituted a watershed for both the political and labour market contexts of labour relations. After sovereignty the Histadrut was transformed for the first time into a fully 'corporatized' intermediary; but from the very beginning the disciplinary capacities of this new corporatism were incomplete.

The social policy transition

Israel's establishment as a sovereign political entity dissolved the contradiction between the aspirations of the Histadrut and other Yishuv institutions to perform state *functions*, and their profoundly limited state *capacities*. As a result the dependence of the Zionist political centre on the intermediary role of the Histadrut was in principle at an end. Those who remained at the helm of the labour organization took a different view. They now expected to reap the benefits of the successful struggle for national liberation, in the form of delegation of state authority and a flow of other privileges to strengthen the Histadrut and its allied institutions.

In the event, despite a strong inclination to concentrate authority and resources in the new state apparatus, its leadership recognized that the old partnership with the Histadrut still had its uses. For macroeconomic reasons, the Histadrut was needed for restraining workers' demands. The labour organization's affiliated enterprises, which had become a major economic power during the Second World War, constituted a flexible means of steering the economy in the service of state objectives. Finally, straddling both Histadrut and state was the party. The Yishuv experience had demonstrated the value of the Histadrut to Mapai as a potent instrument for mobilizing both resources and voters. These advantages were now as crucial as they had ever been. The decade or so prior to sovereignty had already posed new challenges to the labour movement, notably the growing size and self-confidence of the urban Jewish working class and the partly related rise of left-wing opposition to Mapai. To these the attainment of sovereignty added the loss of labour's indispensability to the national cause now that this cause was won; and a new and much enlarged population over which Mapai had no *a priori* claim.

Given this vector of political and economic incentives for keeping the Histadrut intact, a compromise was reached over the role of the labour organization in performing quasi-state functions. While the Histadrut did not emerge unscathed, 'nationalization' bypassed both the Sick Fund and the Provident Funds. The former proved to be remarkably effective in bringing newcomers into the Histadrut and Mapai's sphere of influence. The significance of the Provident Funds was limited at first, but grew rapidly. They provided for a variety of contingencies (sickness, layoff) which otherwise would have been candidates for state social insurance. And they spawned the supplementary pension scheme which soon came to embrace more than half of all wage-earners, locked in by their employers under the terms of national collective agreements. The authorities permitted the Histadrut to exploit much of its vast accumulation of pension fund contributions as a convenient means for financing new investment in the labour organization's own economic enterprises. In this way, the survival of 'voluntarism' in social policy became part of the political-economic virtuous circle around which Mapai reconstructed its political dominance in the post-sovereignty era.

Sovereignty not only posed the issue of whether social policy functions would now be taken over by the state, but in principle also raised the spectre of an end to the politicized and particularistic ethos of pre-1948 social policy. A small cadre of policy advisers inside the Histadrut indeed urged the labour movement to embrace a Beveridge-type programme; but the implications of transition to a universal, social insurance-based 'citizen's wage' would have been intolerable to Mapai. For one thing, the division between Arab and Jewish citizens would have been rendered irrelevant and invisible, whereas the state was anxious to apply the nationality criterion to social policy as an aide in the subordination of Arab citizens to Jewish territorial and political domination. Discrimination against Arabs was moreover temptingly easy to carry out, as a result of the willingness of the Zionist institutions of the Yishuv era to continue raising funds and supplying services on a Jewish-only basis.

The state's reluctance to embrace a comprehensive citizen's wage did not originate solely in the national conflict. Material motives were also at work. As a result both of prejudice (Eastern Jews were simply assumed to be work shy) and the formulation of plans for labour-intensive industrialization, the political elite was anxious to maintain economic discipline among the Jewish poor. Consequently, for more than two decades the state successfully resisted the introduction of unemployment insurance. Benefits under social assistance and the preferred solution, relief works, were deliberately held below the minimum market wage. Since both the Mapai leadership and its most powerful mass constituencies were composed of pre-1948 veterans, public policy was at the same time naturally sensitive to veterans' economic interests. Given the desperate straits and lower customary living standards of both Arabs and Eastern Jews, established workers had good reason to fear labour market competition. Bifurcating social protection between a residual welfare state and a sheltered labour market segment with privileged access for veterans was a way of assuaging these fears. It was also a means of ensuring that employers (including those within the labour movement family) would retain their access to cheap labour.

Its approach to the distributional conflicts inherent in the meeting between veterans and Jewish and Arab 'newcomers' is illustrative of the wider political problem faced by Mapai, of how simultaneously to retain the loyalty of its former supporters while drawing masses of new citizens into the party's orbit. Had social policy moved in a more 'institutional' direction, it would have taken most of the sting out of the clientelism on which Mapai was so heavily reliant. Instead, the party's far-flung network of officials in the public and Histadrut bureaucracies, working closely with street-level 'bosses', was able to bargain life-chances for votes with considerable political effect. The most susceptible clients were the groups which were most disorganized and impoverished, and the least familiar with their surroundings – Eastern immigrants and the remnant of the former Arab majority. Mapai also found ways of cementing the effect of dependency on political loyalty – by appealing to the national sentiments of the Easterners and by exploiting the system of military rule imposed on the Arab population (which lasted until the mid 1960s).

The economic transition

With the acquisition of sovereignty by the Jewish political centre, and the transformation of the Palestinian Arabs into a subordinate minority, the balance of power between capital and organized Jewish labour in the market arena moved sharply in labour's favour. Together with the new powers now enjoyed by Mapai from its perch atop the state apparatus, this might have been expected to spur plans for the nationalization of private enterprise. That the labour movement actually failed even to raise the issue of nationalization must be understood first and foremost as a political choice.

The classic economic barrier to eliminating private ownership – the state's dependence on private investors for the performance of crucial economic functions – was far from imperative. Existing investors were at a premium, and there was little objective hope of attracting foreign investment capital because of Israel's obvious economic handicaps: its small domestic market and isolation from customers elsewhere in the region, lack of exploitable natural resources and high labour costs (despite low real wages), as well as an uncertain future. The real economic issue in Israel's early years was not whether to appropriate the appropriators, but how to divide up the means of capital formation suddenly concentrated in the hands of the state as a result of nationalization of Palestinian refugees' former land and property, economic aid from world Jewry and foreign states, and the extensive regulatory powers acquired by the authorities.

The state responded with a shareout which respected the existing 'pluralistic' (public, Histadrut and private) ownership structure and encouraged a loose division of labour between them. Newly created *state* enterprises were utilized mainly to build and administer infrastructure. *'Movement'* enterprises (Histadrut factories, agricultural collectives, and related institutions) were encouraged insofar as they were expected to give the politicians control over the economy's true commanding heights; and no less important, because of their capacity to furnish the party with funds, spoils, and a sizeable captive audience of workers and settlers. Finally, Mapai opted to maintain the status quo *vis-à-vis* the large existing sector of small and medium-sized *private* business, also making it possible for some big new private concerns to flourish provided they embraced the sponsorship of the party-state.

Why did Mapai choose not to break with its traditional policy of respect for the private sector? Past experience had demonstrated that coexistence with private capital helped perpetuate the weak and fragmented political mobilization of the right. Other political motives also played a part. Externally, there was the danger of compromising Israel in the eyes of allies it was anxious to court, namely the government and the Jewish community of the United States. Inside the labour movement Mapam, a rising coalition of Zionist parties to the left of Mapai, was the most significant champion of extending collective ownership. But in the early years Mapai preferred to continue its historic co-operation with clerical and bourgeois parties rather than yielding to more far-reaching Mapam demands for portfolios and programmatic changes. One further internal factor seems to have sealed the cordial relations between Mapai's key economic policy-makers and private big business. This was the fear of the former that if granted a monopoly over the business sector, the managers of labour movement enterprises would become (even more) impervious to party influence.

The early post-sovereignty years saw the formation of the main lines of economic policy as well as structure. It soon became evident that the economy was in danger of being permanently crippled by severe balance of payments deficits. Largely ignoring economists' advice, the government by the early 1950s had forged its own solution to the problem, in the form of foreign 'unilateral transfers'. The mechanisms were varied: new forms of fundraising in Jewish communities overseas; American gratitude for Israel's effusive support in the Korean conflict; and above all, the government's sponsorship – in the face of intense political controversy – of an agreement under which $700 million worth of West German machinery and merchandise were to reach Israel over a 12-year period as collective compensation for the Holocaust.

With the major sources of both liquid capital and physical plant reaching the country from abroad via Mapai-controlled public bodies, the party-state became the dynamo powering the country's economic engine. The government and its economic ministries were consequently in a strong position to manage distributional flows in the interests of the governing party. Among the symptoms were a pronounced electoral business cycle; generous overt and covert funding of Mapai and its friends; and the ability to grant economic favours to individual citizens or whole communities. So far as business interests were concerned, by virtue of its near-monopoly over new sources of investment finance and ability to give or withhold access to a vast array of government contracts, concessions, exemptions and incentives, the state also acquired 'the potential power to destroy any firm or to make it extremely profitable' (Aharoni, 1976, p. 357). The consequences for the macroeconomy of the new political-economic regime put into place after 1948 are starkly clear from a single datum: between 1954 and 1965 per capita GNP rose by an average of 7 per cent a year in real terms. Without question, this exceptional performance resulted from the encounter between the extensive inflows of gift capital reaching the state, and the rapid growth of consumer demand and labour supply attendant upon mass immigration (also subject to state discretion).

The transformation of labour relations

In the Jewish Yishuv between the two world wars, trade unionism and collective bargaining were highly decentralized. A Histadrut policy of obliging employers to recruit labour solely through its employment offices was only partially successful, and small rival labour organizations and an unorganized minority belied its pretensions to a monopoly of representation. Together with the threat of Arab competition, this placed the Histadrut's unskilled members (by far the majority) in a highly exposed labour market position. Employers relied on this weakness, together with the readiness of the authorities to come to their defence, to act as brakes on labour militancy. They therefore had little interest in organizing or bargaining along corporatist lines, even though the Histadrut leadership would have been delighted to extend its preferred highly centralized organizational model to the sphere of labour relations. During the Second World War the British authorities for the first time acquired a direct interest in limiting trade union struggles because of their reliance on the Yishuv economy for the supply of goods and services critical to the regional war effort. They sponsored some rudimentary forms of economy-wide wage bargaining and political exchange with the Histadrut and the organized manufacturers. But this corporatist evolution was nipped in the bud as a result of hesitation on the part of both employers and the British authorities.

ISRAEL'S DOMESTIC POLICY REGIME

Sovereignty changed this. The state took a variety of steps aimed at strengthening the Histadrut's political capacities and its authority in labour relations. These included the award of various statutory monopolies of representation, the medical care arrangement which automatically brought newcomers into the Histadrut, and the crushing of some dramatic instances of rank and file initiative. Inside the Histadrut, Mapai used its voter majority to exert control over all of the organization's key bodies, including most national and local unions. Successfully fending off Mapam and other left-wing parties, Mapai installed its own 'keymen' in the majority of Workers' Committees.

The 'corporatization' of trade unionism was completed by a national wage policy, negotiated between top Histadrut officials and government ministers within closed party forums. Within this framework, Mapai's Histadrut leaders periodically acceded to Treasury demands for wage restraint in the form of freezes, foregone indexation rights, and so forth. Unlike post-war neo-corporatist developments in Western Europe, government-union political exchange in Israel has not been based on the sacrifice of bargaining power for a full employment commitment – since, as was pointed out earlier in this chapter, this commitment was dependably strong for quite different reasons. Nevertheless, Histadrut leaders genuinely advocate worker self-sacrifice in the name of the national interest, on similar grounds to those advanced in Olson's (1982) theory of 'encompassing' interest organizations. But other, less universal reasons for wage moderation cannot be ignored: the fact that until 1977 the Histadrut's officials owed their positions to the ruling party; the Histadrut's built-in appreciation of employer interests as a result of its own substantial role as an employer; and the leverage enjoyed by the Treasury as a result of the dependence of Histadrut economic institutions and social services on state subsidy.

From the beginning, this system produced only limited labour peace. In the early years there were well-organized veteran workers supported by the left opposition who forced the top leadership to embrace their demands, or else pressed these demands independently. At that time the labour market position of the Easterners and Israeli Arabs who rapidly became the mainstay of the unskilled manual labour force was very precarious, and they were either excluded from Histadrut union protection (formally for Arabs for some years) or brought under the tutelage of party appointees. The major disciplinary problem for both the Histadrut and the state (which for the most part was their employer) originated among the rapidly-growing white-collar labour force, especially salaried professionals. The enormous expansion of state activity after sovereignty, not least in the 'absorption' of the mass immigrations, had transformed educated labour into an economic and political pressure group of major importance. Confronting the Histadrut's insistence on representing the entire spectrum of wage-earners within a single comprehensive framework, upper-level public employees repeatedly went to bat over the issues of wage differentials and union autonomy. Their pressure paid off, but not before the eruption of many bitter labour disputes.

From Sovereignty to Crisis

Before moving on to contemporary issues, let us sum up the implications of the transition from settlement to statehood. The 'system of 1948' in some respects reinforced and in others modified the basic thrust of earlier policy legacies. In social protection the transition to sovereignty had particularly conservative effects. The state was impressed more by the benefits than the costs to itself and to Mapai of perpetuating the Histadrut's triple role as bearer of the functions of state and capital as well as working class representation. The temptation to exploit segregated and selective social policy for exerting political and economic control over subordinate groups further closed the potential opening to a universalistic welfare state and reinvigorated the old ideology of 'constructivism'. In contrast, access to the powers of state fundamentally changed the role of the political centre in relation to the economy and the labour market, by making it possible for the political elite to realize aspirations hitherto beyond the realm of the possible. The economic role of the state was enlarged far beyond its former dimensions (except in wartime). The importation of people and capital continued to drive economic growth but acquired new forms. With state stimulation, immigrants poured into Israel while concurrently, institutional transfers took over the earlier role of personal assets in the import of capital. Buoyed up by the state's redistribution of these transfers, private business became in effect just one more client of the party-state.

For the purpose of explaining the major Israeli policy outcomes in the areas of social policy and the labour market, developments since the formative period of statebuilding are more important for form than for substance. The welfare state in time became more generous, less politicized and less selective; yet without altering the broad lines of Israel's comparative distinctiveness. Except for child allowances (an instrument of population policy as well as social security) the state continued to provide relatively low levels of income support. Social protection remained partially segregated among *Ashkenazim*, Easterners and Arabs. The role of 'voluntary' (Histadrut) and employment-linked provision grew rather than contracted. The basic features of the labour relations system formed after 1948 also remained unchanged. Although the authority of party and state over the Histadrut, and of the Histadrut over its rank and file declined over the years, labour market dualism flourished, and labour militancy and attempts at corporatist discipline were increasingly confined to the public sector. It is thus only the area of *economic* policy – specifically, Israel's response to the global problems of economic stagnation after 1973 – that exhibits a notable contrast to the earlier period, at least in terms of outcomes. The economy's severe structural problems and dismal performance, except in the area of employment, clearly and dramatically point to what had changed – in a word, the transformation of the state's role in the political economy, from a precondition for growth to a hindrance to economic adaptation.

The two decades prior to the eruption of contemporary economic problems in the 1970s did see significant changes in the political-economic context. The most visible cluster of new developments reflected a pronounced decomposition of the labour movement. With rapid economic growth and the transition to full employment undermining the authority of both the Histadrut and Mapai, the government in the mid 1960s felt obliged to unleash the full brunt of an economic slowdown in order to reimpose discipline on workers and voters. Afterwards, during a period of renewed prosperity in the late sixties and early seventies, new challenges were mounted from below – notably, in the form of rank and file labour organization and militancy, on the one hand, and poor people's protests on the other. The labour movement's institutional and political control over the mass public was seriously challenged by these extraparliamentary mobilizations, and it was this challenge which provided the major stimulus for welfare state reform in the late 1960s and early 1970s. The Labour Party's decomposition was capped by a voter realignment which came to the fore in the 1977 elections, when the party was ousted from office for the first time. Labour was deserted by large sections of all three of the new constituencies which had been successfully incorporated after 1948 – Eastern immigrants, Israeli Arabs and the state-made middle class.

The clashing normative visions of Israel's left and right are well known in relation to the national conflict, which has increasingly come to monopolize the very meaning of the left-right continuum. In the field of domestic policy, party rhetoric reflects something of the usual polarities on the classic issues of the role of the market and the desirable scope and form of the welfare state. But the Labour Alignment and the Likud are also equal partners in the full employment consensus, and are divided primarily by their conflicting interests in the continued vesting of key economic and social functions in the Histadrut. (Hence the amusing spectacle of the right vigilantly advocating 'nationalization' of the health system and attacking the Histadrut's role as an employer on the grounds that it compromises the interests of rank and file workers.) The 'political upheaval', as the 1977 change of government came to be known, had surprisingly little impact on the distinctive features of domestic policy with which this chapter has so far been concerned. The Likud took office seemingly determined to savage the Histadrut, but in the short run often found it prudent to avoid head-on confrontation. In economic affairs Likud ministers at first embraced the cause of deregulation, but subsequently introduced a series of sharp policy zigzags in response to the exigencies of the electoral cycle and to tensions between the party's bourgeois and populist wings. Two Likud terms of office and four finance ministers failed to delimit the breadth of state involvement in the economy or to turn back the tide of inflation and stagnation.

While, irrespective of its political stewardship, the state was seemingly incapable of preventing serious economic failures this should not be interpreted as evidence of the irrelevance of the state. It was not the sheer weight of the 'exogenous' blows inflicted by post-1973 conditions which determined the economy's fate. On the contrary, these new constraints served to exacerbate an ongoing process of transformation of formerly successful motors of growth and distribution into fetters on economic success. Assuming that the main lines of economic orthodoxy are correct, the state needed to do two things after 1973 for successful economic adaptation to occur. It needed to be able to discipline civil society – to restrain the demands of capital, organized labour, the poor and so on. And it needed to discipline itself – to cut back public expenditure and employment and the authorities' domination of money and capital 'markets'. The fact that it failed on both counts can be explained in terms of the same three motive forces – political, distributional and national – which repeatedly reared their heads in our account of the historical origins of Israeli policy distinctiveness.

Populism   Earlier, we elaborated the importance of political clientilism and the unique institutional triumvirate of Histadrut, party and state in the formation of Israel's domestic policy regime. But it was also pointed out that despite the potency of the system of 1948, the labour movement's very successes gradually eroded its chief instruments of power. Not only did the material dependency of the electorate diminish in the face of rising prosperity, but Mapai's internal coherence suffered from its achievements in co-opting opposition parties and containing challenges from a new generation of would-be leaders. Meanwhile, the right reorganized, embraced new issues (especially the future of the occupied territories) and turned into both a mouthpiece for anti-establishment sentiment and a respectable contender for power. The results of these changes in the political constellation were growing factionalism, party competitiveness and extraparliamentary mobilization. These in turn stimulated the rise of a widely-remarked 'populism' in the economic and social interventions of the state. From the late 1960s, public policy responded defensively to political flux by resanctifying the full employment norm, enlarging the welfare state, and indirectly supporting rising private consumption and increasing income inequality. Combined with increases in state expenditure contingent on arms acquisitions and the high price of oil, this is the most common explanation of Israel's crisis scenario. It is a line of thinking that will surely be familiar to non-Israeli readers from contemporary debates in their own countries.

Dualism We have argued that historically, distributional conflicts between Eastern and Western Jews, and between Jews and Arabs, bear much of the responsibility for the dualism which pervades the welfare state, the labour market and industrial relations in Israel. By the time of the economic crisis there had been a firming up of the convergence between sheltered (versus exposed) labour market segments, elaborated (versus minimal) social protection, and labour militancy (versus peace). A striking if incomplete coincidence became apparent between these different forms of dualism and the public-private sector split. Among public employees the always restive professional workers were now joined by newer *loci* of economic privilege and union autonomy – manual and technical workers employed in state-owned and exclusively Jewish workplaces lying on the most sensitive nodes of the political economy (like transport and communication, energy, and the giant state arms and aircraft factories). There is no doubt that the difficulty of imposing corporatist restraint on these powerful sections of the labour force helps explain why the state failed to cut public sector employment and wages, and contributed thereby to the perpetuation of economic destabilization.

Nationalism Zionism and the national conflict, linked to some extent with the pursuit of economic interests, have had a variety of secondary implications of major importance for the economy. In different ways, Israel's military success in 1967 and near-failure in 1973 delegitimized Labour and catalyzed the right, thereby reinforcing the political trends – fear of electoral punishment, intensified coalition bargaining, and responsiveness to organized pressure groups – which fed 'populist' economic policies. The national conflict has also been directly incorporated into the economy, with definite consequences for Israel's economic decline. The occupation since 1967 of the West Bank and Gaza reinforced 'traditional' elements of the economy by opening up new but relatively unsophisticated markets and sources of labour. But at the same time, escalation of the Arab-Israel arms race stimulated the growth of hi-tech military industries. The opportunities created by military industrialization and the benefits of the occupation were key parameters of a new formula for economic growth which, until 1973, succeeded in replacing the former and by now unworkable model based on the import of inexpensive human and financial capital. But this transition also resulted in a deepening of the structural splits within both labour and capital, and declining state capacities to steer the economy.

The State and Capital

The foregoing intentionally provides no more than a suggestive overview of the range of political, distributional and national dynamics which led policymakers in Israel to preside over more than a decade of spiralling inflation and stalled growth. In this final section of the Chapter, we shall focus upon an issue which in Israel is invisible in most accounts of the state's role in the (mis)management of the economic crisis, and yet is arguably the most theoretically and substantively important factor of all: the changing balance of forces between business interests and the state. The theoretical context for the discussion is well known and a brief rehearsal will suffice to set the scene. The fusion of liberal democracy with an economic system which places the power to autonomously determine the economic fate of the mass of citizens in the hands of a tiny minority of resource-rich investors, raises the perennial issue of the scope for public policy-makers to determine public policy. The debate over state autonomy has increasingly recognized that the mechanisms by which capitalist priorities are reconciled with democratic ones cannot be fruitfully analyzed without recognizing the historical and national specificity of 'capital' and 'the state', the scope for varieties of interaction between them, and the varying degree to which the power of each is mediated by working class mobilization, position in the world system, and a host of other factors. In many respects Israel under what we termed 'the system of 1948' may be considered a limiting case of extreme state autonomy *vis-à-vis* capital. It is the contention of this Chapter, however, that by the 1970s this relationship had been turned on its head, with the consequence that the state's lack of autonomy is possibly the most profound, and certainly the least recognized, reason for the failure of the Israeli state to steer the Israeli economy away from destabilization in the decade following the shocks of 1973.

The system of 1948 and after

Let us recall, to begin with, the forces which protected the state from becoming hostage to the 'private investment climate' under the conditions prevailing after the transition to sovereignty. Foremost among these were: (1) a paucity of large-scale private investors, and their dependence on the state to bankroll entrepreneurial activites; (2) the direct accountability of the most concentrated and strategic sectors of capital (public and Histadrut-linked enterprise) to political masters; and (3) the extensive regulatory powers and highly centralized structure of the state apparatus. At the level of ideology, it was if anything the state rather than capital which could be identified with the most urgent universal interests of society. The new Israeli state had an extremely broad and fateful agenda – populating and defending territory, attracting and absorbing masses of immigrants; and it had powerful allies external to the domestic system who were willing to provide the financial means for carrying out this agenda. To this must be added a cohesive political party apparatus with hegemony over all of the society's key institutions, with little or no obligation to private capital for material or ideological resources, and with its own internal networks of elite recruitment and interchange.

Yet the system of 1948 did not end here. For a variety of economic and political reasons which have already been touched upon, the political elite recoiled from exploiting its position of strength in order to eliminate private capital or even to discriminate against private interests in the state's patronage of the business sector. Moreover, state sponsorship was not only conditioned by the sectoral 'key' of the pre-1948 political economy, but also had the effect (to some extent intended, and to some extent the result of the system itself) of privileging *big* business and of encouraging various forms of co-operation between the large enterprises of the different sectors. As this system matured, the political and bureaucratic elites not infrequently found themselves hard pressed to maintain control over some of the 'institutional entrepreneurs' at the head of state and Histadrut-owned enterprises, to neutralize 'robbers' coalitions' among the different wings of big business, or to prevent private investors from appropriating capital subsidies without fulfilling their obligations to create new jobs and help ease balance of payments problems. Nevertheless, Mapai's influence over all the sectors of business remained very strong, both because of capital's dependence (political, economic or both) and because of the continuing elements of competition between the private and collective sectors and within the private sector as well.

The turning-point for both the structure of capital and its relationship to the state occurred in the 1960s. During the first half of the decade the flow of German reparations ground to a halt, and there was also a slowdown in some of the state's other external sources of revenue. As a result, dependence on foreign loans and overseas investors to finance the import surplus grew sharply. Lacking the resources to maintain past levels of subsidy to business, the state attempted to wean it of this dependence in the framework of the 1966–7 recession. By depressing the domestic market, squeezing the bloated construction industry and permitting unemployment to skyrocket, the recession was expected to strengthen industry and encourage exports. As it turned out, the realization of these goals was contingent on several additional forces which emerged during the recovery – the new opportunities for profit-making created in the aftermath of the Six Day War, and a renewed rise in the state's resources and readiness for capital subsidy.

In retrospect it is clear that the mid-sixties recession signalled a new balance of forces in the political economy. Capital was greatly strengthened by the weakening of both state autonomy and labour assertiveness. One symptom of the new constellation was the rising concentration and 'conglomeration' of industrial capital, the result of a slowdown-induced shakeout. Another symptom was a new cohesiveness and militancy in the associational activity of private industry, with the covert encouragement of the state. Mapai's top economic policymakers further acted to strengthen capital's orientation towards accumulation by selling off government companies (other than those devoted to infrastructure or armaments) and by installing a new and aggressively profit-seeking managerial cadre at the head of the Histadrut's industrial and financial corporations.

In the same period (between the wars of 1967 and 1973) the state intensified its stimulation of big business. Along one political-economic axis the country's longtime economic policy czar, Pinhas Sapir, concluded countless informal deals with major local and foreign investors for the exchange of diverse forms of state largesse in return for entrepreneurial activity and political support. Along a different axis, identified with future Prime Minister Shimon Peres, the state spurred the growth of local production for the rapidly growing military establishment. The maturation in the early 1970s of a third axis, the 'special relationship' with the United States (in which Peres' long-time rival, Yitzhak Rabin, played an instrumental role), helped to free the state's capacity for capital subsidy from the burden of financing arms imports.

By the time Israel had to confront the problems of commodity price rises, stagnating world trade and escalating military commitments in the 1970s, both the structure of capital and its standing *vis-à-vis* the state had altered inexorably. As the sole empirical study of the period concluded, not only had the economy become increasingly split into a competitive periphery and a dominant core of big conglomerates, but

The big companies and ownership groups have a great deal of influence on economic policy and on the manner in which the resources of the state are allocated, and the state apparatus is often turned into being dependent on them when it wants to implement some action or other. (Aharoni, 1976, p. 118)

It was this political economy, revolving around increasingly powerful concentrations of capital, which can now be seen to bear much of the responsibility for Israel's slide into extreme stagflation and fiscal crisis, and the counterproductive role of state policies. This case will be presented in broad outline for the two most important divisions of the business sector: industry and banking.

The pillars of industry

During the decade of economic stagnation which followed the shocks of 1973, industry's share of output and employment declined. Yet in this same period, official Israel was busy promoting the manufacturing sector as the indispensable centrepiece of healthy economic growth. Industry, it has long been argued, holds the key to creating 'productive' employment, driving economic growth, and weaning the country of reliance on foreign gifts and loans for balancing its chronic external deficit. Table 4.1, which brings together diverse indicators of the fate of the manufacturing sector

Table 4.1 Israeli industry before and after the crisis of 1973

	1965–1972	1973–1980
Profits		
1 Overall rate of return	18.1	19.8
2 Profits of Big 3 conglomerates (% GNP)	0.4	1.0
Performance (% change)		
3 Real output	10.0	3.0
4 Total factor productivity	1.6	0.5
5 Labour productivity	5.3	4.7
6 Capital utilization	2.2	−1.9
Structure		
7 Capital-intensity (% change)	2.3	6.7
8 Three-firm concentration ratio	50.3	49.1
9 Size (employment per plant)	43	57
10 Export to output ratio	23.0	31.8
11 Military branches as % of exports	16.1	36.8
Role of the state		
12 Public consumption as % of output	15	21[a]
13 Public subsidy as % of investment	7.3	27.8
14 Public funding as % of investment	27.9	42.6
15 Export subsidies (% GNP)	2.0	3.1
16 Credit subsidy (% GNP)[b]	0.7	5.9
17 Price subsidies (% GNP)[b]	1.9	2.9
18 Index of protection	1.41	1.23

For notes and sources, see appendix 1.
[a]1973–75 only. (Average for 1976–83 = 15%)
[b]Lines 16 and 17 are subsidies applying to goods sold on the local market.

before and after the turning point in the macroeconomy, helps explain this gap between theory and praxis. The table shows that, as the result of a growing but badly under-utilized stock of capital equipment, the growth of industrial output fell drastically after 1973 in spite of continued increases in labour productivity. Moreover, this unimpressive performance occurred even though industry modernized (larger and more mechanized factories) and became far more export-oriented (accompanied by a shift from 'traditional' to 'hi-tech' exports). To explain these paradoxes, it is necessary to reckon with three closely related institutional characteristics of industry in Israel which have already been hinted at: first, its dualistic structure; second, the scope of the government subsidies which it enjoys; and third, its increasing reliance on defence-related production.

A dual economy Israeli industry has long been characterized by coexistence between a growing 'big economy' and a multitude of small firms and self-employed proprietors. By 1985 the reported turnover of the hundred largest industrial firms was said to be equivalent to fully 40 per cent of Israel's GNP.[3] A handful of government-owned producers of arms, aircraft, electricity and minerals accounted for more than one quarter of the combined activity of the Top 100. The share of the enterprises owned by Koor, the Histadrut conglomerate, was also close to one quarter. Two of the three largest banks, one owned by the Histadrut and the other privately controlled, hold most of the shares in Koor's rival, the Clal conglomerate (with nearly one tenth of Top 100 turnover). Each of the big banks also has a direct stake in individual manufacturing firms.

Within industrial branches the concentration of both domestic sales and export production in the leading firms is extremely high. But the full extent of capital concentration is in fact far more pronounced than this, since in most cases the key firms in each branch are owned by the economic giants – the Histadrut, the government and the banks. Each of these 'pillars' embraces somewhat different priorities and strategies (limited however by real difficulties of exerting centralized control over salaried executives), and their economic empires sometimes compete fiercely among and even within themselves. Nevertheless, irrespective of their parent pillar the senior managers of 'core' firms share a common business philosophy, the same social milieu and very similar levels of remuneration. The pillars are also closely linked by 'complex ownership/ control ties among the holding groups, reciprocal buying and selling arrangements, financing relations among the banks, the government and the industrial groups, property rights enjoyed exclusively by the largest groups and, finally, explicit collusion' (Rowley, Bichler and Nitzan, 1988, p. 15). Increasingly, state and Histadrut-owned firms also participate alongside major private industrialists in Israel's most important business interest organization, the Manufacturers' Association. The literal bottom line of the network of interlocks which bind the seemingly disparate pillars of industrial big business is the convergent level and trend of their profits.[4]

Implicit industrial policy   As table 4.1 shows, despite industry's record of stagnating productivity and output after 1973, its overall profitability emerged unscathed; while the profits of the big industrial conglomerates linked to the Histadrut and the banks *increased* dramatically. The largely implicit industrial policy of the state can explain this puzzling combination. The core of that policy, which was oriented almost exclusively to big industry, had two planks: orders from the defence establishment, and direct subsidy.

Lavish increases in government subsidies on credit, investment and in many cases even production costs made it profitable for firms to keep producing and to buy equipment they did not need. Even production for the local market (officially a low priority) was treated generously, in part as compensation for the increased exposure to imports necessitated by new trade agreements. Exporters, meanwhile, enjoyed both their own earmarked subsidies and privileged access to incentives to new investment. This wealth of state aid undoubtedly bolstered corporate profits, but it was of dubious effectiveness in advancing the declared goals of public policy. By the end of the seventies subsidies had reached the point that the cost in local currency of an additional dollar of export earnings was estimated to be fully 30–40 per cent higher than the market price of a dollar bill.[5] The target of attracting manpower out of the services and into manufacturing was also badly missed. Whereas in the early 1970s the industrial labour force had been growing at the healthy rate of 5 per cent a year, in 1973–80 it expanded by an average of only 1 per cent. This achievement compares poorly with the rapid (5–6 per cent) growth of banking and public services. In the event it was the welfare state and even more so the *warfare state* which had to bear most of the burden of job creation.

The warfare state was also decisive for the profitability of big industry. During the difficult first few years after the shocks of 1973, military procurement played an indispensable counter-cyclical role in buoying up the manufacturing sector in the face of depressed consumer demand. Following a temporary falloff, procurement resumed its upward course after the Likud took office in 1977. Throughout, orders were directed almost exclusively to firms affiliated to the 'pillars' (although with an eye to awarding each of them a fair share of the action), and were based on generous cost-plus arrangements which the authorities proved unable (and for the most part unwilling) to control. The result, as we can see in figure 4.4 was that until 1983 the collective profits of the big industrial groups followed the trend of local defence spending with quite extraordinary fidelity.[6]

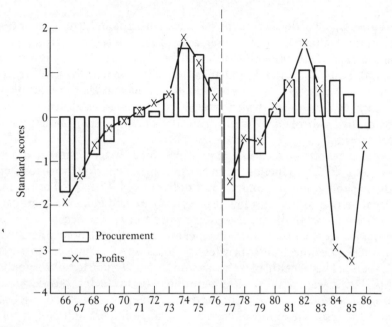

Figure 4.4 Israel: local defence procurement and profits of the big three conglomerates

The surge in domestic procurement attendant on the Yom Kippur War and the re-equipment and redeployment which followed accelerated a process, dating from the war of 1967, of rapid military industrialization led by expanding local demand. In the interregnum between the wars, military-related industries also began turning to export markets on a significant scale. The additional burst of local demand for weaponry after 1973 again facilitated export growth, including diversification into related hi-tech product lines for civilian uses. The volume of exports by the branches of manufacturing closest to military production quadrupled twice over – once in the first flush of growth (between 1967 and 1970) and again in the course of the 1970s. By all accounts, the profits were fabulous. Much of this was due to the state. It not only helped arms exporters find lucrative niches in the world market, but also showered them with subsidies and allowed them a lucrative free ride on the infrastructure created by local orders.

From autonomy to paralysis

These developments of the first post-1973 decade point to a notable imbalance in the relationship between industrial capital and the state. Big industry profited enormously from public contracts and subsidies, yet failed in return to meet the state's objectives of expanding industrial output and employment and made progress in exports only at very high cost to the state. The big manufacturers became bigger and more dependent on the public purse than ever – and the state's capacity to economically and effectively steer them in the direction of its policy goals declined considerably. Responsibility for this decline ultimately belongs to two trends, working in interaction, which came to the fore after 1973. One of these might be called the 'sorcerer's apprentice effect'. Having built up an industrial sector characterized by an extremely concentrated core, acute dependence on patronage and subsidy, and intimate formal and informal links with the political elite, the state had unwittingly created a centre of power capable of making compelling claims on its resources. The other factor was of course the shrinkage of these very resources. And what is particular to the Israeli case in this respect, is the fact that the material constraint was not primarily the result of the fiscal implications of declining economic growth (although those implications were certainly real enough). A more fundamental limit to state autonomy, and one which had already surfaced a decade before the shocks of 1973, was the decline of *discretionary* capital inflow and the rise of non-discretionary gifts tied to Israel's military commitments.

The transformation of the state's external sources of revenue may be vividly charted by a single comparison.[7] In the latter half of the 1950s, the time of Israel's first wave of industrialization, the state was the beneficiary of foreign aid equivalent to about one sixth of GNP. Half of this sum comprised donations and loans from world Jewry, a third was reparations from Germany, and the remainder consisted of cheap loans and grants from the US Government. These funds would have sufficed at the time to cover the defence budget *and* most of the investment bill of the entire business sector.

By the mid 1970s a very different pattern had emerged, one of greatly enlarged foreign assistance (approaching a quarter of GNP) which, except for Jewish philanthropy (down to a quarter of total aid), was dominated by the United States Government. The most salient feature of the US aid package has been its close relationship to the cost of Israeli purchases of American arms.[8] As a result, the largest chunk of Israel's foreign gift capital is mortgaged to the purchase of US weaponry (along the way, contributing to the prosperity of US weapons-makers). But in addition, American support for Israel is premised on the strategic value of an alliance with the strongest military force in a sensitive region. This strength has depended not only on advanced foreign-made armaments, but also on a roughly matching level of *domestic* spending to cover the costs of manning the armed forces and purchasing locally-made supplies and materiel. In other words, because of Israel's role as a regional power wedded to the United States (a role which Israel has of course embraced with enthusiasm), the burden of the state's military spending is far in excess of the gifts it receives from the US.

Two important consequences follow. First, instead of having a major portion of foreign assistance at its disposal with which to direct economic development, the state routinely turns over the entire inflow of aid for military purposes. Second, in order to reap macroeconomic benefits (and political goodwill) from local military procurement, the state sponsored a process of military industrialization. This process tied up the economy's most advanced equipment and manpower in an industry with an unstable foreign market and surging domestic demand that could not grow indefinitely. It also enhanced the power and autonomy of the big defence contractors, thus further undermining the directive capacities of the state *vis-à-vis* the industrial pillars and major public corporations. The growth of Israel's 'military-industrial complex', it must be stressed, was no doubt assisted by the perceived unreliability of external suppliers, extensive career mobility linking the various arms of the complex on the personal level, and other factors routinely considered in the burgeoning literature on the subject. The present analysis instead gives pride of place to the *profitability* of defence-related production. And what is then seen as most notable about this profitability, is firstly its roots in privileged treatment as well as favourable market conditions, and secondly (and hardly unrelatedly), the concentration of military-based profits in the big pillars of capital and their singular importance for big industry's prosperity.

The big banks

Israel's big banks are of great significance not only as stakeholders in industry, but also in their own right. Like industry, banking underwent a long-term process (accelerated by the mid-sixties recession) of growing concentration, a process which was actively supported by the authorities. By the 1980s the three largest commercial banks together cornered some 90 per cent of both assets and deposits, and monopolized almost the entire gamut of financial functions. Of the Big Three, one, the smallest, is privately controlled. The other two, officially the wards of the Histadrut and the Jewish Agency, are for the most part effectively run by their salaried top executives. All three had long enjoyed a special relationship with the authorities, under which they were obliged to channel the vast majority of their deposits and other funds to the state, and in return were provided with opportunities to profit and grow. Under the conditions which came to prevail after 1973, this framework was highly conducive to a mutually reinforcing spiral of inflation on the one hand and aggrandizement of the big three banks on the other, in the course of which the growing weakness of the state in relation to the Big Three became painfully apparent.

The new inflation after 1973 received perhaps its most important boost from the first economic initiative of the Likud-led government which took over from Labour in 1977. Until that time, stabilization policy had followed conventional remedies for a balance of payments crisis – principally, devaluation, wage freezes and restraint of domestic demand by fiscal means. Only five months after taking office, the first Likud finance minister (the leader of the pro-business Liberal Party) introduced a dramatic shift in economic policy emphasis by announcing far-reaching surprise measures to 'liberalize' Israel's foreign currency regime. Potentially the most significant aspect of this programme of deregulation was the simultaneous elimination of the system of multiple exchange rates (a traditional indirect means of encouraging exports) and administrative barriers to 'free trade' (import levies and export subsidies). The immediate fate of the programme affords eloquent testimony to the state's inability to impose market discipline on the business sector. The actual fixing of new exchange rates was distorted so as to preserve the heavy protective shield enjoyed by domestic producers. At the same time, since exporters gained little or nothing from bringing the new uniform exchange rate to the old 'premium' level, the authorities immediately authorized a compensatory increase in off-budget export subsidies. Deregulation did however have dramatic effects on the monetary system. With the removal of hindrances to the import of foreign funds, 'hot money' streamed into Israeli banks in pursuit of high interest rates. At the same time, since Israelis were now free to purchase dollars the Treasury came under pressure to increase the attractiveness of its bond issues, the mainstay of public debt service. The authorities were effectively left with almost no means of restraining interest rates, the money supply, or the erosion of foreign currency reserves.

The liberal economics brought in by the Likud 'revolution' came at the close of a year in which inflation had been high (34 per cent), although no more so than over the preceding 12 months. But during the year which followed, prices rose considerably faster (54 per cent), marking the beginning of an acceleration which was to continue (with a temporary interruption at the beginning of the eighties) until the Stabilization Plan of 1985. The banks were the most spectacular winners from this unleashing of inflation. By 1980 their share of Israel's barely growing GNP was nearly double the level of four years earlier, and the same period also saw a tripling in real terms of the collective net profits of the Big Three. Yet instead of reining in the banks, the state increasingly gave them its business. The big banks became the conduit for the rising tide of local and foreign funds needed to service the public debt and maintain foreign currency balances. When added to their pivotal role as investors, these developments generated considerable sympathy for the banks' requirements on the part of the authorities. By leaving tax loopholes open and failing to enforce legal prohibitions on the banks' manipulation of their own share values, politicians and senior public officials knowingly became implicated in the soaring growth of bank profits – as an official commission of enquiry later revealed in devastating detail, following the stock market collapse caused in the fall of 1983 when the bank share bubble finally burst.

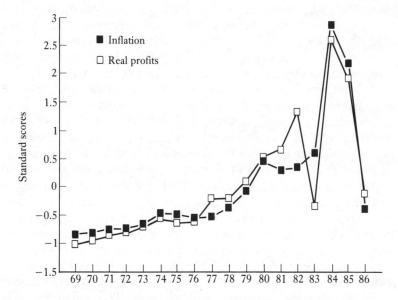

Figure 4.5   Israel: inflation and the profits of the three largest banks

Until the 1983 crash, the profits of the big banks showed a trend in close proximity to Israel's accelerating inflation (see figure 4.5).[9] Yet it bears emphasis that the banks' growing size and profitability were not merely mechanical reflections of accelerating inflation. Certainly the awesome scope for holders of liquid assets to turn a profit, as well as the desperate need of ordinary citizens to manage their money, vastly expanded the scope for banking services as inflation reached double and then triple-digit levels. Yet it was the state which furnished the most important preconditions for expanding bank profits. Countless 'preferred' beneficiaries could borrow unlinked money from the authorities while receiving linked interest on government bonds. This generosity was in no small part due to the necessity for the state to compete with alternative destinations for the public's savings – and above all, the share issues of the major banks. Despite severe problems of external and internal indebtedness in the post-1973 period, the state made no move towards capital market reforms. It proved almost powerless to profit from inflation because of the preservation of arrangements 'unique to the Israeli economy' which prevent the central bank from covering deficits by 'printing' more money in inflationary periods (Meridor, 1987, p. 11). Though much of the resultant burden was deferred to the future, by the early 1980s debt repayment had climbed to a quarter of the government budget, double the level of 1970 and equivalent to the entire cost of the social services. In other words the state was obliged to bear the consequences of its folly in permitting the rise in hyper-inflation. And the burden became ever-greater as higher deficits further enriched the financial sector and further reinforced the inflationary momentum which aggravated the fiscal crisis.

The Economic Crisis – and Beyond

For roughly a decade after the shock waves of 1973, the state's stewardship of the Israeli economy had the effect of aggravating rather than warding off destabilization. The present account has demonstrated the important role played by the changing pattern of capital-state relations in generating these policy failures. Emphasis has been placed on the growing concentration of capital and the blurring of the lines between the different sectors of Israel's once-'pluralistic' economy, in favour of the rise of closely linked 'pillars'. Ironically, the growing concentration and power of business were for the most part the result of the state's own policies. The economic crisis of 1973, and the political crisis which was already in the making before then, heightened the state's dependence on capital and reduced its ability to use capital's own dependence as a source of leverage. Nevertheless, not only the economic structure and conjuncture were behind eroding state autonomy. As we have pointed out, the declining role of discretionary gift capital from abroad, and the linkage of the state's post-1973 receipts to military aggrandizement, deprived economic steering of many degrees of freedom. Finally, big business succeeded in magnifying its relative power by political means. Three of these have been particularly significant: the increasing importance of the Histadrut, since the end of Labour Party dominance, as an instrument for transmitting the common interests of private and 'collective' capital to the state; the growing economic, organizational and political strength of the workforces of big business; and the much enhanced presence of business interest organizations, especially the Manufacturers' Association, as participants in policy networks.

Let us now close the circle by focusing more explicitly on the puzzle of Israel's distinctive pattern of economic performance after 1973. This pattern, it will be recalled, combined low/no growth and high/hyper inflation with comparatively full employment.

Israel's relatively *low unemployment* can be readily explained by returning to the 'defence economy'. The role of the armed forces alone is so substantial that for Jewish prime-age (18–55) men, the *civilian* labour force constitutes only 80 per cent of the total.[10] Not surprisingly then, the overall military labour market (including manpower absorbed by arms-related industries) has been Israel's most important antidote to unemployment – although not the only one. Particularly in the initial few years of crisis several other mechanisms operated, either to cut supply (the rapid growth of the commuter labour force from the occupied territories was temporarily halted), or to create demand (most notably in the form of new public sector jobs in education and health).

Our analysis offers several pointers for explaining the *growth slowdown*. Expansion of the state's military and civilian activity undoubtedly contributed to the measured stagnation of the economy, since this type of activity always translates conservatively into estimates of economic output. No less important, as we pointed out earlier, the core of the productive economy, the non-financial business sector, absorbed a declining share of labour while acquiring excessive new stocks of capital equipment – hardly a recipe for expansion. State subsidies (and also the captive markets and manpower provided by the occupied territories) kept the non-military economy afloat but discouraged efficiency. Meanwhile, as inflation rose the bigger resource-rich firms found it more profitable to devote those resources to speculation in financial markets (including the 'grey' and black markets not reflected in the national accounts) than to production, especially since subsidies were freeing up their cash flow.

Inflation, lastly, was stoked by the self-defeating cycle of costly public borrowing and rising public expenditure – the most significant non-defence items of which derived from capital subsidies and the cost of debt service. Large firms and the banks were able to make immense profits from investing resources freed up by state subsidy in an inflationary 'casino capitalism', even as the overall profit rate and the size of the national product stagnated. The fact that wages as well as interest-rates were pegged to the cost of living also played a role. Both Labour and Likud governments repeatedly attempted to exploit inflation in order to cut real wages, only to discover that in the face of a well-organized labour force and heavily cushioned employers in big business and the

Table 4.2 Israel: selected fiscal indicators for three periods (proportions of national product)

	1962–1966	1968–1972	1976–1983
Total expenditure	35.2	58.1	72.0
Financed domestically	31.0	49.0	54.3
Financed abroad	4.2	9.1	17.8
Of which, gifts	(2.9)	(3.4)	(10.8)
Major expenditure components			
Transfer payments	2.9	6.9	21.9
Other civilian expenditure	15.2	14.3	15.1
Military expenditure	11.3	23.1	25.6
Of which, imports	(5.3)	(10.5)	(10.6)

For notes and sources, see appendix 1.

public sector, induced price shocks had at most only a transient restraining effect on labour costs.

The most concrete and telling indicator of the paralysis of the state's capacity to steer the economy out of crisis, and the pivotal contribution of the changing balance of power between the state and capital, may be found in fiscal trends. By 1985, when the deficit peaked, Israel's domestic public debt was approaching one and a half times its GNP and the government had to set aside more than 40 per cent of its budget for the settling of past obligations. But even if transactions contingent on the 'rolling over' of debt are disregarded, as they are in table 4.2, it is apparent that the share of national resources allocated by the state had been expanding. More precisely, it rose to new plateaux following two major wars – an increase of some 40 per cent after 1967, and a further rise of nearly one quarter after 1973. Now if we set aside (as the table does) what happened in the unrepresentative years immediately following 1973, it emerges that since the crisis only one of the big ticket items of public expenditure other than debt service has risen substantially – namely, transfer payments. This evolution in turn is to a great extent due to the spectacular growth of the welfare state for business. Transfers to households did increase – but much less dramatically, and to the accompaniment of increased taxes (notably when an income tax overhaul in 1975 converted the child deduction into a child allowance).

In any case, the jump in income maintenance in the mid 1970s only added a one-time increment of about three percentage points of GNP to public expenditure. A good portion of the larger amount conventionally interpreted as destined for households actually consists of payments to nonprofit organizations like universities and the Sick Funds. It follows that the lion's share of the global rise in transfers, of the order of ten points of GNP, reflects a rise in 'income maintenance' for business. To this may be added at least another four points to reflect the sharp rise in off-budget credit subsidies serving the same purpose. Moreover, the growing burden of transfers and other forms of support for business was not balanced by any offsetting rise in tax receipts. On the contrary, the opportunities for tax avoidance under inflation actually diminished the contribution of the corporate sector to financing its own benefits. This also helped to complete inflation's magic circle: higher deficits leading to more profitable opportunities in money markets and more inflation, leading to more profits from unlinked government loans and tax benefits, leading once again to higher deficits.[11]

The climax came in the middle of the 1980s. Inflation-weariness was tiring even many of the winners. But in addition, the 1983 share market crash put paid to a major instrument by which the big banks had profited from inflation. In parallel, declining military procurement after Israel's withdrawal from Lebanon and a glut in the international arms market hampered the growth and profitability of the military economy. The state, for its part, came under great pressure to intervene or else see its own stability thrown into question – by economic trends (expansion of the budget deficit and contraction of foreign currency reserves), by pressure exerted by the United States, and by declining public confidence in parliamentary government. The political deadlock imposed by the 1984 general elections, and the Labour Party's success in Histadrut elections the following year, cleared the way for a suspension of competition between the major parties and a revival of corporatist co-operation between the Histadrut and the state. These circumstances created a climate in which inflation could be almost literally stopped in its tracks by a combination of imposed freezes (of wages, prices and the exchange rate) and *ad hoc* developments which relieved balance of payments pressures (including very substantial US aid over and above the cost of Israel's arms purchases). Not only did stabilization prove to be more durable than anticipated, but it was also accompanied by a vigorous struggle by the state to regain its autonomy. This struggle took place on several fronts, including cuts in capital subsidies, a successful showdown with the country's largest arms manufacturer, adamant refusals to bail out failing companies, and a sharp rise in tax collection from the business sector. These events are however too fresh, and their outcome still far too open, for any serious consideration of whether a new turning point has been reached in Israel's political economy.

Conclusions

No apologies are made for eschewing prediction – for the task of this chapter has been to make sense of the past rather than to foretell the future. The paradoxical aspects of the Israeli policy regime which have been the central concern of the essay are a reminder that typological abstractions are precisely that – abstractions from nationally distinctive contexts which were formed by specific historical trajectories. The comparative study of political economy has increasingly recognized these confounding truths: that there exist diverse roads to similar outcomes; and that polities sharing an apparently similar morphology may well generate dissimilar outcomes. The disjuncture in the Israeli case between the apparent strength of working class mobilization and the major thrust of domestic policy is a case in point. An attempt has been made to show the indispensability of a historically and institutionally grounded perspective for unravelling such a paradox. Israel's departures from the norms of social democratic corporatism can only be understood in terms of the peculiar origins and formative experiences of the labour movement, the particular purposes and modalities which it attached to the state in the context of overarching national and distributive conflicts, and the highly ramified interactions (immigration, capital import, and geopolitical alignment and dispute) between Israel and the international system.

In Israel both social democracy and the welfare state have developed more along *dualist* than socialist lines. The most fundamental form of dualism reflects the deeply embedded cleavage between Arabs and Jews, the legacy of an entwined economic and national conflict which was internalized and institutionalized in the organizational and political mobilization of the Jewish working class in Palestine/Israel. In addition, a pronounced ethnic dualism among the Jews themselves became particularly salient after sovereignty. The dominant (European-born) veterans in many ways shut out new immigrants from North Africa and the Middle East from affluence and mobility in the market arena. Coinciding with the Labour Party's inclination to exploit social policy as an instrument of clientelistic voter mobilization, this distributional struggle resulted in a dual system of social protection: market-based economic advance and security backed up by an array of social entitlements for the stronger groups of wage-earners; and a particularistic and tight-fisted public welfare system for the needy. For more than two decades following the attainment of sovereignty in 1948, Labour succeeded in reaping sufficient political credit from both groups to sustain an unchallengeable multiclass base.

Complementing the peculiarities of Israel's variant of social democracy is the flawed character of Israeli neo-corporatism as a paradigm of politico-economic stability. In spite of theoretically favourable precon-ditions for corporatist intermediation by the peak labour association, labour relations are comparatively – though not uniformly – unruly. In those sectors where labour peace is the norm, this is in large measure due, first, to direct collaboration between private business and the Histadrut (which itself is a major employer); and second, to the exposed position of workers in the lower tier of the labour market. The incomplete scope and effectiveness of political exchange between Histadrut and state is one of the reasons why it took more than a decade to engineer a political consensus around a comprehensive economic stabilization policy for the post-1973 era. In the interim, Israel's long spurt of rapid economic growth abruptly ceased, and *monthly* inflation rose to double-digit levels.

An even more important, though less noticed reason for the inefficacy of economic policy, has been a dearth of corporatist self-sacrifice on the side of capital. Both the underlying structure of the business sector and its associational activity have become increasingly concentrated in recent decades. After growing to maturity in a secure climate of massive subsidy and support from the state, capital in Israel is even less inclined than labour to exercise self-restraint. Undoubtedly, all major classes were the beneficiaries of policies which stimulated rising (although increasingly unequal) living standards during the decade of crisis which followed the first oil price shock and the Yom Kippur War. But even more dramatic was enlargement of the already generous welfare state for big business. When combined with the profound consequences of the militarization of economic aid and industrial development on the one hand, and on the other the intensifying dependence of the state on the big banks, this had the effect of greatly aggravating other motors of inflation and fiscal crisis. After three years of successful disinflation and budgetary restraint it remains an open question whether the Israeli state will be capable of breaking free of a debilitating contradiction: that it has steadfastly remained the centre of gravity of the political economy, while lacking the capacity to steer itself or the principal actors in civil society along a policy path of fundamental restructuring.

Notes

Certain ground rules adopted in this chapter should be indicated from the outset. In order to avoid cluttering the text with references, these have been kept to a bare minimum – in general, only those called for by direct quotations. A parsimonious guide to further reading on Israel may be found in appendix 2. Where data is cited in the text, no reference is given if the source was a standard one – viz, the *Statistical Abstract of Israel* (a yearbook published by the Central Bureau of Statistics) or the Bank of Israel's *Annual Report*. Finally, notes and sources for tables and charts have been collected in appendix 1.

1   Three years into the era of stabilization, its future is uncertain. At the time of writing (summer 1988) both inflation and the balance of payments deficit remain at disturbingly high levels and there have been persistent indications of impending recession. The successes of the Emergency Plan were heavily dependent on fortuitous (and therefore potentially fragile) conjunctures in both the international economy and domestic politics. Many economists question whether the long-run structural objectives of stabilization are in the process of realization. So far there has been no material increase in the relative size of the tradeable sector of the economy, nor any end in sight to Israel's need for massive import of capital.

2   Income distribution follows the national/ethnic hierarchy with striking regularity. One reasonable indicator of inequality is the ratio of per cent in the top quintile to per cent in the bottom quintile of the distribution. The Central Bureau of Statistics *Survey of Incomes* for 1980 (limited to urban wage-earners and calculated on a 'per standard equivalent adult' basis) yields the following ratios: Veteran (immigrated pre-1948) *Ashkenazim* 8.1, other *Ashkenazim* 2.8, Eastern Jews 0.3, Arab citizens 0.1 (comparable data are unavailable for Arabs in the occupied territories). Contrary to once-prevalent 'melting pot' expectations, the gap between *Ashkenazi* and Eastern parents (immigrants since 1948) is almost identical to the gap between their Israeli-born children.

3   Dun and Bradstreet, publishers of the 'Top 100' listings, define 'industry' to include not only manufacturing but also electricity generation and mineral extraction and processing (but not oil refineries and distribution). Dun and Bradstreet make no mention of it, but their 40 per cent estimate is almost certainly inflated by the inclusion of complete turnover figures for partly-owned subsidiaries.

4   Building on the work of Bichler (1986), Rowley et al. (1988) document this convergence both within and between the three top banks and the three largest non-governmental industrial conglomerates. They withhold judgement regarding government corporations due to lack of reliable information on profits and the fact that public sector business sometimes appears to function as a 'loss leader' in the service of the private sector.

5   This was the conclusion of a detailed re-analysis of the financial reports of a sample of large industrial firms (Levy and Lerman, 1984).

6   As Bichler (1986) demonstrates with the help of econometric tests, 1977 (the year of the Likud's ascent to office) marked a 'structural break' in the relationship between conglomerate profits and defence spending. For that reason, in Figure 4.4 'standard scores' were calculated separately for the pre- and post-1977 periods.

7   The data cited hereafter are annual averages for two periods, 1955–60 and 1975–7. The principal sources were Halevi (1983) and Bank of Israel annual reports. Dollar values were converted to proportions of GNP using 'effective' exchange rates.

8   If the aid package for a given year is defined as the sum of grants and loans (irrespective of their designated purpose) less the cost to Israel of servicing past debts, then over most of the 1973–87 period aid has exceeded arms imports by an average of only 10 per cent. (Excluded from this calculation are years of special-purpose aid – the 'Camp David supplements' of 1979–80, and the emergency economic aid of 1985–6.)

9   As Figure 4.5 indicates, the otherwise close relationship between the rate of inflation and real bank profits was suspended between 1981 and 1983 – as a result first of the climax and then the collapse of the banks' 'regulation' of prices of their own shares.

10 This figure is based on estimates of conscripts and career soldiers published by the International Institute for Strategic Studies (London), together with data on reservists on active duty gathered by Israel's Central Bureau of Statistics in the framework of its Labour Force Surveys. The reference is to early in the 1980s, before the Lebanon War.

11 Sources for this paragraph include Meridor (1987), Berglas (1986), and Kop. (1987).

Appendix 1

About the tables and charts

Unless otherwise stated all figures cited in the text were derived from two sources: The Bank of Israel's *Annual Report*, or the Central Bureau of Statistics'*Statistical Abstract of Israel*. This note also does not specify the source of data in tables and figures if they were drawn from one of these standard reference works.

Table 4.1   Most of the data were derived from tables constructed by Bregman (1986), located at the following pages. Lines 1, 3, 9, 10 at page 54; Lines 4 to 7 and line 13 at page 20; Line 8 at page 32; Lines 14 and 18 at page 13. In addition, Line 2 is taken from Bichler (1986, Appendix 1) and an update which he provided. Line 11 uses data published by the Ministry of Industry and Commerce (1987, p. 27). Line 12 is from the Bank of Israel's 1986 Report (p. 134 of the Hebrew edition). Sokoler (1984, p. 21) is the primary source of Line 16. Lines 15, 17 and (in part) 16 are from Berglas (1986, pp. 3, 32).

Following Bregman, the 'before' period is 1965–72 and 'after' is 1973–80. (In most cases it would have been impossible to avoid this confounding of somewhat disparate subperiods.) There are certain exceptions to the periodization, in addition to the major one noted in the table itself. Lines 4 to 7 and line 13 compare 1965–72 with 1972–9. Line 8 is available only for two benchmarks, 1965 and 1979. Similarly, Line 11 refers to 1970 and the average of 1975 and 1980. Line 16 compares 1966–72 with 1973–80. Lines 15 and 17 relate to the standard dates, but the 'before' averages had to be calculated by combining average figures for 1966–9 with annual data for the other years.

Nearly all indices refer to the manufacturing sector exclusive of diamonds (a high-export, labour-intensive, small-plant, low-value-added branch with often deviant conjunctural behaviour). Full details on construction of the indicators are available in the source works. The rate of return (Line 1) is total value added less labour costs, as a proportion of capital stock. Line 2 is based on the collective net profits of Koor, Discount Investments and Clal, essentially as published in their balance sheets. Capital utilization (Line 6) is measured by electricity consumption per unit of equipment. The three-firm concentration ratio (Line 8) is the three largest establishments' share of sales of locally-produced output (the figures cited here are weighted averages for 95 detailed industrial branches). As Bregman points out, an index calculated solely in relation to domestic output ignores the growth over time of competing imports (as indicated in Line 18). Line 11 aggregates the Metals and Metal Products, Machinery, Electronics, and Transport Equipment (aircraft) branches. The proportion of investment publicly funded (Line 14) takes account of only two forms of funding, explicit investment grants and 'development loans'. Public subsidy (Line 13) is the *cost* of these two instruments, which for loans is the deviation from market rates of interest. Line 15 is the sum of direct 'export supports' and the implicit subsidy in special loans to exporters granted after 1977. Line 16 was constructed by deducting Berglas' figures for the credit subsidy to exporters, from Sokoler's figures for total long-term credit subsidy to business (not including housing finance). Line 18 comprises estimates of the ratio of local to international prices of protected goods.

Table 4.2 The data were adapted from Meridor (1987), principally tables 1 and 5, and are documented and defined in the source. They are original estimates which attempt to reconcile government budgetary data with broader national accounts statistics. In principle, 'the state' includes the central bank, the Jewish Agency and other quasi-governmental bodies; in practice, this was apparently not entirely feasible. (For instance, 'directed credit' distributed by the Bank of Israel was not included.)

As noted in the text, the 'rolling over' of debt is unaccounted for in this table – i.e. debits due to the repayment of debts which are refinanced, and the matching revenues from the new loans, are both ignored.

The category 'transfer payments' comprises transfers to households and non-profit organizations (other than interest), and the subsidy implicit in budgeted loans to investors. It does not include off-budget credit subsidies, or price subsidies (which benefit consumers as well as producers).

Figure 4.1 To graph all three series on a common scale, the following transformations were performed: Inflation (the natural log plus 2); per capita GDP (thousands of constant 1980 shekels); percentage unemployment (no change).

Figure 4.2 The data are based on the ratio of the mean for 1973–9 to the mean for 1968–73. (Except for the growth rate, where the ratio was reversed in order to measure the *decline* since 1973.) For each indicator, these ratios were then standardized as a percentage of the mean for the seven OECD countries. Thus, the chart shows that after 1973 Israel experienced a decline in growth more than three times (309 per cent) greater than OECD, but unemployment rose by less than half as much as in OECD countries. Note that the growth indicator used here is the year-to-year change in real per capita GDP. Except for Israel, data are from OECD Economic Outlook, *Historical Statistics 1960–1985* (Paris, 1987) (hereafter *Historical Statistics*). Unemployment figures have been 'standardized' by the OECD.

Figure 4.3 Figures for both series are percentages of GDP. The social security data are for expenditure on *benefits* as defined by the ILO in its most recent survey (for 1980, published in 1985 by the International Labour Office in Geneva under the title *The Cost of Social Security*). Public 'consumption' is government expenditure other than transfer payments or investment. Civilian expenditure was calculated as a residual, after deducting military spending (as reported in 'The Military Balance', published by the International Institute for Strategic studies in London) from total expenditure (drawn for OECD countries from '*Historical Stratistics*').

Figure 4.4 Data on the cost of local defence procurement (including expenditure on construction) are as published in various Supplements to Israel's *Monthly Bulletin of Statistics*. The 'big three conglomerates' are Koor, Discount Investments and Clal. Their pooled net profits are reported by Bichler (1986, Appendix 1) and Rowley, Bichler and Nitzan (1988). Both series were calculated in constant 1980 shekels and then converted to standard scores (standard deviations from the mean).

Figure 4.5 Inflation is the year-on-year change in the consumer price index. The collective net profits (in constant 1980 shekels) of the three leading banks – i.e. Leumi, Hapoalim and Discount – were calculated by Bichler (1986, Appendix 1) and Rowley, Bichler and Nitzan (1988). Both series were converted to standard scores.

Appendix 2

Literature on Israel

An essay of this nature necessarily relies on the accumulation of research findings. Nevertheless, for the sake of economy references in the body of the chapter have been kept to a bare minimum. The purpose of this note is to furnish a selective reading list on Israel comprising items which have served as important sources in the preparation of the essay and/or would be appropriate for the English-speaking reader seeking further information.

For general institutional background on politics and policy in Israel, see Shimshoni (1982). The most important social cleavages are analysed by Swirski (1984) and Rosenfeld (1978), and an indicator of social inequality (comparable data on income inequality in Israel and OECD countries) is provided by Ringen and Uusitalo (forthcoming).

The historical development of the labour movement (the Histadrut and Mapai) is treated at length in my forthcoming volume *Labour and the Political Economy in Israel*; see also Shafir (forthcoming), Shalev (1988) and Shalev (forthcoming a), which includes a sizeable bibliography on labour politics in Israel. The structure of the Histadrut is described by Shirom (1980). On its role in the economy and social policy, see Kleiman (1987) and Doron (1988) respectively.

The most penetrating analysis of labour relations in Israel is Grinberg (1985; English version in preparation). Friedman (1976) and Avrech and Giladi (1973) remain useful; see also Artstein and Sussman (forthcoming) and Shalev (1984).

On social policy in Israel, see the overviews by Shlonsky (1971) and Shalev (1984). The work of Abraham Doron (e.g. Doron, 1967; Doron and Kramer, 1976) is useful for following the development of policy over the last four decades. Klein (1959) is indispensable regarding the 1960s; see Avizohar (1978) and Hoffnung (1982) for the innovations of the early 1970s, and reports of the National Insurance Institute and of the Center for Social Policy Studies in Israel (e.g. Kop, 1987) for subsequent developments. Haidar (1987) has published a pioneering survey of the treatment of Arab citizens in Israel's welfare state.

The single most comprehensive source on the Israeli economy (which however focuses mainly on the 1970s) is a collection edited by Ben-Porath (1986a). Within the extensive literature on policy responses to the economic crisis following 1973, Yoran (1987), Ben-Porath (1986b) and Tov (1988) were particularly helpful. Developments following the stabilization plan of 1985 have been reviewed by Bruno and Piterman (1987).

Critical studies of the Israel economy in the political economy tradition are rare. Yago (1977) is a classic work on capital import. The structure of the business sector and its implications for symptoms of economic crisis is a central theme in the work of Shimshon Bichler (Bichler, 1985; Bichler, 1986). Other investigations of industry and its relationship with the state are Schechter (1972) and Jerusalem Institute of Management (1987). The most insightful parallel source in relation to the banks is the 'Beijski Report' (Commission of Inquiry, 1986). For samples of the sizeable literature on the military economy, see Mintz (1987) and Halperin (1986). In the Hebrew literature, Barkai (1987) points out the role of the profit motive in the rise of Israel's military industries, a role made explicit in Bichler's (1986) pioneering work; and Hadar (1988) details the operation of state sponsorship and subsidy.

References

Aharoni, Yair 1976: *Structure and Performance in the Israeli Economy* (in Hebrew). Tel-Aviv: Cherikover.
Artstein, Yael and Sussman, Zvi forthcoming: Wage Policy in a High-Inflation Economy: The Israeli Experience. In V.L. Urquidi (ed.), *Incomes Policy*. International Economic Association

Avizohar, Michael 1978: *Money for All: The Development of Social Insurance in Israel* (in Hebrew). Tel-Aviv: Yariv & Hadar.

Avrech, Isaiah and Dan Giladi (eds) 1973: *Labour and Society in Israel*. Tel Aviv: Tel Aviv University, Department of Labour Studies.

Barkai, Haim 1987: The Defense Industries at a Crossroads (in Hebrew). Research Paper no. 197, Falk Institute for Economic Research in Israel, Jerusalem.

Ben-Porath, Yoram (ed.) 1986a: *The Economy of Israel: Maturing through Crisis*. Cambridge, Mass.: Harvard University Press.

Ben-Porath, Yoram 1986b: Public Sector Employment and Wages in the Process of Adjustment. Paper presented at the conference on Economic Issues and Policy in Israel 1985–1986, Falk Institute for Economic Research in Israel, Jerusalem, June 15–16.

Berglas, Eitan 1986: Taxes and Transfer Payments, 1975–1985 (in Hebrew). Discussion Paper 86–12 (September). Tel-Aviv University: Sapir Center for Development.

Bichler, Shimshon 1985: Insights into the Tsena [Austerity] Period (in Hebrew). Unpublished seminar paper, Hebrew University of Jerusalem.

Bichler, Shimshon 1986: *The Political Economy of National Security in Israel: Some Aspects of the Activities of the Dominant Blocs of Capital* (in Hebrew). Unpublished MA Thesis, Hebrew University of Jerusalem.

Bregman, Aryeh 1986: *Industry and Industrialization Policy in Israel: Central Issues (1965 to 1985)* (in Hebrew). Jerusalem: Bank of Israel Research Department.

Bruno, Michael and Sylvia Piterman 1987: Israel's Stabilization: A Two-Year Review. Discussion Paper 87.05, November. Bank of Israel Research Department.

Castles, Francis G. 1978: *The Social Democratic Image of Society*. London: Routledge and Kegan Paul.

Commission of Inquiry into the Regulation of Bank Shares 1986: *Final Report* (in Hebrew). Jerusalem: Ministry of Justice.

Doron, Abraham 1967: *Development of National Insurance in Israel, 1948–1965*. Unpublished PhD Dissertation, London School of Economics.

Doron, Abraham 1988: The Histadrut, Social Policy and Equality. *The Jerusalem Quarterly*, 47, 131–44.

Doron, Abraham and Ralph M. Kramer 1976: Ideology, Programme and Organizational Factors in Public Assistance: The Case of Israel. *Journal of Social Policy*, 5(2), 131–49.

Friedman, Abraham 1976: Union Structure and Rank and File Revolt: The Israeli Experience. *Relations Industrielles*, 31(2), 261–83.

Goldthorpe, John (ed.) 1984: *Order and Conflict in Contemporary Capitalism*. Oxford: Oxford University Press.

Grinberg, Lev Luis 1985: *The Revolt that Never Was: The 'Forum of Thirteen Workers Committees'; a Test Case for Israeli Corporatism* (in Hebrew). Unpublished MA thesis, Hebrew University of Jerusalem.

Hadar, Shmuel 1988: *Blurring of the Boundaries between Public and Private in Relations between State and Industry* (in Hebrew). Unpublished PhD dissertation, Hebrew University of Jerusalem.

Haidar, Aziz 1987: *Social Welfare Services for Israel's Arab Population*. Tel Aviv: International Center for Peace in the Middle East.

Halevi, Nadav 1983: The Structure and Development of Israel's Balance of Payments. Discussion Paper 83.02, January, Falk Institute for Economic Research in Israel, Jerusalem.

Halperin, Ariel 1986: Military Buildup and Economic Growth in Israel. Paper presented at the conference on Economic Issues and Policy in Israel 1985–1986, Falk Institute for Economic Research in Israel, Jerusalem, June 15–16.

Hoffnung, Menahem 1982: *Social Protest and the Public Budgeting Process: The Effect of the 'Black Panther' Demonstrations on Allocations to Social and Welfare Needs* (in Hebrew). Unpublished MA thesis, Department of Political Science, Hebrew University of Jerusalem.

Jerusalem Institute of Management 1987: *Export-Led Growth Strategy for Israel: Final Report*. Tel-Aviv: J.I.M.

Kleiman, Ephraim 1987: The Histadrut Economy of Israel: In Search of Criteria. *Jerusalem Quarterly*, 41, 77–94.

Klein, Philip 1959: The Ministry of Social Welfare in Israel: Proposals on Program and Administration Prepared for the Government of Israel. Mimeo, March.

Kop, Yaakov (ed.) 1987: *Israel's Social Services 1986–87*. Jerusalem: The Center for Social Policy Studies in Israel.

Levy, Haim and Zvi Lerman 1984: Estimates of Capital Costs in Israeli Industry, 1971–1980 (in Hebrew). Discussion Paper 84.05. Falk Institute for Economic Research in Israel, Jerusalem.

Meridor (Rubin), Leora 1987: The Financing of Government Expenditures in Israel, 1960 to 1983 (in Hebrew). *Seker Bank Yisrael*, 62, 3–31.

Ministry of Industry and Commerce 1987: *Industry in Israel 1986* (in Hebrew). Jerusalem: The Center for Industrial Planning, Ministry of Industry and Commerce.

Mintz, Alex 1987: Arms Production in Israel. *The Jerusalem Quarterly*, 42, 89–99.

Olson, Mancur 1982: *The Rise and Decline of Nations*. New Haven, Conn.: Yale University Press.

Ringen, Stein and Hannu Uusitalo (forthcoming): Income Distribution and Redistribution in the Nordic Welfare States. In Jon-Eivind Kolberg and Gosta Esping-Andersen (eds), *Between Work and Social Citizenship, Volume III: The Impacts on Society*.

Rosenfeld, Henry 1978: The Class Situation of the Arab National Minority in Israel. *Comparative Studies in Society and History*, 20(3), 374–407.

Rowley, Robin, Shimshon Bichler and Jonathan Nitzan 1988: Some Aspects of Aggregate Concentration in the Israeli Economy 1964–1986. Working Paper 7/88. McGill University: Department of Economics.

Schecter, Stephen B. 1972: *Israeli Political and Economic Elites and Some Aspects of their Relations*. Unpublished PhD Dissertation, London School of Economics.

Schmitter, Philippe C. 1981: Interest Intermediation and Regime Governability in Contemporary Western Europe and North America. In Suzanne Berger (ed.), *Organizing Interests in Western Europe*. Cambridge: Cambridge University Press, 285–327.

Shafir, Gershon (forthcoming): *Land, Labour and the Origins of the Israeli–Palestinian Conflict, 1882–1914*. Cambridge: Cambridge University Press.

Shalev, Michael 1984: Labour, State and Crisis: An Israeli Case Study. *Industrial Relations*, 23(3), 362–86.

Shalev, Michael 1988: Jewish Organized Labour and the Palestinians: A Study in State/Society Relations in Israel. In Baruch Kimmerling (ed.), *The Israeli State and Society: Boundaries and Frontiers*. Albany, NY: State University of New York Press, 93–134.

Shalev, Michael (forthcoming a): The Political Economy of Labour Party Dominance and Decline in Israel. In T.J. Pempel (ed.), *Uncommon Democracies*. Ithaca, NY: Cornell University Press.

Shalev, Michael (forthcoming b): *Labour and the Political Economy in Israel.* Oxford: Oxford University Press.

Shimshoni, Daniel 1982: *Israeli Democracy: The Middle of the Journey*. New York: Free Press.

Shirom, Arie 1980: Political Parties and Democracy in the Histadrut. *Industrial Relations*, 19(2), 231–7.

Shlonsky, Hagith 1971: Welfare in Israel in a Comparative Perspective. Mimeo, Center for the Study of Welfare Policy, University of Chicago, November.

Sokoler, Meir 1984: The Inflationary Tax on the Monetary Base, The Inflationary Subsidy Implicit in Cheap Credit, and Their Influence on The Inflationary Process in Israel (in Hebrew). Discussion Paper 84.05, June. Bank of Israel Research Department.

Swirski, Shlomo 1984: The Oriental Jews in Israel. *Dissent*, Winter, 77–91.

Therborn, Göran 1986: *Why Some Peoples are More Unemployed than Others*. London: Verso.

Tov, Imri 1988: The Economic Upheaval of 1977 – Implementation of Operational Goals (in Hebrew). *Rivon L'Kalkala*, 135–136, 33–47.

Wilensky, Harold L. 1975: *The Welfare State and Equality: Structural and Ideological Roots of Public Expenditure*. Berkeley, CA: University of California Press.

Yago, Glenn 1977: Whatever Happened to the Promised Land? Capital Flows and the Israeli State. *Berkeley Journal of Sociology*, 21, 117–46.

Yoran, Yosef 1987: An Economy in Structural Crisis: Israel since the Oil Crisis and the Yom Kippur War (in Hebrew). *Rivon L'Kalkala*, 131, 827–54.

5

Japan's Creative Conservatism
Continuity under Challenge

T.J. Pempel

Introduction

In a famous radio broadcast in 1939, Winston Churchill offered his now celebrated assessment of the Soviet Union. The country, he suggested, 'is a riddle wrapped in a mystery inside an enigma'. Were the classic phrasemaker monitoring the world of the mid 1980s he might well have applied the designation to Japan. Despite its industrial prowess, its parliamentary democracy and its cultural modernity, Japan continues to strike most Westerners as perplexingly different from the other industrialized democracies. To many Europeans, the country is too culturally distant for understanding; to Americans looking at Japan, what is striking are Japan's differences from their country's own presumed normalcy; to Japanese familiar with their country's centuries of linguistic, ethnic and cultural uniqueness, any parallels to other industrialized nations are easily dismissed as superficial. This impression of Japanese singularity is continually reinforced by those analysts of Japan who treat the country in isolation, typically using an idiosyncratic vocabulary rooted heavily in culturally specific jargon. Indeed, the manufacture and marketing of Japanese inscrutability has become an export industry success second only to that country's cars, semiconductors and video recorders.[1]

Japan's behaviour like that of any other country, surely has its components of uniqueness. These are not to be denied. At the same time, many aspects mirror to a greater or lesser extent those in other countries of the world. The arduous research task is to isolate just what is different from what is similar, and more importantly to analyse the particular way in which the two are combined. The true uniqueness of any country lies in the ways it has woven combinations of the many possible common threads of historical experience to create its own particular and discrete pattern.

Doing this for Japanese public policy presents three interwoven perplexities. First, Japan does indeed offer a historical profile of public policies quite different in important ways from its counterparts in Western Europe and North America. In the most simplistic formulation, Japan's economic growth rates have been far higher and its social welfare spending far lower than the rest of the industrialized world. From this perspective, Japan represents an extreme version of the pro-business, anti-welfare capitalist state. Secondly, even within that universe of industrialized democracies, Japan is especially confounding because many of its policies and their consequences do not appear to follow logically from the overwhelmingly conservative character of its government. And finally, Japanese public policy defies easy characterization because it has undergone several striking transformations radically at odds with its past policies. Thus, deciding what is unique about Japan in part requires one to determine which of its changes separate it from other countries, which bring it closer, and which can be ignored as no more than superficially interesting.

I will argue that these three sets of problems can best be understood as connected rather than separate. Indeed they are intricately woven together, representing a set of interlocking puzzles the solution to one of which demands an understanding of all three. Once the three are outlined, I will argue that they can best be understood as the outgrowths of historically rooted choices that have led Japan to what truly distinguishes it from the other industrialized countries, namely, its particular pattern of 'creative conservatism' (Pempel, 1982). In turn, this pattern has made Japan's political economy one that is 'structured for change'.

Three Sets of Puzzles

The two aspects of Japan that are most immediately striking to students of comparative public policy are Japan's tremendous economic growth and its low public spending for social welfare. The data on Japan's economic performance are widely known and do not demand excessive repetition. Consider only several items. Japan's Gross National Product grew at an average annual rate of about 11 per cent from 1952 until 1973. The cumulative effect was a total improvement of some six and a half times, a figure unmatched by any other OECD country and one which took Japan from being one of the smallest medium-sized economies to being the second largest among the industrialized democracies. National productivity soared and Japan's share of world trade rose from about 2 per cent to about 8 per cent.

Even more striking has been Japan's economic performance since the breakdown of the Bretton Woods monetary system in 1971 and the quadrupling of world oil prices by OPEC in 1973. While GNP growth rates slowed, they still exceeded those for most of the other industrialized democracies. Japan's annual growth in GNP placed the country fifth of sixteen major OECD nations from 1974 to 1979, while from 1980 to 1984 its performance was once again the best among these advanced economies. Moreover, Japan's trade balance became highly positive; its currency gained in world strength; domestic inflation remained low; gross investment soared. The overall extent of Japan's successful macroeconomic performance was evidenced in numerous ways, from the formal statistical compilations of the OECD which invariably put Japan at or near the top on most of its comparative economic indicators; to the rush of attention paid by world leaders to the pluses and minuses of Japan's economic performance for their own countries; to the rash of efforts by American and European managers to 'Japanize' their companies' managerial practices; to the surge of mass appeal paperbacks lauding or lambasting the Japanese economic miracle, with titles ranging from *Japan as Number One* (Vogel, 1979) to *The Japanese Conspiracy – the Plot to Dominate Industry Worldwide – and How to Deal with It* (Wolf, 1983).

At the same time, Japan has been uniformly branded a welfare laggard. Part of this is due to the overall low level of government funding for all activities. As late as 1967–9, Japan's total public expenditure for social welfare as a percentage of GDP averaged only 19.2 per cent annually, by far the lowest among the industrialized democracies, with only Switzerland and Australia spending less than 30 per cent (Castles, 1982, p. 49). In 1980, the figure was up to 30 per cent, an allotment still dramatically below the Scandinavian high spenders (mostly over 50 per cent) as well as the moderate spenders such as France, Germany, Britain and Italy (42–45 per cent). And it still lagged behind the next lowest spenders, the US and Australia, both of whom were over 33 per cent. Public expenditure for social welfare explicitly is similarly low. In the mid 1970s the government of Japan spent only 8.9 per cent of GDP for all welfare measures. Only Australia was below 15 per cent. Indeed the OECD country closest in level of spending to Japan was Spain (which had a GNP equal to only one-sixth that of Japan) (Poullier, 1982, p. 620; Kokuseisha, 1984, p. 105). Moreover, since nearly 70 per cent of Japan's governmental expenditures on social measures are for health and retirement insurance, government spending on such measures as family or child allowances, public housing, unemployment insurance and relief payments show Japanese social welfare policies to be even further away from programmes adopted elsewhere in Europe and North America.

Such a picture presents a strong counter-argument to notions of some automatically positive correlation between economic growth and social spending, and a convergence in social policies among countries with comparable economic levels (e.g. Pryor, 1968; Wilensky, 1975; though cf. Shalev, 1983).

On the other hand, it would seem intuitively compatible with neo-classical economic interpretations arguing that low levels of government spending for social welfare present a vigorous market stimulus to the private sector. In effect, this argument goes, the less money 'wasted' on such social measures the more vigorous a nation's economy will be.

And although it is not precisely the target of their explanations, the essentially pro-business, anti-welfare character of Japanese public policy is certainly compatible with political explanations such as those of Hibbs (1978), Crouch (1977), Panitch (1979), Stephens (1979), Cameron (1978), Przeworski (1985) and Schmidt (1982) among others. To a greater or lesser extent all of these authors provide arguments that link the level of a country's social expenditures to the strength of its labour movement and/or to the duration of socialist governments. A strong labour movement, they argue, combined with a socialist or labour party that controls some or all cabinet seats for sustained periods of time will be able to develop and institutionalize social welfare programmes that remove some of the economic sting of a 'pure' market. The social safety nets thus created are stronger than in countries with weaker labour movements and less long-standing socialist governments.

An important, but also compatible, variation on this logic is offered by Castles (1978, 1982) who argues that it is less the strength of the left to implement programmes, but more the strength of the right to oppose them, that explains major variations in the extent of governmental spending for social welfare among industrialized democracies.

In either case, however, Japan would appear to fit, having had uninterrupted conservative government from 1947 to the present (and, as I have noted elsewhere, if one excludes the six-month socialist coalition government that ruled under the watchful eye of the American military during 1947, one could argue that Japan has had conservative, or right-of-centre governments since its industrialization began in the late nineteenth century) (Pempel, 1982; Pempel and Tsunekawa, 1979).

Yet there are two important problems with such plausible surface level explanations for Japan's most important elements of distinctiveness: first, they do little to explain the massive changes that have taken place both in Japan's economic and social welfare policies, particularly over the period since 1971 or 1973. And second, they do nothing to account for the numerous exceptions to the pro-business, anti-welfare image in Japan's public policy profile.

Consider first the widespread changes that Japan has undergone in the last decade or so. From the 1950s until the early 1970s, macroeconomic policy relied among other things on a fixed and artificially depressed exchange rate, tight government control over the credit and money supply, high levels of protection for agriculture and industry combined, severe restrictions on capital movements into and out of the country, low government expenditures, minimal public debt and overbalanced budgets. (Patrick and Rosovsky, 1976; Pempel, 1978b; Yamamura, 1967; Boltho, 1975; Kanamori, 1967 *inter alia*.)

In the mid to late 1980s, these had given way to a floating and ever more highly valued yen, sustained by periodic Bank of Japan intervention; an expansion of borrowing opportunities for industries at home and abroad; lower tariffs and fewer quotas on manufactured imports than could be found in almost any other industrialized country; liberalization of the capital, bond and securities markets; the widespread expansion of Japanese investment and manufacturing operations throughout the world; as well as a startling increase in government spending as a proportion of GNP, in public debt and in deficit financing (Yamamura and Yasuba, 1987; Okimoto, 1988; Pempel, 1987; Murakami, 1982). Tax policy which once rested heavily on highly visible (though often unevenly administered) income taxes as well as much less visible luxury taxes also came under debate with strong government pressure for a total tax system overhaul aimed at minimizing loopholes and creating a value added tax.[2]

Change is also demonstrable in the area of social welfare. The country that had been uniformly labelled a welfare laggard in the 1950s and 1960s suddenly, in the early 1970s, undertook the effort to create a 'Japanese style welfare state' (Japan, Economic Planning Agency, 1979; Campbell, 1977; 1984; Rose and Shiratori, 1986). The new label was matched by sudden budgetary expansion for old age 'medical' and pension care and a variety of other programmes. As a consequence, between 1973 and 1981, government expenditures for welfare pension payments rose five times; social security expenses were up four times; state subsidies for construction of primary and secondary schools increased five times, while those for the operating expenses of private schools were up eight times (Kumon, 1984: p. 147).

Perhaps even more striking in a comparative context, in the middle years of the 1980s, the government reversed these policies once again as it engaged in a concerted effort to attack 'the welfare state' that it had yet to create. With the government's moves towards 'administrative reform' and fiscal austerity, items such as social security, health and education began to shrink as percentages of the total government budget; medical expenditures for the elderly ceased to be fully covered by government programmes and initially 10 per cent and later 20 per cent of all expenditures were to be borne by the recipient. Overall, the government gave numerous indications that it sought to undo a number of the policies instituted only a decade or so earlier, and that it wished to reverse the trajectory of increasing social welfare policy expenditures.

In the absence of a change in the governing party to account for such policy shifts, their explanation is not readily attributable to one of the most typical causes of policy change. The new directions in economic policy certainly resulted in part from the breakdown of Bretton Woods and the OPEC oil shock. But the wholesale and extremely rapid redirection of the wide range of economic policy measures that had hitherto been successful is neither politically nor economically easy to understand. A similar difficulty is posed by the sudden and dramatic introduction of social security measures during the same period. While rollbacks in social welfare spending became the common currency of conservative (and a few social democratic) regimes in the 1980s, and are thus by no means counter-intuitive either in comparative terms or in terms of Japan's overall conservative character, the interesting question is why Japan ever began its big move toward higher social welfare spending.

If the political interpretation of social welfare is correct – namely that some combination of a strong, union-based left and a disunited right is essential to the creation of a social welfare state, then Japan is an oddity. When the social welfare initiative began in the early 1970s labour union membership was comparatively low and on a continual decline; the Japan Socialist Party was only drawing about 20 per cent of the popular vote, well off its post-war highs of 33 per cent two decades earlier and by no means comparable to socialist parties in most of Western Europe; the LDP, while less solidly entrenched in parliament than it had been in the early 1960s, was still the largest party by a 2:1 margin.

In addition to the questions posed by Japan's policy changes, even more puzzling are several inconsistencies that arise in the context of Japan's overall pro-business, anti-social welfare image. Three of these are particularly striking.

First, Japan has consistently maintained internationally low levels of unemployment. Whereas the majority of governments in the industrialized democracies watched over steadily escalating unemployment rates in the mid 1970s and then again in the late 1970s and early 1980s, only five major countries were exceptions. Countries with left-of-centre governments and long-term public commitments to full employment such as Sweden, Austria and Norway accounted for three of these. Switzerland, with its conservative government, had a ready if only partial solution to the employment problem in its small country: it deported some 10,000 of its foreign guestworkers. Japan's adherence to low levels of unemployment thus stands as an exception to the general pattern among the industrialized countries, and more importantly provides a stark challenge to the expectations usually associated with the image of 'pro-business, anti-welfare' (Therborn, 1985).

A second puzzle relates to Japan's relatively high level of income equality. Over the last 30 to 40 years, Japan has ranked extremely low on the Gini index, a standard measure used to compare income equality among different countries. Sawyer (1976) in a famous study of ten major countries found Japan to be the second most egalitarian country in income equality before taxes and the fourth most egalitarian after taxes. Bronfenbrenner and Yasuba (1987), Verba et al. (1987) and Kosai and Ogino (1984) found similar results using different time periods. In effect all such studies have shown that on the question of income equality Japan looks more similar to social democratic Sweden and Norway than to conservative Canada, the US, the UK or Germany.

Nor is such 'equality' some artefact of income statistics. In a number of other areas, such as education, infant mortality, crime, health care and elsewhere, comparative statistics show Japan to be a relatively egalitarian country in which a citizen's day-to-day experiences with such matters are not as extremely differentiated by class as they are elsewhere. So too are figures on the distribution of capital goods such as cars, colour television sets, telephones and other items. From such statistics it is no wonder that 90 per cent of Japan's citizens typically identify themselves as 'middle class' (Murakami, 1982). Japan hardly fits the expected cross-national behaviour of a conservative country.

A third anomaly concerns labour conflicts. Labour-management relations were hostile in Japan in the years immediately after the end of the Second World War and strike rates were high in comparative terms. Korpi and Shalev (1980) found that from 1946 to 1976 Japan ranked sixth of eighteen industrialized countries in strike involvement. Starting in 1955 Japanese labour's bargaining tactics over wages rested heavily on 'the spring offensive', a phrase designed to capture the broad array of public protests, threatened mass strikes and conflictual behaviour that were at the heart of unionized bargaining (Hanami, 1979; Harari, 1973). During the 1960s and early 1970s Japan's strike rates remained relatively high, placing the country in the middle ranks of the OECD countries in terms of both number and duration. As late as 1974 and 1975, Japan's hours lost to strikes put it ahead of relatively high strike countries such as the UK, Canada and France.

Yet, by the early years of the 1980s, Japan had one of the industrialized world's lowest strike rates. This is particularly interesting since most other conservative regimes (Italy, US, Canada, UK) have continued to have high strike rates. Low strikes have been most closely associated with countries in which there were national institutions of corporatist bargaining between business and labour such as Austria, Norway, Sweden, or even Germany; none of these institutions were present in

Japan. (Indeed, for the period 1975–80, Japan's industrial disputes were lower than those for corporatist Sweden (Koike, 1987, p. 292; cf. Cameron, 1984)).

To sum up, Japan is a country which looks to have followed public policies consistent with many interpretations of political conservatism. It has been a country with a highly successful macroeconomic performance and with a low level of state action in social welfare. Yet this image of unbridled conservatism is confounded by the fact that Japan has pursued these policies by changing means and, in social welfare at least, seemingly different goals. It has also done so with varying levels of commitment and success, making it much harder to grasp what is historically continuous and distinctive about Japan's public policy profile. Furthermore, in several areas of labour-management relations and matters of social and economic equality, Japan appears to defy its own conservative image. It follows many policies intuitively contradictory to the image of conservatism or with expectations from right-of-centre governments. Elsewhere, I have labelled this specific mix as Japan's 'creative conservatism' (Pempel, 1982).

The Core of Creative Conservatism

'Creative conservatism' is a phrase that includes several important elements. In its 'conservative' mode it refers, among other things, first to the explicitly close co-operation between the Japanese state, major Japanese corporations and financial institutions. Second, it involves a 'small' but activist state. Third, and quite importantly, it indicates a highly competitive, even if often highly oligopolistic, domestic market. Fourth, it refers to the low levels of institutionalization of social welfare and redistributive mechanisms, and a reliance instead on labour market adjustment measures and a social safety net that relies primarily on the firm and the family. A number of other traits could be identified as 'conservative' in Japan, including the government's historical ties to agriculture and small business, social mores, respect for hierarchy, and so forth. But for present purposes the above four traits are most vital.

A brief elaboration on each seems in order. Relations between the Japanese state and the business and financial sectors have been subject to a great deal of analysis. Marxists treat the country as a relatively typical case of monopoly capitalism where such ties are taken for granted (Iida, 1976; Steven, 1983; Halliday, 1975). Others debate the relative importance of the Japanese government's actions, particularly in industrial and financial policy, for business success (Okimoto, 1988; Johnson, 1982; Magaziner and Hout, 1980; Zysman, 1984; Zysman and Cohen, 1983; Pempel, 1978b; Kaplan, 1972; Patrick and Rosovsky,

1976; Lincoln, 1984; Samuels, 1987; Friedman, 1988; Horne, 1985 *inter alia*). There are undoubtedly adherents of the view that Japanese big business would have done well without much help from the Japanese government, a view with which I personally disagree. But there seems to be no one contending that in Japan business and government are anything like enemies. Far more apt in conveying whatever differences divide them is Samuels' term, namely 'reciprocal consent' (1987, 1). And, as I will argue below, the evidence is strong that particularly until the early 1970s government actions were extremely helpful to Japan's big business and big finance institutions.

Empirically there is no doubt that the Japanese state is small. Comparing numbers of government employees as a proportion of the total population, or of the labour force, shows Japan to be one-third or more smaller than almost all the other major industrialized democracies (e.g. 9 per cent of the labour force versus 14–20 per cent elsewhere). The same is true for governmental expenditures, with Japan's spending as a percentage of GNP about 33 per cent compared to figures of over 40–50 per cent in most of Western Europe.

There has, however, been a good deal of debate lately about the relative strength or weakness of the Japanese state (in addition to the above citations on the links to business, see Muramatsu and Krauss, 1987; Krauss and Muramatsu, 1984; Otake, 1979; Inoguchi 1983, *inter alia*). When one looks at areas of state power other than simply economic policy, such as police effectiveness, the small size of the underground economy, the ability to restrict drugs and immigration, the stringency of anti-drunk driving provisions, regulation of health and safety and so forth, it is hard to conclude that the Japanese state is not a comparatively strong one (though compare Nordlinger, 1981).

Japan's domestic market is highly competitive. At one level it is a competition among Goliaths – Japan's giant banks, manufacturing firms, trading companies and industrial groups battling one another for market share, price competitiveness and product improvement. Particularly during the 1960s there was a great consolidation of ownership and cartelization in Japan's big industries. Today, Japan is unquestionably the home to more economic giants than any other country in the world. Some 94 of its firms are capitalized at over $5 billion, compared to 81 in the US, 18 in Britain and 12 in West Germany (*The Economist*, 14 November 1987). These account for over 60 per cent of Japan's market capitalization, compared to roughly 40–50 per cent for the other three. In addition, Japan has 152 companies in the Fortune International 500; it has the world's six largest trading companies and the world's five largest banks.

Unquestionably, there is a certain degree of market fixing, collusion and co-operation among these erstwhile competitors. But at the level of the giants, Japan is by no means a country of pure monopoly; in virtually no major industrial field does a single company or two companies control the bulk of sales; more typically four, five or more companies are in competition with one another (Kokuseisha, 1984, p. 348) and they compete fiercely. Moreover, there is virtually no movement of executives from one firm to another. As Dore (1986, pp. 72–3) so aptly put it 'Toyota could no more think of employing an ex-Nissan executive, for instance, than the wartime British army would have inducted a captured German officer into its ranks.' A final measure of Japan's business competition lies in the fact that its top 100 firms account for only 26 per cent of retail trade, compared to 41 per cent in the US and 45 per cent in West Germany.

Within the overall business structure of Japan, there are still quite high numbers of small and medium-sized firms, representing a larger number and proportion than in most of Europe and North America. These firms are often linked through subcontracting or financial ties to the larger firms. Large numbers are in the areas of distribution and service. Though politically linked to the conservative camp, about 1500–1600 such firms go bankrupt each month, still a further indication of the competitiveness of the Japanese market.

Finally, as has been noted at length above, the Japanese government has resisted taking an active role in redistributive policies, either through direct transfer payments or in the creation of an elaborate social safety net. In this sense, Japan is a prototype of what Titmuss has called the 'residual welfare state' (1958), a state whose commitment to the provision of social benefits is limited to those at the extremes of destitution and uncared for by family or friends.

While Japan is conservative, however, it has also been 'creative', breaking with traditional ideological positions dearly embraced by conservative regimes in other countries. Adjusting to changing international and domestic conditions has been critical to the national economy's development and to the success of Japan's conservatives in maintaining office. And with an ideologically hostile electoral camp ready to take office and radically overhaul entrenched policies should the conservatives fail to maintain their electoral majority, the incentives for conservatives to be flexible are far greater than where the likelihood of electoral defeat is less likely to result in massive policy revisions.

Thus, Japan's elite is relatively open, so long as the appropriate rites of passage have been made. A Tokyo University degree, even when held by the son (though rarely yet the daughter) of a labourer or a clerk, counts far more in the circles of business or politics than does a high class birth. And with about 90 per cent of Japan's youth finishing high school and with 40 per cent of Japan's relevant age cohort attending higher educational institutions, even the class biases inherent in the high cost of the 'best' educational opportunities are partly overcome.

Further, policies adopted at one time in Japan are often scuttled later should there be good enough reason politically to do so. This is not to suggest that bureaucratic entrenchment of vested interests and individual lethargy do not impede change; surely they do. But ideological adherence to a policy seems to count for far less. Consequently, Japan's conservatives have been relatively quick to adopt as their own many popular policy proposals put forward by their opponents, including environmental reform measures, regional development proposals, educational revisions, and so forth. In essence, Japan's conservatives have little of the class-bound encrustations of many of their European counterparts; they resemble far more the pragmatists of the Italian Christian Democrats than the entrenched class defenders found among French or British conservatives. In this they are far more frequently 'creative'.

When one finally returns to the original question of what differentiates Japanese public policy from that of the other industrialized democracies, and more importantly, why, the answer must be somewhat complex. But I will argue that the heart of the difference lies in the ways in which these elements at the core of Japan's creative conservatism have combined to shape the broad public policy profile of the country. They help to account for all three parts of the puzzles first posed: Japan's pro-business, anti-welfare orientation; rapid changes in economic and social welfare policies in the last decade and a half; and, finally, the anomalies of relatively low unemployment, high equality and low strike rates.

Important as the seemingly new policies are, they contain within themselves elemental continuities to policy directions of the past. In effect, what appears as change may camouflage continuity. Moreover, much as it may appear that Japanese public policies have not been 'truly' or 'consistently' conservative, the core of Japan's policies has been both highly consistent and unmistakably beneficial to its conservative political supporters, even though the kinds of challenges faced, the specifics of the regime's responses, and the overall distribution of burdens and benefits within the country may be different from those of its conservative counterparts in the West. Understanding the core of Japan's creative conservatism enables one to unravel this set of puzzles and to understand how Japan has come to be 'structured for change'. For all of the component parts are deeply rooted in Japan's political and historical evolution.

The Historical Roots of Creative Conservatism

Most public policies pursued in any country are the outgrowths of a series of root and branch decisions. Specific choices once made delimit future options; subsequent choices again create further restrictions. Just as the individual climbing a tree can always back down half way up and move off in new directions, so individual countries are not completely the prisoners of their past actions. But policy inertia is difficult to overcome in practice (Heclo, 1974; Wilensky, 1975).

In the case of Japan, options offered and paths taken during the pre-war period sharply circumscribed post-war possibilities. Furthermore, certain key directions marked off in the years immediately following the Second World War also provided a secondary momentum that was difficult to reverse. This historical legacy affected both public policy and the socio-economic groups that most influenced Japan's policymakers.

As I have argued elsewhere, what makes Japan truly unusual in historical terms is the fact that, alone among the industrialized democracies, it has been a country which has never had a government owing its election in whole, or in large measure, to organized labour.[3] As such, many components of the social welfare state that have become more or less the norm elsewhere due to labour and/or social democratic party strength have remained, at most, marginal to the Japanese policy agenda, as odd to Japan as chopsticks to Copenhagen.

At the same time, the institutionalization of political democracy, particularly after the Second World War, has made it essential for Japan's long ruling conservatives to remain sensitive to public opinion and electoral expediency. Indeed, the length of conservative rule in Japan is partly attributable to the very ability of Japan's policymakers to anticipate, refine, shape and accommodate changes in public and interest group demands, and to balance these with the ongoing requirements of their long-standing support base. This talent is at the heart of many recent policy changes and is at the core of the conservatives' creative balancing act that maintains a capitalist economy on the one hand and protects the nation's citizens from its most brutal and extreme potentialities on the other.

The pre-war history of Japanese public policy was shaped largely by elite perceptions of international vulnerability. From the arrival of Commodore Perry's Black Ships in 1853, through the reluctant signing of the unequal commercial treaties with countries from Russia to Holland to England and Peru, and on into the series of wars that marked Japan's foreign relations through the middle of the twentieth century, Japan's political elite struggled with the perception of national weakness and vulnerability. In the late nineteenth century, the warships and traders coming to Japan were remarkable testimony to the industrial, military and commercial backwardness that had resulted from Japan's 250 years of self-imposed isolation. Military victories over China, Russia and Germany helped assuage some of this collective sense of vulnerability. A strong national culture and social integration also mitigated worries about international inferiority. But the driving perception among elite policymakers was undoubtedly close to that of Yamagata Arimoto, an early leader of the Meiji Restoration, prime minister, principal architect of the nation's army and long-time adviser to the emperor. Geopolitics, he argued, was structured against Japan. Weak in natural resources, shut out of many of the world's most profitable markets, and facing an international arena in which the existing imperial powers had already divided up most of the world into spheres of influence, Japan must anticipate that the West would gang up against it, and must, in turn, prepare for this inevitability (Hackett, 1971).

While Japan hardly followed a linear course of action, and while individual policies ebbed, flowed and conflicted with one another as often as not, the overarching impression of pre-war public policy is that of major effort devoted to rapid economic modernization with a strong component of bureaucratic initiative. Early state creation and ownership of factories in munitions, shipping, communications, textiles, railways and the like gave way by the 1880s to private ownership of the nation's economic, industrial and financial core. Government leadership was complemented by private sector oligopolistic initiative. The largely family-owned, interlocking mega-corporations, known as *zaibatsu*, became key collaborators in much of the country's industrial and financial development. The national government in its fiscal, monetary and exchange rate policies served as a close and willing partner to the private sector. During this period, the issue was far less whether business or government was the more powerful; rather it was how powerfully the two could co-operate to structure an increasingly vibrant national economy, to develop overseas markets and to hold down the socio-political demands of the labour force and the rural peasant.

Parliamentary institutions were introduced in 1890 but the parliament's powers were heavily circumscribed by a number of restrictions, the most important of which was its lack of power to determine the composition of the cabinet. That right was reserved for the emperor. Sovereignty too was vested in the emperor. Not until 1925 did most males acquire the right to vote (Scalapino, 1953; Marshall, 1967; Hoston, 1985). Party cabinets were only a brief, decade-long episode during the 1920s, bracketed by oligarchic rule on one end and 'whole nation cabinets' on the other. It would be a mistake to ignore the democratic potential inherent in Japan's pre-war institutions and to assume an inevitable trajectory between the limits placed on democracy and the country's ultimate spiral into authoritarianism and war. Yet unquestionably, Japan's political institutions, modelled as they were largely on Bismarck's Prussia, were designed for authority, decisiveness and a concentration of power, not for democratic debate, division of power and minority rights. Economic growth and expansion abroad were the principal driving forces in the pre-war period. Citizens' rights, the protection of workers and the implementation of the social welfare state were not.

As has been well chronicled, throughout the pre-war period Japanese labour unions were late to develop, organizationally divided and subject to a restrictive blend of paternalism and overt suppression by both managers and government. It was only in the late 1910s that unions began to take form. The efforts of workers to organize in many key industries led to certain limited successes during the early 1920s but, as Gordon has demonstrated so well 'By the end of the 1920s, managers had contrived to banish almost all strong, independent unions from major shipyards, machine factories, and steel mills.' (Gordon, 1985, p. 125). A central trade union bill was defeated in the House of Peers in 1931, trade union membership never went above 8 per cent of the work force through the 1930s and the various socialist and workers parties operating in the electoral arena garnered at most 10 per cent of the vote as late as 1936 and 1937. It is true that during the late 1930s and the war itself a number of government measures were passed to provide some degree of wage stability, job security and retirement benefits to workers. Informal bureaucratic pressures also led certain firms to institute health care benefits. But, for the most part, these were restricted to the limited number of employees holding 'permanent' status, and were counterbalanced by restrictions over the rights of workers in heavy industry to change jobs, and, during the war, by restrictions on wage hikes as well. Few of the pre-war benefits entailed major transfer payments by government or had important redistributional effects on incomes. It was not until the end of the war and the initial efforts of the US occupation to stimulate unionization and to provide Japanese workers with guarantees of the right to organize, bargain collectively and to strike that the situation took on anything like the shape of labour management relations in the rest of the industrialized democracies.

In the area of social welfare the situation was correspondingly bleak. There was very little substantial social welfare legislation passed prior to the First World War, and very little between the wars (Maruo, 1986, p. 65). The national health system did not begin until 1925. Only in 1929 was a law passed that made it the responsibility of local officials to care for the poor. The Ministry of Health and Welfare was not created until 1938, the same year in which health insurance for the self-employed and pensions for the elderly were introduced as national policy. Again, the pre-war story is largely the story of very little and very late. Hence, while

Japan made significant gains in economic growth during the pre-war years and was recognized as one of the world's five major powers by the end of the First World War, in its labour and social welfare legislation it bore little relationship to countries such as Germany or England (Briggs, 1961; Polanyi, 1944).

One of the important historical differences between Japan and much of Western Europe can be traced also to the First World War. Even though Japan fought in the war and won major territorial concessions from Germany, the war wreaked none of the havoc on Japanese society that it did in Europe. There the impact of the war has been seen by many as a major catalyst in the improvement of social welfare measures. Lacking this stimulant, the social well-being of individual citizens, whether the old, the unemployed, the sick, the orphaned or the infirm, continued to be seen by the Japanese government, and by its ruling politicians, as predominantly the responsibility of the family, the neighbourhood and the local community. Social welfare was largely an outgrowth of personally developed human networks; it was not a *right* of citizenship. Quite obviously, Japan bore no relationship whatsoever to the emerging welfare states in Scandinavia (and, one might add, New Zealand and Australia by the turn of the century) where unionization levels were astronomical, labour was becoming 'decomodified' (Korpi, 1983; Esping-Andersen, 1984; Rein et al., 1986) and a wide variety of social benefits were becoming available on a universal scale without stigma to their recipients.

Thus, throughout the pre-war period, one sees the early roots of both parts of Japan's pro-business, anti-welfare policy orientation. The state and the major industrial and financial sectors collaborated for rapid economic development to meet international challenges and opportunities. Private competition was strong, particularly among the *zaibatsu* giants. Suffrage came late and union organization and socialism were officially thwarted and slow to develop on their own.

At the same time, rigid and inherited class status played a diminishing role in Japanese society during the same period. Rural landlords were a powerful force politically and economically, especially at the local level. A House of Peers gave formal recognition to the advanced social status of members of the Imperial family, retired bureaucrats, ex-*samurai* and others. But at the same time the military caste system had been eliminated in the late 1800s. Economic success afforded social prestige to the *nouveau riche* and the new industrial and financial tycoons. Most importantly, in the area of educational opportunities, Japan was far more egalitarian and advanced in its policies than many other industrialized countries. If Japan was to industrialize quickly and retain its national autonomy in world affairs, it needed to draw on all its resources – regardless of class background. Consequently, from the first days of the

Meiji Restoration, the government required that local communities provide universal schooling for children aged 6–15. In addition, secondary schools and national universities were created by the state. By the early 1900s a far larger proportion of Japanese children were in primary schools than was the case in England or on much of the Continent. Certainly, the economic status of one's family correlated positively with high school and university opportunities, but meritocratic passage of the entrance exam quickly became a far more significant criterion than family ties. A skilled populace meant at least a somewhat egalitarian approach to the development and identification of talent on a non-class basis.

Furthermore, it is important to recognize also that Japanese business leaders, both collectively through the Japan Industrial Club, local chambers of commerce and other employers' associations, and individually in their capacities as managers, took a number of forward steps in reducing tensions in industrial relations. In particular, by the end of the First World War, a number of managers in heavy industry, though by no means all, recognized the dangers in using massive layoffs of employees as a basis for controlling the costs of production and of relying on short-term hiring of skilled but itinerant craftsmen. In addition to catalyzing the drive toward unionism and precipitating radical confrontations between business and labour, plus being costly, such moves could easily deprive managers of workers who had developed important skills or else put them at their mercy. Far more beneficial, many of them argued, to hire recent graduates of elementary or high school, to give them the implicit guarantees of long-term employment, encourage their skill development and loyalty to the company, and blackball those who sought to move to competing companies (Gordon, 1985; Garon, 1987; Okochi et al., 1973). Though such moves clearly benefited business in guaranteeing a loyal and skilled work force, they also contributed to economic equality and to limited unemployment in ways that did not derive directly from the economic or political power of a comprehensive and militant labour movement (cf. Hibbs, 1978; Cameron, 1984). Here, too, a component of social equality was the outgrowth of economically motivated business decisions.

This historical legacy of a state favouring economic development and impeding both labour rights and a state-supported social welfare system, but counterbalanced by components of egalitarianism, has continued to leave its mark on Japan in the 1980s, although the period of the US occupation provided important radical overhauls in components of Japan's total public policy mix.

In the briefest terms, the US occupation began in 1945 committed to the 'demilitarization and democratization' of Japan. As a consequence, it restructured Japan's political institutions in a radical manner, including the introduction of popular sovereignty, the universalization of suffrage to males and females over the age of 20, and the requirement that the cabinet be formed by parliamentary vote and be made up of a majority of parliamentarians (Ward and Sakamoto, 1987; Takemae et al., 1977).

In public policy terms, the Americans introduced a series of economic measures initially designed to break the power of the largest financial houses and to redistribute economic wealth. Among other things, holding companies were disallowed, shares in several major companies were transferred to the public, and limits were placed on total shareholding by an individual (Aoki, 1987, p. 269). Land reform and radical inflation wiped out the economic muscle of many of Japan's pre-war powerful. Labour leaders, socialists and communists were freed from prisons and, in the first years of the occupation, the Americans took a number of steps to encourage union formation, including the passage of a series of laws modelled on the Wagner Law in the US. In just a few years, unionization rates soared to over 50 per cent; radical redistributive demands were widely pressed; and socialist and communist parties gained legitimacy and a component of popular support.

In many respects, this initial trajectory begun under the US occupation might well have meant a fundamentally restructured power balance that would have created the conditions for social democracy in Japan. A defeated and fragmented right would have confronted an invigorated and union-based left that could take advantage of legalized strikes in the workplace and free elections and mobilization power in the political arena to advance their agenda, much as had been done in the early years of the century in New Zealand or Australia (Castles, 1985), in the 1930s in Northern Europe (Korpi, 1983), or in 1945–51 in Britain.

In what has come to be called the 'reverse course', however, the direction of American policy shifted fundamentally due to changes in US domestic politics, the outbreak of the Cold War, the revolution in China, and a growing perception on the part of many American leaders that an economically strong (and conservative) Japan would be far more desirable than the potentially social democratic regime that seemed on the verge of emerging. Thus, by 1948–9 America had begun to throw its political weight toward Japan's conservative political leaders and its financial and industrial giants. It ended the anti-*zaibatsu* programme, fixed the foreign exchange rate at Y360, required tight fiscal measures, and lent both legitimacy and tanks to the battle against inflation and wage hikes (Hadley, 1970; Yamamura, 1967). Union rights were curbed, including checks on the right of public employees to strike, curtailment of the political liberties of union leaders and a host of measures reflecting the Taft-Hartley Act that had just been passed in the US (Takemae, 1977).

The Americans also laid the groundwork for a military alliance with

Japan, several components of which had an important impact on subsequent economic policy in Japan. Essentially, the United States provided a variety of economic assistance for Japan's military and security ties. As part of America's overall efforts to create an international monetary system and a free trade regime (Maier, 1978; Gilpin, 1987; Krasner, 1978), it acted as Japan's advocate in the international arena. US sponsorship was critical to Japan's becoming a member of a variety of international organizations including the UN, the IMF, GATT, the OECD, and so forth, thereby reducing the otherwise steep political barriers to Japan's commercial activities. In addition, US strategic interests loomed sufficiently large and its position as economic and military leader was so relatively secure that America willingly tolerated a massive imbalance in its economic activities with Japan, allowing Japan extremely favourable access to US markets, technology, capital and raw materials as a means of underwriting the anti-communist and pro-business orientations of the Japanese government. This was to play a large role in integrating Japan's economy with that of the US during the first two decades after the war, laying the groundwork for what Gilpin has referred to as the Nichibei economy (Gilpin, 1987).

In the area of social welfare, even though several steps were taken to advance the guarantees of social welfare it was clearly the American model of private insurance schemes, rather than the British or Scandinavian model of state guarantees, that provided the principal inspiration. Thus, in this area at least, the pre-war Japanese legacy and the post-war American legacy were highly congruent (and American policy was relatively consistent).

Several other legacies of the occupation have an important bearing on the contemporary policy mixture in Japan. The most obvious political contribution involved the institution of parliamentary supremacy, popular sovereignty, universal suffrage for both males and females, as well as the freedoms of speech and free organization. These quite clearly made post-war Japanese politics a far more democratic process than had been the case under the pre-war system, and gave far more importance to citizen demands and popular politics than was the case earlier.

Furthermore, even though the occupation eventually reinforced many of the powers of the big financial and industrial organizations, and eventually turned its weight against the most radical elements in the union movement, its positive stimulus to the Japanese left must also be recognized. Indeed, though weakened in the later years of the occupation, Japan's labour movement nonetheless continued to be strong enough in the 1950s and 1960s to secure job security and wage hikes for the one-third or so of Japan's workers who were union members. But possibly the biggest contributions toward social equality by the Americans came as a result of the land reform, the partial *zaibatsu* dissolution and the massive confiscatory inflation that followed the war. Established wealth was drastically reduced and large portions of the Japanese citizenry found themselves more equal, even if only in their collective immiseration. This contribution toward social equality was bolstered by the Americans' radical restructuring of the educational system, opening up opportunities even further than they had been in the pre-war period. In this sense, then, much of Japan's contemporary egalitarianism is the direct legacy of occupation policies.

Thus, the historical bias with which Japan entered the 1950s was one highly congruent with the overall pro-business, anti-welfare orientation that characterizes it today. Japan began its industrialization comparatively late in international terms. Facing relatively weak pressures for political and economic equality at home, but a hostile strategic situation abroad, Japan's political and business leaders were quick to choose, and steady in their adherence to, a policy course that concentrated the limited amount of national resources available to them on the goals of rapid economic growth, improving the country's international terms of trade and strengthening the country's military capabilities. Given these competing priorities, an expansion of political rights, the creation of a public sector safety net or the curtailing of oligopoly were neither politically necessary nor economically affordable.

At the same time, unlike the case in the conservative market economies of Britain, the United States and various countries on the continent, the Japanese business community had made certain tentative commitments to keeping a relatively stable work force. For very self-interested and less than altruistic reasons, Japanese business leaders in most of the major firms came to the conclusion that it was better business and social policy to develop an internal labour market, to hire at least a large part of their workforce with the expectation of keeping them on permanently, to retrain them internally, and to avoid massive layoffs during periods of excessive production.

The military component was struck from this equation after the war ended; economic equality was increased as a result of the land reform and the massive post-war inflation; and the political rights given to labour and the political left broadened the spectrum of political choice considerably. At the same time, the economic devastation wreaked by the war, Japan's unfavourable terms of international trade, resurgence of political conservatism, economic oligopolies and bureaucratic power all served to give new life to many of the policy orientations of the pre-war period. There is no denying the changes in political and economic power that took place under the US occupation; at the same time these did not result in a full scale recalibration of the nation's public policy profile, particularly as regards such key policies as economic growth, social welfare and unemployment.

Like the political leaders in virtually all of the industrialized countries whose industrial might had been obliterated by the war, those in Japan were confronted with the necessity of rapid economic restructuring and rebuilding. But unlike Germany, Austria, France, England or the Benelux countries, all of which had residual pre-war commitments to state directed social welfare, Japan's leaders had no such bureaucratic or policy legacy. At the same time, they had a much more meritocratic heritage in terms of educational opportunities and rights to employment than was the case in most of these. To this extent, Japan's post-war policy choices began from a starting-point historically and politically quite different from that of the other industrialized democracies.

Structured for Change: Creative Conservatism in Action

For roughly the first twenty-five years after the war, Japan's political economy adhered to a relatively consistent course. It was highly protectionist of agriculture, domestic manufacturing and finance, although open to the relatively free import of most non-agricultural raw materials. It was supportive of manufactured exports. It rested heavily on low state expenditures for social welfare. Such statements are suggestive of a rather static, closed and reactive political economy, but in fact, at both the level of the state and the level of the firm, Japan's political economy was highly dynamic, adaptive to international market opportunities, and flexible in its labour market policies. These characteristics were particularly conducive to the many rapid adjustments that were made during the early to mid 1970s.

From the outbreak of the Korean War until the quadrupling of world oil prices in 1973, Japan's GNP grew at rates vastly greater than in the other industrial countries, allowing Japan to make a remarkably rapid transformation from an agrarian-based to an industrially-based economy and catapulting the country quickly up the ranks of comparative economic performance in the OECD statistics. (As late as 1950 nearly half of Japan's work force was in the primary sector; by 1980 it was less than 10 per cent.) Yet, for the bulk of the high growth period, as has been noted throughout, Japan remained a low spender for welfare and state transfer payments were minimal. It was not only social welfare that received small shares of the total budget. Military defence and security also trailed that of the other industrials by a large margin.[4] For many, Japan was the quintessence of the 'economic animal', a country in which economic growth was relentlessly pursued at all levels – government, industrial sector, firm, and individual – to the virtual exclusion of all other priorities.

Key Japanese government agencies, including the Ministries of

Finance, International Trade and Industry, Construction and Transportation, among others, worked closely with business federations, industrial groups, the banking sector, private firms, trading companies and local governmental agencies to expand Japan's industrial base through an elaborate mixture of public policies and private initiatives. In the phrase of Chalmers Johnson (1982), Japan was a 'developmental state'.[5] Among other things, the government provided a policy mixture that included tax incentives for favoured industrial sectors, protective restrictions on foreign imports of capital and goods, an ample supply of cheap capital for R&D (Research and Development) and investment by targeted firms and sectors, favoured and fixed foreign exchange rates, an extensive expansion of the industrial infrastructure from roads to railways to air transportation, plus harbours, communications networks, and the like. The government also encouraged 700–1000 new mergers and cartels per year during the 1950s and 1960s. These plus collusive short-term interest rate fixing by banks and administered prices in highly concentrated industries were largely exempted from anti-monopoly regulation. Rapid industrial transformation and export-led growth were at the centre of these specific policy actions.

Important as government policies and plans may have been, it is important to stress that they were largely market-compatible (Samuels, 1987; Okimoto, 1989). There were no equivalents to the French 'national champions'. Japanese firms operated within this context in a highly complementary fashion that led to widespread success for many of them and in turn to national economic gains as well. Among other things, firms gained international competitiveness by holding down wages, but more importantly by preventing increases in wages and prices from being reflected in export prices. This was accomplished by at least two key components of labour market policy.

On the one hand, large Japanese firms relied heavily on subcontract labour and part-time employment to create flexibility in their labour costs without heavy reliance on layoffs and unemployment. Expanding during times of boom and contracting during times of slowdown, subcontract and part-time work afforded Japanese firms the flexibility to pass on many of the costs of adjustment to one segment of labour without having to confront its stronger, unionized segment.

Meanwhile, firms' own core workforces, often only 30 per cent of the total workforce, made it possible for them to adjust through rationalization and the introduction of new technologies and operational methods as well (Kyogoku, 1987, p. 33).[6] So-called 'permanent employees' enjoyed relative guarantees of employment until age 55 or so, systematic promotions and wage increases, a series of bonuses and subsidies related to family size and need, as well as to company profitability, plus a wide array of company services ranging from vacation spots to health care facilities to marriage counselling services. In some firms, these benefits were the result of collective organizing. In others, the benefits were introduced in an effort to prevent the emergence of unionization. In either case, the result was horizontal, rather than vertical, fragmentation in the work force – permanent employees and their benefits versus non-permanent employees and their relative lack of such benefits. The sharp line between labour and capital stressed by Marxists was replaced by countless blurred shades of hierarchy widely perceived as a modest approximation of homogeneity and a vaguely generalized equality.

Rationalizations on the shop floor were assisted greatly by the organization of the core labour force within most large manufacturing companies. Enterprise unionism, the bonus system, and at least some implicit guarantees of long-term employment linked the fortunes of unionized workers to that of their firms. Management gained wage flexibility, without the need for layoffs. Workers were treated as resources to be developed and utilized rather than commodities to be bought and used up. By developing what Koike (1983, 1987) has labelled an internal labour market, these firms could also retrain their own workers for flexible use on different jobs, without confronting the serious limits of union-based job classification that prevailed in the US or Britain for example. By the early 1960s, after management control had been established, the introduction of new processes was rarely used to 'rationalize' the work force through layoffs; instead, the core workforce was constantly being retrained to increase the firm's productivity and profits. Skill development, flexible job classifications, wages linked to company profitability and relatively secure employment made large segments of Japan's blue-collar work force similar to the white-collar work forces in other countries (Koike, 1987). Concurrently, contracting plants were aided in achieving similar flexibility and technical upgrading. In this way they developed what Piore and Sabel have called a 'tradition of permanent innovation and organizational plasticity' (1984, p. 225). The overall result was typically better products and more highly skilled workers. Furthermore, the system reduced labour-management tensions in the market place and assisted Japanese firms to adjust more freely to domestic and international market opportunities (Dore, 1986).

Thus, large parts of the labour force benefited from low unemployment, retraining and an overall jump in absolute economic well-being, even though Japanese wages lagged well behind increases in industrial productivity. Between 1955 and 1970, Japanese productivity rose approximately 3.6 times while real wages rose only about 2.3 times (Boltho, 1975 p. 181; Pempel, 1978b, p. 172). This lag was far greater than that in other industrial countries (Pempel, p. 173).

The extent of government initiative and the importance of 'administrative guidance' from Japanese government agencies has undoubtedly been overstressed as the central source of Japan's macrolevel success. At the same time, the workings of the market have been given excessive applause by economists. Surely the complementary blending of government and business was essential for the success. Despite the many specific battles pitting know-it-all government regulators against creative entrepreneurs, or, conversely, far-sighted spokesmen for the national interest against recalcitrant and unimaginative managers, the overall impression that emerges of economic policy during the period is that of a government pursuing market-enhancing economic incentives that helped many Japanese companies to profit, and of private industries that competed vigorously with one another to achieve market shares and product innovation, while at the same time resting comfortably on the assurance that collectively all of them could count on an unabashedly pro-business government to set favourable macroeconomic policies.

At the heart of government policy during this period was a confluence of measures that essentially, in the period from 1952 until 1971 (the breakdown of the Bretton Woods monetary system), provided a protectionist hothouse for industry as well as a protectionist fortress for agriculture and small business. Japanese sovereignty kept the outside world of more competitive products and more capital-rich, technologically and managerially sophisticated firms at bay, thus allowing Japanese products to dominate the expanding domestic market and creating an industrial structure that could eventually withstand foreign competition at home and then ultimately compete with it abroad.

Low social welfare spending and a small state were integral components of the government's macroeconomic policies. By keeping down the amounts spent elsewhere, the government was able to focus its initially limited resources on key sectors of the economy. And by restraining the extent to which government programmes provided a social safety net and by restricting the ability of Japanese capital to move out of the country, the government encouraged savings and investment rates unmatched among the other industrialized countries.[7] In the absence of a social welfare net, Japanese citizens had few choices but to save large amounts to provide for personal expenditures in health care, retirement, education, and the like. The absence of government assistance in the area of housing subsidies, mortgage underwriting and consumer credit meant an additional stimulation to savings from those desiring expensive capital goods. And by insulating Japan's savings market from international competition, and by artificially holding down the interest rates paid to Japanese savers, government policy generated large pools of capital that were available at low cost to financial institutions and industrial borrowers (Zysman, 1983; Pempel, 1978b; Johnson, 1982).

This overall, pro-business, anti-labour bias to economic and social policy should not be particularly surprising given the fact that during this entire period (and indeed into the mid 1980s as well), Japan had exclusively conservative governments. But conservative dominance was not maintained simply by the strength of big business and finance. Indeed, critical to LDP predominance was the support of agriculture and small business. This post-war coalition in Japan is far from self-evidently logical, particularly given the rapid industrialization of Japan and the high domestic costs of the protection afforded to Japanese industry. Moreover, with the exception of Australia, New Zealand and possibly Italy, it is difficult to find electorally successful examples of such coalitions among the OECD nations continuing into the 1970s and 1980s. Quite typically the exigencies of an industrialized economy make it difficult to maintain such coalitions without the superimposition of overt police or military force (Moore, 1966).

In the Japanese case the coalition was sustained by the somewhat selective nature of the protectionist policies followed and their benefits to both segments of the economy: protection was against agricultural imports and manufactured imports but *not* raw materials. The overall terms of Japanese trade, particularly during this period, but even afterwards, have been marked by the virtual absence of primary exports and by extremely low levels of manufactured imports. Japanese imports in the early 1970s were nearly 70 per cent primary, a proportion generally 20 per cent higher than most other industrialized countries, while its exports were over 90 per cent manufactured, again considerably higher than other countries. Consequently Japanese manufacturing benefited from a policy of cheap imports of raw materials, and from protection against most foreign manufactured goods.[8] Meanwhile agriculture did not suffer heavily from these barriers to manufactured imports. Rather, the government maintained an extensive system of price subsidies to Japanese farmers, as well as unnecessarily high levels of government spending in rural areas, both of which kept farming incomes as high as those in urban and manufacturing areas (Donnelly, 1984, pp. 350–4). The government could afford to do this in turn because overall economic growth remained high, while expenditures for other forms of social welfare and defence were low. Thus, as Japanese industry developed goods for the home market, the Japanese farm family could enjoy the luxuries of television, refrigerator, air conditioning, car and the like along with their urban counterpart, with no particular collective clamour for lower tariffs in the expectation of significantly cheaper or higher quality foreign goods, even if that might well have been the result.

Much the same strategy prevailed with regard to small business. Self-employed workers and unpaid family workers constitute a far larger proportion of the labour force in Japan (29 per cent) than in France (17 per cent), Germany (14 per cent), the United States (9 per cent) or the

United Kingdom (8 per cent) (Patrick and Rohlen, 1987, p. 335). Moreover, in manufacturing, 46.5 per cent of Japanese workers are employed in establishments with fewer than 50 employees, significantly higher than most other industrialized countries, with the possible exception of Italy (44.4 per cent) (Patrick and Rohlen, 1987, p. 336). Thus the small sector of business is potentially critical to both the national economy and to the political fortunes of those who seek their votes. In much the same way as agriculture, small business benefited from the combination of protectionism and subsidies that prevailed into at least the early 1970s. Large retailing establishments that would compete with smaller shops were essentially prohibited as well. Similarly the government largely followed a 'hands off' policy toward smaller businesses in the enforcement of tax laws, and labour and environmental standards.

In this regard, the internationally inefficient Japanese agricultural, manufacturing and retail sectors were insulated from market competition by a wide variety of favoured policies. Retaining these policies became increasingly costly. Yet, so long as growth rates remained relatively high, and the more competitive segments of Japanese industry could enjoy cheap raw materials and a secure platform from which to export, the total costs of sustaining such inefficient sectors seemed a small price to pay for the large number of votes that could be delivered to the LDP which in turn could continue to support pro-business policies, including protection. (Surely big business had no reason to expect better treatment from any alternative government.) Thus, the coalition could hold quite well.

The situation of labour and the consumer was very different. And yet, the LDP stayed in power and was able to continue policies whose major effects worked against both sectors. Why were there not major gains in unionization; why no greater electoral support for the opposition parties; in short, why did Japan not begin to look politically more like Western Europe? A number of factors obviously played their historical part, ranging from government repression of radical unions, especially in the 1950s and early 1960s, to the standard difficulties of union organizing; from gerrymandered electoral districts to the complexities of information gathering by union organizers; from speed of industrial development to moves away from large scale manufacturing where labour unionizing has traditionally been easiest, and undoubtedly a host of other factors. Yet, several country-specific factors should be noted.

In addition to the well-noted fragmentation in the Japanese left, including several major federations competing for union affiliation at the national level, no one of which could claim to represent more than one-third of the nation's union members, and at least three political parties claiming to represent the interests of organized labour, two additional features stand out. First, the Japanese unions, particularly in the public sector, and more importantly, their main electoral vehicle, the Japan Socialist Party, remained committed to a totalist political strategy of class revolution. Moreover, the party rested a good deal of its public appeal on foreign policy attacks against the US even as the Japanese economy grew by double digits annually, as domestic consumption soared, and as the Japanese public continued to express widespread admiration for the US in world affairs. As Otake (1989) has demonstrated, a critical juncture was reached in Japan early in the 1960s when the JSP, following successful mass mobilizations and protests against the ratification of the Japan-US Security Treaty, and under heavy influence from radical party functionaries and labour organizers, opted for a policy line and a strategy of anti-conservative attack dramatically at odds with the more accommodative policies adopted by the German SPD at Bad Godesburg. Under such influences, the JSP became increasingly marginalized, attempting with decreasing success to appeal to voters under a radically marxist economic banner, and with its principal focus on foreign and military affairs rather than domestic social and economic programmes. Both leftist voter support and union membership dropped steadily over the 1960s and 1970s.

The internalization of the labour market and the role of subcontract and part-time workers noted above also played a part in keeping down collective power by the national union federations.

One additional point should be made in this regard. In many other industrialized countries, the most marginalized workers typically form a reproducing lower class, often further distinguished by race and ethnicity. Some sectors of business urged a liberalizing of immigration laws in the 1950s in an effort to acquire cheap labour. This approach was rejected and since then exceptionally strict immigration regulations have left Japan with virtually no foreign immigrants in the work force. Nor is race or ethnicity particularly relevant. Moreover, economic distinctions in Japan are primarily intra-familial, rather than between one family and another. Occupational discrimination in Japan has its most negative effects on women,[9] the elderly (that is, those over the low 'retirement' age of 55),[10] on younger workers, on subcontract employees, on seasonal workers, and the like (Wood, 1980, p. 4). A not atypical working-class family in Japan could easily include a 43-year-old husband with permanent employment earning a relatively good salary and benefits at a major firm, his wife doing piece-work for much lower pay and few benefits in a small assembly plant, perhaps his semi-retired father working at a reduced salary for a subsidiary of his previous employer, and two children, one of whom might be doing part-time night work as he or she attends a college or technical school, and the other a low paid newly employed worker in a department store. In addition, the husband's brother and his family might well be partially dependent on some form of *ad hoc* financial help during downturns in the business performance of their small family-run bread shop or subcontracting factory. The image could be extended more broadly, but the central point is that many of the most important wage discriminations present in Japan affect individual family members in highly differentiated ways, ways far more important than their general effects on families as collective economic entities. The end result is a further blurring of class divisions as some of the most important traditional divisions are reflected within the same families in Japan.

A final factor weighing heavily in the success of Japan's conservative coalition and its ability to outflank the opposition and attract popular support lies with the United States. The domestic trade-offs among agriculture, small business and big business were particularly facilitated by the co-operative behaviour of the United States during the 1950s. American foreign policy interests in Asia, and in particular the anxiety to keep Japan as a close ally, led the US to provide widespread assistance to the conservative coalition governing Japan. This was particularly the case with regard to economic policy and security. As was noted above, US sponsorship was vital in Japan's becoming a member of such international organizations as the UN, the IMF, the OECD and the GATT. As a result, many barriers to Japanese trade dropped around the world. Despite certain product specific disputes in areas such as textiles during the 1950s, US markets remained largely open and receptive to the purchase of growing numbers of Japanese products.[11] More importantly, while US companies invested heavily in Western Europe from the end of the Second World War until the present and were able to protect their technological advantages from European competitors, investments in Japan were minimal until the mid 1970s and sales of their technologies proved to be bargain basement giveaways for Japanese industry. A large measure of this was undoubtedly due to Japanese barriers erected against foreign investment, and partly resulted from a mistaken perception by many American companies that Japan offered poor potential both as a market and as a competitor. But the major role of the US government in providing assistance to Japan in developing its export markets, in acquiring foreign technology, and in keeping its borders closed must also be acknowledged as a major aid to Japan's economic success (Krasner, 1987). Even more importantly, the US provided military and defence protection for Japan that allowed the country to keep its own military budget quite low. Patrick and Rosovsky (1976, p. 45), for example, calculate that European levels of defence spending might have reduced Japan's annual growth rate by about 2 per cent per year – instead this was a vast sum left over for civilian investment. In short, the US government by its actions proved to be a major prop for the conservative coalition within Japan. It is hard, particularly, to imagine that the coalition would not have divided along some version of agricultural-business lines had the US pressed its comparative economic advantages in Japan in the same way as it did in Western Europe during the 1950s and early 1960s. It is also difficult not to imagine internal splits over military spending and/or greater electoral support for the left if the Japanese government had attempted significant increases in its defence budget. Even more significantly, it is hard to imagine that the conservatives would have remained in power for as long, and with the margins they enjoyed, had the overall policy of rapid economic growth behind protectionist barriers not been at least tacitly endorsed by the American government.

Creative Conservatism under Challenge

The policy and politics that worked so harmoniously for Japan's conservative coalition during the first twenty-five years or so following the Second World War came under serious challenges in the last few years of the 1960s and the first years of the 1970s from three major sources, most of them traceable to the very successes that had been achieved. Within Japan, the population became more urbanized, reducing the voting and economic significance of the agricultural sector. In addition, increasing citizen affluence led to heightened perceptions of the costs of rapid economic growth in areas such as environmental pollution, as well as of the low levels of social infrastructure and social welfare provisions compared to other countries of comparable wealth. In effect, there was an electoral threat from a citizenry no longer content to accept the basic orientations of high economic growth and protectionism if the costs were to be a polluted environment, minimal social welfare, higher domestic prices and trickle-down economics.

Abroad, Japan's export successes led to a widespread attack from the other industrialized nations on the closed character of the Japanese market and demands for export restraint and market access. No longer was Japan able to draw international sympathy with its pleas of being a resource-poor nation needing special treatment from its allies in order to sustain economic growth and, by implication, to ward off the domestic threat from the left.

The third challenge came from OPEC in the form of the massive increase in world oil prices. As is well known, Japan depended for virtually all of its energy on oil, almost all of which was imported (Caldwell, 1981; Morse, 1981; Samuels, 1987).

These combined pressures forced the conservatives to strike out in several new policy directions to placate critics at home and abroad, and to do so in a manner that would ensure electoral success as well. Thus, to meet the domestic demands, as noted above, spending for a wide variety of social welfare measures increased rapidly, generally from 1972–3 to the early 1980s. It is worth noting, however, that the introduction of these measures came primarily from a conservative government anxious to forestall electoral changes, rather than from a socialist government anxious to institutionalize them. In this regard the measures were more Bismarckian than Beveridgite. The government also undertook an anti-pollution campaign that was initially unpopular with industry's captains, but which headed off the growing protests from environmentalists, and ultimately undermined the possibilities for a serious electoral threat from Japanese Greens. This was in contrast to Western Europe, and particularly West Germany, where more rigid party lines led frequently to an inability on the part of existing political parties to adapt to the environmental challenge.

The costs of these changes, however, were met largely through government borrowing. Japan's domestic budget deficit soared, particularly after the drastic rise in world-wide oil prices, deficit spending being a politically more palatable prescription than most alternatives. The deficit dependency ratio which had been just over 4 per cent in 1970 rose rapidly to the 11–16 per cent range for 1971–4, then to just below 30 per cent in 1976 and 1977, and finally up to 37 per cent in 1978. For the next two years it continued at over 30 per cent (Yamamura, 1985, pp. 497–8).

To meet the trade and anti-protectionist demands of Japan's industrialized, and to some extent its less industrialized, trading partners, policy was shifted massively in other ways as well. Thus, part of the deficit expansion during the late 1970s was due to pressure from Western nations for Japan to become one of the three locomotives, along with the US and West Germany, whose domestic demand expansion was to pull the world's economy out of recession. But, in addition to expanding its fiscal policies, the Japanese government, along with big business, began a concerted effort to move from an industrially-based to a knowledge-based economy, and to concentrate investment in higher value-added production where Japan could still compete effectively with other producers (JETRO, 1975). The introduction of numerically controlled machine tools, robotics, and other high technology production methods was undertaken on a large scale at home.[12] Even Japan's so-called depressed industries remained 'progressive' in that they put a fair proportion of their investment into rationalizing through labour-saving and cost-cutting measures, as well as into replacement investment (Dore, 1987, p. 41).

In addition there was a major expansion in overseas investment, with the total investment for the four years 1973–6 being nearly double that for the previous twenty years (Keizai Koho Center, 1987, p. 56). Import regulations were liberalized as were those for foreign investment. Tariff levels for manufactured imports to Japan dropped quickly to become probably the lowest in the industrialized world, while actual quotas were the lowest. By the early 1980s Japan had some of the world's most liberal statutes on imports, capital investment and overseas movement.

Finally, to meet the massive rises in world oil prices (and in other commodities following the massive inflationary period of the mid 1970s), Japan followed a twofold strategy. One part of the strategy was to expand its exports in real terms, something that was aided by the internal adjustments going on in Japan's factories. Between 1973 and 1982 Japan had to double her exports in real terms just to import 7 per cent more in real terms due to the change in world prices (Dore, 1986, p. 45). So Japan remained a major exporter, but an exporter adjusting quickly to a changed environment. This expansion of exports aided the domestic Japanese economy of course while it simultaneously exasperated its much slower moving trade partners. Indeed, between 1970 and 1980 there was nearly a 10 per cent rise in total domestic employment (Kokuseisha, 1981, p. 31).

The second major step Japan took to meet the jump in foreign prices, particularly oil, involved a major agreement with its private sector trade unions. In 1975 what some have labelled a '*de facto* incomes policy' was reached. Under its terms, private sector labour unions agreed to moderate their wage increases (which in the previous year had been 32.9 per cent contributing to, as well as responding to, the massive inflation in Japan during that year). Agreement was facilitated by the fact that most union contracts were set annually at the time of the 'spring offensive' so that collective union action was possible, and leapfrogging contract demands were avoided. In addition, a one year's delay could quickly be evaluated collectively twelve months later to guarantee that all parties were playing their respective parts.

Under the terms of the agreement unions moderated their wage demands in exchange for job security from employers and low taxes and anti-inflationary policies by the government. The annual wage increases achieved through the spring offensive fell from 32.9 per cent in 1974 to 13.1 per cent in 1975, and then dropped further to the 5–6 per cent range by the end of the decade and into the early 1980s (Shimada, 1983; Shinkawa, 1984) Tsujinaka, 1986; Kume, 1988 *inter alia*).

In many respects this agreement made a major contribution not only to the ability of Japan's manufacturers to adjust quickly and at low cost to the changing international conditions, especially massive rises in world prices, and to curtail inflationary pressures at home. It also played a big role in reducing the strike rates, especially within the private sector, as well as allowing income levels to remain relatively equal and unemployment to remain low.[13]

At base, then, a number of important new directions have appeared in Japanese public policy during the past 15 years or so as the conservative coalition has reacted to and at times anticipated domestic and international pressures that did not exist during the heyday of its early reign. Electoral vulnerability led to some of these policy changes; accommodation to OPEC, the US, the EEC and to multinational firms and banks has necessitated others.

The cumulative picture of these changes might well be applauded as dramatic, flexible, smart and humane. After all, Japan's economy has continued to grow rather steadily, and has done so with lower inflation and lower unemployment than the other industrialized countries. Indeed, Japan has the best economic performance in the OECD on several comparisons (Schmidt, Ch. 3, this volume *inter alia*). Social democrats might be disturbed by the pace, but certainly not the direction of social security expenditures, by the overall expansion in jobs and the low levels of formal unemployment, and quite possibly the apparently more harmonious relations between business and labour.

Several more negative consequences have accompanied the above successes, however. Three of these are likely to have profound effects on the future direction of Japanese public policy, and also on the character of Japan's political economy.

Creative Conservatism: The Attempt to Survive

The first consequence that must be noted is that the commitment to social welfare has not been institutionalized. Faced with massive deficit spending burdens, Japan carried out a number of measures collectively labelled 'administrative reform' in the early 1980s. The national railway system, the telecommunications system and many public corporations have been privatized. Extreme fiscal austerity has been introduced for the national and local governments (Kumon, 1984; Campbell, 1985). Several of these have had devastating effects on Japan's major public sector unions.

In addition, the cutbacks have been used to roll back the embryonic efforts at state support for social welfare. Social welfare spending was curtailed in the early 1980s and several components of the health care programme were substantially rolled back. Social security benefits were made more restrictive and the rapid increases in overall transfer payments that took place in the 1970s slowed down dramatically in most areas, and actually witnessed absolute reductions in others such as social welfare. Overall, the policy measures carried out as a result of 'administrative reform' led to serious rollbacks in the trend line of budget deficits, transfer payments, medical care programmes, and social security and retirement provisions among other things. Carrying out these changes has also loosened the long standing ties between many of the most important segments of Japan's business and financial community on the one hand and the government on the other.[14] But it is largely because Japanese business has become so internationally competitive that the once strong paternal ties are no longer needed. In declining industries such as aluminium, steel and shipbuilding, the government continues to maintain active policies of adjustment that include labour market, tax and cartel arrangements designed to speed adjustments (Boyer, 1983). And in higher technology industries such as high speed computers, new industrial materials, semiconductors, biotechnology, teleoptics, microelectronics, fibre optics and a variety of others, government-business collaboration looks more like it did in traditional industrial sectors during the 1950s than like the free working out of market competition along principles of *laissez faire*. In short, government and business continue to work closely together, albeit in frequently different forms and with different policy measures than were pursued two decades ago. But international competitiveness for Japanese industry and finance remains the principal policy objective to which specific measures are directed.

Other long-standing elements at the core of Japanese conservatism remain as well. The several laws that were enacted between 1974 and 1977 to provide formal benefits to the work force were not followed up by substantial additions in the decade following (Kume, 1988). Moreover, employment guarantees gave way to the relatively unthinkable 3 per cent unemployment rates of 1986–87.[15] Although it is not dramatic, Japan's Gini index is on the rise, indicating a slight lessening of overall income equality (Economic Planning Agency, 1984, pp. 25–7). Most importantly, in the public sector labour has suffered major setbacks as a result of government policies to privatize the telecommunications system, the railways and several other monopolies where public sector unionism had once been extremely strong. Labour particularly in the private sector, won some, perhaps permanent, victories in the 1970s, but it has by no means ensured itself a permanent place in national policymaking on a level anywhere near that in most European countries.[16] However this would appear to be a more open question as some consolidation of private sector unions has been taking place with the formation of the new labour federation, Rengo. Any real improvements made by private sector unions would appear to be separate from those for the public sector unions, with the result that union unity in one sphere may have been achieved at the expense of progress in another.

With the budget cutbacks, the size of the Japanese government in personnel and in budgetary spending either held constant or shrank in the 1980s, and in effect returned to its earlier, smaller and more natural shape, still a further indication of the relative permanence of creative conservatism's core.

The reasons for most of these changes can be traced quite simply to the conservatives' electoral successes. Whereas in the middle years of the 1970s the LDP clung to the thinnest of parliamentary margins and seemed destined to be forced at least to share power with one or more of the minor parties, starting in 1979, but most notably in the 1980 dual elections, the party reversed its previous declines. By 1986 it seemed destined to retain office for another thirty-odd years.[17] Certainly no opposition party or coalition appeared likely to provide a significant challenge. Conservative electoral strength has allowed for policy reversals in important areas, helping both to explain the changes of the 1970s and their many reversals in the 1980s. Yet not all of the changes have been ephemeral.

If one part of the economic linkage looks similar, another is vastly different. Economic liberalization in particular has begun to erode the close collaboration between agriculture, small business and big business that in the past depended so heavily on protectionism. For example, as part of the administrative reform effort, the once politically critical subsidy programmes for agriculture and small businesses have been reduced, thereby threatening part of the conservative electoral base. At the same time, while barriers to manufactured imports have been quick to tumble, those against agricultural products have been far more resilient. In this respect, Japan does not look quite as bad as France, but its agricultural tariff structure is far more restrictive than that of West Germany, England, Italy or Canada. Government subsidies for agricultural products have begun to erode; a curb has been placed on rural funding; and in many product areas, such as beef, tobacco and citrus fruits, liberalization has begun, even if the speed and extent has not fully pleased foreign exporters or many Japanese business leaders. Consequently, the harmony between Japan's advanced and its retarded sectors that was so critical to conservative success in the first twenty-five years after the war, when growth was high and economic inefficiencies could be tolerated as a political necessity, is far more dubious today.

The domestic coalition that has been at the heart of Japan's creative conservatism has begun to change as a result, consciously or not, of the policy direction the conservatives have pursued. At the macrolevel, agriculture is decreasing in significance and seems destined to be further burdened by economic liberalization. Meanwhile, urban consumers and blue-collar unionized workers, particularly in the most export-oriented segments of Japan's manufacturing sector, are beginning to benefit from the policies of economic liberalization, job guarantees, and social infrastructure creation. The conservatives have begun to shift their electoral base, with decreasing reliance on the diminishing rural areas and an increased support level within the cities and metropolitan areas

(Miyake, 1985). This coalitional shift has been reflected in certain redirections in the policy nexus of the country.

Cumulatively viewed, therefore, the current picture of Japanese public policy undoubtedly reflects important changes in numerous functional areas over the past two decades or so. Many of these have been taken against conservative interests and are quite contrary to expectations of a conservative regime, rooted as it has been in business, finance, big industry, small merchants and agriculture, and simultaneously almost totally devoid of support from organized labour. But the changes of the 1970s were in many respects tactical shifts designed to head off even greater changes, or possibly even a loss of governmental power. Many of them returned like rubber bands to their original shape once the electoral pressure was removed. Precisely such creativity in Japan's conservatism has been at the heart of its survival.

Equally striking though is how resilient the core of conservatism has been, particularly in the manner in which Japan's economic policies adapted to the vastly different circumstances of the 1970s and 1980s, providing continued assistance, but in a vastly different form, to Japanese business and finance. These firms and sectors have benefited enormously from their past protection. Such protection allowed them to develop market shares, increase capital and labour stock and gain international competitiveness. Where once head-to-head competition with the world's best would have been impossible, today such competition is more easily withstood. Indeed, the now far more modernized domestic manufacturing and financial sectors, plus the internationalized and overseas based operations of many of Japan's companies, seem far more 'structured for change' in the future than they were a decade and a half ago. When viewed in comparison with the other industrialized democracies, it is this combination of 'core' and 'creativity' in the politics and policy of Japan that constitutes the true uniqueness of the country.

Conclusion

Two separate sets of questions arise from the above analysis. The first concerns whether or not Japan can continue to follow the general directions it has been taking in most areas of public policy. Will there not be new international or domestic challenges that will force major reversals? If so, in what areas? The second set of questions concerns that of 'lessons for other countries' and for theories of political science and public policy. At this point it would be difficult to pursue both lines to their complete conclusion, but it seems clear that answers to both hinge on two major factors: organized labour and international pressures.

Without question international pressures will continue to confront

Japan. These will have a particularly important effect on the nation's economic strategy, and on its international competitiveness. In particular, competition with the United States and US demands for further monetary revaluation and market liberalizations are sure to accelerate economic changes if they do not lead to a total rejection by Japan of US demands, as seems certainly unlikely. The US it must be remembered, is not simply Japan's number one market for exports, but it accepts some nine times more exports than Japan's number two trading partner (West Germany or South Korea, depending on the year).

Moreover, international learning will surely serve to increase public perceptions of social welfare and consumer conditions in other countries, thus putting potential pressure on future governments to expand the resources allocated to such areas.

Yet international economic pressures may also make it very difficult for the current conservative coalition to remain intact. External economic pressure is sure to exacerbate tensions between Japan's internationally capable sectors and those unlikely or unable to adjust to increased monetary and trade liberalization pressures. Japan's major banks and trading companies are far more likely to withstand such pressures than are the typical family-owned grocery shops or farms that have traditionally been at the heart of the LDP's electoral support.

In this regard, it is hard to ignore the evidence suggesting a permanent historical defeat for organized labour in Japan and with it the likelihood that the future course of policy action will be very different from that in Western Europe and in those states that have actively or reluctantly embraced the welfare state model. As Japanese industrial structure moves from manufacturing to services and information-based areas where the unions have barely penetrated and where the likelihood of unionization based on comparative information seems dim, it is hard to see major pressures building for massive government involvement in the provision of a widespread publicly guaranteed safety net. Far more probable would be the demand for increasingly individualized benefits and market opportunities.

Yet, labour's defeat in the traditional sense may well mean its accommodation and absorption into the conservative coalition. In particular, if Japan's domestic manufacturers continue to do well in world markets their unionized work forces seem well poised to share in such profitability. This in turn is likely to lead to even closer relations between such workers and the ruling conservatives, in part providing the conservatives with an important replacement for lost farmers and small businessmen. Japanese conservatives may soon benefit, as did their British counterparts, from the generation of 'working class Tories'. Indeed, results of the 1980 and 1986 elections suggest a big jump in the support by labour for the LDP (Miyake, 1985, p, 16 *inter alia*).

This is hardly an absolute certainty. It does, however, suggest that Japan may well be on its way to a very different policy profile than that seen in most other industrialized countries. Indeed, if the re-emergence of market conservatism in the US, Britain, New Zealand, Australia and possibly other countries is any indication, Japan may well be historically 'ahead' of many such countries, rather than lagging behind. At the same time, it is far more to be questioned whether such prototypes of the new right will in fact embrace Japan's orientation to low unemployment and minimal social inequalities.

Notes

1 In Japanese, see the various Nihon-jin-ron scholarship. In English, there are numerous popular books and articles that take such positions on Japanese uniqueness. Consider only the wave of publications linking Japanese business success to the samurai ethic.

2 At the time of writing (Winter 1988) the tax reforms had just been passed in parliament.

3 This point is developed at length in Pempel (1982) and Pempel and Tsunekawa (1979). In essence, the only possible claim for a labour-based government in Japanese history would be the brief coalition government of 1947–8 in which the Japan Socialist Party was the principal component. Japan was under military occupation by the US at the time, and ultimate authority rested with the occupation forces. This, plus the short duration and limited power of the coalition, made it impossible for the socialists to implement more than a small portion of their pro-labour, social welfare agenda.

4 It should be noted that Japanese defence and military expenditures are counted in a way that makes the percentage of GNP seem smaller than it would if Japan followed more standard accounting procedures, but by any calculation Japan is still a low spender for military matters (Drifte, 1985; Otake, 1979).

5 I use this phrase more generally than does Johnson. He utilized it to refer primarily to the actions of the Ministry of International Trade and Industry; I would apply it to a number of other economic ministries. A somewhat similar phrase is that of Okimoto who treats Japan as a 'network state' (Okimoto, 1988). Elsewhere I have used the phrase 'state-led capitalism' (Pempel, 1982, ch. 2).

6 As noted above, this was a feature begun in the pre-war period, but refurbished vigorously in the 1950s and early 1960s in an effort to reduce union appeals and in particular union radicalism.

7 Japanese family savings rates typically exceeded 20 per cent until the mid-1970s and indeed have been near 20 per cent ever since. This compares to rates of below 10 per cent in the US shrinking to 5–6 per cent or lower in the 1980s and to rates of 10–12 per cent in most of the countries in

Western Europe. The Japanese government also contributed heavily to capital formation until the mid 1970s. Gross domestic investment was over 35 per cent from 1960 to 1974.

8 It is also worth noting that, given Japan's trading companies, and given the low profile Japan sought in foreign affairs, most industrial raw materials could be purchased at world market prices, free of the complexities of 'buying from one's allies'.

9 Japanese women even as late as 1985 earned on average less than half the wages of their male counterparts (Keizai Koho Center, 1987, p. 70).

10 It is worth noting in this regard that between twice and three times as many Japanese over 65 continue to work as their counterparts in other industrialized countries.

11 Lynch, (1968) deals with early textile negotiations between the US and Japan, and notes the early relevance of product specific, voluntary export quotas in solving politically sensitive export issues.

12 Today, Japan leads the world in the total number of robotics on line with nearly five times as many as in the US and ten times as many as West Germany. On a per capita basis, Japan follows behind Sweden as the number two user.

13 It should be noted that Japan's adjustments included many labour saving measures, including reductions in hours worked, semi-forced early retirements, lower hiring rates, limitations on overtime and so forth (Shimada, 1983). At the same time, from a normative standpoint, such measures seem far less draconian than straight layoffs on a 'last hired, first fired' principle.

14 See the declining role of administrative guidance, the growing importance of international capital flows, the increased competitiveness of these Japanese industrial and service companies and so forth.

15 Actual unemployment and underemployment is in fact far higher in Japan, and probably is over 6 per cent by some calculations, but there is little doubt about the fact that there is more unemployment, particularly among males, in important sectors of manufacturing in the mid 1980s than there was in the mid-1970s (Shimada, 1983).

16 See the creation of Zenryokyo, later Rengo, as a major break in the union movement in Japan, pitting public sector (and declining private sector) unions against at least stable private sector unions, particularly in the export-oriented industries.

17 I personally do not subscribe to this view, but it has become a popular one in the media, and certainly the LDP looks secure electorally into the 1990s. More importantly, its success has allowed it to 'act strong' and to reverse electorally popular programmes with relative impunity (Sato and Matsuzaki, 1986).

References

Aoki, Masahiko 1987: The Japanese Firm in Transition. In Yamamura and Yasuba (eds) *The Political Economy of Japan*, 263–88

Barnhart, Michael 1987: *Japan Prepares for Total War*. Ithaca NY: Cornell University Press.

Boltho, Andrea 1975: *Japan, An Economic Survey 1953–1973*. London: Oxford University Press.

Boyer, Edward 1983: How Japan Manages Declining Industries. *Fortune*, 10 January, 58–63.

Briggs, Asa 1961: The Welfare State in Historical Perspective. *European Journal of Sociology* 2, 221–58.

Bronfenbrenner, Martin and Yasukichi Yasuba 1987: Economic Welfare. In Yamamura and Yasuba (eds) *The Political Economy of Japan*, 93–136.

Caldwell, Martha 1981: Petroleum Politics in Japan: State and Industry in a Changing Context. Unpublished dissertation, University of Wisconsin.

Cameron, David 1978: The Expansion of the Public Economy: A Comparative Analysis. *American Political Science Review*, 72, 1243–61.

Cameron, David 1984: Social Democracy, Corporatism, Labour Quiescence, and the Representation of Economic Interest in Advanced Capitalist Society. In John H. Goldthorpe (ed.) *Order and Conflict in Contemporary Capitalism* Cambridge: Cambridge University Press.

Campbell, John Creighton 1983: Medical Care for the Japanese Elderly. *Pacific Affairs*, 57, 53–64.

Campbell, John C. 1977: *Contemporary Japanese Budget Politics*. New York: Columbia University Press.

Campbell, John C. 1984: Policy Conflict and Its Resolution within the Governmental System. In Krauss et al. (eds) *Conflict in Japan*.

Castles, Francis G. 1978: *The Social Democratic Image of Society*. London: Routledge and Kegan Paul.

Castles, Francis G. 1981: How does Politics Matter? Structure or Agency in the Determination of Public Policy Outcomes. *European Journal of Political Research*, 9, 119–32.

Castles, Francis G. (ed.) 1982: *The Impact of Parties: Politics and Policies in Democratic Capitalistic States* London: Sage.

Castles, Francis G. 1985: *The Working Class and Welfare*. Wellington: George Allen and Unwin, Port Nicholson Press.

Crouch, Colin 1977: *Class Conflict and the Industrial Relations Crisis*. London: Heinemann.

Donnelly, Michael 1984: Conflict over Government Authority and Markets: Japan's Rice Economy. In Krauss et al. (eds) *Conflict in Japan*, 335–74.

Dore, Ronald 1986: *Flexible Rigidities*. Stanford University Press.

Drifte, Reinhard 1985: *Japan's Growing Arms Industry*. PSIS Occasional Papers, 1/85.

The Economist, 14 November 1987.

Esping-Andersen, Gösta 1984: *Politics Against Markets*. Princeton NJ: Princeton University Press.

Friedman, David 1988: *The Misunderstood Miracle: Industrial Development and Political Change in Japan*. Ithaca, NY: Cornell University Press.

Garon, Sheldon 1987: *The State and Labor in Modern Japan*. Princeton, NJ: Princeton University Press.

Gilpin, Robert 1987: *The Political Economy of International Relations.* Princeton, NJ: Princeton University Press.
Goldthorpe, John H. (ed.) 1984: *Order and Conflict in Contemporary Capitalism.* Oxford: Oxford University Press.
Gordon, Andrew 1985: *The Evolution of Labor Relations in Japan; Heavy Industry 1853–1955.* Cambridge, Mass.: Harvard University: Council on East Asian Studies.
Hackett, Roger F. 1971: *Yamagata Aritomo in The Rise of Modern Japan.* Cambridge, Mass.: Harvard University Press.
Hadley, Eleanor M. 1970: *Antitrust in Japan.* Princeton, NJ: Princeton University Press.
Hall, Peter 1986: *Governing the Economy.* New York: Oxford University Press.
Halliday, Jon 1975: *A Political History of Japanese Capitalism.* New York: Pantheon.
Hanami, Tadashi 1979: *Labor Relations in Japan Today.* Tokyo: Kodansha International.
Harari, Ehud 1973: *The Politics of Labor Legislation in Japan.* Berkeley CA: University of California Press.
Heclo, Hugh 1974: *Modern Social Politics in Britain and Sweden.* New Haven: Yale University Press.
Hibbs, D. 1978: On the Political Economy of Long-Run Trends in Strike Activity. *British Journal of Political Science*, 8, 153–75.
Horne, James 1985: *Japan's Financial Markets: Conflict and Consensus in Policymaking.* Sydney: Allen & Unwin.
Hoston, Germaine A. 1986: *Marxism and the Crisis of Development in Prewar Japan.* Princeton, NJ: Princeton University Press.
Iida, Seietsuro 1976: Nihon Keizai no Kiko to Kodo Seicho no Shikumi. In Ienaga Saburo et al. (eds) *Showa no Sengoshi* IV. Tokyo: Sekibunsha.
Inoguchi, Takashi 1983: *Gendai Nihon Seiji Keizai No Közu.* Tokyo: Töyö Keizai.
Japan, Economic Planning Agency 1979: *New Economic and Social Seven-Year Plan.* Tokyo: EPA.
JETRO 1975: *Japan's Industrial Structure.* Tokyo: Japan External Trade Organization.
Johnson, Chalmers 1982: *MITI and the Japanese Miracle.* Stanford, CA: Stanford University Press.
Kanamori Hisao 1967: *Nihon Keizai O do Miru ka?* Tokyo: Nihon Keizai Shimbun.
Kaplan, Eugene 1972: *Japan: The Government-Business Relationship.* Washington, DC: US Dept. of Commerce.
Katzenstein, Peter J. (ed.) 1985: *Between Power and Plenty.* Madison, Wis.: University of Wisconsin Press.
Keizai Koho Center 1987: *Japan 1987: An International Comparison.* Tokyo: Japan Institute for Social and Economic Affairs.
Koike, Kazuo 1987: Human Resource Development and Labor-Management Relations. In Yamamura and Yasuba (eds), *The Political Economy of Japan*, 289–330.
Kokuseisha, (annual) *Nihon Kokuseizue.* Tokyo. Yano.

Korpi, Walter 1980: *The Working Class in Welfare Capitalism*. London: Routledge and Kegan Paul.

Korpi, Walter 1983: *The Democratic Class Struggle*. London: Routledge and Kegan Paul.

Korpi, Walter and Michael Shalev 1980: Strikes, Power and Politics in The Western Nations, 1900–1976. In Maurice Zeitlin (ed.) *Political Power and Social Theory*, vol. 1 Greenwich, CT: JAI Press, 301.

Kosai, Yutaka and Yoshitaro Ogino 1984: *The Contemporary Japanese Economy*. Armonk, NY: M.E. Sharpe.

Krasner, Stephen D. 1978: *Defending the National Interest: Raw Materials Investments and U.S. Foreign Policy*. Princeton NJ: Princeton University Press.

Krasner, Stephen D. 1987: *Asymmetries in Japanese–American Trade*. Policy Papers in International Affairs, 32. Berkeley CA: University of California Press.

Krauss, Ellis, Thomas P. Rohlen and Patricia G. Steinoff (eds) 1984: *Conflict in Japan*, Honolulu: University of Hawaii Press.

Kume, Ikuo 1988: Changing Relations Among the Government, Labor and Business in Japan after the Oil Crisis. *International Organization*, 42, 4 (Autumn), 659–87.

Kumon, Shumpei 1984: Japan Faces Its Future: The Political–Economics of Administrative Reform. *Journal of Japanese Studies* 10, 1.

Kyogoku, Jun-ichi 1987: *The Political Dynamics of Japan*. Tokyo: University of Tokyo Press.

Lincoln, Edward 1984: *Japan's Industrial Policies*. Washington, DC: Japan Economic Institute.

Lindberg, Leon and Charles Maier (eds) 1985: *The Politics of Inflation and Economic Stagnation*. Washington, DC: The Brookings Institution.

Lynch, John 1968: *Toward an Orderly Market: An Intensive Study of Japan's Voluntary Quota on Cotton Textile Exports*. Tokyo: Sophia University.

Magaziner, Ira C. and Thomas H. Hout 1980: *Japanese Industrial Policy*. London: Policy Studies Institute.

Maier, Charles S. 1978: The Politics of Productivity. In Peter J. Katzenstein (ed.) *Between Power and Plenty*, 23–50.

Marshall, Byron K. 1967: *Capitalism and Nationalism in Prewar Japan: The Ideology of the Business Elite; 1868–1941*. Stanford, CA: Stanford University Press.

Marshall, Byron K. 1987: *Capitalism and Nationalism in Prewar Japan*. Stanford, CA: Stanford University Press.

Maruo, Naomi 1986: The Development of the Welfare Mix in Japan. In Rose and Shiratori (eds) *The Welfare State East and West*, 65.

Miyake Ichiro (ed.) 1985: *Seito Shiji no Bunseki*. Tokyo: Sokobunsha.

Moore, Barrington Jr. 1966: *Social Origins of Dictatorship and Democracy*. Boston Mass.: Beacon Press.

Morse, Ronald A. 1981: *The Politics of Japan's Energy Strategy*. Berkeley: University of California, Institute of East Asian Studies.

Murakami, Yasusuke 1982: The Age of New Middle Mass Politics: The Case of Japan. *Journal of Japanese Studies* 8, 1.

Muramatsu, Michio and Ellis S. Krauss 1987: The Conservative Policy Line and the Development of Patterned Pluralism. In Yamamura and Yasuba (eds.) *The Political Economy of Japan*, 516–54.

Muramatsu Michio, Tsujinaka Yutaka and Ito Mitsutoshi 1986: *Sengo Nihon no Atsuryoku Dantai*. Tokyo: Toyo Keizai Shinposha.

Nordlinger, Eric A. 1981: *On the Autonomy of the Democratic State*. Cambridge: Harvard University Press.

Okimoto, Daniel 1989: *Between MITI and the Market*. Stanford, CA: Stanford University Press.

Okochi, K., B. Karsh and S.B. Levine (eds) 1973: *Workers and Employers in Japan*. Tokyo: University of Tokyo Press.

OECD 1985: *Social Expenditure 1960–1990*. Paris: OECD.

Otake Hideo 1979: *Gendai Nihon no Seiji Kenryoko Keizai Kenryoku*. Tokyo: Sanichi Shobo.

Otake Hideo 1989: Defense Controversies and One Party Dominance: The Opposition in West Germany and Japan. In T.J. Pempel (ed.) *Uncommon Democracies: One Party Regimes*. Ithaca: Cornell University Press.

Panitch, Leo 1979: The Development of Corporatism in Liberal Democracies. In Schmitter and Lehmbruch (eds), *Trends towards Corporatist Intermediation*, pp. 119–46.

Panitch, Leo 1981: Trade Unions and the Capitalistic State. *New Left Review*, 125, 21–43.

Patrick, Hugh T. and Thomas P. Rohlen 1987: Small-Scale Family Enterprises. In Yamamura and Yasuba (eds) *The Political Economy of Japan*, 331–84.

Patrick, Hugh T. and Henry Rosovsky (eds) 1976: *Asia's New Giant*. Washington, DC: The Brookings Institution.

Pempel, T.J. 1978a: *Patterns of Japanese Policymaking*. Boulder, CO: Westview Press.

Pempel, T.J. 1978b: Japanese Foreign Economic Policy: The Domestic Bases for International Behavior. In P.J. Katzenstein, *Between Power and Plenty*, 139–90.

Pempel, T.J. 1982: *Policy and Politics in Japan*. Philadelphia, PA: Temple University Press.

Pempel, T.J. 1987: The Unbundling of 'Japan, Inc.'. The Changing Dynamics of Japanese Policy Formation. *Journal of Japanese Studies*, 13, 2.

Pempel, T.J. and K. Tsunekawa, 1979: Corporatism without Labor? The Japanese Anomaly. In P.C. Schmitter and G. Lehmbruch (eds), *Trends Toward Corporatist Intermediation*. Beverly Hills, CA: Sage.

Piore, Michael J. and Charles F. Sabel, 1984: *The Second Industrial Divide*. New York: Basic Books.

Pryor, F.L. 1968: *Public Expenditures in Communist and Capitalist Nations*. London: George Allen and Unwin.

Polanyi, Karl 1944: *The Great Transformation*. Boston, Mass.: Beacon Press.

Poullier, Jean Pierre 1982: Social Expenditure Growth in Selected Industrialized Countries: France, Germany, Japan, Sweden, United Kingdom, United States. *Journal of Institutional and Theoretical Economics*, 138, 618–28.

Przeworski, Adam 1985: *Capitalism and Social Democracy*. London: Cambridge University Press.

Rein, Martin, Gösta Esping-Andersen and Lee Rainwater (eds) 1987: *Stagnation and Renewal in Social Policy*. Armonk, NY: M.E. Sharpe, Inc.

Rein, Martin and Lee Rainwater, (eds) 1986: *Public/Private Interplay in Social Protection*. Armonk, NY: M.E. Sharpe, Inc.

Rose, Richard and Rei Shiratori (eds) 1986: *The Welfare State East and West*. New York: Oxford University Press.

Samuels, Richard 1987: *The Business of the Japanese State*. Ithaca, NY: Cornell University Press.

Sato Seizaburo and Tetsuhisa Matsuzaki 1986: *Jimintō Seiken* Tokyo: Chuo Koron sha.

Sawyer, Malcolm 1976: *Income Distribution in OECD Countries*. Paris: OECD.

Scalapino, Robert A. 1953: *Democracy and the Party Movement in Prewar Japan*. Berkeley, CA: University of California Press.

Schmidt, Manfred G. 1982: The Role of Parties in Shaping Macroeconomic Policy. In F.G. Castles *The Impact of Parties*, 97–176.

Schmidt, Manfred G. 1983: The Welfare State and the Economy in Periods of Economic Crisis; A Comparative Study of Twenty-Three OECD Nations. *European Journal of Political Research*, 2, 1–26.

Schmitter, Philippe and Gerhard Lehmbruch (eds) 1979: *Trends towards Corporatist Intermediation*. London: Sage.

Shalev, Michael 1983: The Social Democratic Model and Beyond. *Comparative Social Research*, 6, 315–51.

Shalev, Michael and Walter Korpi 1980: Working Class Mobilization and American Exceptionalism. *Economic and Industrial Democracy*, 1, 31–62.

Shimada, Haruo 1983: Japanese Industrial Relations – A New General Model? In T. Shirai *Contemporary Industrial Relations in Japan*, 3–28.

Shinkawa Toshimitsu 1984: Senkyuhyaku Nanajugonen Shuntoto Keizai Kiki Kanri. In Otake Hideo (ed.) *Nihon Seiji no Shoten*, Tokyo: Sanichi Shobo.

Shirai, Taishiro (ed.) 1983: *Contemporary Industrial Relations in Japan*. Madison, WI: University of Wisconsin Press.

Skocpol, Theda and Edwin Amenta, 1986: States and Social Policies. *Annual Review of Sociology*, 12, 131–57.

Stephens, John D. 1979: *The Transition from Capitalism to Socialism*. London: Macmillan.

Stephens, John D. 1988: Democratic Transition and Breakdown in Europe, 1870–1939: A Test of the Moore Thesis. In Dietrich Rueschemeyer et al., *Economic Development and Democracy*, London: Polity Press.

Steven, Rob 1983: *Classes in Contemporary Japan*. Cambridge: Cambridge University Press.

Taira, Koji 1970: *Economic Development and the Labor Market in Japan*. New York: Columbia University Press.

Takemae Eiji and Amakawa Akira 1977: *Nihon Senryo Hisshi* vol. 1. Tokyo: Asahi Shimbun sha.

Therborn, Göran 1986: *Why Some Peoples Are More Unemployed than Others*. London: Verso.

Titmuss, Richard M. 1958: The Social Division of Welfare. In *Essays on 'The Welfare State'* London: George Allen and Unwin, 34–55.

Tokunaga Shigeyoshi and Joachim Bergmann (eds) 1984: *Industrial Relations in Transition*. Tokyo: University of Tokyo Press.

Tsujinaka Yutako 1986: Rodo Dantai. In Nakano Minoro (ed.) *Nihon Keiseisaku Kettei no Itendo*, Tokyo: Toyo-Keizai.

Verba, Sidney et al. 1987: *Elites and the Idea of Equality*. Cambridge, Mass.: Harvard University Press.

Vogel, Ezra F. 1979: *Japan as No. 1*. Cambridge, Mass.: Harvard University Press.

Ward, Robert and Yoshikazu Sakamoto (eds) 1987: *Democratizing Japan*. Honolulu: University of Hawaii Press.

Wilensky, Harold 1975: *The Welfare State and Equality: Structural and Ideological Roots of Public Expenditures*. Berkeley, CA: University of California Press.

Wilensky, Harold L., Gregory M. Leubbert, Susan R. Hahn and Adrienne M. Jamieson 1985: *Comparative Social Policy*. Berkeley, CA: University of California Press.

Wolf, M.J. 1983: *The Japanese Conspiracy – The Plot to Dominate Industry Worldwide – and How to Deal with It*. New York: Empire.

Wood, Robert 1980: Japan's Multitier Wage System. *Forbes*, 18 August, 53–8.

Yamamura, Kozo 1967: *Economic Policy in Postwar Japan*. Berkeley, CA: University of California Press.

Yamamura, Kozo 1985: The Cost of Rapid Growth and Capitalist Democracy in Japan. In Lindberg and Maier *The Politics of Inflation and Economic Stagnation*, 467–508.

Yamamura, Kozo and Yasukichi Yasuba (eds) 1987: *The Political Economy of Japan Volume 1: The Domestic Transformation*. Stanford, CA: Stanford University Press.

Zysman, John 1984: *Governments, Markets and Growth: Financial Systems and the Politics of Industrial Change*. Ithaca NY: Cornell University Press.

Zysman, John and Stephens Cohen 1983: Double or Nothing: Open Trade and Competitive Industry. *Foreign Affairs*, September.

6

'Pillarization' and 'Popular Movements'

Two Variants of Welfare State Capitalism: the Netherlands and Sweden

Göran Therborn

Welfare States and Private Capital

Public policy has a high profile, or at least a sizeable importance, in the Netherlands and in Sweden, the two countries of the Western world in which public expenditure is greatest. For 1980–5, public outlays averaged 64.5 per cent of GDP in Sweden and 60.4 per cent in the Netherlands (OECD 1987a, p. 64). The Dutch and the Swedes have pioneered a new variant of advanced capitalism and of private/public socio-economic relations. In the Netherlands since 1975, and in Sweden since 1976, public income transfers to households have been above the sum of the operational surplus of unincorporated enterprise and of property income accruing to households (OECD, 1986 and 1987e, national tables 8; Det økonomiske råd, 1984, pp. 80–1).[1]

In 1986 public transfers (of all sorts) to households constituted about 27 per cent of Dutch GDP and about 19 per cent of Swedish GDP. (Centraal Planbureau, 1986, p. 28; Tweede Kamer, 1987–8, p. 254; Finansdepartementet, 1987, p. 152; 1988, p. 19). Total public social expenditure by the broadest definition exceeded 40 per cent of GDP in the Netherlands in the early 1980s, and approached the 40 per cent mark in Sweden. In the trough of the recent depression, in 1982, Dutch social expenditure went up to 43 per cent of GDP.

That the Dutch have constructed the world's most extensive welfare state is not that well known and fits rather uneasily into current explanatory frameworks. In fact, neither the Swedish nor the Dutch case of welfare state trajectory fits very well with general structural explanations of welfare development, whether they are couched in terms of the strength of the working class or of Social Democracy (Korpi,

Table 6.1   Public social expenditure in Western Europe in 1980 (percentage of GDP)

Austria	32.6
Belgium	36.0
Denmark	32.8
Finland	24.8
Germany	31.0
Ireland	29.0
Italy	27.0
Netherlands	40.2
Norway	26.1
Sweden	37.9
Switzerland	19.7
UK	24.5

Public social expenditure includes income maintenance programmes, health care services or payments, education, housing benefits, retraining and public works programmes.
Source: Flora, 1987b, national tables.

1983), the weakness of the right (Castles, 1982), the impact of an open economy (Cameron, 1978) or others. Wilhelmine Germany pioneered modern social insurance, and in the inter-war period Germany and Britain were the most generous providers of social services, with both Sweden and the Netherlands well behind (Flora, 1983, ch. 8). After the Second World War, British (Beveridgeian) ideology and German largesse (and war victims' compensation) led the way until about the mid 1960s. Only in the second half of the 1960s did the Netherlands and, then, Sweden overtake these nations. A clear Swedish superiority over Germany established itself only in the second half of the 1970s. In 1960 Swedish social expenditure was virtually equal to that of Britain (Flora, 1987a, pp. 42, 325, 393, 720).

Traditionally, the most open economies of Europe were the Netherlands, Norway – neither of them trail-blazing welfare states – and, until the Depression, the UK. In the 1950s and 1960s Belgium, Ireland and Switzerland moved close to the top of the openness league table. The Austrian economy is also somewhat more open than the Swedish, the latter having a roughly comparable level of trade exposure to the low-spending New Zealand economy prior to 1973 (Flora, 1987b, ch. 6; Centraal Bureau voor de statistiek, 1979, pp. 144–5; OECD 1987a, p. 67).

From the point of view of political forces, the period of special welfare state expansion looks rather anomalous in both the Dutch and the Swedish cases. In the Netherlands, expansion got going in the fourteen years (1959–73, except for one year in 1965–6) that the Social Democrats were out of office and the economically most right-wing party (the liberal VVD) was in government. In Sweden, public welfare began to expand appreciably only at the end of the long Social Democratic era 1932–76, and even accelerated when the Social Democrats were in opposition. Katzenstein's (1985, p. 105) distinction between 'liberal' and 'social corporatism' does not appear very persuasive in this context either. 'The liberal corporatist' Netherlands is closest to 'social-cum-liberal corporatist' Sweden, while the former is very different from fellow 'liberal corporatist' Switzerland, as is Sweden from 'social corporatist' next-door neighbour, Norway.

Katzenstein's perceptive analysis of Western European small states does, however, imply another Dutch-Swedish puzzle. Both countries, he notes, have strong, internationally oriented, centralized business communities – which is why he calls their 'corporatism' liberal – although, because of her simultaneously strong labour movement, Sweden's corporatism is also 'social'. A crucial question is, therefore, how have the Dutch and the Swedes managed to combine the world's most generous welfare states with internationally competitive big business? That question or puzzle is a major focus of analysis in this chapter.

Table 6.2 gives a few measures of the comparative importance of Dutch and Swedish capital.

Private capital accumulation appears quite vigorous in the extensive welfare states, seemingly faring well in comparison with the world's leading capitalist economies. In relation to the size of the countries, the number of large private industrial corporations in the Netherlands and in Sweden is quite impressive.

This phenomenon highlights the limitations of a purely public approach to public policy. Public power and policy should also be seen and analysed in relation to private powers and policies, and with a view to the complex pattern of interdependence, co-operation and conflict they jointly constitute. In an otherwise most penetrating policy study of Sweden (Heclo and Madsen, 1987), this private-public constellation is completely lost sight of, leading the authors to the unqualified and, in this writer's opinion, unwarranted conclusion of 'labor's hegemony' in Sweden (p. 322). In any case, an understanding of the functioning and the viability of the contemporary political economy of Sweden and the Netherlands requires that we examine the imbrication of welfare state and capital accumulation in these countries.

History and Social Action

Policies are made or pursued by actors. Dutch and Swedish politics have in this respect at least one important feature in common. In each country, twentieth-century politics has largely been shaped by a single politically

Table 6.2 Comparative profits and big business in the Netherlands, Sweden and leading capitalist nations in the mid 1980s

	Netherlands	Sweden	US	Japan	FRG
Operating surplus as % of GDP[a]	29.0	19.3	19.3	24.3	23.3
Gross operating surplus as % of gross value added in manufacturing[b] business	28.9	27.0	24.3	42.2	26.9[c]
Number of domestic private corporations among the world's 50 largest industrials/million inhabitants[d]	2[e]/14	0/8	21/239	6/121	7/61
Ditto among the largest 500 non-US[d]	7[e]/14	17/8	—	151/121	42/61
Ditto among the 100 largest non-US banks[d]	3/14	1/8	—	31/121	9/61

a 1985.
b 1980–85.
c 1980–84.
d Industrial corporations ranked by sales and banks by assets, in 1986. Population figures for 1985. Subsidiaries of foreign companies, public and co-operative enterprises excluded.
e Anglo–Dutch Shell and Unilever have together been counted as one Dutch corporation.
Sources: Rows 1 and 2 and population figures from OECD, 1987a, pp. 14ff., 18, 74. Rows 3–5, *Fortune* 3 August 1987, pp. 18–19, 183ff., and 208ff.

dominant acting force. In Sweden, it has been the Social Democratic labour movement: initially, a part of the governmental coalition in 1917; subsequently, providing a series of minority governments in the 1920s, and then governing the country between 1932 and 1976, and again since 1982. Less spectacular, but more constant, has been the influence of the Dutch Catholics. They have been part of every single Dutch cabinet since September 1918; since 1977 as the major force in the inter-confessional Christian Democratic Appeal (CDA) and previously as an exclusively Catholic party. Since December 1977, and for a total of 35 of the 70 years from 1918 to 1988, the Catholics have provided the Prime Minister. Their share of the vote has, however, always been smaller than that of the Swedish Social Democrats. While the vote of the latter has oscillated around 45 per cent since the 1930s (never below 40 per cent but occasionally above 50 per cent), the Dutch Catholic party received around 30 per cent until 1967, which is about what the interconfessional CDA obtained in the period 1977–86. The Catholics have not dominated Dutch politics in the sense the Social Democrats have in Sweden, but they have constituted the pivot of Dutch political life. In the making of social and economic policy they have played a crucial part. For many purposes, the Catholics have formed a central part of a bloc of confessional parties (two Calvinist and one Catholic plus some splinter parties), which from 1918 up to and including 1963 scored an absolute majority in every single parliamentary election. That bloc is now the interconfessional party, the CDA. Before 1945, the most pronounced confessional leadership in Dutch politics was provided by the fundamentalist Calvinist party, the Anti-Revolutionaries.

The reasons for this long-term single party dominance in Sweden and the Netherlands must first be sought in the historical socio-political contexts from which it emerged, contexts that also shaped and continue to shape party and governmental policy-making. A major objective of this chapter is to demonstrate the extent to which the public policy profiles of Sweden and the Netherlands took their characteristic form and development potentials from an interaction between the forces of capitalist development and social structures inherited from the past. Ultimately, these profiles converged towards what may broadly be characterized as exemplary development of the welfare state, but, as we shall see, that convergent public policy outcome simultaneously masks a diversity of origins, developmental sequences, institutional and ideological forms and modes of accommodation with capitalist accumulation.

The Making of Modern Politics in Sweden and in the Netherlands

Sweden: the politics of 'popular movements'

The most important forces of twentieth-century Dutch and Swedish politics emerged in the last quarter of the previous century. The main issues were largely the same: the place of revived religion, the working class and the 'worker's question' and the suffrage. But the frontlines, the temporality, and the relations of force differed vastly, and with them the outcome.

Sweden was the poorest (Maddison, 1982, p. 21), the least politically modernized of the two countries, and the one with the most entrenched and united right.

The first parliamentary cabinet was set up only in 1905, during the breakdown crisis of the union with Norway. The constitutional monarchy was governed by high civil servants – 85 cabinet members out of 95 for the 1867–1905 period between the substitution of a bicameral diet for an estates system and the establishment of parliamentary government (Therborn, 1982, p. 27). The unitary state itself was very old, and the Lutheran Church was part of the state apparatus. The franchise for the Second Chamber covered about 10 per cent of the adult population above the age of 20, twice the size of the Dutch before 1888, equal to the latter till 1897 when the Dutch franchise jumped to surpass the 20 per cent mark. By 1885 the British electorate comprised about 30 per cent of the adult population, a figure reached in Sweden only in 1911 (Flora, 1983, pp. 131, 141, 148).

The country's rural pre-modernity and the ancient autonomy of its farmers gave the latter a very important voice in the Second Chamber. However, rural interests shrank from demanding governmental power, and their parliamentary base was counterbalanced by the aristocratic entrenchment in the co-equal First Chamber. By 1879, 63 per cent of the elected First Chamber MPs were nobles, a proportion which stabilized at around a third from 1890 until the First World War and its democratic aftermath (Therborn, 1982, p. 25). For the first two decades of its existence, the bicameral political system of the constitutional monarchy was mainly preoccupied with the conflicts between the farmers and the 'lords' (herrarna), the former demanding the abolition of the continuance of military obligations and taxation upon non-noble land. The parliamentary club called the Yeoman Party provided the political clout which the non-establishment forces had in these years, and urban radical MPs rallied to it too.

Then, at the end of the 1880s, a post-feudal market conflict became central, in the form of conflict over the tariff, mainly on grain. The tariff issue split the farmers, between the grain producers of the south and the grain consumers in the north and in the central forest areas, and has largely coloured the country politically to this day, between a right-wing south, outside strongly industrial areas and a (mainly) radical north (Carlsson, 1953 and Korpi, 1983: pp. 112ff.). However, the tariff – which was carried because of an electoral technicality – did not lead to any lasting political organization, although it spawned contacts and networks of some organizational importance, particularly on the protectionist right. It should be emphasized, that in Sweden the tariff was overwhelmingly a pre-industrial issue, seeking, for the most part, to protect the grain farmers and, to a lesser extent, the small pre-industrial iron works of central Sweden. Protectionism had little meaning to the key sectors of Swedish industry, now taking off under the lead of exporters of timber and wood products. It hardly touched the working class outside a couple of textile towns, and the incipient organizations conceived of it as an instrument of agrarian reaction.

In the 1880s and 1890s new forms of social mobilization and organization developed very rapidly in Sweden. In Swedish political parlance they are usually referred to as 'popular movements' (folkrörelser), which has the double connotation of large democratic associations, and of voluntariness and autonomy from the state (Johansson, 1954; Lundkvist, 1977; Thörnberg, 1943). The concept denotes first of all dissenting religious denominations, the temperance movements, and the labour movement, in particular the trade unions. The concept was never one of an explicit political strategy, and in part it expresses a vision of the origins of social modernity, a vision largely deriving from the time of the Social Democratic breakthrough of the 1930s. Nevertheless, freed of its ideological trimmings, the notion captures a decisive aspect of the making of modern Swedish politics.

Modern Swedish politics was constituted along a clear frontline between a conservative, authoritarian, pre-industrial, and largely pre-bourgeois state establishment and a new associational world of large groups of deeply concerned people collectively grappling with basic questions of human life and of life beyond death. The popular movements were not united, their relations among themselves were competitive, conflictual or simply ignorant, as well as co-operative. But a common enemy often brought them together. The control of the state church over the school system hurt both the religious dissenters and the anti-clerical radicals. All three major popular movements were engaged in organizing the politically disenfranchised. An extension of the franchise would weaken the hold on society of the state establishment and would favour both social reform and religious freedom. The temperance movement was central to the early complex of popular movements, being then the largest – peaking at about 350,000 members in 1910, almost a seventh of the total population (Lundkvist, 1977, p. 67) – as well as a meeting ground of the free church people and labour movement cadres.

The reasons for the sudden upsurge of mass popular organizations – from 36,000 members in 1880, to 200,000 in 1890, and 373,000 in 1900 (certainly, with some overlapping memberships, but all of them individual enrolments) – are still not quite clear, largely because research in this area has rarely had a cross-national frame of reference. My guess is that the enormous expansion of these organizations was due to particularly acute potential conflict between, on the one hand, the *ancien régime* of the Church and the central state, and on the other, a wide diffusion of social skills among the population, and almost complete literacy, widespread farming property, old traditions of municipal/ parochial secular autonomy and of local judicial participation (cf. Therborn, 1984a, pp. 540ff.). When changing economic conditions and new modes of communication shook the old local order and when a thin central state enlightenment loosened the repressive powers of the Church, there appeared a cultural and social void which relatively resourceful farmers or farmers' sons, artisans, small businessmen and skilled workers could fill with organizational efforts. The economic conjuncture is likely to have spurred the spread of the movements of reform and protest in the 1880s. The processes of modernization just started encountered the effects of the international depression and declining national income in the second half of the 1870s, and in 1884 and 1887. Mass emigration ran parallel to the rise of popular mobilization (see further Therborn, 1988 with references to Swedish popular movements).

Rapid industrialization and urbanization soon eroded the positions of the old state establishment which had no reserves to draw upon. Ancient peasant autonomy deprived the landowners of any mass base, although the tariff had driven the farmers in the south to the right. As a state bureaucracy, the Lutheran church was singularly inept at dealing with unruly and anonymous communities which could not be ruled from the pulpit on Sundays, and its increasingly militant and authoritarian stance in the last two decades of the nineteenth century (Rickardson, 1963, ch. VI) alienated it even further from the people. The geopolitics and the historical traditions of Sweden gave little room for any nationalist, not to speak of imperialist, mobilization around the turn of the century. To preserve the dynastic union with Norway by force was never seriously considered in ruling circles, and the whole issue had little popular appeal (Vedung, 1971).

The timing of the rise of the popular mass movements and the division of the religious ones gave the labour movement clear advantages over possible political contenders for the leadership of the succession to the

Oscarian *ancien régime*. There were two conceivable contenders, Liberalism or some variant of non-socialist radicalism and a Christian democratic or social party. Cultural and political underdevelopment, including clerical control, had prevented the emergence of national political movements and any independent religious mass movements before the 1880s. The three major movements began almost at the same time. The temperance organisation (IOGT) was founded in 1879, the year after the Mission League, which soon became the most important free church, broke with the state church. Social Democratic agitation began in 1881, leading to the founding of the Social Democratic Workers' Party in 1889. The first national trade unions constituted themselves in 1886, the decisive Iron and Metal Workers' Union was set up in 1888. Social Democratic agitation was crucial to the launching of the latter.

On a national level, the Social Democratic labour movement then preceded Liberalism. A Liberal parliamentary party was founded in 1900, four years after the first Social Democratic MP had been elected, and a Liberal national electoral organization only in 1902. Locally, in Stockholm in particular, there were earlier Liberal organizations, but the superior organizational capacity and strength of the Social Democrats was already obvious in the joint Liberal and Social Democratic universal suffrage campaign, the 'people's parliament' election in 1893 (Vallinder, 1962, pp. 90ff.). Liberalism became an important political force in the first almost universal male suffrage election in 1911 and the largest political party in the country. But it was then mainly a rural force, of teetotallers, religious dissenters, rural radicals and free-traders, while the town and city population was primarily divided between the Right and the Social Democrats. Sweden was for a long time an agrarian and, even more, a rural country. In 1870 72 per cent of the population were in agriculture, forestry and fishing. In 1910, the figure was 49 per cent, and in that year 66 per cent were living in 'sparsely populated rural areas' (Therborn 1984a, p. 547). But rural Liberalism was hardly a competitive route toward twentieth-century modernity.

The Christian Social alternative never took off nationally, although it did score some local victories and even one at provincial level. The reasons were many. The Evangelical movements were divided among themselves, on grounds of religious doctrine. Their most immediate political adversary was most often the State Church, the controller of public education and their competitor in the interpretation of and in the recruitment for Christianity. With the powerless urban cultural radicals there were no immediate conflicts, but a source of support for religious freedom. In a common anti-statism, there was also an affinity with Liberalism. Liberalism therefore became the main political outlet of religious dissent. There was, however, a Low Church movement within the State Church, and a part of the Free Church movement was doctrinally not very distant from the former. These two tended to be the most right-wing and anti-socialist of the new religious movements and served as a basis for attempts at anti-Social Democratic working class organization and for the launching of a right-wing Christian party. But internal heterogeneity could only be overcome in a few places and areas, and the increasing nationalization of politics doomed such efforts from the start (cf. Palm, 1982; Ericsson, 1987).

The popular movements of the founding period of Swedish political modernity had a long-term and still enduring impact upon twentieth-century politics in Sweden: its popular but not populist character, based upon well-structured, resourceful mass organizations (cf. Pestoff, 1977), and the movement dynamic of these organizations, derived from the concerns, the collective studies and the deliberations of members in a myriad of local branches. Social Democracy became the main carrier of the popular movement tradition, but the political success of the former depended upon its using the resources of the latter in key policy choices. It was also important that the popular movements constituted an open world of overlapping memberships and/or associational contacts and co-operation on the local level. 'Left co-operation' (as the Liberal-Social Democratic co-operation for democratic rights and democratic institutions was called) petered out after its success in 1918, religious dissent and temperance declined, and Liberalism became more economic. However, in the 1930s, a new popular movement arose. This was a new kind of farmers' movement which included a trade union (RLF), co-operatives, and a whole network of political and cultural organizations of farmers and the farm-related rural population. The most successful of these was the Youth of the Swedish Countryside, the youth organization of the Farmers' League party, which around 1950 for a while overtook the Social Democratic Youth organization as the country's largest, each having about 100,000 members among a population of 7 million. The Farmers' League became the new 'popular movement party' alongside the Social Democrats, and, like the Liberals earlier, was ready to collaborate across party lines.

The Netherlands: the politics of 'pillarization'

Modern mass organization is in the Netherlands referred to as 'pillarization' (*verzuiling*) (cf. Lijphart, 1982; Stuurman, 1983, with a large bibliography; Righart, 1986, who provides a comparative cross-national analysis of Catholic pillarization). It is as a central aspect of the phenomenon of pillarization that confessional parties have come to dominate Dutch politics. The political power of the confessional forces has been used to institute public policies of further pillarization, through which confessional power has been reproduced. Even more than 'the popular movements' in Sweden, pillarization is engraved in the structure of Dutch socio-economic institutions.

A 'pillar' as a sociological concept is a set of closed, tightly interlocking organizations held together by a common cultural orientation. In the Netherlands, three or four such pillars are distinguished: the Catholic, the Calvinist, the Socialist, and, sometimes (rather inappropriately), a Liberal pillar. The 'pillars' have five things in common with the original Swedish 'popular movements'. Both are founding movements of modern associational mobilization of the ruled classes, petite bourgeoisie and other 'middle classes', farmers and workers. Both emerged at about the same time (the last quarter of the nineteenth century) in some countries of Western Europe. In the rise of both, religious revival and the social question in emergent market economies and industrial capitalism are interwoven. Both create large, well-structured, ideologically committed and enduring associations. Finally, the connotation of both is plural, referring first of all to a pattern of social organizations, not only to a single organization. As such the pillars and the popular movements are mutually exclusive.

The most important difference is one of associational openness or closure. A popular movement is a large, voluntary organization for a specific purpose, the members of which may also for other purposes be members of other organizations, unconnected or even competing with the first. The world of popular movements is an open, pluralist field of large associations. The pillars, on the other hand, constitute a hierarchically structured marching ground of columns closed off from each other. A member of an organization for one purpose can only legitimately choose an organization for another purpose within the same pillar. A pillarized organizational pattern resembles what Philippe Schmitter (1978) has called 'corporatism', without any necessary state recognition and state control.

A complex of popular movements in the Swedish sense may be found also in Denmark and Norway. Belgium and Austria, together with the Netherlands, are clear examples of pillarization, as to some extent also is Switzerland (Righart, 1986). The popular movements were counterposed to a pre-modern regime of state and (state) church and seem to have arisen out of the immobility of the old regime and the widely diffused social skills of the ruled classes, derived from traditional rights and organizational experience. The constitutional perspective of popular movements was a democratization and a liberalization of the central state. The pillars, on the other hand, are more bent on defending a separate social world against the state, not least against the liberal state. The pillars were also counterposed to each other. The full effect of pillarization is a society and state organized as a confederation of pillars –

or civil war – and successful pillarization presupposes a weak central state and involves a political perspective of a marginal or subsidiary state. Further, the much more far-reaching organizational structuration involved in pillarization requires huge organizational resources. The latter have been met, it appears, only by an international or an officiously national (but not state) Church and by a certain kind of labour movement, the 'Germanic'.

The Dutch state by the mid-nineteenth century was a thin superstructure, only loosely linked to a society in fundamental restructuration. After the defeat of the French Revolution, and of the Batavian regime with it, the oligarchic Dutch republic had become a monarchy surrounded by a flimsy layer of a newly created nobility. The king came from the House of Orange which had provided military and often political leadership throughout most of the republican era since the Eighty Years' War against Spain. But the conservative Vienna Congress monarchy was a novelty to the Netherlands, the *ancien régime* of which had been a confederation of city-dominated provinces run by local patricians with experience of popular rebellions and participation in the affairs of cities and parishes. The secession of Belgium in 1830 was an early defeat for the new state. The country was urban and commercial, without yet being significantly industrialized. There was no important landed upper class. In the wake of European revolutions, a liberal cabinet was installed in 1848, opening a process of political reform. After a half-hearted attempt at a royalist reaction had petered out in the 1850s, moderate liberalism, of numerous shades, was, on the whole, the largest tendency of Dutch pre-democratic parliamentary politics until 1918. Dutch Liberalism was neither a pillar nor a popular movement. It was an agglomerate of the enlightened wing of the urban bourgeoisie, provincial intellectuals and notables, and some sectors of the middle strata. This Liberalism constituted the bulk of the Establishment, against which the mass mobilizations of the late nineteenth century were most immediately directed.

The terrain of conflict was the relationship between state and church, a running theme in the Netherlands since the revolt against Spain. The focal issue, however, was rather new to the nineteenth century: popular education, or rather the extent to which it was to be subject to confessional control. The intensity of the conflicts is not always quite easy to understand for a modern outside observer. The bone of contention was neither public versus private, nor secular versus religious education. Even the Batavian School Act of 1806, taken over by the Vienna Congress monarchy, allowed private confessional school and church-controlled religious education in the public schools (de Bruin, 1985, pp. 191ff.). Rather, the issue was whether public education should have any advantage or at least assumption of priority over denominational schools. After a protracted series of battles and partial victories, the confessionals won a complete triumph in 1917. Public taxation would finance denominational schools fully and equally on the same basis as the public schools. In Sweden, the process was the reverse, a gradual substitution of lay state control for clerical state control over education started in 1897. The modesty of the Swedish 'Free Church Movement' was remarkable. On the whole, it accepted the public school system and limited itself to cautious parliamentary motions, for instance that primary school teachers need not necessarily be members of the State Church. Even the non-reactionary Second Chamber rejected that motion by a two-thirds majority in 1886 (Rickardson 1963, pp. 347ff.).

The Dutch School conflict is crucial to an understanding of twentieth-century politics and policy in the Netherlands because it was in that conflict that the process of pillarization emerged and developed. The driving force was not the Catholic Church. The spearhead of pillarization was orthodox Calvinism. Not only was the Dutch state weak, the institutionalization of the national faith was also fractured. The Reformed Church had an official standing, but it was not a state bureaucracy, as was the Swedish Lutheran Church. Since the 1830s a fundamentalist Calvinism had been gaining strength, within as well as separate from the official church. In contrast to religious dissent in the Nordic countries, this fundamentalism laid claim not only to the true interpretation of the Bible, but also to being 'the doctrine of our fathers', the carrier of the spirit of the nation from the anti-Spanish war and the Golden Age (cf. de Bruin, 1985, pp. 61, 89). The bitter divisions within Calvinism irrevocably put an end to whatever slight chances a traditional Conservative bloc might have had in the Netherlands after 1848 (cf. Stuurman, 1983, pp. 120ff.). At the same time, however, the very absence of a strong traditional Establishment meant that no common terrain between religious and secular popular mobilization, no alliance between religious dissent and cultural radicalism, could emerge, as occurred in Sweden. Instead, the fundamentalist Calvinist minority and the Catholics found themselves on the same side in the fight for publicly financed confessional schools.

In 1879, the Calvinist fundamentalists created the first modern political party of the Netherlands, the Anti-Revolutionary Party. It was so called because it was ranged against the secularism and the individualism of the French Revolution. Few countries have had as strange a route to political modernity as the Netherlands. The background was a Liberal School Bill, against which the Calvinist fundamentalists gathered 305,000 signatures and the Catholics 164,000 (Stuurman, 1983, p. 132). The same school conflict led to a split of the first Dutch trade union confederation, the Liberal ANWV, set up in 1871. In 1876, the Calvinists decided to install their own working men's association, Patrimonium.

The first clearly confessional cabinet, of Anti-Revolutionaries and Catholic notables, took office in 1888.

Confessional mass mobilization and organization depended on socio-economic changes with concomitant resources and skills of communication and association which in previous centuries had been too scarce and limited to be able to countervail against the oligarchy of Regents. The new 'Workers' Question' of the last third of the nineteenth-century further stimulated tight and extensive denominational organization of their flocks. In such a fashion, religious pillarization in the Netherlands was related to a similar socio-economic dissolution of an old agrarian and urban order and its transformation into industrial capitalism as occurred in Sweden. But whereas in Sweden the labour movement soon came to appear as the model type for religious and other mass movements, conceived as Popular Movements, Dutch confessional organization came to serve as the model for class organization.

The Socialist labour movement was only the second modern mass organization in the Netherlands, and it had a slow and difficult start. There was a section of the First International but, like all other sections, it left no continuous organized legacy. Socialists left the Liberal ANWV two years after the Calvinists and the first party, the SDP, began in 1881, also two years after the foundation of the Anti-Revolutionary party. But in contrast to the ARP, the SDP gradually became politically irrelevant as a more or less Anarchist organization. Social Democratic party foundation took place only in 1894, and a Social Democratic trade union confederation (NVV) emerged in 1906. The original backbone of both were the highly skilled, mostly Jewish, diamond workers in Amsterdam (cf. Harmsen and Reinalda, 1975).

The Catholic pillar was organized somewhat later, having first to overcome the non-mediated rule of the Church hierarchy and of lay notables. Catholics comprised about a third of the population, most of them poor or disadvantaged. In the eastern industrial areas, Catholic pillarization also had to defeat German-inspired, inter-confessional, Christian trade unions. By the First World War, social change had tipped the balance within the Catholic world in favour of the renovators, and vigorous episcopal intervention had crushed most of inter-confessionalism. But only in the mid 1920s was the Catholic pillarization complete. When the last inter-confessional union (of the Limburg miners) disappeared, the Catholic trade unions were given a unified organizational structure, and Catholic politics became formally structured as a political party (cf. Righart, 1986, ch. V; Stuurman, 1983, ch. 4).

Popular and pillarized policies

While the outcomes of mass mobilizations at the time of emergent Industrial capitalism and of steam powered transport in Western Europe depended considerably upon the character of the state inherited from previous history, these outcomes in their turn significantly affected, and, in some respects, determined, the structure and policies of twentieth-century states. Most directly, the character assumed by mass mobilizations structured the foundations of the welfare state established in the late nineteenth or early twentieth centuries; foundations which, by and large, still continue to this day. Via that institutional groundwork, as well as unmediatedly through current political forces, popular movements and pillarization continued to shape the controversies around and the development forms of socio-economic policy. The different historical forms of political organization and the dynamics/inertia of the particular institutional legacy have, nevertheless, also converged in the creation of two very extensive welfare states. The different kinds of welfare states which emerged out of these founding moments of mass politics are now described.

The 'people' in the Scandinavian sense of 'people's/popular movements' (*folkrörelser*) consisted of individuals – in the case of trade unions, of a particular class – spread across a territory bounded by the external and internal boundaries of the state. The 'pillar' (*de zuil*), in the conception of the tone-setting Calvinist and Catholic pillarizers, was certainly not a collection of individuals, but a set of families, and, particularly in Catholic eyes, of members of 'estates' (*standen*) or different social rungs and occupations, who were citizens of a particular state, but also, and above all, members of a community of faith. State–citizen relationships were explicitly and generally (that is, not just in questions of faith and salvation) 'subsidiary' or secondary to pillar-member relations. 'Subsidiarity' was a Catholic term; the Calvinist fundamentalists used another, more striking, for the same idea of social organization, 'sovereignty in one's own circle'. The 'people' conceived of itself as an organization of and for enlightenment and betterment. The confessional 'pillar', on the other hand, tended to be primarily pre-occupied with the twin problems of social integration and social segregation, integrating the 'estates' of the pillar and keeping them uncontaminated by other pillars.

The organization of social services brings out these ideal typical differences between 'people' and 'pillar' very clearly. Very illuminating examples are the systems of health care, health insurance and old age pensions. A system of public provincial hospitals (*lasarett*) for the poor was gradually installed in Sweden in the second half of the eighteenth century, further motivated by the spread of venereal disease in the wake of the Napoleonic wars. A liberal constitutional reform in 1862 set up provincial parliaments as a preparation of a general liberalization of the state. These new provincial parliaments (*landsting*) almost accidentally obtained the financial and administrative responsibility for public somatic health care (Gustavsson, 1987, p. 298), a responsibility they still have. In the same year, the municipalities had their competence widened and, most importantly, obtained fiscal autonomy. The municipalities were in charge of poor relief. Voluntary health insurance societies developed in a variety of forms, but they never coalesced into ideological patterns. In 1931, legislation of extensive public support could therefore easily and consensually reorganize the friendly societies into territorially delimited, non-competitive 'recognized' societies, most often *de facto* run by Social Democratic trade unionists, though originally there had been an important Liberal input into the 'health insurance movement' (*sjukkas-serörelsen*) (cf. Lindeberg, 1949, Broberg, 1973).

The world's first universalist social insurance, the Swedish old age pension of 1913, is perhaps the most telling illustration of a public policy expression of a 'popular' conception of society. It goes back to a parliamentary amendment in 1884 urging the need to investigate 'workers' insurance'. The question of amendment was tabled by the leader of the Yeoman Party, and called for an investigation into the needs of 'workers and with them comparable persons'. The Royal Commission which was established provided a class analysis to the effect that all but '5.75% of the total population' had to be counted as 'workers and with them comparable persons' or as their family members (Arbetarförsäk-ringskomitén, 1888, p. 48). The proposal of obligatory old age insurance was not legislated at that time, but the idea of a non-categorical pension stuck. The pension insurance of 1913 became fully universalist only in the final parliamentary debate on the government bill and probably mainly for reasons of administrative simplicity and efficiency. But both the government bill and the Social Democratic party motion had proposed that only the very wealthy should be excluded. It was called the 'people's pension' and was to be administered by municipal boards (see further Elmér, 1960; for the intricacies of full universalism, Therborn, 1986a, pp. 52ff.; a general overview with extensive references is Olsson, 1987).

Pillarization also shaped social policy and institutions in characteristic ways. Indeed, the very word 'pillar' (*zuil*), in its socio-political sense, seems to have emerged in the field of social policy; that is, as a concept designating, in the second half of the 1930s, the different ideological orientations of organizations taking care of and applying for state subsidies for their care of unemployed youth (de Rooy, 1979, pp. 223, 245n.). A weak state and strong and militant churches manifested themselves already in the Dutch Poor Law of 1854 which explicitly laid down the principle that care for the poor was primarily the responsibility of church and lay charity, and that the municipality was only the last resort. This subsidiarity principle was reproduced in the Poor Law of 1912, formally in force till 1963, although public charity surpassed private in terms of expenditure by 1905 (Centraal Bureau voor de statistiek, 1979, p. 186). The idea that children 'belonged to their fathers', and not the state (de Bruin, 1985, p. 248) meant that there was little interest in and much resistance to compulsory primary education in any form. Obligatory schooling was legislated only in 1900, about the same time as conscription – ending the system whereby you could buy someone to soldier for you – both decisions passed against the large majority of Catholic MPs (Righart, 1986, p. 246).

As modern hospitals have grown out of institutions for indoor poor relief, it is not surprising, given the nature of the Dutch Poor Law, that the state, locally as well as centrally, was rather passive with regard to health care. Most hospitals were built and run by private charities, and by the time of the latest available figures (for 1977), only 18 per cent of hospital patients in the Netherlands are taken care of in public hospitals (Ministerie van Volksgezondheid, 1977, p. 78). Health care insurance developed in organizationa/ideological channels mainly in insurance funds connected with the Social Democratic trade unions and in funds run by the Catholic pillar or by the association of physicians. Preventive care and hygiene, subsequently and right up to the present, and, in particular, pre-natal care and preparation were handled by special charity organizations, the 'cross associations', the neutral Green, the Catholic White-Yellow, and the fundamentalist Calvinist Orange-Green Cross (see further Juffermans, 1982 and Querido, 1973).

Social insurance started as workers' insurance only and was administered corporatistically. Its founding legal principle (*rechtsgrond*) was not any conception of citizens' rights or public obligation, but a 'just wage' (among the Catholics) or protection of the weaker part of the labour contract (as the Calvinists put it) with a view to guaranteeing an income in cases and times of incapacity to work. As late as in the aftermath of the Second World War, the confessional majority, including the confessional unions, explicitly rejected the idea that the state had any obligation to shoulder men's 'risks of life'. Wrangles about the exact form of corporatist administration and about the maximum public supervision acceptable complicated and delayed social politics enormously. The proper form of corporatist administration delayed the implementation of a sickness insurance bill from the passing of its social security content in 1913 to the finding of its administrative form in 1930. No significant old age insurance for workers was established before the Second World War (see further Roebroek and Berben, 1987 with extensive references).

The structural effects of the two different patterns of modern popular mobilization in Sweden and in the Netherlands seem to create a dynamic paradox of their own. How could pillarized subsidiarity possibly lead to one of the world's most extensive welfare states? Why did the popular movement tradition in Sweden for so long fail to produce a generously extended public welfare system – throughout the whole first generation of continuous Social Democratic government – and how did it overcome its original inhibition?

Two Routes from Laggard to Vanguard

Affluence and the latent dynamic of confessionalism

The Dutch started late and slowly. By 1956, among 13 Western European countries only three devoted less of their national product to social security than the Netherlands (Switzerland, Norway, and Finland) (Flora, 1983, p. 456). The later expansion rested upon a change of the economic and demographic parameters. The Netherlands had been hit hard by the Occupation and the war, harder in economic terms than Denmark and Norway, but less so than France and the vanquished countries. GDP per capita in 1950 was clearly lower than in the UK, Switzerland or Scandinavia; slightly lower than in Belgium, higher than in France or Germany (Maddison, 1982, pp. 232–3, 21, respectively). About 25 per cent of the Dutch labour force was in manufacturing in 1947, less than in the UK, Germany, Belgium or Sweden, but about the same as in Denmark, and more than in France, Italy or Norway (Flora, 1987b, ch. 7).

In other words, the Netherlands was neither particularly poor nor particularly under-industrialized by the rather demanding standards of Northwestern Europe. Nevertheless, early post-war Dutch policy was governed not just by an idea of reconstruction, but a conception of Dutch underdevelopment. A major reason for this view was the demographic situation and the prospects of labour supply. The Netherlands had the fastest population growth in Western Europe in 1946–8, at the extraordinary rate of 2 per cent a year, more than two-and-a-half times higher than, for example, England and Wales (Flora 1987b, ch. 1). Second to Belgium, it was also the most densely populated country of Europe. Added to economic-cum-demographic concern was uncertainty about the future of the Dutch East Indies. In 1913 an estimated 10 per cent of the Dutch national income derived from the latter, one way or the other. Colonial profits and importance declined after that, but by 1938 14 per cent of Dutch national wealth was still invested in the East Indies (Kossmann 1978, pp. 418, 670). Under intense international pressure, the Netherlands had to give up her attempt to keep her main colony by armed force and to set Indonesia free in 1949.

Industrialization and emigration then became the catchwords of Dutch macroeconomic and macro social policy of the late 1940s and the 1950s. A 'guided' low wage policy and a policy of investment promotion with a state Directorship General for Industrialization were to support industrialization, and emigration was to be encouraged and facilitated (cf. Böhl et al., 1981, and Blekker, 1952). The Netherlands was an emigration country before the First World War, but not at all on the same scale as Sweden. From 1922 to 1934 immigration surpassed emigration. But while Sweden definitely turned into an immigration country in 1930, net emigration from the Netherlands began again in 1935 and, the years of return from Indonesia apart, accelerated after the Second World War (Flora, 1987b, pp. 65ff.; cf. Therborn, 1987a).

A period of industrial accumulation and of fostered emigration expresses a (conception of) scarcity hardly conducive to social policy generosity. In fact, no major social security reforms were passed in the first decade after the war. An Emergency Regulation of Old Age Provision in 1947 offered some stopgap aid to the poorest of the elderly. In spite of its meagreness, it was immensely popular in a situation of dire need. The regulation was named after the Labour Prime Minister Drees, and its beneficiaries as *Dreestrekkers* ('Drees recipients'). It took nine years for regular old age pension legislation to be passed, and even so this was only meant as a 'floor contribution' to subsistence (*bodemvoorziening*), not enough to live on by any standard of normal modesty.

Post-war austerity ended about 1960 in the Netherlands. The relative volume of work in manufacturing (and mining) peaked in absolute terms in 1965. In 1961 the Netherlands became an immigration, a labour-importing, country. Real wages started to rise considerably in 1959, and in 1964 the 'guided wage policy' blew up. Having stagnated in 1949–52 and in 1955–8, national income per capita began to grow steadily from 1960 up to and including 1973 (Centraal Bureau voor de Statistiek, 1979, pp. 27, 68, 144, 174, 183). In 1963, the first major discovery of natural gas was made (Lubbers and Lehckert, 1980).

The latter half of the 1960s and the early 1970s saw a cultural landslide in the Netherlands. The hard crust of pillarization broke up and the religious grip of the population loosened dramatically. Between 1961 and 1975 the proportion of Catholics attending Sunday mass declined from 71 to 33 per cent (Thurlings, 1969, p. 489). In 1963, the three major confessional parties lost their parliamentary majority which they had had since 1918. They got 49.2 per cent of the votes; by 1972 their share had slumped to 31.6 per cent. The Catholic party lost most. From its second best electoral score ever, 31.9 per cent in 1963, it went down to 26.5 per cent in 1967, 21.9 per cent in 1971, and finally to 17.7 per cent in 1972. Previously its worst result since 1918 had been 27.9 per cent in 1933. In 1963, 85 per cent of Dutch Catholics voted for the Catholic People's Party; in 1972 only 38 per cent (Bakvis, 1981, p. 176). The Catholic trade unions broke off from the pillar altogether and merged with the Social Democratic unions in 1976. The Protestant union remained. The Catholic party merged with the fundamentalist and with the theologically moderate Calvinist party in 1977. From the mid 1960s Amsterdam became a European centre of free-wheeling youth culture. The Dutch birthrate was more than halved between 1970 and 1975.

To explain the virtual collapse of the Catholic pillar is outside the scope of this chapter. But three coalescing factors seem to have been important: the particularly dramatic arrival of international mass consumption and the mass media society in the previously sealed-off Dutch pillars, the simultaneous radical changes in the Vatican signalized by *Vatican II*, and a sudden change into modernism of the Dutch Catholic Church (see further Bakvis, 1981).

Depillarization was not unimportant to the expansion of the Dutch welfare state, but its influence was indirect and mediated in a complex way. The confessionals were governing. The post-war period of Labour-Catholic coalitions, mostly under the premiership of Labour leader Drees, had ended in 1958. In the period 1959–72, the Catholics and the fundamentalist Calvinists, the Anti-Revolutionaries, supplied all Prime Ministers and all Ministers for Social Affairs, and for 13 of the 14 years the Labour party was in opposition. The leading spirit of the social advance was the Catholic G.M.J. Veldkamp, Social Minister in the decisive years of 1961–6. He was an academic with previous vice-Ministerial experience (as *staatssecretaris*), and had long been a progressive social policy advocate with important links to the Catholic labour movement.

The most expensive and by far the most controversial step in the Dutch welfare state expansion was the raising of the old age pensions to a liveable 'social minimum'. The bill was passed in 1964 and went into force on 1 January 1965. The subsidiarity principle was done away with as far as social assistance was concerned in a new Social Assistance Act of 1963, and a Children's Allowance Act became effective in the same year. Other major pieces of legislation formed part of this mid-sixties social policy surge, an increase in unemployment insurance and a new provision for the long-term unemployed were passed in 1964, a generous invalidity pension – supplanting the old workmen's compensation legislation (for work accidents) – in 1966, and an Exceptional Medical Expenses Act in 1967, publicly funding long-term medical care. Finally, minimum wage legislation was carried in 1968. (An overview in English can be obtained from Roebroek and Berben, 1987, pp. 680ff.; cf. Veldkamp et al., 1978, pp. 118ff.)

The success of Veldkamp's resolute and Florentine action was made possible by three structural co-ordinates brought together by the conjuncture of the 1960s. One was the inherent expansionary potential of confessional political principles and politics. Added to that were now, secondly, the loosening of confessional orthodoxy and the crumbling of the pillars, and, thirdly, the new resources of affluence.

The confessional tradition had at least four components which, under favourable circumstances, would tend to further social policy expansion. It is hardly possible to rank them in any order of importance, but in the Netherlands in the 1960s and 1970s they seem to have made their most important impact in the following sequence. First, the corporatist principles of social organization, common to Calvinists and Catholics, created a broad institutional terrain for debating, defending and, possibly, expanding social rights. Trade unions and employers' organizations were drawn into a framework in which all sorts of social issues were put on the agenda. The expansionary effects fell, of course, upon the unions, but also employers learnt to deal continuously with questions of social policy. On the other hand, corporatist institutions and confessional ideology actively discouraged and hindered a trade union option of concentrating on wages and industrial militancy. The pillarized division also weakened the industrial muscle of trade unionism, making a purely industrial social wage policy rather unattractive, in view of direct union access to state policy-making. Post-Second World War corporatism had created a Socio-Economic Council consisting of representatives of trade unions and of employers' organizations and of 'Crown members' (government appointees, who were usually senior academics) according to informal rules of rough party proportionality. Every piece of intended socio-economic legislation had to be officially presented to the Council for formal 'advice'. In this way, social policy became a normal preoccupation of the trade union leadership, and pillarization meant that each pillar had trade unions to take into account.

Secondly, another expansionary potential resided in the classical confessional conception of public social policy. This was the idea of a 'just' or 'necessary' wage, capable of ensuring the livelihood of a family even in times of sickness, invalidity and old age. It was expressed in publicly ordered insurance connected with the wage level. As such, social policy was linked to the general evolution of wages, and not, as in the Anglo-Saxon tradition, caged into a concern mainly with the alleviation of poverty. To the workers below the wage level to which it applied, the compensation rate of Dutch social insurance was high from the very beginning. The Disability Act of 1901 paid 70 per cent of the applicable wage, raised to 80 per cent in 1930, together with the inauguration of sickness insurance. As the applicable wage had a low limit, and as the compensation was not indexed, this did not mean high expenditures by post-war standards, but an institutional form favourable to growth was there.

Thirdly, the liberal emphasis on economic incentives which, as far as social security is concerned, means disincentives to social generosity, is alien to confessional social thought. Classical confessional doctrine certainly stressed the religious and moral duty of individuals and of family heads to provide for themselves (and for their families). But to ensure the latter by deliberate social harshness would imply that religious and moral teaching were non-effective and that only material interests counted.

Finally, the idea and practice of self-governing administrations of social insurance – manifestations of basic confessional principles of subsidiarity and corporatism – were financially open-ended. The industrial branch organizations running the 1930 sickness payment insurance, for instance, could set their premiums to cover their costs, subject to the proviso that they made no profit and were subject to ministerial control. This method was carried over into the post-war period, with premiums for social insurance adjusted yearly – the Minister for Social Affairs having the final word – to cover expected expenditure. Social insurance expenditure was thus cost-led instead of based on actuarial funding. The effects of this were most important in sustaining the expansion, once started.

The expansionary social policy potential of confessionalism was held back by two other powerful aspects of confessional doctrine and politics which had to be removed before expansion could take place. First, orthodox subsidiarity (and 'sovereignty in one's own circle') prevented the use of general taxation for social security other than as residual social assistance, and of social insurance other than for (poor) workers. That would be 'state socialism'. This opposition was a major reason for the delay of any adequate old age provision (cf. Royers and Winters, 1984). The Old Age Insurance Act of 1956 was a compromise still heavily marked by orthodox confessionalism: covering the whole population, but financed by premiums from the insured only, and the pension was in any case not intended to be sufficient to live on in itself. Of course, finance by non-redistributive premiums put severe restraints on the social security that the neediest parts of the population could afford to pay for. For a long time Veldkamp had held heterodox views on this topic and had been active in the League for State Pensioning, as the organization (run mainly by Social Democrats and left Liberals) for publicly supported pensions was called. But only with the secularization process of the early 1960s did such views carry the day in confessional politics. In 1962, the leading Catholic social politician of the 1950s, the Minister of Social Work, M. Klompé, presented a bill whereby the Poor Law of 1947 with its subsidiarity principle was replaced by a recognized right to social assistance. In the government declaration of the new, again confessional-dominated and Catholic-led, Marijnen cabinet in 1963, it was stated that the government did not look upon the co-financing of social security by public funds as a question of principle (that is, therefore to be rejected), but as a pragmatic issue (Veldkamp et al., 1978, p. 127).

The second internal hindrance to an unfolding of the confessional potential to welfare state expansion was the balance of power within the pillars. Pillarization, in its classical form, meant that the 'higher estates' governed the 'lower' of each confessional pillar with the help of the clergy, which was much more important in the Catholic than in the Calvinist pillar, although it was also true that pillarization implied that the former had to pay attention to the needs and demands of the latter. In the early 1960s, the confessional unions, and the Catholic ones in particular which organized many more ordinary workers, became restive and autonomous. In the post-war deliberations about social policy, the confessional unions had sided with the confessional employers in setting the subsidiarity principle before everything else. Now, they sided with the Social Democratic unions, demanding general social expansion and, in the key test case, raising the old age pensions to a social minimum. (The best study of this development is Berben and Jansen, 1982.)

Within the confessional political parties, polarization between right and left increased in the 1960s. The active backing of the unions and of progressive media was a crucial support to Veldkamp in his violent clashes with the right-wing of the Catholic leadership (Maas, 1982, pp. 118ff.). Concern with trade union reactions also became important among the Anti-Revolutionaries, traditionally the major party of pre-Keynesian financial orthodoxy and strictness and the leading party of nationalism and imperialism (Indonesia, New Guinea). A new generation of strongly socially committed intellectuals gained influence at the expense of the thin Calvinist business elite (Maas, 1982, pp. 79ff.; v. Enk, 1986).

The strengthening of labour on the tight labour market and the general cultural change tipped the balance of power within the crumbling pillars. But confessionalism did not cease to be of importance. In the foundation of the new interconfessional Christian Democratic Appeal party, it was made clear, above all at Calvinist insistence, that Christian principles remained central, and that the party therefore was different from the German CDU, seen mainly as a right-wing party with little religious meaning (v. Enk, 1986, p. 158).

Affluence does not *per se* lead to welfare state growth. It is quite logical to argue, and so it has been argued in a number of countries, including Sweden and the Netherlands around 1960, that affluence makes public social security superfluous or at least less necessary (Berben and Jansen, 1982, p. 102). The Dutch employers' organizations were also strongly against a rise in the old age pensions and against the use of redistributive general taxation for purposes of social security. However, in a situation where the affluent economy left ample room for profits as well as for wages and social security, resistance to strong social demands tends to wane rapidly. While on and off expressing worries about increasing costs, the Dutch employers' representatives in the Socio-Economic Council, on the whole, supported the rest of the welfare state expansion in the 1960s. Occasionally, they even came to declare their principled support of extensive social insurance, for social reasons and for reasons of counter-cyclical economic policy (see Berben and Jansen, 1982, pp. 113, 118).

Once the expansionary potential of confessionalism had got started, it acquired a momentum which confessional politics was singularly inept at reining in. This was not only because of the cost-led social insurance organization, but also, and even more importantly, because of the extreme intricacy of the political game of the confessional Netherlands. The contours of this complicated game may be sketched as follows. In spite of the basically stable and socially deep-rooted party system – in motion in the late 1960s and early 1970s – Dutch confessional politics had no clear leadership structure and no clear party line on issues other than confessional fundamentals. The perennial coalition politics had made elections of minor significance in deciding government composition which, instead, emerged out of protracted negotiations among the political elite. Furthermore, Dutch parliamentary politics preserved a significant amount of dualism between cabinet and parliament, always making it far from certain that a government proposal would be accepted by the parliamentary groups of the government parties. In the past, this complexity had significantly contributed to the delay of social reform. Since the mid-1960s, it has worked the other way around, making it extremely difficult for continuously strong conservative forces to stop public expenditure from growing.

They have certainly tried. In 1966, the right-wing of the Catholic party brought down the Catholic-Social Democratic government with a motion calling for a tighter budget. The ensuing confessional-Liberal cabinet, presided over by a previously little-known Catholic naval officer, intended to stop further social expansion and even declared its intention to make some reductions in existing social rights. In fact, however, no cuts were made, and some previously prepared social reforms were passed. The next government, under a moderately conservative Anti-Revolutionary and composed of confessionals, right-wing Liberals and a right-wing breakaway from the Labour party, had inflation control and a restrictive budget on its programme, but in the end progressive confessionals succeeded in vetoing cuts. The only real victory for these efforts at restraint came through the old negative policy of blocking major new institutional changes. Veldkamp's proposal of establishing health insurance for the whole population was finally buried. But for the rest, no sufficiently consistent and persistent right-wing policy could be put together (Maas, 1982; v. Enk, 1986; Veldkamp, 1978).

On the other hand, this devious mode of expansion also meant, that no political force was clearly and unequivocally identified with it, credited for it, and therefore prepared to make a principled stand in defence of the extensive welfare state. The two confessional parties that had provided most of the input (the Catholics and the Calvinist Anti-Revolutionaries) also contained some of the most prominent opponents of the expansion. The Labour party had supported the expansion, certainly, but mostly from the opposition benches. Depillarization also meant that the Labour party lost its organic links with the unions and increasingly became a party staffed by academics.

The Labour-led coalition of 1973 began with high social ambitions but, under the impact of the 1974 crisis, a more restrictive social and economic policy was announced. The architect of this turn was a Social Democrat, the Finance Minister Duisenberg. But this government had the same experience as the ones of 1967–72, that budgeted cuts were extremely difficult to bring about. It has been estimated, that only 14 per cent of intended cuts were realized. A more biting policy ensued with the confessional-right-wing Liberal coalitions of 1977–81 and since 1982. (See further Roebroek et al., 1988). We will return to economic crisis policy later. But the previous momentum did not stop abruptly. Although an inheritance from the previous government, the final piece of basic social generosity was legislated by the Christian Democratic government of Van Agt. In December 1979, the level of social assistance and of unemployment benefits was set equal to the net minimum wage, which was also equal to the old age pension (Roebroek and Berben, 1987, pp. 690, 694).

Dutch confessionalism has always been patriarchally sexist, a legacy which has spread to Dutch Social Democracy as well. The compromise on old age pensions had a remarkable sexist slant to it. All old persons got a right to a pension, except married women. Married couples did get more than singles, but this all went to the husband, in contrast to Sweden where it was always self-evident that half of the pension of a married couple should be paid to the wife. The Dutch bill was actually written and presented by a Labour party Social Minister. Only in 1985, under intense European Community pressure, was the sexist pension clause done away with.

A good part of the special character of the Dutch welfare state is expressed in two Dutch keywords referring to it. One is *uitkering* and its derivative *uitkeringsgerechtigd*. *Uitkering* is an everyday word designating a (public) transfer payment, and its derivative means 'entitled to a transfer benefit'. An *uitkering* can be both a social insurance entitlement, a pension, an unemployment benefit and so on, and a social assistance payment. Dutch language makes no distinction between the two, which implies a probably unique lack of stigmatization of people 'on welfare' or 'on the dole'. The other word is *verzorgingsstaat*, which is the usual Dutch word for welfare state. In contrast to the latter, however, it has slightly negative connotations. Literally it means 'provision state', a translation from the French *État de Providence*. It came into common use only in the latter half of the 1970s, and then primarily in contexts like 'the stagnating . . .', 'the crisis of . . .', 'the /uncertain/ future of . . .', 'the aftermath of . . .'. It expresses the lack of any principled legitimacy of the totality of the generous Dutch social policies, brought about piecemeal in the meandering manner of confessional reform politics.

Popular conservatism and the Swedish dynamic of class and municipality

Public social insurance was neither a labour movement invention nor a working class demand originally (Therborn, 1984a, 1986a). Once it was put on the agenda, it tended to get supported by the labour movement sooner or later, but other tasks might very well have a higher priority. In the early 1920s, the social issue to which the Swedish labour movement gave priority was agrarian reform. The trade union congress passed resolutions in 1922 and in 1926 proposing public facilitation of the acquisition of agrarian property as the main solution to the problem of unemployment (references in Therborn, 1986a, p. 21, a work in which other references on the history of Swedish social policy can be found; cf. also Olsson, 1986 and 1987). In spite of a vigorously growing manufacturing industry, Sweden was, until the 1930s, a predominantly agrarian and rural country.

Social insurance was introduced as a major Social Democratic idea in 1926 in a series of bills on health insurance and a plan for unemployment insurance put forward by the Social Democratic minority government, and in the electoral campaigns of Social Democracy in the 1926 (municipal and provincial) and 1928 (parliamentary) elections. In the campaign brochure of the latter, 'a welfare state' was called for. Quoting Ferdinand Lassalle (the nineteenth-century German labour leader), the leading Swedish Social Democratic social politician Gustav Möller (1928, p. 5) asserted, 'The state should not only be a nightwatchman's state but also a welfare state'. Nothing came out of this, however. The government was defeated over the rules governing the access to public relief works in cases of highly indirect connections with industrial conflict, an issue of class principle in reality involving only a handful of workers. In the electoral campaign, social insurance turned out to be no asset. It met with general indifference, and the 1928 election was dominated by a successful aggressive, anti-socialist mobilization by the right, freely extrapolating from a Social Democratic inheritance tax proposal. The term 'welfare state' did not stick and virtually disappeared from the political language of the period, although the Lassalle-Möller

connection adds an interesting branch to the genealogy of the welfare
state concept indicated by Peter Flora and Arnold Heidenheimer (1981,
pp. 18ff.). The radical yeoman tradition with its conception of farmer-
worker equality had won farmers' support for people's pensions, but for
the rest, the ancient farmer concern with public thrift was enshrined in
the Farmers' League (and among the strong farmer MP contingents of
the popular movements, Liberals and the Right) and in the general rural
culture of the country. There was still a significant non-monetarised
economy, not only among farmers and farm workers, but also among
workers for the combined enterprises of forestry, timber processing and
iron and steel-making who were paid partly in kind.

The 1930s was an important period in Swedish social policy. A new
momentum was gathered, and a characteristic orientation emerged. The
Depression put unemployment into focus and, in September 1932, the
Social Democrats into government office. Social policy was defined very
broadly, and policy-making was very powerfully staffed. Social insurance
now had only a minor part in this conception, 'a set of social insurance
schemes' constituting one of ten points in which the Minister for Social
Affairs summarized social policy. Unemployment policy, work safety,
working-time regulation, child care and housing were other important
items, all of them handled by the Ministry of Social Affairs which also
had the tasks that in most other countries fall to a Ministry of the Interior
(police and internal administration). This Ministry was headed by the
number two in the SAP leadership, Gustav Möller.

Earlier aspects of the public policy profile were reinforced and
modernized, and one new one was added. In the course of the 1920s a
broad consensus had emerged in Sweden about the appropriate policy
stance for coping with unemployment. That is, through the provision of
relief work, for which a municipally anchored central administration had
existed since the First World War. This was called 'the work line' and
was distinguished from 'the cash line', that is, the provision of
unemployment benefits in cash. The heavy emphasis on relief work did
not exclude traditional poor relief, nor several investigations into the
establishment of public unemployment insurance, but it gave all policy
debates and initiatives a special character. The 'work line' may also be
seen as an embodiment of the old Lutheran ethic and of farmers' values.
The controversial issues of crisis policy were working conditions (always
harsh), wages (below the lowest market wage for unskilled workers), and
the extension of public works. The deal between the Social Democrats
and the Farmers' League involved the support of the latter for unskilled
market wages and for starting general public works with normal
conditions, in return for Social Democratic support of farm protectionism
and acceptance of continued severe conditions for relief work (Therborn,
1984a). The pensions sytem was unified as an institution for public age

grants to the whole population, doing away with the insurance organization and with a number of separate pension funds for different categories of public employees. A rise (by later standards, modest) in the pension amount also took place and figured in the 1936 election. Part of the continuity of policy was that public expenditure was kept rather low. As a percentage of GDP, social expenditure was actually lower in 1938 than in 1932. GDP was considerably higher in 1938, but the growth of expenditure after 1932 was only marginally higher than in the 1920s (Flora, 1983, p. 428). No new expensive income maintenance programmes were created.

Novel, however, was a policy of family care and of regulating family consumption and gender relations. This new turn was brought about by Alva and Gunnar Myrdal (1934) with a tremendously influential book, *Crisis in the Population Question*. In a real *tour de force*, the Myrdals used demographic concerns with the low marriage and birth rate of Sweden as a platform for radical, and for its time feminist, social reform proposals. The population was a social resource, the quality as well as the quantity of which had to be enhanced. This was in contrast, not only to the Dutch conception of the population as a social burden to be diminished by emigration, but also to French and Nazi German concern with the breeding of future soldiers. The Myrdals' proposals, a large number of which were accepted and carried out, centred on two characteristic features: making marriage and child rearing a more attractive option for women, and bettering the quality of children and of their life environment. (The quality conception also included an eugenic component, explicit in the Myrdals' book and implied in an actual practice of forced sterilization of people considered unfit and demented (Elmér, 1958, pp. 161–2).) Measures taken included abolition of the remaining gender-specific salary scales in state employment; prohibition of the employer's right to dismiss anybody because of betrothal, marriage or pregnancy; a liberalization of contraception and, more modestly, of anti-abortion legislation; a maternity allowance; provision of public infant and mother care and health checks; favourable loans for and public advice to couples setting up a home; public support for better housing; provision of public housing for large families; the beginning of an extensive system of compulsory housing construction norms; free school meals for better nutrition (implemented later); elaborate plans for – but in the post-war period abandoned – public production of children's clothes and shoes.

The population policy had broad political support and central political status. It was through his work in a wartime Population Committee, planning post-war social policy, that Tage Erlander earned his spurs, which in 1946 took him to the positions of Social Democratic party leader and Prime Minister. The universalist, 'popular' conception had become deeply rooted. In the first wave of post-Second World War social policy debates and legislation, universalism was most firmly sustained by the bourgeois parties, with the support of the employers' confederation. Under financial pressure, the Social Democrats wanted to give priority to a means-tested increase of the 'people's pensions', but when the SAP parliamentary group found it shameful to stand for means-testing in the face of bourgeois universalism, the SAP cabinet backed down. The logic behind this line-up, so different from most Anglo-Saxon ones, is the following. Going back to the 1888 official class analysis referred to above, means-testing in Sweden meant mainly that the wealthy or prosperous minority should be excluded. For farmers and employers, who were going to have to foot much of the bill anyway, the argument was that if taxes must be paid, they too might as well get some benefit.

In view of all this, however, the late quantitative expansion of the Swedish welfare state looks puzzling. As has been pointed out above it is only in the second half of the 1960s that the Swedish welfare state looks big by international standards. One reason is the different orientation of Swedish social policy, emphasizing prevention and regulation above income maintenance. These qualitative aspects of the Swedish welfare state are scarcely visible from afar, embedded, as they tend to be, in the general polity and administration: municipal politicians applying housing norms, assessing pension claims and organizing family support; labour market board and other social boards officials implementing central policies of labour market balancing and social regulation. But that orientation, a remarkable mixture of conservative Lutheran puritanism and radicalism, is nevertheless only a secondary reason.

The absence of large-scale income maintenance programmes was not a voluntary choice of Swedish social politicians. The initiatives of Möller in the late 1920s were frustrated. At the SAP congress in 1932 another front-rank Social Democratic social politician, Bernhard Eriksson, compared with regret the high social insurance premiums paid and considered acceptable by German, Danish and French workers with the miniscule contributions of Swedish workers to the people's pensions insurance. In 1953, when the then Social Minister Gunnar Sträng presented his health insurance bill, he pointed out that by international comparison Sweden 'stood rather badly' as far as social insurance was concerned.

Finance was the bottleneck. This major reason for Swedish social lag depended in its turn upon three factors. Neutrality in the two world wars meant that the size of the Swedish state had not been extended as it had in the belligerent countries. In the UK, for example, between 1913 and 1918 public expenditure rose from 12.7 to 48.4 per cent of GDP, after which it never went below 23 per cent; from 1938 to 1944 it increased from 28.6 to 62.5 per cent of GDP, staying above 35 per cent for the rest of the 1940s, then to decline to a post-war low of 32 per cent in 1955. Swedish public expenditure grew from 10.4 per cent in 1913 to 14.3 per cent in 1918, a level at which it stayed in non-Depression years till the mid-1930s. During the Second World War it went up from 17.7 per cent in 1938 to 29.4 per cent in 1940, decreasing to 25.9 per cent in 1944, and to 19.3 per cent in 1946. Then expenditure climbed slowly, but reached the British post-war trough only in 1962 (Flora, 1983, pp. 426–7, 440–1). Before the First World War, general government taxes in Sweden took a larger part of GDP than in Germany and almost as much as in the UK. But in the 1920s the Swedish tax rate vacillated around 10–12 per cent of GDP, whereas the British tax was about 18–20 per cent and the German 15–16 per cent. Between 1938 and 1950 Swedish taxes rose from 13.9 per cent to 20.9 per cent of GDP, but the British from 18.7 per cent in 1935 to 33.2 per cent in 1950 (via 35.2 per cent in 1945). The other Scandinavian countries and, on a somewhat higher level, the Netherlands show a pattern similar to the Swedish one (Flora, 1983, pp. 262, 264).

Secondly, fiscal prudence was part of the legacy of the Farmers' Estate, strongly reproduced by the people's movement around the turn of the century, and the absence of wartime necessities had done little to change it. In the post-Second World War period, a 'tight' fiscal policy has been a central notion of Social Democratic policy in Sweden. This policy was theorized by the trade union economists Gösta Rehn and Rudolf Meidner, but it was firmly entrenched well before they acquired any significant political influence. It should probably be seen as part of the popular cautiousness and conservatism (with a small c) which Social Democracy inherited. Financial caution meant that a bill on compulsory universal health insurance passed in 1946 was only meant to take effect in 1950; in 1948 it was postponed till 1951; and, in 1950, Prime Minister Erlander told Parliament that because of the financial situation the health insurance scheme had to be postponed indefinitely.

The financial bottleneck was also due to a third factor, the removal of which was decisive for the later expansion. Added to the weakly extended financial capacities of the state and to the reproduction of traditional popular fiscal prudence was the particular mode of revenue-raising for social services in Sweden. Compulsory social insurance had never been a popular issue. It was originally a social Conservative, Liberal or, as in the Netherlands, a confessional conception, at first opposed by the labour movements of the pioneering countries (Therborn, 1984a). Largely accounting for the opposition was the non- or only marginally-redistributive nature of finance out of contributions by the insured. Indirect taxation was also an old popular grievance because of its regressive incidence. Because of popular influence, Swedish social security was financed overwhelmingly out of general public taxation, of which income taxes made up the major part. In 1949, 77 per cent of total social security – in the Netherlands 25 per cent and in the UK 62 per cent – and 64 per cent of social insurance were financed by general taxation. Income taxes constituted 63 per cent of general taxation in Sweden, as against 39 per cent in the Netherlands and 36 per cent in the UK (Flora, 1983, pp. 319, 329, 339, 520, 534, 548). According to the 1946 bill, 79 per cent of the new health insurance was to be paid for by general taxation. When health insurance was proposed again in 1953, this time taking effect, the state and the employers would pay one quarter each and the insured half. This was explicitly presented as a solution to the financial straitjacket, and it won the support of the main opposition party (Therborn 1984a, p. 43). At the given level of tax experience, a change in the structure of finance was clearly a political precondition for social policy expansion. Employers' contributions have since then become increasingly important to the Swedish welfare state. Another financial barrier was also broken. In 1959, traditional labour resistance to indirect taxation was overcome and a sales tax was adopted, later changed into a VAT.

The removal of the financial bottleneck did not, of itself, provide a positive dynamic for expansion. Compulsory health insurance was no clear success. On the contrary it was even believed that it contributed to the electoral reverse of the Social Democrats in the 1956 election, the reason being that it meant some disadvantages to white-collar employees who had sickness insurance schemes negotiated with their employers. The political turn to social policy offensive took place after 1956. By 1960 the battle was decisively won, but it took a few more years before it showed up in the statistics. In almost every single aspect this Swedish social expansion differed from that of its Dutch counterpart, whose similar expansion was taking place almost simultaneously (a few years earlier). The Swedish thrust forward was pushed by the Social Democrats on an explicit class issue involving a confrontational, albeit smartly tactical, form of politics.

Swedish old age pensions were flat-rate, but this derived from their conception as a demogrant and was not part of any principled ideology, unlike the situation in Britain. The Dutch issue of 1964, whether pensions should be enough to live on, had been settled in Sweden in principle in 1947, and in practice in the early 1950s. The principle was that no pensioner should need to take recourse to social assistance, and when it was found that this was still the case, the pensions were raised. However, what resulted was no more than what the Dutch called 'a social minimum'. Most white-collar employees and some workers had additional occupational pensions. The manual workers' trade unions now began to demand occupational pensions for all workers and for this reform to be effectual through legislation, as it seemed impossible to reach an agreement with the employers' confederation. This issue became the leverage point of welfare state expansion.

The Swedish supplementary pensions scheme, ATP, was probably the most controversial social policy issue of post-war advanced capitalism. It broke up the coalition between Social Democracy and the Farmers' League, it was the object of a (consultative) referendum (in 1957), of an extra parliamentary election (in June 1958), and the key issue of at least two other elections (municipal in September 1958, parliamentary in 1960). The victory for the Social Democratic alternative was very narrow, in spite of a massive mobilization by the manual workers' confederation and of the full support of the Communists. The referendum gave no majority, only a plurality, but the Farmers' League had an incentive to distance itself from the other bourgeois parties with a view to transforming itself into a Centre Party, so the referendum involved three alternatives. The extra parliamentary election saw an advance of the SAP, but no majority. Only the abstention of one 'worker-Liberal' MP, a remnant of the old people's movement lib-lab current, saved the ATP bill in 1958.

As far as social issues are concerned, the 1960 election was the most clearly polarized one in Swedish post-war history (see further Therborn, 1983). On one side, the Social Democrats were arguing for what they called 'the Strong Society', meaning a strong public sector; on the other, the three bourgeois parties for individual initiative, tax reduction and a more liberal economy. ATP was kept in the forefront by the Social Democrats, while the Liberals and the Centre Party now were prepared to acquiesce in the parliamentary outcome of 1958. The electoral verdict was clear: the SAP got its second highest vote ever in a parliamentary election, 47.8 per cent, second only to its extraordinary victory in September 1940. As the Communist Party got 4.5 per cent (and parliamentary representation), the three bourgeois parties, which had received an electoral majority in 1956, were roundly defeated. For the remaining elections of the 1960s and 1970s, the bourgeois opposition refrained from demanding tax cuts. Ironically enough, this period of oppositional silence on taxation was precisely the time at which Sweden first became an internationally high tax country.

Part of the Social Democratic electoral victory was the beginning of a realignment of white-collar employees. The ATP legislation had given white-collar trade unions a formal option of staying outside the public occupational pensions scheme. Actually, this was not intended to be a practical option (to be inferred from declarations of social Minister Nilsson at meetings of the SAP parliamentary group and the Party Executive). Negotiations between the employers' confederation and the main private sector white-collar union proved this to be the case. The result was a twofold gain for the SAP. The employers agreed to pay the employees' salary increases commensurate to what had been set aside in previous private pensions agreements, which meant in the short run that the bourgeois parties were proved wrong in their predictions of stagnant real salaries and wages due to direct and indirect effects of ATP. In the longer run, the inclusion of white-collar employees in the ATP system broadened and solidified the welfare state coalition. Private entrepreneurs soon tended to find it advantageous to join the ATP scheme too.

The extension of the revenue base by massive resort to employers' contributions – the sole finance of ATP pensions for workers and employees – and indirect taxation created the financial means, and the working class mobilization for occupational pensions for all manual workers provided the impetus and the political clout for Swedish welfare state expansion. The dynamic was sustained and kept up for two decades owing to at least three important explanatory forces.

One had to do with the resounding political victory with which the whole process had started and the very large part of the population directly benefiting from it. Against such a background, it was unlikely that all three rival bourgeois parties would come round to a common anti-welfare position. They have not done so to this day, and the frontal opposition of each party by itself is futile, given the size of Social Democracy. It is in this political context that the rapid ageing of the Swedish population must be seen, with concomitant social rights and care needs of the elderly. The ATP system went into effect in 1960 and the first pensions were paid out in 1963. Then there were 16,000, in 1970, 393,000, and in 1980, 1,227,000 (Olsson, 1987, p. 56), and by the beginning of the financial year 1987–88 they amounted to about 1,700,000 (Finansdepartementet, 1988, p. 151).

The third explanatory force is the mode of finance. ATP is a funded insurance scheme and is therefore capable of running into deficit and calling forth restraining mechanisms. Debate about its long-term viability has started, but so far eventual problems have been located in the next millennium, thereby, as yet, inciting no political action. The rest of Swedish social insurance is *de facto* not based on insurance principles and has, therefore, like the Dutch, a cost-led expansionary dynamic with revenues adapted to cover costs. But the Swedish welfare state also has another, more particular financial dynamic. That is the provinces (*landsting*) and the municipalities, both with important income taxing powers. The provinces run most of the country's health care, and the municipalities provide child daycare, non-medical care for the elderly, a wide supply of leisure facilities, social assistance, public housing and housing subsidies. Under tight central supervision and with central money the latter also administer the comprehensive school system. Local direct taxes have increased their share of total public revenue, from 19 per cent in 1962 to 26 per cent in 1980, while the proportion of central direct taxes has gone down from 26 per cent to 12 per cent in the same period (Olsson, 1987, p. 53). Out of total public expenditure, provinces and municipalities have increased their share from 47 per cent in 1960 to 56 per cent in 1980 (Olsson, 1987, p. 14). The average Swedish municipality is rather big. A forced merger in the early 1970s brought the number down to 278, the norm being that none should have fewer than 8000 inhabitants. The immediate reason for that norm was the recruitment to a full comprehensive school system, but an important implication is a relatively large tax base upon which to build an extensive municipal apparatus.

Sweden has 23 provinces (and the cities of Gothenburg and Malmö and the island of Gotland, in which cases the municipality also has provincial competence). The overwhelming part of their task consists of health care administration, for which they pay by levying an income tax. Health care has expanded and become enormously more expensive everywhere. Swedish health care administration faces much less financial restraint than in most other countries, however. Provincial elections take place on the same day as municipal and parliamentary ones, and few citizens pay much attention to provincial politics. In a general ambience of welfare state expansion, this tends to foster provincial expansion without much concern. Second to the USA (with its mainly private set-up) Sweden has the most expensive health care system in the world (OECD, 1985, pp. 11, 31, 32). Bourgeois and Social Democratic provinces have increased their expenditure at basically the same pace in the period 1960–80, controlling for demographic structure and tax-base (Therborn, 1987b, p. 41).

Market Voice and Market Exit: Two Supplements to Market Loyalty

The extensive and socially ambitious polities of Sweden and the Netherlands coexist, as we noted in the first section, with vigorous private capital accumulation. However, this cohabitation of public sector and private markets is not without problems. It calls for means of accommodating state, capital, and labour. This question is often dealt with theoretically by invoking 'corporatism', on which Sweden and the Netherlands both score 'strong' (Lehmbruch, 1984, p. 66) or 'high' (Schmitter, 1981, p. 297). Occasionally, the two countries are qualitatively differentiated among those with a heavy dose of corporatism: the Netherlands as 'liberal corporatist', having strong capital and weak labour, and Sweden, having both strong labour and capital, as being 'social' as well as 'liberal corporatist' (Katzenstein, 1985, p. 105). In reality, the corporatist amalgamation is rather confusing, and the 'liberal corporatist' characterization of the Netherlands rather misleading. To see Sweden as liberally-cum-socially corporatist is more apt, but it is not a very fruitful base of comparison with the Netherlands. Instead, the suggestive distinction by Albert Hirschmann (1970) of exit, voice, and loyalty seems more promising. The public policies of Sweden as well as of the Netherlands have developed on the basis of a fundamental loyalty to the capitalist market economy. But on that common basis the two countries have diverged in their mode of accommodating this loyalty to important non-market principles of public policy-making. It is in capturing the core of these modes that Hirschmann's distinction is helpful. The Swedish manner of bringing markets and public policy goals into viable coexistence is to regulate who may speak in the markets, at what pitch, and at what time, and to raise a strong state voice in the market. The Dutch mode, on the other hand, is to provide, to organize, or to facilitate exits from markets. The Swedish public authorities are anxious not to leave the marketplace to the free marketeers, and the Dutch to keep the public voice low or quiet. Metaphors aside, what is meant is that Swedish public policy is oriented towards regulating the parameters of market action and to intervention in the market, while the Dutch concentrate on public adaptation or compensation for the market. Differences are not pure and absolute, but are ones of emphasis. Contrary to what the 'liberal corporatist' label suggests, the latter may turn out more subversive of liberal market rationality than the former kind of policy.

Two key markets are the money and the labour markets. The former was crucial to the distinctive crisis policies of Sweden and the Netherlands in the 1930s as well as in the 1970s and 1980s, the second to social reform as well as to crisis policies in both nations. From the money market, there is no real exit for a capitalist country, but the extent to which the option is for voice or loyalty very strongly affects the burden upon exit or voice in the labour market.

Means or end? The national currency on the world market

With regard to their currency policies, Sweden and the Netherlands maintained policy continuation in the crises of 1929 and of 1973. The Swedes devalued their currency unashamedly in both crises. In 1931 Sweden immediately followed the British off gold, and also devalued against the pound. In the 1970s Sweden undertook a series of devaluations for reasons of external adjustment and then, as the initial move of the Social Democrats back in office, in 1982 a 16 per cent competitive devaluation. Over the period of international 'stagflation' from 1973 to 1985, among comparable developed economies only Australia, Italy and New Zealand devalued their currency more than

Sweden's 26.5 per cent. The Dutch, on the other hand, revalued their currency by 26.4 per cent, surpassed only by Switzerland, Japan and Germany (OECD, 1987b, p. 169). In the 1930s the Netherlands was part of the 'Gold Bloc', the small group of countries sticking to the gold standard, after Britain, and others with her, had abandoned it. Only in September 1936, a year after Belgium, and after the French, and in view of impending Swiss defection, did the Dutch authorities go off gold.

The effects of the currency option chosen were the same in both crises: alleviating the pressure of international competition and creating more room for domestic expansion in Sweden, increasing external pressure in the Netherlands. However, the immediate reasons for the national choice seem to have been rather different in the two crises. The Swedish 1931 devaluation was a swift adaptation to new market conditions, a consensual step following the lead of the country's major trading partner (Myrdal, 1931). But the 1982 one was part of an offensive move by the new Social Democratic government. Dutch resistance to the British example in the 1930s was an assertion of monetary independence, although with the *de facto* meaning of doing nothing – while at the same time explicitly calling for a policy of 'adaptation' at home (v. Oenen, 1982, ch. VI). In the 1970s and 1980s, on the other hand, the hard guilder policy involved an adaptation to the German mark and to French needs of veiled franc devaluation.

Common to the national options in both crises, however, was a characteristic conception of the currency. In Sweden, the currency was in both cases seen as an instrument for achieving ends of international competitiveness. When the end was endangered, appropriate means had to be adopted and the public authorities had to intervene in the market. To the decisive Dutch actors the currency had an intrinsic value. In the 1930s gold standard orthodoxy was defended by arguments such as that of the President of the Nederlandse Bank that 'We are no counterfeiters' (v. Oenen 1982, p. 250). Prime Minister Colijn and the Finance Ministers of the period held the same view. In the recent crisis, the hard currency, no foreign loan policy (in spite of mounting public deficits) is justified by the assertion that an easy currency and external loans would entail beggaring one's neighbour (National Bank President Duisenberg in an interview). The Dutch National Bank, although not constitutionally sovereign in the manner of the Bundesbank (cf. ch. 3 this volume), is more autonomous and prestigious in relation to the government than the Swedish National Bank. In this case, however, the position of a specific institution seems less a policy cause than the effect of a policy conception with a broader social base. In both crises, monetary orthodoxy has been embraced by political leaders as well as by the bank.

It seems that the basic reason for these different national modes of relating to the currency market is the type of capitalism. As was indicated above, Swedish capitalism is heavily industrial, and the currency tends to be regarded as a means to industrial international competitiveness. Dutch capitalism, on the other hand, is traditionally mercantile and colonial; largely *rentier* in the eigtheenth century, and in modern times with powerful private banks and international financial operators, all involving key actors for whom the currency tends to acquire a value in itself. An instrumental view of the currency is conducive to intervention, to raising one's voice in the market; an intrinsic respect for the currency is a market loyalty which necessitates a more extensive exit or louder voice in other markets.

'Parties' and 'partners' – two kinds of institutionalized industrial relations

Prevailing language is symptomatic of social relations. In the Netherlands, unions and employers are 'social partners'. In Sweden they are 'the parties of the labour market'. Partnership constitutes an exit from market rivalry; partisanship an organization of it.

The Dutch conception derives from Catholic and Calvinist conceptions of social ordering. It culminated in the post-Second World War process of labour market institutionalization. In order to understand the Dutch confessional idea, the English reader should be reminded of a Continental European legal distinction between public and private law. The former pertains to the state and to the general public order, the latter to relations between members of civil society. Continental European law gives special weight to and provides special procedures for public law. The Business Organization Act of 1950, which was the instrument of labour market institutionalization, was a public law regulation of business. A Socio-Economic Council of representatives of capital, labour and 'the Crown' (in effect, the major political parties via senior academics) was installed as an official advisory body to the Cabinet and as the top organ of branch-specific organizations of capital and labour. The latter were to constitute a public ordering of private enterprise and of capital-labour relations. The intention was twofold: to supersede capital-labour conflict and to mitigate goods market competition. In fact, the market reasserted itself against corporatist organization with the momentum of the post-war boom and only the advisory body actually materialized. Another possible exit from the market set-up, but never really opened, was the establishment in 1947 of a Central Plan Bureau, originally as the chief agency for managing what was going to be a 'guided economy'. The Catholic politicians clipped its wings from the beginning, although they were crucial to bringing it about at all, as had also been the case with the Public Law Ordering of Business. The Plan Bureau became an influential body for sophisticated econometric modelling of an increasingly liberal orientation, but in no sense an agency of economic planning (see further Böhl et al., 1981, pp. 229ff. and Beld, 1979).

More powerful was the Collegium of National Mediators, the government-appointed implementers of the 'guided wage policy', the cornerstone of Dutch macroeconomic policy after the war, effectively determining post-war wages until the mid 1960s. The guided wage policy originally had broad support and was considered a key instrument of post-war reconstruction, and industrialization. Confessional as well as Social Democratic political forces saw it as the primary means of reordering of the economy. When it came under pressure, it was first abandoned by the employers, then by the confessional unions. The Social Democratic unions defended it to the end, regarding it as the best available means to wage equalisation (Hueting et al., 1983, pp. 239ff.). Part of this post-war policy was a *de facto* delegalization of strikes. Only in the late 1960s did this become obsolete in practice, after an interest in a relegalization had been expressed by the confessional Social Democratic Cals coalition government in 1966, and subsequently supported by official advice from the Socio-Economic Council in 1968.

Employee rights, most recently expressed in the Enterprise Councils Act of 1979 conferring powers on councils elected by all employees, whether unionized or not, provide paths outside the market. Appeals may be made to the Amsterdam Court of Justice over enterprise decisions, and the enterprise council has the right to veto a nomination to the Board of Directors, with the Socio-Economic Council having the final word (see further the standard work by Windmuller et al., 1983 and Teulings, 1981).

The Swedish system of industrial relations, alleged 'corporatist' commonality notwithstanding, is a mirror image of the Dutch. 'Freedom of the labour market' is conceived as a fundamental democratic right. Although practised *sotto voce*, 'incomes policy' is still officially taboo, and the Dutch notion of a 'guided wage policy' would in Swedish have connotations similar to 'guided democracy'. Since 1936 in the private sector, since 1965 in the public sector, the law has guaranteed the right to collective bargaining, and with bargaining the right to strike and to lockout is explicitly recognized. Conflict rights in the public sector are more extensive in Sweden than in most countries. The conflictual principle is underlined by the Swedish 1974 Constitution's guaranteeing the right to lock out as well as the right to strike (para. 17). These rights are severely regulated, however. According to legislation passed in 1928, only when a collective contract has elapsed and due notice has been given is a strike or lock-out legal. The 'Basic Agreement' between the confederations of employers and of trade unions in 1938 laid the basis for post-war institutionalization of collective bargaining. The organiz- ations of employers as well as of workers and employees are publicly asked for their opinion about official investigations and government proposals, but the organizations are asked separately, without any machinery whatsoever for attempting to create consensus. In contrast to their Dutch counterparts, the Swedish Social Democrats have not set up a Plan Bureau. The Ministry of Finance has always been the key economic policy-making body of Swedish Social Democracy. A succession of long-lived, popular as well as powerful Social Democratic Finance Ministers – Ernst Wigforss, Gunnar Sträng, Kjell-Olof Feldt – have all catered to the sound functioning of markets, while themselves skilfully and innovatively acting on them.

Under Social Democratic auspices, government policy towards industrial relations has largely been to provide a legal voice for the unions. Early post-war investigations into a general unemployment insurance were finally buried because the unions wanted publicly financed union-run insurance instead (see further Therborn, 1986a). In the 1950s and the 1960s neither the unions nor the employers wanted any government interference in industrial relations. The trade union economists Gösta Rehn and Rudolf Meidner developed a new labour market model in order to cope with macroeconomic management under conditions of full employment in which, instead of intervening in the wage-bargaining process, the government should stiffen employer resistance to wage increases by high taxation. For reasons of equality as well as of labour rationality, the unions should pursue a centralized 'solidaristic wage policy' aimed at reducing differentials between enterprises and industries. (The unitary Swedish trade union movement with its high organizational density could realistically hope to achieve wages equalization by centralized market bargaining without having recourse to the state in the manner of the divided and pillarized Dutch trade unions.) To the extent that such a policy tended to result in unemployment because of lay-offs from low productivity enterprises, public measures should support and stimulate labour mobility into high productivity areas. (For an interesting autobiographical account of the development of, and of the political fight for, this model, see Rehn, 1977.)

In the 1970s Swedish unions changed their minds about labour legislation. In the first half of the 1970s there ensued a spate of legislation on employee (read union) representation on the board of directors, on employment protection, on the work environment and on co-determination. The character of the legislation is in a sense summed up in the latter which gives the plant level unions the right to be informed and to bargain about all decisions of the enterprise, and the public authority, employer. It does not provide for any consensus-making council. Bargaining between two labour market actors is the key content, and the law provides additional resources, in the form of legal rights, to the weaker party in the labour market, and pecuniary penalties for employers – including political bodies – who take major decisions without prior bargaining. However, after all bargaining, at the end of the day, the employer decides. The ground and the rules of capital accumulation on the market are left intact, but the position of labour is bolstered (see further Schiller et al., 1987).

The relative effects of these policy emphases on legal exits from and legal voice in the labour market are hard to assess. Given the vast superiority of votes and of industrial muscle of the Swedish labour movement, the most noteworthy feature is that the superiority of benefits to Swedish workers is not at all clear-cut. There are certain demands made by the Dutch unions which the Swedes alone have been able to realize: a legal occupational pensions system for all workers, a share in the accumulation of capital. The ATP scheme in effect from 1960 realised the former, the wage earners' funds legislation of December 1983 the second, while similar Dutch demands in the 1970s came to nothing. Swedish safety stewards have the legal right to stop work which they consider dangerous. On the other hand, the same social conditions for workers as for employees were established in big Dutch enterprises in the 1960s (I am here indebted to S. Stoop), but are not yet a fact in Sweden (which also has strong white-collar unions). Most Dutch workers receive 100 per cent sick payment, 80 per cent by law and the rest by collective agreement, whereas the first sickness wage agreements for manual workers in Sweden were concluded in early 1988. The Dutch had a serious industrial and political conflict about an attempt to do away with that right in 1981–2, a conflict won by the unions. Since the 1965 Philips agreement, Dutch workers have indexed wages, a demand only obliquely raised by Swedish unions and always firmly rejected by the employers. In terms of real wages, Swedish workers have been the OECD losers in the 1973–85 crisis, with zero increase in real hourly earnings. Only US workers have been worse off. New Zealand workers come third in the back row, and the Dutch fourth, having real wages increases, but by less than 0.1 per cent a year from 1973 to 1985 (OECD, 1987a, p. 90).

Employment or alternatives to employment

The different unemployment outcomes of the 1973–85 crisis – in the Netherlands, 10.6 per cent unemployment in 1985, 9.9 per cent in 1986, 9.4 per cent in the third quarter of 1987, and for Sweden the corresponding figures being 2.8 per cent, 2.7 per cent, 1.9 per cent (OECD, 1987c, p. 190) – reflect to a large extent the differential strength of labour in the two countries. The institutionalized Swedish commitment to full employment, fully accepted and successfully maintained by the bourgeois governments of 1976–82 (they actually had to bear the brunt of the crisis in Sweden), was initiated by post-war Social Democracy. Such a commitment, and a corresponding policy-making instrument, was clearly lacking in the Netherlands (see further Therborn, 1986b). The positive effects of mass unemployment with regard to wage moderation, changes in labour legislation and cutting down the collective sector were pointed out by leading Dutch business-men, high civil servants and former leading centre-right politicians in key interviews that my collaborators Wessel Visser and Rien Wijnhoven made in 1987. The attempts of Labour leader den Uyl, as Minister of Social Affairs and Employment in 1981–2, to do something about soaring unemployment were incomprehensible to and competely frus-trated by the dominant Christian Democratic coalition partner (cf. Galen, Jansen and Vuisje 1985, pp. 42ff., 223).

However, the Dutch outcome was only in part a failure in relation to Labour efforts and to the solemn ends of public macroeconomics, and still less a consequence of deliberate right-wing pressure on labour market action. It was also a choice of exit from the labour market, rather than of intervening in it. The post-war use of exit mechanisms had begun already with the promotion of emigration in the late 1940s and the early 1950s. Characteristically, the first post-war social insurance legislation concerned unemployment compensation, passed in 1949, and effective from 1952. The exit policy took new forms in the handling of the structural rationalization of the economy in the 1960s. Many people laid off were classified as disabled. Between 1963 and 1973 the number of 'disabled' in the Netherlands rose by about two thirds, from 183,000 to 303,000, then surged to 720,000 by 1982 (Roebroek and Berben 1987, p. 732). By 1 January 1987, there were 792,000 'disabled' Dutch adults below the pension age, equivalent to 13.2 per cent of the labour force (Centraal Bureau voor de statistiek, 1988).

The Netherlands ceased to experience full employment in 1975, during the Labour-led den Uyl government. In that cabinet there was no battle-line between Social Democrats and Christian Democrats over (un)employment. There was for a time a conflict between a restrictive Minister of Finance and a more expansive Social Minister. But the former was a Social Democrat and the latter a Christian Democrat (Gortzak, 1978, pp. 18, 31ff.). In opposition in the 1980s, the Social Democrats have been more concerned with preserving the purchasing power (*de koopkracht*) of transfer beneficiaries and minimum wage workers than with combatting enduring massive unemployment.

Working-time reduction has been a major crisis policy of the unions, encouraged by the state, and at least formally accepted by the employers in the central agreement of 1982. Unemployment benefits are generous and easy to get, even for young school-leavers. In spite of a decline in the

1980s, the development of purchasing power in the period 1974–86 has been much more favourable for people drawing a transfer payment than for employed workers; about 10 per cent total increase to the former, standstill (as annual income) to the latter (Tweede Kamer, 1986–7, pp. 197–8, 2:24). (Although, at least for old age pensioners, similar trajectories for benefits and wages took place in Sweden from 1975 to 1984 (Vogel et al., 1987, p. 116).)

Comparatively little effort has been put into supplying jobs and training in the 1980s, trainees usually comprising less than 1 per cent of the labour force (Centraal Planbureau, 1986, p. 70). For the handicapped there is, however, an extended work programme, in 1987 comprising about 1.3 per cent of the labour force. If those measures are included, about 2 to 2.2 per cent of the Dutch labour force have been touched by such schemes (Ministerie van Sociale Zaken, 1987).

Swedish works and retraining programmes, on the other hand, are renowned, and surpassed 3 per cent of the labour force in 1978, and peaked in 1984. In that year, they amounted to 4.6 per cent of the labour force (Statistika Centralbyrån, 1988, pp. 176, 193). The Swedish government takes pride in labour market entry. The high rate of employment in Sweden, as well as the low rate of unemployment, are highlighted by the government in a rare international comparison in the latest budget (Finansdepartmentet, 1988, p. 111).

The Swedish special labour market policy is no substitute for regular employment. On the contrary, in the mid 1970s a secular trend of a diminishing volume in the total number of paid working-hours a year – a decline due mainly to the increase in pensioners and to work-time reduction – was broken. After a few years of stability, the volume of paid work began to rise in Sweden. In 1985, it was 1.9 per cent higher than in 1975 (Statistika Centralbyrån, 1986, p. 15), and the growth continues. In the Netherlands, the work volume counted in annual hours was 9.5 per cent lower in 1985 than in 1975 (Tweede Kamer 1987–8, p. 39; Centraal Bureau voor de Statistiek, 1979, p. 68; OECD 1987d, p. 200). The upward turn of the Swedish labour market in the international crisis is remarkable, but not unique. A similar trend in the employment volume occurred in Finland and Norway also (see further Therborn, 1987c). The turnaround in Sweden's historical trend is entirely due to the expansion of the municipal and the provincial welfare state, mainly in the areas of employment in health care, care for the elderly and daycare of children (Statistika Centralbyrån, 1986, p. 25). The actual trajectory of (un)employment is, of course, not reducible to deliberate policy choices. However, the former is very significantly affected by the latter (see further Therborn, 1986b). The reasons for the Dutch choosing mainly a labour market policy of exit and the Swedish of voice are no doubt complex. But a certain pattern emerges out of the historical record.

Three elements appear to have been crucial, an ideological tradition, an institutional legacy, and a policy experience.

There is a Dutch Catholic tradition of exit policies going back to the 1930s at least, the roots or possible causes of which might be seen in the fact that the Catholic Church originated in times before capitalism and labour markets. The proposals (most of them not carried) of the Catholic Ministers Romme and Stenberghe at that time included work programmes, but had a characteristic exit slant: work-time reduction, exclusion of married women and some other categories from the labour market, prohibition of mechanization and rationalization (de Rooy, 1979, p. 179). Romme was the political leader of post-war Dutch Catholicism in the 1940s and 1950s. That a job was not an important human right was stressed by the Catholic Premier Van Agt in a parliamentary debate in the autumn of 1980. Van Agt took Labour leader den Uyl to task for ·implying that by demanding full employment, 'you can only completely, humanely and socially function in society when you have a paid job' (Tweede Kamer, 1980–1, p. 200).

It might, however, be asked how this ideological stance rhymes with the Protestant Ethic of Calvinism. The answer is that orthodox, fundamentalist Calvinism (that of the Anti-Revolutionaries) was always against state organization and at the height of its power (in the inter-war period), pre-Keynesian liberal in fiscal and monetary policy, without believing that society should be left to the market. In other words, the pillarized anti-statism of Calvinism prevented it embracing an active public labour market policy, while refusing to give market outcomes a principled endorsement. In the ensuing vacuum, support, or at least tolerance, of exit policies could develop.

Patriarchy is an important part of the religious tradition, and Dutch patriarchy has kept women at home. When the grip of patriarchy loosens, this tends to imply an ambiguous attitude to employment as it is so overwhelmingly a male attribute. By 1974, the Netherlands had the lowest female labour force participation of all the OECD countries, a mere 29.7 per cent. Any female right to labour market participation has not been established, although women's emancipation has led to a considerable participation increase, to 41.2 per cent in 1985 (Sweden 78.2 per cent) (OECD, 1987a, p. 35).

The relativization of paid employment in the Dutch confessional view of society comes out clearly in the current institution of 'work with right of public benefit' (*werk met behoud van uitkering*). It gives a new twist to charity work, and refers to unpaid voluntary work for municipalities or non-profit organizations, for which the worker is legally allowed to keep his or her public benefit. In 1984 there were officially 50,000 unpaid workers of this kind (Sociaal en Cultureel Planbureau, 1986, p. 86).

Sweden has no comparable tradition. On the contrary, as was noted above, an employment provision approach to unemployment was firmly entrenched by the 1920s. There was also from early on a different perspective in the Social Democratic labour movement. In spite of the official line of the European labour movement, both the Swedish trade union leadership and the Social Democratic Party refrained from proposing work-time reduction as (part of) a solution to the unemployment crisis. This difference was clear at the LO Congress in 1931, at the SAP congress in early 1932, and in the SAP parliamentary 'crisis motion' of 1932, that is, before the Social Democrats had got into office (Therborn, 1984a). The rural Lutheran work ethic and the fact that the unemployment situation was not as desperate as in Central Europe may perhaps explain the stance, vigorously repeated in the 1970s and 1980s. The Dutch Plan of Labour of 1935, on the other hand, included calls for work-time reduction, as has Dutch Social Democratic and trade union policy in the 1980s.

In spite of ideology, cash was the most frequent help given to the Swedish unemployed until 1934, 56 per cent of all help in 1933 (calculated from Gustafsson et al., 1974, p. 128). This was less than in the Netherlands, where the dole constituted between 69 and 81 per cent of support to the unemployed (Goudriaan, 1986, p. 30). But the most important difference was that Swedish unemployment support was concentrated in one central body that was revamped in 1940 for tasks of wartime labour allocation. Out of the experience of the 1930s and out of the 1940 Labour Market Commission came a vision of a special labour market policy as part of post-war planning. The top priority of the SAP-LO joint Postwar Programme was full employment, and two of its wide-ranging 27 points dealt with labour market policy. In 1948, a new Labour Market Board was set up, a context in which the so-called Rehn-Meidner model and the 'active labour market policy' concept could develop. This increasingly powerful and well insured body ran the local job exchanges, furthered mobility and retraining, and was delegated all means to organize public relief works. But it had nothing directly to do with unemployment compensation (see further Rothstein, 1986).

No similar central institution existed in the Netherlands at the outbreak of the Depression. One was later proposed, but its implementation was delayed until 1939 and it left no heritage for the post-occupation era (de Rooy, 1979, pp. 179ff.; Goudriaan, 1986, p. 69). When Jan Tinbergen (1946) drew the conclusions of the inter-war period, the need for a specific labour market policy was not among them. The penalizing relief works petered out in the 1950s, and little of a modern labour market policy followed it. By the time of the post-1973 crisis, the post-war Central Plan Bureau was a bulwark against selective public economic policies and produced much material arguing that any public works programme was counterproductive (see further

Therborn, 1986b, pp. 153ff.). An autonomous municipal and provincial labour market expansion was impossible in the Netherlands, as these bodies have only minor taxation rights and receive 95 per cent of their income from the central state (Tweede Kamer, 1987–8, p. 222). On the other hand, the Dutch social security system with its low thresholds provided an open door out of the labour market when the pressure on the latter mounted.

A third part of the explanation, after the ideological and the institutional, is that exit policies can constitute a way out of market failure and market weakness when no other policy is very credible by experience. The Depression decade ended very differently in Sweden and the Netherlands. In Sweden, the end of the 1930s consolidated the triumph of Social Democracy which was given credit for its crisis policy. Registered unemployment (relief-seekers) in 1939 were only 15 per cent of the 1933 peak (Therborn 1984a, p. 565). That unemployment could be prevented was a central part of Swedish political self-confidence, reinforced by successful labour market policy interventions in the pre-crisis recessions after the war. The Netherlands, on the other hand, was by the end of the 1930s just beginning to find a route out of the right-wing, confessional, 'Antithesis' bloc to a 'Roman-Red' Catholic-Social Democratic Coalition, with no positive innovations and an unemployment figure still 55 per cent of the 1936 peak. After the war, scarcity of labour and full employment soon emerged, rather unexpectedly. The temporary rise in unemployment in 1958 and in 1967–8 was hardly met with any labour market countermeasures, and soon once again appeared unnecessary (Centraal Bureau voor de Statistiek, 1979, p. 69). When the avalanche of unemployment got rolling in the early 1980s – aggravated by the maturing of the last high birth-rate cohort – an honourable exit from the labour market was also the most visible solution. It should be emphasized that Dutch labour market exit policy has no nationalistic streak to it. Unemployed immigrants have been given support to return to their native countries when they so wished, but the rise of unemployment was not accompanied by expulsions and special termination of immigrant labour contracts (see further Therborn, 1987a).

Sweden and the Netherlands have both created combinations of advanced, multinationally competitive private capitalism and extended, generous welfare states. In its current scope, this combination is in both cases an achievement of the 1960s. The forms of their welfare states differ, however, and derive from two historical patterns of popular mobilization and organization at the time of the rise of modern capitalism – from 'pillarization' and from 'popular movements'. Dutch Catholicism came to constitute the developed model of the former. Swedish labour came to epitomize and to further, more than elsewhere, the popular movement tradition.

Both states provide both their private multinationals and local capital with a supportive home base. But this loyalty to international and to domestic markets has been combined differently. Sweden has opted for a 'voice' policy in the labour market, promoting and regulating labour market action: promoting female and youth entry into the labour market, keeping full employment, furthering mobility, recognising-cum-regulating collective market action by autonomous parties. The Dutch have pursued an 'exit' policy, trying to replace collective labour market action with institutionalized collaboration, and generously compensating for employment by disability, unemployment, and social assistance benefits and by encouraging unpaid work outside the labour market.

Both policies pose problems for private capital accumulation, by raising the voice of labour and by providing exit from labour respectively. Both are potentially costly to the rate of profit. The ways that the two countries go about handling these problems are different but functionally roughly equivalent. In the Swedish case an active currency policy enhances international competitiveness, while trade union power in the labour market .is accommodated by the mobility and the technical adaptability of individual workers and employees and by the market flexibility of individual wages and salaries (OECD, 1983, p. 48; Åberg, 1984). The Dutch exit policies accommodate capital interests by restraining state interventions in markets, refraining from an instrumental currency policy and from controlling financial markets, reining in public employment, and holding down public investment.

These ways of linking welfare state and capital accumulation are not necessarily stable. The linkages are no more stable than the bases of the states and of the capitals. They do, however, give both countries their intriguing duality of public welfare and private capital. A labour movement social state connecting with exit policies with regard to the labour market would be explosively difficult to accommodate to private capital. A confessionally shaped state playing by the ground rules of labour markets would, on the other hand, probably be more manageable, but also more conventionally capitalist. And what Sweden and the Netherlands today have in common is precisely that both exemplify a welfare state capitalism beyond the conventions of pro and anti.

Notes

1 Social insurance and social assistance surpassed entrepreneurial and property income in Norway in 1977 as an isolated recession phenomenon. According to the OECD National Accounts, the same was the case in France from 1980 onwards. However, the French transfers figures include the value of services in kind provided by social insurance, e.g., health care (INSEE, 1987, p. 174).

References

Åberg, R. 1984: Market-Independent Income Distribution: Efficiency and Legitimacy. In J. Goldthorpe (ed.), *Order and Conflict in Contemporary Capitalism*. Oxford: Clarendon Press.

Arbetarförsäkringskomitén 1888: *Betänkande*. Stockholm.

Bakvis, H. 1981: *Catholic Power in the Netherlands*. Kingston and Montreal: McGill and Queen's University Press.

Beld, C.A. v.d. 1979: *Het Centraal Planbureau: zijn invloed, zijn macht en zijn onmacht*. The Hague: CPB Reprint Series.

Berben, T. and Jansen, G. 1982: *De vakbeweging en sociale zekerheid in Nederland*. Nijmegen: Instituut voor Politicologie.

Blekker, R.J.P. v. Glinstra 1952: *Industrialisatie- en emigratiebeleid*. The Hague: CPB Reprint Series.

Böhl, H. de Liagre et al. 1981: *Nederland industrialiseert*. Nijmegen: SUN.

Broberg, R. 1973: *Så formades tryggheten*. Stockholm: Försäkringskasseförbundet.

Bruin, A.A. de 1985: *Het Ontstaan van de Schoolstrijd*. Barneveld: Ton Bolland.

Cameron, D. 1978: The Expansion of the Public Economy: A Comparative Analysis. *American Political Science Review*, 72.

Carlsson, S. 1953: *Lantmannapartiet och industrialismen*. Lund: Gleerups.

Castles, F. (ed.) 1982: *The Impact of Parties*. London: Sage.

Centraal Bureau voor de Statistiek 1979: *Tachtig jaren statistiek in tijdsreeksen*. The Hague: Staatsuitgeverij.

Centraal Bureau voor de statistiek 1988: *Nederland statistisch gezien*. The Hague.

Centraal Planbureau 1986: *Macroeconomische Verkenning 1987*. The Hague, Staatsuitgeverij.

Det økonomiske råd 1984: *Dansk økonomi*. Copenhagen: Akademisk Forlag.

Elmér, Å. 1958: *Svensk socialpolitik*: Lund: Gleerups.

Elmér, Å. 1960: *Folkpensioneringen i Sverige*. Lund: Gleerups.

Enk, P.L.v. 1986: *De Aftocht van de ARP*. Kempen: Kok.

Ericsson, H.-O. 1987: *Vanmakt och styrka*. Lund: Arkiv.

Finansdepartementet 1987: *Långtidsutredningen 1987*. Stockholm.

Finansdepartementet 1988: *Regeringens budgetförslag 1988/89* Stockholm.

Flora, P. (ed.) 1983: *State, Economy, and Society in Western Europe 1815–1975* vol. I. Frankfurt: Campus.

Flora, P. (ed.) 1987a: *Growth to Limits* vol. 4. Berlin: De Gruyter.

Flora, P. (ed.) 1987b: *State, Economy, and Society in Western Europe 1815–1975*, vol. II. Frankfurt: Campus.

Flora, P. and Heidenheimer, A. (eds) 1981: *The Development of Welfare States in Europe and America*. New Brunswick, NJ: Transaction Books.

Fortune, 3 August 1987.

Galen, J. Jansen v., and Vuijsje, B. (eds) 1985: *Joop den Uyl*. Weesp: Van Holkema en Warendorf.

Gortzak, W. (ed.) 1978: *De kleine stappen van het kabinet Den Uyl*. Deventer: Kluwer.

Goudriaan, F.G.W. 1986: '*Geef ons Nederlanders toch werk*'. The Hague: Staatsuitgeverij.

Gustafsson, B., Pihkala, E. and Tönneson, K. 1974: Perspektiv på den offentliga sektorn under 1930-talent. In *Kriser och krispolitik i Norden under mellankrigstiden*. Uppsala: Almqvist o. Wiksell.

Gustavsson, R. 1987: *Traditionernas ok*. Stockholm: Esselte.

Harmsen, G. and Reinalda, B. 1975: *Voor de bevrijding van de arbeid*. Nijmegen: SUN.

Heclo, H. and Madsen, H. 1987: *Policy and Politics in Sweden*. Philadelphia, PA: Temple University Press.

Hirschmann, A. 1970: *Exit, Voice, and Loyalty*. Cambridge, Mass.: Harvard University Press.

Hueting, E., de Jong, Edz, F and Neij, R. 1983: *Naar Groter Eenheid*. Amsterdam: Van Gennep.

INSEE 1987: *Rapport sur les comptes de la nation*. vol. II. Paris.

Johansson, H. 1954: *Folkrörelserna*. Stockholm: Ehlins.

Juffermans, P. 1982: *Staat en gezondheidszorg in Nederland*. Nijmegen: SUN.

Katzenstein, P. 1985: *Small States in World Markets*. Ithaca, NY: Cornell University Press.

Kossmann, E.H. 1978: *The Low Countries 1780–1940*. Oxford: Clarendon Press.

Korpi, W. 1983: *The Democratic Class Struggle*. London: Routledge and Kegan Paul.

Lehmbruch, G. 1984: Concertation and the Structure of Corporatist Networks. In J. Goldthorpe (ed.), *Order and Conflict in Contemporary Capitalism*. Oxford: Oxford University Press.

Lijphart, A. 1982: *Verzuiling, pacificatie en kentering in de nederlandse politiek*. Amsterdam: De Bussy.

Lindeberg, G. 1949: *Den svenska sjukkasserörelsens historia*. Lund: Gleerups.

Lubbers, R. and Lenckert, C. 1980: The Influence of Natural Gas in the Dutch Economy. In R. Griffiths (ed.), *The Economy and the Politics of the Netherlands since 1945*. The Hague: Martinus Nijhoff.

Lundvkist, S. 1977: *Folkrörelserna i det svenska samhället 1850–1920*. Stockholm: Sober.

Maas, P.F. 1982: *Kabinetsformaties 1959–1973*. The Hague: Staatsuitgeverij.

Maddison, A. 1982: *Ontwikkelingsfasen van het kapitalisme*. Utrecht: Specturm.

Ministerie van Sociale Zaken en Werkgelegenheid 1987: *Arbeidsmarkt December 1987*. The Hague.

Ministerie van Volksgezondheid 1977: *Compendium Gezondheidsstatistiek in Nederland 1977*. The Hague.

Möller, G. 1928: *Trygghet och säkerhet åt Sveriges folk!*. Stockholm: Tiden.

Myrdal, A. and Myrdal, G. 1934: *Kris i befolkningsfrågan*. Stockholm: Tiden.

Myrdal, G. 1931: *Sveriges väg genom penningkrisen*. Stockholm.

OECD 1983: *Economic Outlook 33*. Paris: OECD.

OECD 1985: *La santé en chiffres*. Paris: OECD.

OECD 1986: *National Accounts 1960–1984*. vol. II. Paris: OECD.

OECD 1987a: *Historical Statistics 1960–1985*. Paris: OECD.

OECD 1987b: *Economic Outlook 41*. Paris: OECD.

OECD 1987c: *Economic Outlook 42*. Paris: OECD.

OECD 1987d: *Employment Outlook*. September. Paris: OECD.
OECD 1987e: *National Accounts 1973–1985*. Vol. II. Paris: OECD.
Oenen, G.J.v. (ed.) 1982: *Staat en klassen in het interbellum*. Amsterdam: University of Amsterdam, Subfaculteit der Algemene Politieke en Sociale Wetenschappen.
Olsson, S.E. 1986: Sweden. In P. Flora (ed.), *Growth to Limits*. vol. 1. Berlin: De Gruyter.
Olsson, S.E. 1987: Sweden. In P. Flora (ed.), *Growth to Limits*. vol. 4. Berlin: De Gruyter.
Palm, I. 1982: *Frikyrkan, arbetarfrågan och klasskampen*. Uppsala: Uppsala University.
Pestoff, V. 1977: *Voluntary Associations and Nordic Party Systems*. Stockholm: Stockholm University.
Querido, A. 1973: *De Wit-Gele vlam*. Tilburg: Wit-Gele Kruis.
Rehn, G. 1977: *Finansministrarna, LO-ekonomerna och arbetsmarknadspolitiken*. Stockholm: Institutet för Social Forskning.
Rickardson, G. 1963: *Kulturkamp och klasskamp*. Gothenburg: Akademiförlaget.
Righart, H. 1986: *De katholieke zuil in Europa*. Amsterdam: Boom Meppel.
Roebroek, J. and Berben, T. 1987: Netherlands. In P. Flora (ed.), *Growth to Limits*.
Roebroek, J., Therborn, G. and Berben, T. 1988: Netherlands. In P. Flora (ed.), *Growth to Limits*. vol. 3. Berlin: De Gruyter (forthcoming).
Rooy, P. de 1979: *Werklozenzorg en werkloosheidsbestrijding 1917–1940*. Amsterdam: Van Gennep.
Rothstein, B. 1986: *Den socialdemokratiska staten*. Lund: Arkiv.
Royers, T. and Winters, W. 1984: *100 jaar pensioenstrijd in Nederland 1884–1984*. Leeuwarden: Wielsma.
Schiller, B. 1987: *Arbetarna, arbetsgivarna och medbestämmandet*. Göteborg: Göteborgs Universitet, Historiska Innstitutionen.
Schmitter, P. 1978: Still the Century of Corporatism? In P. Schmitter and G. Lehmbruch (eds), *Trends Toward Corporatist Intermediation*. London: Sage.
Schmitter, P. 1981: Interest intermediation and regime governability in contemporary Western Europe and North America. In S. Berger (ed.), *Organizing Interests in Western Europe*. Cambridge: Cambridge University Press.
Sociaal en Cultureel Planbureau 1986: *Sociaal en Cultureel Rapport 1986*. The Hague.
Statistika Centralbyrån 1986: *Kvinnor och män på arbetsmarknaden*. Stockholm.
Stuurman, S. 1983: *Verzuiling, kapitalisme en patriarchaat*. Nijmegen: SUN.
Teulings, A. 1981: *Ondernemingsraadpolitiek in Nederland*. Amsterdam: Van Gennep.
Therborn, G. 1982: The Making of A Bourgeois-Bureaucratic State in Sweden. Paper presented to an international conference on 'States and Social Structures'. Mt Kisco, NY, so far unpublished.
Therborn, G. 1983: Electoral Campaigns As Indicators of Ideological Power. In S. Hänninen and L. Paldán (eds), *Rethinking Ideology*. Berlin: Argument.
Therborn, G. 1984a: The Coming of Swedish Social Democracy. In *Annali della Fondazione Giangiacomo Feltrinelli*. Milan: Feltrinelli.

Therborn, G., 1984b: Classes and States: Welfare State Developments 1881–1981. In *Studies in Political Economy*, 14.

Therborn, G. 1986a: The Working Class and the Welfare State. A Historical-Analytical Overview and A Little Swedish Monograph. In P. Kettunen (ed.), *Det nordiska i den nordiska arbetarrörelsen*. Helsinki: Finnish Society for Labour History and Cultural Traditions.

Therborn, G. 1986b: *Why Some Peoples Are More Unemployed Than Others*. London: Verso.

Therborn, G. 1987a: Migration and Western Europe: The Old World Turning New. In *Science* vol. 237, 4 September.

Therborn, G. 1987b: Den svenska välfärdsstatens särart och framtid. In I. Karlsson (ed.), *Lycksalighetens halvö*. Stockholm: FRN-Framtidsstudier.

Therborn, G. 1987c: Tar arbetet slut? Och post-fordismens problem. In U. Björnberg and I. Hellberg (eds), *Sociologer ser på arbete* Festskrift till Edmund Dahlström. Stockholm: Arbetslivscentrum.

Therborn, G. 1988: Hur det hela började. När och varför det moderna Sverige blev vad det blev. In U. Himmelstrand (ed.), *Sverige mellan vardag och struktur*. Stockholm: Norstedts.

Thörnberg, E.H. 1943: *Folkrörelser och samhällsliv i Sverige*. Stockholm: Bonniers.

Thurlings, J.M.G. 1969: De ontzuiling in Nederland. In *De Sociologische Gids*, 6.

Tinbergen, J. 1946: *De les van dertig jaar*. Amsterdam: Elsevier.

Tweede Kamer 1980–81: *Handelingen der Staten Generaal*. The Hague.

Tweede Kamer 1986–87: *Financiele Nota Sociale Zekerheid 1987*. The Hague.

Tweede Kamer 1987–88: *Miljoenennota 1988*. The Hague.

Vallinder, T. 1962: *I kamp för demokratin*. Stockholm: Natur och Kultur.

Vedung, E. 1971: *Unionsdebatten 1905*. Uppsala: Statsvetenskapliga föreningen.

Veldkamp, G.M.J., 1978: *Sociale zekerheid*. vol. 1. Deventer: Kluwer.

Vogel, J. 1987: *Ojämlikheten i Sverige*. Stockholm: Statistiska Centralbyrån.

Windmuller, J.P., de Galan, C. and v. Zweden, A. 1983: *Arbeidsverhoudingen in Nederland*. Utrecht: Aula.

7

The United Kingdom
Paradoxes of an Ungrounded Statism

Patrick Dunleavy

In public policy research routine inductive reasoning and 'surface correlation' studies can take us only to a first stage of analysis. To go further we need to bring to the surface deeper conundrums or anomalies which are problematic given an existing frame of reference. Cross-national studies can throw into question phenomena previously considered straightforward within a single-country mode of explanation, making them appear as difficulties or paradoxes in the light of new information. Studying variations over time can also yield insights into the character of contemporary public policies by countering the normal temptation to construct ineluctable patterns of development culminating in current configurations. Major policy shifts shake up such historicist accounts and underline the contingent quality of those policies subject to rapid change. They also emphasize the more deeply rooted characteristics of programmes which withstand major pressures for their termination or reconstruction. In the British case both comparative policy research and recent changes under the Thatcher government suggest three fundamental questions about the nature of post-war public policies.

First, is the United Kingdom unusually 'statist' by comparison with other West European countries and, if so, in what respects and why? By 'statist' policy-making I mean that, for a given scale of government intervention, the strategies adopted have implied:

- a relatively heavy institutionalization of governmental machinery for implementing social and economic policies (including strategies which produce comparatively high levels of direct public ownership and state provision of collective services); and
- a relatively low reliance upon either non-governmental intermediary

bodies (such as interest groups, communal organizations, or QUANGOs) or on transfers as mechanisms for delivering public policies.

Second, how was this long-run 'statist' configuration created when the political conditions in the UK apparently should have operated against it? A 'statist' approach appears 'ungrounded' in the kinds of causal factors which comparative policy studies have associated with more vigorous public intervention in other industrialized societies.

Third, why has this established pattern proved relatively easily reversible by the Thatcher government? Does the scale of policy changes in the 1980s support the interpretation of previous 'ungrounded statism'? Or are recent shifts no more significant than previous policy alternations?

The 'Statism' of Post-war Public Policy

In Britain as in most democratic countries there has been a wide margin of political debate about the extent to which government intervention is necessary or effective. But in many policy areas until the late 1970s state intervention seemed stable and permanent. And the *pattern* of intervention in both the welfare state and the mixed economy was consistently statist, committed to direct governmental control of enterprises or service provision. Establishing the accuracy of these propositions entails a brief overview of the main forms of intervention in the UK; a consideration of how state expenditures have grown over time; and an effort to situate Britain in comparative perspective.

Patterns of institutionalization

In the sphere of *industry policy* full public ownership of industries on the model associated with Herbert Morrison was the basic form of government economic intervention for most of the post-war period. The public corporation form was first adopted in the 1920s by Conservative governments for the BBC and a few other special case interventions, and was only legislated on a large scale in the 1945–51 period. At that time the Labour government clearly rejected all the alternative strategies for socializing control of production industries – such as state shareholding in conventionally structured companies on the Italian model, or attempts to secure public guidance on social issues via extensive regulation on the American pattern. Subsequently there were some significant debates about the appropriateness of the public corporation form for particular industries. The denationalization of road haulage and of the iron and steel industry by the Conservatives in the early 1950s might have been expected to inaugurate a sweeping programme of privatization. In fact, although there were some aftershocks, such as the restructuring of an initially integrated nationalized transport firm into separate public corporations, the boundaries of the public ownership of industries either remained stable under Tory governments or expanded under Labour administrations thereafter until the 1980s. In 1978, when public corporations were most numerous, one in twelve of all employees worked for them. In that year the government effectively controlled all of the following industries – coal, steel, gas, water, electricity, railways, nuclear power, telecommunications, mail services, shipbuilding, aerospace and new town corporations. Other public or municipal corporations accounted for most bus services, docks, almost all airports, and parts of the armaments industry and North Sea oil industry. In addition the government had controlling shareholdings in quoted companies covering large parts of the car industry, computer industry, and aero-engineering, mainly built up during the 1970s (Rees, 1973).

In the public corporation form the assets of whole industrial sectors were nationalized; their boards became nominated by the government, and their workforces became public sector employees (Rees, 1973; Tivey, 1973). The type of social ownership chosen vested no effective controls in the trade unions or in corporatist structures, nor did it create any noticeable increases in consumers' rights. 'As far as relations between employers and employees and between producers and customers are concerned, few changes have occurred which enable the individual to distinguish the nationalized industries from private enterprise.' (Hill, 1976, p. 42). However government intervention in the running of these industries was considerable. Ministers directly approved investment programmes, set rate-of-return targets, vetted major pricing decisions and administered extensive subsidies. In addition governments pressurized the industries' managers to adhere to general government policies – especially avoiding some politically sensitive job losses, 'Buying British' and limiting their charges and wage increases to stay in line with governments' implicit or explicit prices and incomes policies.

Direct state provision of *welfare state services* has also made British social policy distinctive with only a minimal role for voluntary provision, intermediate quasi-public bodies, or subsidized private service provision. The origins of this stance can be traced to the strategies adopted for managing conflicts over state schooling. The first large-scale public services were poor law workhouses and hospitals and highways, both of which developed with little political conflict under local government auspices in the early nineteenth century (Foster et al., 1980, pp. 102–26). But primary education grew to be a major local service in the closing decades of the century despite the religious controversy between the established Church of England and non-conformist Protestant creeds about state funding of church schools. The 1902 Education Act established predominant control by local authorities and government inspectors over all church schools and severely reduced the established Church's role in shaping educational policies. Since then education has always absorbed at least 20 per cent of local government spending (Dunleavy, 1984, pp. 51–4). Together with the strong secularization of British society in the ensuing decades, this pattern ensured that there was no growth of *distinctive* 'communal' provision along religious or interest group lines in a key policy sector. The Church of England bodies ran nearly 8000 schools and retained some curriculum control until the 1944 Education Act, and the Catholic Church developed its own schools system funded in the same way. But in the modern period the education provided in state and church schools has been virtually indistinguishable except on explicitly religious matters.

Education in turn became a model for the public provision of housing and health care. There was a significant voluntary housing movement in the last quarter of the nineteenth century founded on moral or religious philanthropic sentiments which sought to provide decent housing for working class people – while making a 'reasonable' rate of return (Tarn, 1973). The movement's role was gradually by-passed by the slow growth of permissive local authority powers from the 1880s to 1914. Then, in 1919, the legislation associated with the 'homes fit for heroes' election campaign decisively vested complete powers to provide working class housing needs with local authorities. The existing housing associations were relegated to the margins, apparently seen as historical curios whose past adherence to '5 per cent philanthropy' disqualified them from acting as a channel of public subsidies (Emsley, 1987, chs. 1–4; Power, 1987, pp. 7–19). Similarly in the social health field, the inter-war period especially saw a patchwork of insurance and care facilities set up by trade unions, 'voluntary' hospitals, private fee-paying schemes and piecemeal local authority provision (Watkin, 1978, ch. 1). Again all these forms of provision were swept aside when the National Health Service created a completely integrated and public sector administrative solution.

Finally, the UK pattern of *social insurance/income maintenance* has also focused on constructing a comprehensive set of universalized and fully tax-based benefits including pensions, unemployment insurance and 'safety net' social security provision. The systems developed have strongly underscored the direct responsibility of central government for ensuring the basic incomes and living standards of all citizens. Since the late nineteenth century the British welfare state has been greatly preoccupied with poverty issues, as perceived by a small centralizing elite of welfare experts (Ashford, 1986). There were nonetheless two distinct phases of the institutionalization of government's role in the post-war period. The Labour government of 1945–51 created an extended system which built upon the foundations of broadly supported, if previously inadequate, existing policies for old age pensions, sickness insurance and unemployment compensation. Labour added family allowances, a flat rate National Insurance system for income replacement in sickness and unemployment plus more generous state old age pensions, and a means-tested National Assistance (later renamed Supplementary Benefits) system for people falling through the net of other provision (Parry, 1986, pp. 160–3). But in the early 1960s 'as long as the breadwinner was employed, poor families received nothing from the major income support programmes, national insurance and supplementary benefits' (Banting, 1979, p. 66). In the late 1960s and early 1970s broader-based programmes of income supplements and housing benefits were gradually extended to cover employed households as well, partly under the influence of academic social science research into the continued existence of widespread relative poverty. At much the same time the first 'mixed' systems of joint public-private provision began to be established. Such systems started tentatively with public subsidies to private rental tenants in 1973 (previously rental subsidies had only been available for council housing tenants), and opt-out provisions for occupational pensions as a substitute for more extended state schemes.

Long-term trends in state spending

The aggregate implications of this policy history can be traced for the period since the 1890s. Figure 7.1a presents data for 'general government expenditures' expressed as a proportion of gross domestic product. Figure 7.1b shows the percentage of general government expenditure spent on transfers of all kinds, including welfare payments, producer subsidies, grants, etc. (i.e. after excluding all government consumption of goods and services). Both series have been 'median-smoothed' to detect the trends underlying one-off fluctuations in the statistics (Mosteller and Tukey, 1977). In the ten years from 1890 government expenditures grew relatively fast as a proportion of GDP from 9 to 14 per cent, while at the same time the proportion of spending on transfers was falling, from 26 per cent in 1890 to 14 per cent at the height of the Boer War in 1901. From then on until the start of the First World War general government expenditures declined slightly as a proportion of GDP to oscillate around the 12 per cent level, while the proportion of spending devoted to transfers slowly crept up again to a fifth of the total.

The inter-war period demonstrated a qualitatively different pattern which, once established, persisted for all but the closing years of the 1930s when a crash programme of rearmament was already under way (see Peden, 1979). The smoothed figures for general government

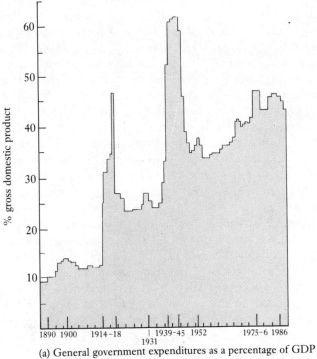

(a) General government expenditures as a percentage of GDP

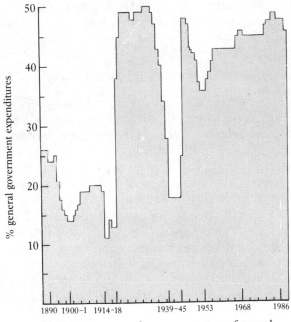

(b) Government transfers as a percentage of general
government expenditures

Figure 7.1 The development of public expenditures in the UK 1890–1986
(computed from *Economic Trends, Annual Survey 1987*, London: HMSO)

expenditures fluctuated between just over 23 per cent of GDP and under 27 per cent of GDP from 1920 to 1937, with mini-peaks in 1920–2 and in the trough of the Great Depression in 1931–2. From 1921 to 1935 the proportion of spending on transfers hovered around the 48–50 per cent range, falling away decisively only in 1938 and 1939 as rearmament dramatically boosted government consumption of goods and services.

After 1945 both government spending and the proportion spent on transfers started at high levels but fell away. The decline in the proportion of GDP absorbed by government was briefly disrupted by the Korean War, but otherwise the smoothed spending figures stayed at between 33 and 37.5 per cent of GDP between 1948 and 1966. From 1967 this figure moved to a base level above 40 per cent, and from 1974 to 1976 peaked sharply just below 47 per cent of GDP. After government spending fell back abruptly to around 43 per cent of GDP in the late 1970s, it almost returned to the mid-1970s record peacetime level in the early 1980s, chiefly because of the government's policy-induced recession. The proportion of government spending on transfers fell steadily from 48 per cent in 1946 to 34 per cent in 1954, but then rose again to 43 per cent by the end of the decade, a level which remained constant for ten years. Transfers grew slightly as a proportion of government spending in 1968–9, but then settled at a new level of 45 per cent of the total public outlays until 1978. The onset of higher unemployment pushed the transfers share up to 48–49 per cent of government spending under the Thatcher government, the first time anything approaching the inter-war split between government consumption and transfers had been seen in the post-war period.

Cross-national comparisons for the early post-war period

For the thesis being developed here, the period from 1945 to the mid 1970s is the most critical one, for which it is fortunately possible to assemble a range of reliable inter-country statistics. In cross-national terms there are a number of distinctive statistical features of post-war government activity in the UK. One of its most persistent and enduring characteristics is the high proportion of gross domestic product devoted to defence spending. Nutter (1978) analysed 16 OECD countries for the period from 1950 to 1974, using a different and more inclusive definition of total government spending. Britain consistently spent well above the median percentage of gross domestic product on defence. In this data set only the USA has ever exceeded the UK defence share since the Korean War, and only France has been close to British levels at any stage, and then only in the early 1950s (see figure 7.2a). Outside the data set the only other (qualified) democracy spending more of its national income on defence seems to be Israel (for obvious reasons). Although the UK defence share fell towards the median figure throughout the 1950–73 period, it has always remained exceptional.

Looking at the government's domestic spending on goods and services, that is, after excluding any transfer payments such as pensions or unemployment pay, Britain is again above the median for Nutter's OECD data set throughout the 1950–74 period (see Figure 7.2b). In the early 1950s Britain was quite exceptional in the high proportion of GDP devoted to domestic non-transfer spending, partly because of direct governmental spending on public health care, council housing provision and state education, but also because of substantial government contributions to nationalized industries, both for investment programmes and as subsidies for operating losses. But in the 1960s and 1970s the UK began to be overtaken by a small group of social democratic-influenced countries committed to radically improving their standards of directly provided public services (Sweden, Norway, and most recently Denmark). Over the whole period, however, 9 out of 16 countries were permanently below UK levels, with a further 3 countries approximating the British pattern temporarily.

By contrast, British government spending on domestic transfers always fell below the median for OECD countries in the 1950–74 period (see figure 7.2c). The UK share clearly grew considerably in these years, in stark contrast to the static minimum figure (for Japan). But as a proportion of the median value in the data set the UK share remained fairly constant or actually dropped a bit. Every West European country in the data set except Switzerland devoted a larger share of its GDP to domestic transfers than the UK, and even the Swiss figure moved ahead by the mid 1970s. One key element in explaining this difference is that the funding of health care in most West European countries retains a considerable transfer element in terms of insurance pay-outs to sick people, whereas in the UK the insurance element has been almost completely decommodified into the free provision of hospital and GP medical services. Nonetheless it is striking that in addition to Japan the only other countries consistently below the British figure for domestic transfers from 1950 to 1974 were the USA and Australia, all three of them countries committed to low welfare spending strategies.

In terms of overall government spending as a proportion of national income the combined effect of the policy characteristics reviewed above has been to maintain the UK's levels very close to the median of the OECD countries in Nutter's data set. In the early 1950s British government spending was some 20 per cent greater than the median, but by the end of that decade it was almost identical with median levels, a

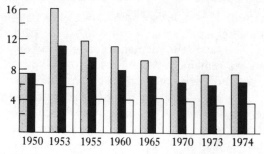

(a) Defence spending as a percentage of GDP

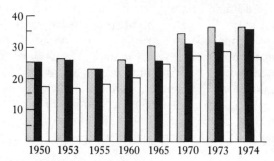

(b) Domestic non-transfer public expenditures as a
    percentage of GDP

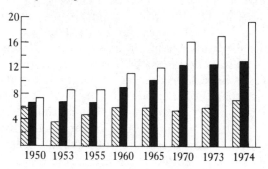

(c) Domestic transfer payments as a percentage of GDP

Key:

☐ median of 16 OECD countries

■ UK figure

▨ maximum figure for 16 OECD countries

▨ minimum figure

Figure 7.2 UK spending on defence, domestic non-transfers and transfer
pyaments, by comparison with 16 OECD nations 1950–1974 (computed from
Nutter, 1978)

picture which changed very little in the next fifteen years. Although the share of national income devoted to overall government spending is not a particularly useful indicator of state size (Heald, 1982, pp. 10–32), these data strongly suggest that the scale of state intervention has not been greatly out of line with levels in other liberal democracies. In the late 1970s overall UK public spending in Nutter's more inclusive measure fell from 55 to 47 per cent of national income, and defence spending drifted down from 6.3 to 5.0 per cent. Domestic transfers shot up from 13.4 to 19 per cent of national income, while other domestic spending fell sharply from 35 to 22 per cent. More recent data is not available on the same basis for the 1980s, but the trend towards domestic transfers has undoubtedly continued, albeit associated with a reversal of the decline in defence spending.

Summing up the features which differentiate British public policy then, table 7.1 suggests that five groups of comparable liberal democracies can be distinguished for the post-war period up to the mid 1970s. The USA is the only country in Nutter's data set with higher defence spending than Britain's, and it also consistently spent a smaller proportion of its national income on either transfers or other domestic spending. Amongst lower defence-spending countries, four countries spent less than the UK on transfers over the whole period, three of them being low government spending countries across the board, namely Australia, Japan and Switzerland. Canada by the 1970s was slightly

Table 7.1 Comparing UK state spending with other liberal democracies in the period 1945–1974

Countries where compared with the UK:				
Defence spending is more (+)	*Defence spending is lower (−)*			
Domestic − *Transfers −*	*Domestic −* *Transfers −*	*Domestic +* *Transfers −*	*Domestic −* *Transfers +*	*Domestic +* *Transfers +*
USA	Australia Japan Switzerland	Canada	Austria Belgium France Italy Luxembourg West Germany	Denmark Netherlands Norway Sweden

Source: Nutter 1978.

above the UK in its spending on domestic non-transfers. All the West European nations assigned a higher proportion of national income to transfers than did the UK, the key distinction being between Scandinavia and the Netherlands (where domestic state spending is also appreciably greater), and the remaining six countries which spent less than the UK on other domestic policies.

There are two other useful clues to the distinctive patterning of post-war British public policy, trends in public employment and patterns of social expenditures, for which the available comparative information is a bit more restricted. In public employment terms, Abramovitz and Eliasberg (1957) demonstrated that the first major growth of public employment took place between 1891 and 1911, when manpower numbers doubled, largely due to the impact of educational reforms and consequent local government growth. The impact of the First World War was to make the UK peacetime public sector a comparatively large one. But it was really the Second World War and the Labour government's post-war reforms which made British public employment much greater than comparable advanced industrial societies in the early post-war period (see table 7.2). In 1951 British public employment was more than half as great again as any of the other five countries. But by 1981 the UK's distinctiveness had completely faded, with all the other four West European countries having comparable state workforces.

Table 7.2 Public employment in the UK and five other liberal democracies since the mid-nineteenth century

Country	1981	1951	Pre-1939	Pre-1914	c.1850s
Sweden	38	15	na	na	na
France	33	18[a]	9	7	5
Britain	31	27	11	7	2
FRG/Germany	26	14[a]	13	11	7
Italy	24	11[a]	8	5	2
USA	18	17[a]	8	na	na

Figures for 1981 and 1951 are slightly varied years and are for percentages of the workforce, while all other years are percentages of the labour force. FRG = Federal Republic of Germany.
[a] For these countries figures before and after 1951 are not strictly comparable. Comparable figures for earlier years are France 16, FRG 12, Italy 10, and USA 12. For a fuller explanation see source.
Source: Rose et al., 1985, pp. 8–10.

The pattern of social expenditures growth in Britian also shows an interesting pattern of lagging increases in education, health care, pensions and unemployment compensation spending in the period from the 1960s (see table 7.3). Both before and after the impact of the mid

Table 7.3 The growth of British social expenditures by international comparison countries, 1960–1981

Average annual percentage growth of deflated social expenditures			*Income elasticity of social expenditures*		
	1960–1975	1975–1981		1960–1975	1975–1981
Japan	12.8	8.4	Japan	3.9	1.8
Norway	10.1	4.6	Norway	2.4	1.1
Canada	9.3	3.1	USA	2.4	1.0
USA	8.0	3.2	France	2.2	2.2
Italy	7.7	5.1	Britain	2.2	1.8
France	7.3	6.2	Canada	1.8	0.9
W. Germany	7.0	2.4	Italy	1.4	1.6
Britain	5.9	3.2	W. Germany	0.8	0.8

Source: Marmor, 1987, p. 13, from OECD, 1985, pp. 21–22.

1970s oil shock, British social expenditures (measured in constant GDP prices) grew more slowly than those in seven other liberal democracies. Much of this effect can be attributed to the concentration of British social expenditures growth into the period before 1960: growth rates from a larger base automatically tend to be smaller. However, part of this effect can also be attributed to slower economic growth in the UK, which can be controlled for by examining the income elasticity figures (defined as the ratio of the growth of social expenditures to the growth of national incomes). On this second criteria, the UK's performance up to the mid 1970s was unexceptional, while the onset of chronic recession in the late 1970s left the UK's income elasticity of social expenditures third only to those of France and Japan.

Paradoxes of the UK's Ungrounded Statism

There are two obvious frameworks of ideas within which one might try to assess the pattern of statist spending growth in the early post-war period charted above. The first is the conventional, rather ethnocentric discussion of the growth of welfare state interventions in the conventional social policy/social administration literature (Fraser, 1973; Marshall, 1950) and the piecemeal creation of a mixed economy with a high proportion of nationalized industries (Middlemas, 1979; Tivey, 1973, chs. 2 and 3). Before the early 1980s most accounts accepted a kind of linear progress myth in which the Victorian heyday of *laissez-faire* ideologies was bound to be challenged by an incipient and untested socialism, producing a period of experimentation in government intervention. Naturally periods of experimentation were closely linked to the two major wars of 1914–18 and 1939–45. But the post-war reconstructions simply condensed and dramatized much longer-term trends in the evolution of ideas and policy practices (Parry, 1986). Out of the post-war period of transition was supposed to have emerged a compromise 'steady state' situation accepted in all its essentials by a 'Butskellite' political consensus. Explanations of the UK's distinctive pattern of intervention have been rare in this tradition. They tend to appeal to particular features of British history, such as the early extension of legal citizenship rights in the eighteenth century (Marshall, 1950); aspects of intellectual life, such as the strength of Fabianism and 'reluctant collectivism' in the first half of the twentieth century (George and Wilding, 1976); or the operations of the party system, such as the growth of a distinct socialist party long after the basic framework for universal suffrage was created.

An alternative approach is suggested by the conventional liberal-conservative assumption of a 'ladder of interventions' in liberal

Table 7.4   The ladder of interventions

Level 0	Policy problem denied.
Level 1	Policy problem acknowledged, but no government intervention because it could not ameliorate situation.
Level 2a	Minimum necessary government intervention accepted to combat market externality effects – adjusting payoffs and costs for market decision-makers, but preserving market interactions/allocations in full.
Level 2b	Need for a higher level of provision of collective, pool or 'worthy' goods accepted – implemented by governmental transfers to market actors.
Level 3	Necessity for qualifying market allocations of resources accepted. Higher level of intervention involves either coercive regulation to block some market exchanges; or a greater governmental role in subsidizing and organizing intermediary bodies to produce services in quasi-markets.
Level 4	Need for direct government involvement in producing goods and services accepted.

democratic policy-making (see table 7.4). This commonplace view suggests that state involvement should proceed in the sequence shown in the table, with higher order interventions being accepted only when lesser solutions have been tried and failed (Stokey and Zeckhauser, 1978, pp. 322–4). There should be strong incentives to minimize governmental involvement because governmental solutions are as prone to failure as competitive markets (Woolf, 1979); because there is a danger of governmental overload (King, 1975; Douglas, 1976), and because state growth erodes the bases of private sector profitability (Bacon and Eltis, 1978). Governments dispose of a wide-ranging toolkit and so are able to choose from a very graduated list of alternative policy technologies, of which direct government provision of benefits is probably the most costly and most prone to creating overlarge bureaucracies (Hood, 1983). Set against this background the problem of post-war British 'statism' is that an unexceptional degree of government intervention has been accomplished in very institutionalized ways. Both in mixed economy and welfare state areas there is a relative scarcity of lower tier forms of intervention and predominant reliance on higher level forms of intervention such as public ownership of industries and extended public sector provision of services in kind.

The ladder of interventions model underpins various unsatisfactory explanations of British exceptionalism associated with the new right (King, 1987; Barry, 1987; Green, 1987). The new right analyse the growth of the state as a symptom of the degeneration of the democratic process into a scramble for public subsidies by vested interests (Green, 1982) – a view increasingly part of the 1980s conventional wisdom in Britain. One major effect of this sea-change in ideas has been to break down the insulating effect of UK-centred explanations of why public policy has its current shape, and to expand the audience for American-orientated market liberal explanations and paradigms (for example, Tullock, 1976; Niskanen, 1973; Buchanan, 1978). Naturally this shift has created Americanized perceptions of the idiosyncratic 'collectivism' of British public policy (compared with the USA), but without providing any plausible causal explanations of it.

The new right explain the past statism of public policy-making only in terms of very high level generalizations about budget-maximizing bureaucracies, the interests of the 'new class' of state professionals, the baronial ambitions of feudally-minded Labour local politicians, and the weakness of will of past Tory administrations in the face of a liberal-socialist welfare orthodoxy. More traditional conservatives appeal to a rag-bag of causal factors supposed to have distorted British public life for the decades between 1910 and the late 1970s, such as the trade union pressure on Labour governments, the intellectual ascendancy of Fabianism, and the long learning curve required for public opinion to accept that nationalization and direct government intervention could not offer any miracle cures for private market failures (Gilmour, 1978).

In some other contexts it would be straightforward to explain why a country's pattern of public policy development should be a statist one. For example, Castles' (1979) analysis of Swedish politics links the development of a strong welfare state to the ideological ascendancy of social democracy, combined with the fragmentation of the right-wing parties and the development of strong and effective corporatist practices. More generally, although left voting strength shows only a relatively weak correlation with levels of social policy interventions by government, the presence of a united right-wing party grouping uniformly tends to depress the level of welfare state provision (Castles, 1982). And the importance of corporatist practices in sustaining long-run economic growth and welfare expansion in some West European states is argued by several studies (Katzenstein, 1985; chapters in this volume by Schmidt and Shalev).

However, similar sorts of reasoning cannot be applied in the UK. Here a statist pattern of intervention was established in a political system characterized by the predominance of the right and the incomplete establishment of social democratic ideas in a non-hegemonic position. It flourished in a society with a notably weak development of corporatism; an absence of policy stability in macroeconomic management; and a low level of substantive welfare benefits provision. In the remainder of this section each of these apparently paradoxical factors is examined in turn.

Conservative predominance

The Conservative party is one of the oldest and most successful unified parties of the right in any liberal democracy. There have been twenty general elections since 1918 (when the Labour party first campaigned nationwide at a general election). The party system in the modern period has been relatively stable. Scottish and Welsh Nationalist MPs were elected in the 1970s; the Liberal vote collapsed in the 1930s and again in the 1950s; the Social Democratic Party was launched in 1981, and partly merged with the Liberals in 1988: but these changes did not fundamentally change the 'two and a half party' system first defined in the 1920s. In competition against Labour and the Liberals the Conservative party has consistently attained the most votes. The median Conservative vote since 1918 has been 44 per cent, with a midspread from 38 to 48 per cent and a top score of 55 per cent (in 1931). Its vote has fallen below 38 per cent of the popular vote in Great Britain only twice (in October 1974, and under the 1918 coalition government arrangement when many Tory candidates voluntarily withdrew in favour of their National Liberal partners). The fluctuations in Conservative voting are lower than those for any other party (see figure 7.3a).

Despite significant periods of two-party alternation in power, the Conservatives have dominated the government, winning elections eleven times with secure majorities in *1922*, 1924, *1931*, *1935*, 1951, 1955, 1959, 1970, 1979, 1983, and 1987. (Italicized years were formally coalitions or 'National Governments' but were in practice Tory dominated.) The party has been a poor second in Parliament for only fifteen years in this period, and has been defeated by significant majorities only twice (in 1945 and 1966). In terms of their control over ministerial office the Conservatives' record dwarfs the Labour party's achievements since 1918 (see table 7.5). The Conservatives have controlled peacetime governments with secure majorities for three-fifths of the period since 1919, and assuming that the Thatcher government stays in office until at least the summer of 1991 the proportion is still rising.

Part of the reason for the Conservatives' success has been the ability to knit together first three and then four very different strands of ideological thinking. The oldest established of these traditions was, first, the traditional Tory paternalism whose version of 'nation-state' Conservatism stressed a diluted form of *noblesse oblige*, a distrust of ideological reasoning, and respect for the accumulated experience of historical practice as a sifting mechanism for validating social institutions

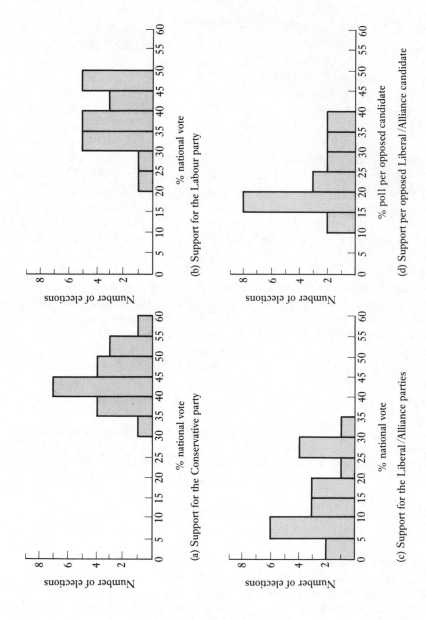

Figure 7.3 Support for the main British political parties 1918–1987

Table 7.5   The major British parties' record in government, 1918–1987

	Conservative	Labour	Liberals (or Lib/SDP)
Total months with ministers in government	569	310	109
% of all months (N = 816)	70	38	13
Excluding wartime coalition	509	247	49
% of total (N = 756)	67	33	7
Months as sole government	460	247	0
% of total (N = 756)	61	33	0
Months with secure majority govt	460	127	0
% of total (N = 756)	61	17	0

(Gilmour, 1978, pp. 74–92, 101–106). A second, equally traditional group were the inegalitarian right who put forward a blanket or unqualified defence of privilege, however 'extreme' or potentially damaging to the maintenance of a social consensus (Scruton, 1981; Oakeshott, 1962; Cowling et al., 1978). In late Victorian times, the far right metamorphosed with an influx of support from the Liberal Unionists and the systematic development of imperialist thinking into a grouping marrying reactionary domestic policies with overseas expansionism, a strong military build-up, economic protectionism and sound currency (albeit accompanied by an abhorrence of other forms of government intervention).

The tension between these wings of the Tory party was blurred after 1918 by the embryonic development of two less aristocratic groups, both based in the overtly 'bourgeois' wing of the party, which slowly expanded to capture the ideological centre-ground in the party during the 1960s and 1970s when aristocratic influences on the Conservative leadership were decisively reduced to residual importance. A 'technological modernizing' form of liberal Conservatism dominated the party first under Macmillan and then Heath. This strand of thinking accepted functional (rather than simply political) arguments for the necessity of a welfare state, and vested government with a key role in modernizing industry and state institutions, with both commitments married to a right-wing version of Keynesian economics (Lindsay and Harrington, 1979, pp. 177–263). The market liberals or 'new right' emerged gradually from the late 1950s onwards as a distinct group from the traditional far right to dominate the first Thatcher government with a strongly developed inegalitarian ideology based on modern social science foundations – such as monetarism, Austrian school economics, public choice theory, and libertarian philosophy. Although they profoundly disagree about the need for social equalization and the viability of welfare state interventions, both technological modernizers and the market liberals are similar in rejecting 'nation state' Conservatism in favour of a generally utilitarian and thoroughly individualistic framework of assumptions (Lawson, 1981).

There has never been any strong *étatist* tradition of right wing thinking about economic issues, such as is found in France. But as with most parties of the right there have been three main exceptions to this rule. The first is Conservative support for large-scale agricultural subsidies, reflecting at root the party's electoral predominance in rural constituencies. The second exception involved maintaining British overseas colonies and the military apparatus to support them. In the heyday of the Empire, which for the traditional far right at least extended to the end of the 1950s, the armed forces and colonial administrations were both major sectors of the state which were dominated by Conservative ideas and protected by the Tory party from scrutiny. A number of pseudo-economic justifications were developed to explain why colonial and military expenditures were consistent with support for a market economy, rationales which were redefined in the post-war period to apply to other kinds of overseas military commitments, such as the Rhine army or the Falklands War. With decolonization, plus the abolition of conscription and drastic manpower reductions in the armed forces, this close military linkage has withered a little. Partly to compensate, Conservatives have placed increasing emphasis on the intelligence services as bastions against 'subversion' in the Cold War and its aftermath. Thirdly, the police force has moved closer to the heart of the Tory pantheon under the pressure of industrial disputes in the 1970s and 1980s. Other aspects of maintaining 'law and order' (such as prison building) have benefited from large-scale financing injections in the 1980s, but without being insulated to the same degree from Tory criticism.

Dominant Conservative attitudes have meant that a strong fetishism surrounding public/private sector differences has always characterized British economic debates. Apart from farming, Empire, defence, and law and order, the British right has always insisted on policing the public/private line as restrictively as possible. In the early post-war period Labour's commitment to the Morrisonian form of nationalization initially served as a strong unifying device for the Conservatives when the homogeneous business opposition to government interference in economic life might otherwise have been dented by a more diversified pattern of intervention. The period of cross-party enthusiasm for growth-orientated economic planning in the early 1960s was too short-lived and too inconclusive to effect any significant change in business or Conservative attitudes. The reaffirmation of free enterprise values in the Conservatives' 1968 Selsdon declaration was in practice shortlived – for the Heath government actually used state power vigorously in pursuit of national modernization objectives, such as the restructuring of the steel industry (Ovendon, 1978). Nonetheless the *ideological* colouring of its programmes was radically different from the 1960s planning era and already foreshadowed Thatcherite themes.

The shallow penetration of the labour movement

The long-term strength of the Conservatives has as its corollary a much weaker penetration of the British social and political system by the labour movement than has been suggested by historical accounts written in the afterglow of Labour's electoral landslides in 1945 and 1966. The top five election performances by the Labour party, in the upper 40 per cent range, are all concentrated in this period. But the midspread of Labour performances since 1918 lies in a band from 32 to 45 per cent, with a median level of 38 per cent, fully six points lower than the Conservative average (see figure 7.3b). The Tory share of the vote has never fallen below 35 per cent (except in the 1918 election for technical coalition reasons). But 7 out of 20 Labour vote shares since 1918 have been in the lower 30s, and the party polled below 28 per cent in 1983, only 6 points above their 1918 launch level.

Contrary to the accepted political science picture of Britain as a two-party system, modern revisionist studies argue that the central reason for Labour's weakness has been its incomplete displacement of the pre-1918 Conservative/Liberal two-party system (Catt, 1988). During the 1920s the Liberal party consistently polled from 23 to 30 per cent of the vote despite its acute factional splits in the early part of the decade (see figure 7.3c). It was only with the formation of the 1931 coalition government that the total Liberal vote (including Liberal National and Independent Liberal support) fell to a catastrophic 11 per cent, and then 7 per cent in 1935. This steep decline chiefly reflected the drop in the number of Liberal candidates from over 500 in 1929 to just 160 in the two 1930s elections. In the post-war period, Liberal candidacies revived for two elections (1945 and 1950) to approximately the 500 mark, but when their share of the poll failed to break past 9 per cent the party organization collapsed for the rest of the 1950s. Thus the levels of national support for the Liberals of below 3 per cent recorded in this decade were artificially produced reflections of the Liberal party organization's difficulties.

The continuing strength of 'third force' support in the electorate throughout the heyday of the 'two party system' can be better gauged by looking at the vote per Liberal/Alliance candidate since 1922 (see figure 7.3d). Median Liberal candidate support over the whole period since the 1920s is 21 per cent, with a midspread from 15 to 28 per cent. The scores below the lower quartile are for 1950 and 1951, and for 1970 and 1979. These statistics put the 1980s combined performance of the Liberals and the Social Democratic Party into perspective, as fairly predictable (if above-median) levels of performance. Thus the picture is one of a basically stable level of third party support, albeit subject to major fluctuations in response to party organizational influences – such as the 1988 split of SDP loyalists from the Social and Liberal Democrats (the merged party which was supposed to bring to an end the half-hearted 'alliance' of the Social Democratic Party with the Liberals).

The consequences of Labour's partial displacement of the Liberals can be read off most clearly in the party's record in government. From 1918 to the end of 1987 Labour has been in government for less than half the time accounted for by Tory governments, and for majority governments Labour's share is under a third of the Conservative's period in office (see table 7.2). Labour has won power only three times with secure majorities, in 1945, 1950 and 1966, but the 1950 government collapsed through the exhaustion of ministers. Two other Labour majorities (in 1964 and October 1974) were wafer-thin, and the party has had three periods of minority government (1923–4, 1929–31 and 1976–9). In all these latter cases the party has been reduced to almost a 'caretaker government' status, with its legislative programme either severely restricted or aborted altogether.

The trade union arm of the labour movement successfully unionized manual workers in large-scale manufacturing from the 1880s to the 1920s. From this base there were two post-war avenues for consolidating and expanding union membership. The first was by the nationalization of many of the most highly unionized industries, and the second involved the large-scale growth of welfare state public services from the late 1950s. These relatively easy but politically dependent areas of expansion contributed, however, to the changing public image of both trade unionism and the Labour party as public sector rather than working class forms of organization. Public sector wage demands also helped sustain a favourable union/non-union wage differential throughout the post-war period, a feature which has even survived the experience of Thatcherism. But a series of major public sector disputes, notably the miners' overtime ban and strike of 1973–4, the 'winter of discontent' in 1978–9, and the miners' strike of 1984–5, have provided some of the most distinctive landscape features on the long road by which Tory/Labour conflicts have been progressively converted from class-based to sectorally-based issues (Dunleavy, 1980; Dunleavy and Husbands, 1985, ch. 6).

The labour movement's weak political entrenchment and dependency upon public sector expansion has been matched by its failure to aim for or achieve the kind of ideological hegemony enjoyed by social democratic ideas in Sweden. The most fruitful period of Labour ideological development was around the turn of the century. By the 1920s the Fabian contribution to Labour's programme for government was virtually complete, with standardized solutions (such as the need for government economic planning and full nationalization of some major industries and public utilities) being chiefly reiterated in the next two decades. The 1945 landslide government adhered very closely to the ideas already current twenty years before, albeit heavily modified in a more 'statist' direction by the experience of wartime mobilization (see pp. 277–8 below). The practical innovations of this period, in the field of counter-cyclical economic management, compulsory social insurance, and the establishment of the National Health Service, did not stem chiefly or even solely from labour movement sources. Many aspects of the critically important Beveridge report and of the introduction of Keynesian economic management policies reflected the impact of debates among Liberal intellectuals in the 1930s and early war years, rather than any strong welling up of new Labour ideas. Six months before its 1945 victory, Labour had no agreed programme and its leadership was bitterly divided by personal and policy disputes.

The post-war development of Labour thinking was marked by no wholesale reappraisal of its intellectual inheritance (Whiteley, 1983, pp. 21–52). The Crosland re-statement of social democracy as an altruistic elite policy of generally egalitarian redistribution financed by faster economic growth came to dominate Labour's social policy proposals by the 1960s (Crosland, 1956). But whether there was a viable and socialist argument for rejecting outright nationalization remained contested and under-developed within the labour movement until the late 1970s. Even when Labour attitudes towards a social market economy were redesigned under the Kinnock leadership in the mid 1980s, it was only the specific device of unified public ownership of industries which was called into question. Labour's traditional faith in the long-run viability of full public sector provision of welfare state services remained intact. The party's most significant policy reappraisal occurred in 1981 when Labour's defence attitudes decisively shifted into a non-nuclear stance. But even this switch represented a long-delayed rerun of a change first signalled and then rescinded at the beginning of the 1960s.

The weakness of corporatism

Few areas of British political and social history have been so affected by the 'backward mapping' of current trends onto earlier epochs than the discussion about the existence and importance of corporatist forms of intermediation. Middlemas's (1979) position accurately reflects the atmosphere of the social contract period by extrapolating the origins of corporatist practices back to the early decades of the century. In particular he locates the crucial origins of low levels of class conflict and the integration of peak associations into a closed, triadic relationship with government as early as the late 1920s and 1930s. Interestingly, too, Middlemas sees the 1960s as a critical period of rupture in pre-existing patterns of social consensus, heralded by the overt involvement of government in wage determination via statutory incomes policies and the escalation and politicization of industrial conflict which followed (see also Marquand, 1988). By contrast, most conventional corporatist accounts describe the years from the first attempt to orchestrate national economic 'concertation' in the 1962 National Economic Development Council through to the demise of the 'social contract' in 1979 as the heyday of state-business-trade union intermediation (Panitch, 1979).

Critics of both variants of the corporatist thesis stress the dramatic fluctuations in government-industry-union relationships across different parties and political leaderships, across different issues, and across different time periods. Pluralist writers suggest that the British experience has principally been one of episodic 'tripartism', in which peak associations have entered into temporary agreements with government. Most of these recognizably 'exceptional' interventions were directed to stabilizing 'crisis' indicators in macroeconomic policy, as with the 'social contract' used to restrain inflation by the Labour government in the 1975–8 period. British peak associations have been quite weakly developed, and constrained by internal divisions. There are two main groups claiming to speak for business, the Confederation of British Industry – traditionally the voice of manufacturing and keen on corporatist relations with government (Grant and Marsh, 1977) – and the more overtly right-wing and market-orientated Institute of Directors. The CBI has consequently been apprehensive about corporate breakaways and weakened by competition from the IoD. The Trades Union Congress has been more successful in maintaining a dominant position and forestalling union disaffiliations, but there remain considerable internal strains (Coates and Topham, 1980, pp. 94–113). The balance of powers between individual interest groups and peak associations has always been heavily biased in favour of the former. Consequently the CBI and TUC have been reluctant or unable to take a particularly strong line except in crisis conditions. The weakness of corporatist arrangements for economic planning, supporting growth sectors, securing co-operative investment financing by different corporations, persuading trade unions that productivity improvements can be acceptable, or controlling inflation, have all contributed to a record of erratic macroeconomic policy.

Erratic macroeconomic policy

All governments in market societies must chop and change their immediate economic policy stance in response to environmental stimuli. But in most liberal democracies it is possible to point to underlying stabilities or constants in macroeconomic policy – such as the anti-inflationary bias of German policy, the corporatist economic management of Sweden or Austria, the productive investment and expanding world market share orientation of Japan, or the growth planning of post-war French governments. The UK resembles mainly the United States in resisting such longer-term characterizations of policy stances. The erratic quality of British policy reflected the lack of any institutionalized consensus about the direction of development for the economy, even though the 1945–60 period as a whole was characterized by historically high rates of growth in industrial outputs, productivity and exports (Blank, 1977). Two key factors seem to underlie this trait: the narrow group of decision-makers involved in macroeconomic policy-making; and the importance of financial markets in the UK's economic life.

The concentration of economic policy control within government has contributed strongly to the short-termism of British economic policy-making. There is no effective pluralism of policy-making institutions such as is found in the USA, nor are there important economic agencies operating with a degree of autonomy from the government of the day such as the Australian Arbitration Commission or the West German Bundesbank. The Treasury has always been the sole economic ministry, apart from a couple of short-lived attempts to establish separate departments for 'strategic' planning. The Treasury controls the allocation of public expenditures across the board, the collection of all central taxes (with operational details handled by two 'semi-detached' sub-ministries), and the overall conduct of the country's external economic relations.

The Chancellor of the Exchequer and his ministerial team are key influences upon Treasury policy-making, together with the internal committee of senior officials (Keegan and Pennant-Rea, 1979; Young and Sloman, 1984). The core of the Treasury has always remained a smallish (1300 strong) staff department, staffed by elite administrators. Within the public expenditure and cash planning processes Treasury approval is the absolutely critical stage, since there is no real capacity for the legislature to scrutinize or change what has been agreed. Within the civil service, the Treasury is additionally influential because it effectively controls most aspects of promotion and personnel at senior levels (following the successive abolitions of two separate departments for the Civil Service which lasted from 1969 to 1986). And in ministerial terms the Chancellor of the Exchequer operates very much on his own, consulting the Prime Minister, but not required to clear major changes with his Cabinet colleagues.

In deciding on financial policies the Treasury shares power with the Bank of England, nationalized in 1946, which regulates the London Stock Exchange and currency markets, mainly relying on 'hands off' forms of socialized controls and internal policing. The Bank of England, however, does not have anything similar to the status or independence of the US Federal Reserve or the West German Bundesbank. Governors can be easily appointed and persuaded to leave by ministers, without any Parliamentary control or possibility of effective resistance from the Bank. Yet the Bank does have a considerable impact on decision-making by virtue of its operational control over implementing financial policies, an influence which it has used systematically to maximize governments' deference to City interests. The Bank staffs regard themselves as advocates of the financial markets' case to government, at least as much as they are government regulators of the market.

The tight concentration of economic decision-making in such a powerful institutional apparatus has insulated most aspects of macro-economic policy-making from any effective control by most domestic social interests. The Treasury and the Bank, and even the Treasury's sub-ministries handling taxation, are all core departments, with no readily identifiable groups of 'clients' – except of course for the financial markets and their associated professions. The closest thing to a Treasury 'policy community' is a small group of financial journalists, plus economists in universities and corporations who model the British economy's performance. As with other professions, status and income hierarchies slanted towards the private sector often influence the flow of ideas in the occupational community (Dunleavy, 1981), a factor which helps explain why monetarist thinking made such a rapid impact upon first the City and then government itself in the mid 1970s. And as with other highly professionalized policy systems, the Treasury has demon-strated a tendency to embrace a rapid succession of 'fashions', involving the cycling and destruction of new ideas and policy directions.

From the late 1940s through to the mid 1970s governments broadly accepted the need for counter-cyclical intervention and manipulated the public sector as an economic regulator. However, any government attempts to 'fine-tune' the economy were complicated throughout this period by the need to consider three key policy variables – inflation, unemployment and the balance of payments. Consequently Moseley (1984) argues that policy changes are best captured by a simple stimulus-response model in which the current macroeconomic stance was preserved for as long as the development of the three policy indices remained within their respective trend rates of development. Only when one of the policy variables strayed out of line with its trend rate of development would decision-makers intervene, and then by minimally adjusting policy so as to bring the deviant policy index back into line. Despite the apparent quietism of Moseley's satisficing model, volatilities in inflation and the balance of payments meant that adjustments were in practice pretty frequent. A greater degree of short-term stability in the economic policy-making process might have been expected from the early 1970s when the floating of sterling on the international exchanges finally removed the obligation to police fixed exchange rates from policy-makers' shoulders. In fact, however, the worsening 'stagflation' conditions of the 1970s saw a rapid succession of policy crises, mostly linked to the control of inflation and to financial crises.

The concentration of economic policy-making under ministerial control might be expected to open up opportunities for the creation of political manipulation effects on economic policy. But in practice the strong professionalization of Treasury policy-making combined with deference to financial market signals has mostly blunted such effects. Britain's 'adversary politics' system of polarized major parties with an electorally almost unrepresented centre ground has been alleged by many critics to produce unnecessary and economically destabilizing adjustments of policy (Finer, 1975). But such accounts are disputed by quantitative studies showing the sporadic nature of economic policy adjustments and the predominant influence of trend rates of development on most economic policy indices (Moseley, 1984; Rose, 1981). It is quite hard to detect major differences in parties' economic policy preferences before 1979, or to pinpoint party alternations in power as crucial turning points in the development of economic indices. Hibbs (1977) has suggested evidence of lower unemployment under Labour rather than Conservative governments, but the difference involved is under 1 per cent and disputed by critics. These unspectacular conclusions may nonetheless disguise the most important impacts of 'adversary politics' in maintaining a lack of attention to long-term macroeconomic strategies (Gamble and Walkland, 1986), thereby contributing to the fractured evolution and ungrounded character of statism in public policy-making.

The importance of financial markets in the economy has always injected extra instability into the policy environment. Britain's international currency position was first weakened by the debt created during the First World War, a period when the gold standard for exchanging sterling was 'temporarily' suspended. By the 1920s the national debt was roughly ten times larger than in the decade before 1914, while UK national income had barely doubled and central government revenues increased between four and five-fold. From the early 1920s onwards the role of sterling as an international reserve currency began to constitute an important additional constraint on financial decision-making (Jay, 1985, pp. 80–

159). The problem partly arose because sterling was used to finance trade with the British Empire, and the sterling area in the inter-war period became a progressively more important mechanism by which the UK implemented protectionist policies. But sterling was also used as a safe currency in which foreign banks and investors could hold their liquid assets, confident that they would not lose out through adverse movements of exchange rates. Churchill's 1925 decision to restore Britain to the gold standard, and to fix on the 1914 high rate of exchange ($4.86 to the £), was a doomed attempt to re-establish the international confidence of an earlier imperial period.

When the National Government was forced off the gold standard again in 1931, the acute currency crisis which preceded their decision achieved something like a paradigm shift amongst British economic policy-makers. Sterling's vulnerability to international spasms of confidence was acutely dramatized, even though the UK's gold and foreign currency reserves in the 1930s roughly balanced the size of sterling liabilities. On the outbreak of war in September 1939 the government took sweeping emergency powers to underpin Britain's international financial position, formalizing the Sterling Area within which stringent exchange controls were imposed, and pegging the value of the pound at $4.03. This system was maintained right through into the late 1940s, buttressed towards the end of the war by the Bretton Woods agreement and the creation of the IMF.

As the UK's national debt tripled during the Second World War the policy constraint imposed by the reserve currency role of sterling was greatly magnified. British decision-makers sought to maintain sterling as a reserve currency, or at least to smooth out its decline, despite the hegemonic position of the dollar in the post-war world economy. But the maintenance of strict exchange controls and production licensing into peacetime could not disguise the weakness which was created for the UK's economic policies. In the early post-war period the Treasury and Bank of England were continuously aware that if sterling entered a 'free fall' in world currency markets the UK could no longer even theoretically cover sterling liabilities more than three times larger than gold and foreign currency reserves. In 1949 the spectre of panic selling of sterling returned with a vengeance, and the Labour government announced a drastic 30 per cent devaluation. The new $2.80 rate laid the foundations for the industrial recovery of the 1950s. Yet, as the succession of stop-go policies in the next fifteen years demonstrated, the problem of sterling's reserve currency role could not be so quickly exorcised. From the early 1960s onwards the $2.80 rate began to be tested on exchange markets again, and in mid 1966 the next Labour government embarked on a dogged defence of the fixed rate, raising interest rates and taxes and announcing a standstill of prices and wages. Intense and repeated speculative attacks on sterling eventually produced a further sterling devaluation (to $2.40) in late 1967.

Four years later the pound was floated following the USA's decision to end dollar-gold convertibility and the collapse of the Bretton Woods agreement. At the same time the reserve currency role of sterling had dwindled away to vanishing levels, so that by the mid 1970s the pound's rating reflected financial market views of the UK's economic prospects alone. But the currency crisis syndrome returned within five years of the pound's being floated when another Labour Chancellor was forced to pull out of a trip to Washington by panic selling of sterling pushing the pound below $1.60. Only the government's capitulation to IMF demands for major public spending cutbacks restored market confidence. By the late 1970s, however, Britain's balance of payments began to be powerfully strengthened by the arrival of North Sea oil, while the petroleum tax revenues greatly eased the government's financing problems – underlying trends which the election of a Conservative government in 1979 allowed the markets to better appreciate.

Britain's low-welfare state

Britain's high profile forms of post-war government intervention to support social welfare have coexisted since the late 1950s with lagging levels of substantive benefits, especially in transfer payments such as pensions, unemployment pay and sickness pay. As table 7.3 demonstrates, the growth in social expenditures in the UK in the 1960s was less than that in most other advanced industrial societies. Provision of services in kind was generally at a higher level until the late 1970s, especially with those services (such as council housing in its early days, school education and the National Health Service) used by the population generally. The chief problems here were the neglect of 'Cinderella services', which left facilities for the elderly and many handicapped or mentally ill people chronically under-funded for several decades. Nonetheless a comprehensive social policy system, providing institutional support for many social contingencies, has survived most open challenges. And major proposals for reducing the welfare state until recently have generally attracted bipartisan opposition and evoked no enthusiasm from voters.

However, one of the most distinctive features of the UK welfare system has been the generally low level of social transfer payments providing income replacement for the elderly, sick and unemployed. Table 7.6 shows the evolution of the main benefits – the old age pension, sickness and unemployment pay, family allowances/child benefits, and social assistance/supplementary benefits – expressed as a percentage of the average male wage over the post-war period. The characteristic pattern for most transfer schemes was of gradual growth in the 1960s,

Table 7.6 Main benefit levels as a percentage of average male earnings, 1951–81

Type of benefit	1981	1975	1970	1965	1960	1955	1950
Unemployment pay (earnings related)	36	43	54	na	na	na	na
Old age pension	39	35	32	35	31	30	30
Unemployment pay (basic)	28	29	32	35	31	30	26
Social assistance (long term)	36	35	32	na	na	na	na
Social assistance (basic)	29	29	31	34	30	30	30
Family allowance/child benefit	12	11	14	18	19	28	28

Benefit levels are those payable to a married couple previously on average earnings; except that the family allowance/child benefit figures are for a family with three children aged under 11. Earnings-related figures assume payments into the scheme at average earnings. The long term social assistance rate is payable to all retired people, and to other claimants after one year: but the unemployed are excluded from this rate. All figures are rounded to the nearest percent.
Source: Parry, 1986, p. 189.

following a generally static picture in the 1950s under Conservative governments. By 1965 unemployment/sickness pay and pensions were respectively 11 and 5 percentage points higher than in 1950, and in the following year earnings related supplements were introduced, giving significantly higher income replacement for those on the scheme. But in the early 1970s all benefit levels showed a decline relative to average earnings, which has continued for most benefits into the 1980s. The exceptions are old age pensions and long-term supplementary benefits (payable mainly to the elderly, sick and disabled) which up to 1981 continued to expand slightly. Finally, the initially very generous levels of family allowance created by Labour in 1945 have tailed off throughout the period. These comparatively low welfare levels in European terms have been viewed as acceptable by voters over long time periods. And public opposition to further welfare state growth has generally grown quite sharply when attempts are made to significantly upgrade transfer or service levels (as in the late 1960s and mid 1970s). Both these points, together with the record of long run stasis in low benefit levels as a share of average earnings, strongly suggest that there is no very marked pro-welfare consensus in Britain (Banting, 1979).

Some new right and even social democratic critics of the British system explain these phenomena as cause and effect. They argue that the costly and ineffective use of statist public policies (such as the provision of goods and services in kind rather than relying on transfers, voucher schemes and a private market) has increasingly reduced the legitimacy of government intervention altogether. Pursuing a strategy of equality by means of direct and heavily formalized public service provision (Tawney, 1937) implies carrying out income redistribution by means of a more than usually leaky bucket. The more explicitly governmental such programmes become, the more median voter leverage power dictates the linking of genuinely pro-welfare measures for needy social groups to pseudo-welfare policies of providing subsidized private goods to the 'middle class' (Goodin and LeGrand, 1987; LeGrand, 1982). Both effects imply taxation costs for achieving a given redistribution which are quite disproportionate to the social benefits secured.

The alternative view adopted by pro-welfare groups and the centre left has been that the development of social policy has been adversely affected by stop-go macroeconomic policies, with public expenditure cuts being used as a mechanism for throttling back an overheated inflationary economy. This effect has been concentrated in particular policy sectors and time periods, such as council housing investment from 1949 to the mid 1970s, which was used as a direct instrument of macroeconomic policy (CDP, 1975; Merret, 1979). But the more generally acknowledged effect of sharp adjustments to economic crises, such as the devaluation of 1967 or the IMF deal in 1976, has been to fracture the coherent evolution of welfare policy for lengthy periods. Instead individual policy sectors and their professions and decision-makers have cultivated a high level of defensiveness about their issue area, contributing to a low level of overall strategy despite a high level of policy institutionalization. One of the first major social policy impacts of the Thatcher government was in cutting back the over-management of services which was the legacy of ambitious management reorganizations in the National Health Service and local government, put through in the early 1970s just before the IMF crisis and worsening unemployment situation scaled down expectations of social policy growth.

Explaining 'Statism'

Because some of the most common foundations for statist forms of government intervention are missing, the British pattern of public policy-making in the early post-war period appears 'ungrounded'. Three main factors can reduce this explanatory gap: the weak organization of British manufacturing business, the impact of extraordinary wartime mobilization strongly led by government, and the dismantling of the British Empire.

The weakness of industrial capital

Conventional accounts of the post-war mixed economy have stressed that by the time of the First World War many features of the British economy marked out a prospect for major industrial decline. Much of the heavy industry base, such as coal mining, iron and steel manufacture, or shipbuilding, already had lengthy records of under-investment and reliance on labour-intensive methods of production. These same industries were maintained under artificial market conditions but with negligible investment during the two world wars, so that some civil servants and ministers by the early 1940s foresaw a lengthy and unsatisfactory period of economic adjustment ahead (Barnett, 1986). The changing international division of labour, itself powerfully boosted by the wartime diversion of 'first world' goods to war production, was bound to create collective action problems and investment demands in industrial sectors like these, factors to which private corporations could not effectively respond. In Marxist accounts the same thesis is expressed as a recognition by 'monopoly' capital that an orderly run-down was needed of such industries which could not be profitably organized by capital owners themselves. Thus the 'exclusion principle' which normally prohibits the state in capitalist society from intervening in production (Offe, 1975) was waived in order for the government to take over these sectors of devalorized capital and manage their run-down in ways which would preserve linkages with other UK industries and minimize the scope for disruptive social implications.

In fact the mix of industries nationalized by Labour in 1945–50 or absorbed piecemeal before or after this period always contained a mixture of major growth industries (electricity, telecommunications, broadcasting), industries which fluctuated from long-term decline to profitable growth (gas, mail), socially necessary industries perhaps no longer financially viable on pure market criteria (railways and public transit systems), and industries facing drastic long-term decline because of changing international specialization of activity (such as coal, steel and shipbuilding). There is no easy pattern to be detected here.

Nor have attempts to extend the same logic to explain the expansion of welfare state services been very successful. Most areas of social policy, even those where government mandates consumption of particular services, do not remotely look like the 'technical' public goods sought by conventional economists in trying to explain government intervention. But equally radical political economy arguments about the development of welfare state programmes directly or indirectly favouring the accumulation of capital seem hard to test (Gough, 1979). Interventions may directly foster business profitability by socializing wage costs (for example, unemployment or health insurance), or by socializing other production costs (such as training costs), or by providing a pump-priming accumulation potential, or by opening up opportunities for complementary consumption growth. On the other hand the constraints on state intervention include a direct accumulation imperative not to see resources diverted into devalorized capital sectors, an imperative under favourable market forces to 'recommodify' services with private capital growth potential (such as medical services at present) and an ideological imperative to preserve the primacy of market forces (Dunleavy, 1983). With such a diversified list of influences available to radical political economy accounts it is not surprising that they can relatively easily 'explain' the growth, stabilization or decline of state intervention in consumption processes.

There are two more promising lines of argument about the specific features of British industrial capital which encouraged statist forms of government intervention:

1 *The lack of any distinctive manufacturing capital ethos* has been seen as a long-term feature of British economic life in many varied accounts. Cultural explanations have stressed the downside of the relatively easy assimilation of new entrepreneurs into the ranks of the British upper classes. British elite attitudes from the late Victorian era showed an increasing suspicion of technical progress, an idealization of the

countryside and a nostalgia for simpler and more stable times standing outside the experience of painful social change.

The accommodation between aristocracy and bourgeoisie (in the Victorian period) meant an adaptation by the new middle class to a comparatively aloof and passive economic role. The rentier aristocracy succeeded to a large extent in maintaining a cultural hegemony, and consequently in reshaping the industrial bourgeoisie in its own image. (Weiner, 1981, p. 10).

However, critics find implausible the view that:

successful entrepreneurs have no sooner established some capital than they are seduced from trade and commerce towards the purchase of country estates, into time-consuming involvement in public administration and concern to establish a non-commercial career for their offspring. (Mather, 1988)

The historical evidence for and against the importance of cultural factors in Britain's long-run economic decline remains contested. But there is little doubt that the assimilation of business into an aristocratic elite in the later nineteenth century at least hindered the emergence of any distinctive or unified manufacturing business ethos in the UK.

In the twentieth century the international prominence of the UK in world trade, allied with the declining but still substantial role of the sterling area, created strong pressures for size increases in the largest British companies from the 1930s through to the 1970s. These pressures were helped along by governments from the 1930s (when amalgamations were seen as averting redundancies from the closure of smaller firms). In the post-war period industrial concentration was often assumed to be vital to fend off US competition, a stance explicitly embedded in the operation of UK monopolies policy. By the 1950s, however, the largest British firms' most important characteristic was their tendency to plough a great deal of investment into diversification and capacity-creation overseas. In addition to worsening the balance of payments problem, the outward flow of investment by large companies reduced their stake in the domestic UK economy, and created a division between their internationalist and free-trade outlook and the potentially more protectionist stance of medium and small capital. In the post-war years:

a serious conflict began to develop between the international priorities of British policy (such as overseas investment, maintaining a UK military presence abroad, etc.) and the needs of the domestic economy. This was sometimes presented as a new clash between manufacturing industry and the financial sector. But the real clash was between the new and often combined operations of British industry and British finance, and the requirements of domestic expansion. (Gamble, 1980, p. 114)

2   *The growth of the City from the 1960s* has tended to create enhanced

deference by policy-makers towards financial market signals – a factor which more than compensates for the decline in sterling's reserve currency role. The world-wide growth in financial services has had a dramatic impact upon the City of London, which has grown and adapted to preserve its role (along with Tokyo and New York) in the top three international centres in financial asset trading. The annual real growth of output in banking, finance, insurances and business services from 1961 to 1983 was 4.3 per cent, more than twice the growth rate for all UK industries, and four times as large as the growth in manufacturing outputs (Johnson, 1985, pp. 34–7). In the same period the share of total output absorbed by finance services almost doubled to 13.4 per cent. Financial services' share of employment more than doubled in the period to 8.6 per cent, with an annual growth in employment of 3.7 per cent, while manufacturing employment fell by 1.3 per cent a year on average. The City's role in generating 'invisible' exports to offset against Britain's chronic albeit fluctuating trade imbalance has expanded in significance from an always considerable influence to a primary factor in economic policy-making. In the 1980s the Conservatives' abolition of all exchange controls, the 'Big Bang' deregulation of financial markets, and massive privatization flotations all combined to produce spectacular growth in the City, strenghening its importance both to the balance of payments and to employment.

As well as its influence on macroeconomic policy, London's role as a world financial centre has also had extensive implications for the workings of industrial capital itself. British companies' performance is directly and intensively scrutinized by a large and sophisticated equity market. Few corporations have effectively insulated themselves from finance market pressures by long-term arrangements with banks or major investing institutions. While industrial corporations in Japan and Germany overwhelmingly seized the opportunities afforded by post-war reconstruction to take a long-term view of their investment programmes, British industrial companies have operated in the main with an immediate profits orientation dictated by the need to maintain their stock market capitalizations in a volatile market. Like Wall Street, the City's dominant approach is to be more concerned about short-run fluctuations in corporate stock market valuations than long-term investment returns. Only a handful of very large corporations (such as ICI) or family firms (such as Pilkingtons) enjoying quasi-monopoly positions in their domestic markets have taken a long view on research and development needs or the development of proper training programmes.

Manufacturing weakness and financial sector predominance both seem to have increased state involvement in the mixed economy and welfare state by reducing the willingness of business to take a leading role in public affairs in a unified or effective way. Most large, internationally-orientated British companies have displayed a characteristic resistance to undertaking any domestic activity 'inessential' to the making of short-term profits. One immediate consequence has been a chronic underprovision of training within UK manufacturing, which throws a considerable extra education burden on to government programmes. Initially handled by the conventional education system, the burden thus created has increasingly been handled by a separate training agency since the mid 1970s, which from 1981 has basically paid firms to provide large numbers of trainee placements. Similarly in the research and development field UK firms have been content to depend to a large degree upon government funding and direct research in public laboratories (much of which is associated with defence programmes). In the welfare state field companies have also done relatively little to create an 'occupational welfare state'. Throughout the 1960s a fifth of private sector employees worked for firms with no occupational pension scheme. And barely half of private sector employees in firms with schemes were actually covered by them, compared with nearly three-quarters in the public sector (*Social Trends*, 1974, table 72). Very similar patterns in respect of sick-pay also existed. Companies rationed their involvement in occupational welfare state benefits, providing them for non-manual employees chiefly as a device for status differentiation, but withholding them from manual workers. Even in the mid 1970s access to such 'fringe' benefits was a major element in defining class distinctions (Westergaard and Resler, 1976, pp. 72–106).

For most of the early post-war period company attitudes towards their manual workforce especially created a vacuum of responsibility in policy areas such as employment protection, health insurance, or sickness pay for working people. While poverty-related and old age provisions in any advanced industrial state involve direct government intervention, Britain is rather unusual in the extent to which government was sucked into this vacuum in meeting the extended consumption needs of people in work. In the mid 1970s a number of developments changed this situation, including the push under both Conservative and Labour governments towards more mixed public/private pensions systems, and the simple expansion of non-manual positions *vis-à-vis* manual workers. Flat-rate incomes policies under the Heath government and the 'social contract' period also dramatically developed company-assisted consumption of car transport, private health care and other services as perks to retain managers from being poached by rival firms, while nominally adhering to government pay norms.

War and state intervention

The UK's experience of 'extraordinary statism' during the Second World War is obviously a period of crucial importance in the development of state growth. Peacock and Wiseman's (1968) survey of a century of public expenditure expansion offered a supply-side explanation in which state growth was primarily caused by the freeing of public officials from normal tax-raising constraints. In the 1939–45 period consumers became accustomed to the restricted availability of opportunities for private consumption, and the near impossibility of organizing some kinds of private investment (such as new house construction or new car purchases). Income earners also became familiar with very high (50 per cent) basic rates of income tax. Thus normal public opinion constraints on state growth were breached – and politicians, civil servants and interest groups acting in pursuit of their individual or sectional interests were quick to exploit the period of decreased resistance to public spending, converting the temporary wartime mobilization of social resources into a permanent peacetime apparatus.

However, this account accords no weight to the demand-side of the equation, elite acceptance and wider public recognition of wartime administration and planning as effective mechanisms for accomplishing social purposes. This positive experience was inaugurated during the First World War when government direction was progressively extended from 'industries essential to war needs' until, by the third year of hostilities, the War Cabinet Report declared in self-congratulatory fashion that:

1917 may be described as a year in which State control was extended until it covered not only national activities directly affecting the military effort, but every section of industry – production, transport and manufacture. (Marwick, 1973, pp. 249–50)

The wartime apparatus thus created at its peak absorbed over 5.1 million personnel, including a central government swollen to more than twice its usual size (Abramovitz and Eliasberg, 1957, table 4). Most of this machinery was quickly dismantled after the war, so that the numbers of government employees in 1921 were a fifth of their figure three years earlier. But although the Lloyd George coalition recreated what Marwick terms 'the same old state', the experience of wartime administration, discreet though it may have been by 1939–45 standards, persisted as a living exemplar of the solutions advocated by Fabian socialism throughout the inter-war period.

With a second major war in Europe, public and elite attitudes in the UK shifted dramatically in two key areas – the need for strong defence, and the perceived inevitability of a great deal more state direction of economic and social life under future peacetime conditions. British administrators almost immediately reactivated a stronger version of the planning machinery for control of economic life used in 1917–18, creating a system of state direction of social life more extensive than that in any other combatant European country except Russia (Marwick, 1974). British controls were appreciably tougher in economic matters than the wartime regime in Nazi Germany – for example, in imposing more restrictive rationing of civilian consumption. The perpetuation of this system into peacetime was not simply the result of inertial momentum. It also reflected a quantum leap in social learning, a recognition of the value of managed social effort for achieving specific and predictable economic and logistical effects. In terms of social policy the reappraisal of state intervention also mirrored a significant change in the pattern of class relations in wartime Britain. Some accounts portray this period as marked by a greatly increased appreciation of the social situation of others (Marwick, 1980, pp. 213–30). Observers using more of a rational choice approach suggest that wartime enthusiasm for income protection and welfare state measures reflected the much greater degree of uncertainty about how people would fare in the post-war epoch whose outlines could only dimly be anticipated (Dryzek and Goodin, 1986). But for whatever reason a change of attitudes affected all levels of public opinion and most political viewpoints, and the perceptual shift involved decayed only slowly with the passage of time and changing social, technological and international conditions. Thus the wartime experience not only created an opportunity for public sector growth in overtly statist forms, it also created a strong and enduring public acceptance of governmental expansion.

Of course, the large-scale evidence of attitudinal shifts under wartime conditions does not imply that we should accept uncritically some of the more embroidered myths of British wartime performance which underpin many conventional accounts of the mixed economy and welfare state. Barnett (1986) argues that central state direction did nothing to reverse declining productivity and long-term investment neglect in manufacturing and coal mining. Even in the new industries boosted by defence needs, British dependency on the USA for many crucial components deepened progressively during the war years, and some of the most famous British war devices (such as the Spitfire fighters) were built using much lower productivity methods than those in Germany or America. However, in explaining public and elite reactions to state intervention despite such shortcomings, Barnett's would-be revisionist account collapses into a long implausible tirade against the 'new Jerusalemism' of wartime social reformers such as Beveridge and the Labour ministers in the coalition government.

The transition from empire

The combined push of wartime supply- and demand-side factors was clearly at its greatest in the late 1940s when the Labour government implemented its major nationalizations, public service reorganizations and expansion of welfare entitlements. The 1950s were generally years of retrenchment under the Conservatives. As Parry (1985, p. 60) notes: 'The range of activities of the modern British state was largely in place by 1951. Public employment actually *declined* absolutely and proportionately in the 1950s, the first decade in the twentieth century in which this happened.'

Yet within this overall decline, the growth of welfare services continued at a fast rate, and a small growth in general administration occurred outside the civil service in local government (see table 7.7). By contrast the public corporations' manpower dwindled, initially via denationalization and later via extensive labour-shedding. The introduction of conscription in 1948 plus the Korean war meant that the 1951 figures for British-based uniformed and civilian defence personnel were effectively at record peacetime levels, far above those of the inter-war period when the country was administering a much more extensive empire. A series of incidents, such as the Suez crisis, the 'emergency' in Malaysia, and a set of decolonization struggles in Africa, Arabia and Cyprus kept up the UK's overseas military engagements throughout the decade. Nonetheless defence personnel fell dramatically in the late 1950s with the phasing out of conscription from 1960.

Table 7.7 Evolution of UK public employment in the 1950s

	1951	1956	1960	1966	Growth (%) 1951–1960	Growth (%) 1951–1966
Social welfare	1284	1438	1684	2103	+31	+64
Administration	1566	1551	1686	1833	+8	+17
Public corps	2206	1969	1732	1494	−22	−32
Defence etc.	1228	1192	838	731	−32	−40

Sources: Parry, 1985, p. 63; Parry, 1986, p. 169

The dismantling of Britain's overseas Empire also had significant effects which do not show up in the figures for UK public employment or finances. The Whitehall staffs of the Colonial Office itself are included in official statistics. But otherwise 'each of the Colonies, Protectorates, and other Territories supervised by the Office has its own budget and is expected to pay for its own civil service . . . These local administrations have always been staffed partly by local recruits, partly by people sent out from this country' (Mackenzie and Grove, 1957, pp. 91–2). Similarly, British armed forces stationed in overseas territories are included in UK public employment, but not locally recruited colonial armed forces or police (often quasi-military in their functions and organization). Hence it is currently impossible to present integrated figures for the decline in the overall size of the imperial administrations being at least partially supervised from Whitehall. Even if only a small percentage of the issues handled by outstation governments was ever referred to London, the load on the central decision-making machinery thus created must have been very substantial. And it seems clear that there were sharp declines in this load at two periods, first in 1947 with independence for India, Pakistan and Burma, and secondly in the late 1950s and early 1960s as a series of UK colonies in Africa, Arabia, Asia and the Caribbean achieved independence. Between these periods Whitehall involvement actually somewhat increased, partly because of the stress placed on fostering economic development of the colonies, and partly due to some vain efforts by the Conservatives to stave off decolonization. But the underlying trend towards disengagement remains clear.

This background helps to explain why the expansion of domestic welfare state programmes could continue throughout the 1950s, and why the retrenchment of public spending under Conservative governments throughout the decade was less severe than might have been expected. As the flow of issues from imperial administrations slackened off and military spending was cut back, so core executive attention and seats at Cabinet gradually fell free. By the mid 1960s, when Labour was returned to government and embarked upon a second main wave of domestic welfare state expansion, a considerable 'underload' or spare capacity seems to have developed within the central government machinery, particularly at the core executive level.

As a result, the steady growth of the welfare services did not confront some of the problems of intense ecological struggle with competing policy sectors for finance and political attention which some pluralist writers have argued will typically beset processes of rapid policy change. Hogwood and Peters (1983) suggest that once slack decision-making and managerial capacity in a governmental system has been absorbed, and general constraints on growth apply, then exponents of new initiatives must either find some vacant 'policy space' or engage in a costly battle of 'policy succession' in which new policy space is created by terminating existing programmes. But in the UK case the transition from Empire, especially from the late 1950s or early 1960s onwards, meant that these constraints did not apply. If the mechanisms for welfare state expansion under the Conservatives were primarily demographic changes rather than significant policy shifts, there was nonetheless some incremental extension of the scope and quality of services. And the sense of spare capacity in government left the Conservatives politically vulnerable to Labour's campaign for a renewed assault on domestic poverty and economic malaise which brought the party its election victories of 1964 and 1966.

The Move Away from Statism in the 1980s

The statist character of British public policy-making in the early post-war period is thrown into sharper focus by the experience of the Thatcher government in the 1980s. The changes in the organization of government intervention have been more dramatic than any shift in the level or scale of government involvement. But it is also possible to point to underlying continuities in the UK's policy configuration.

Post-statism in public policy

The centrepiece of the 'Thatcher revolution' in the 1980s has been the emergence of a hegemonic rolling programme of 'privatizations' of public corporations and state shareholdings (Veljanovski, 1987; Jones, 1987). The privatization programme began almost by accident as a strategy of selling state shareholdings in private companies to raise public finance plus the denationalizing of two industries (aerospace and shipbuilding) which had been controversially absorbed into the public sector only in the 1970s. But the programme was progressively extended in the mid 1980s to apply to long-established and profitable public corporations with a clear public utility character. British Telecom and British Gas have already been converted into quoted company forms and floated on the Stock Exchange. In Thatcher's third term from 1987 two previously non-corporation forms of public authority, the water authorities and the electricity industry, also began metamorphosing into a clutch of publicly quoted companies. In addition to these major changes there has been a fairly continuous process of sales of public assets, state shareholdings, and smaller discrete parts of public corporations' operations (Dunleavy and Rhodes, 1988). The previously accepted apparatus of overt state intervention in production industries has thus been speedily dismantled. The drive towards privatization has also produced continuous government pressure on industries still within the state sector to cut manpower and trim outputs so that public subsidies for operating costs can be reduced or eliminated, with the eventual aim of creating profitable corporations ripe for transfer to the private sector. The combined effect of privatizations and labour-shedding by state industries has been to reduce employment in the public corporations sector by 43 per cent between 1979 and 1986. The public corporations' share of all employees also dropped from 9 per cent at the start of the Thatcher government to 5 per cent by 1986.

However, some of these changes have been accomplished by building up regulatory powers to replace the governmental control previously delivered more informally by public ownership. Especially in public utility areas the government has created small regulatory bodies to police the telecommunications and gas industries, with quite a substantial regulatory agency in prospect for the water industry. Public dissatisfaction with the performance of the privatized British Telecom, which has a clear monopoly position and little effective competition, has prompted an anxiety in the Conservative party to split up the electricity generating industry into two supposedly competing corporations before transferring it to the private sector. The government has also decided to make it mandatory for 20 per cent of all electricity supplied to customers to come from non-fossil fuel sources in order to ensure the survival of a UK nuclear energy programme, which private investors might otherwise have found unattractive. In other ways ministers have also rather belatedly discovered that renouncing the ownership of public corporations or state shareholdings can create new problems. For example, in 1987 the government sold the last of its initial 40 per cent stake in the oil giant British Petroleum, only to find that the Kuwaiti State Investment Office used the occasion to build up a commanding 22.5 per cent stake in BP. Protecting the autonomy of the UK-based management then required considerable British government flexing of other regulatory muscles. These considerations suggest that the form of state intervention in production industries has certainly shifted dramatically under the Thatcher government, but that the level of intervention is still oscillating somewhat as experience of post-privatization performance increases.

In a range of policy areas standing between industrial policy and 'welfare' interventions proper, the Thatcher government has also been successful in reducing the role of central departments and local authorities and building up the 'social' and 'community' involvements of business. This new form of business/government corporatism (rigorously excluding the trade unions) stands in clear contrast to macroeconomic policy where the Conservatives have preferred 'hands off' policy controls such as money supply, exchange rate and interest rate manipulations to overt collaboration with business, still less the prices and incomes policies used by previous Labour and Conservative administrations. But at a microeconomic level the most important organizational forms developed under corporatism were the highly variegated quasi-government agencies (QGAs) which provided the basis for maintaining central control over both the mixed economy and much of the consumption-orientated welfare state. Since 1979 the Thatcher government has greatly increased the policy roles of some pre-existing QGAs (such as the

Manpower Services Commission), and has created a small crop of new QGAs to tackle pressing problems of the 1980s (such as Urban Development Corporations modelled on the new towns corporations first established by Labour in the late 1940s). But the most distinctive initiatives have been in urban and educational policy, where companies have been persuaded to engage in a range of state-sponsored initiatives, such as inner city regeneration schemes, the creation of a special type of urban school (City Technology Colleges), and increased involvement in determining the courses and research output of colleges and universities. In infrastructure policy the government has also shifted to a strategy of 'franchising' major schemes to consortia of private corporations on lines common in France for many years.

For most of the 1980s the Conservatives had a more limited impact in changing the pattern of private sector non-involvement within welfare state services. Only a small diversification of public service delivery channels has developed, together with a limited growth of contracting out (Ascher, 1987). But an extensive revision of social policy has nonetheless taken place. The government has renounced any future role for local authority housing provision which from 1919–79 accounted for nearly 40 per cent of all new construction in every year. Provisions for council tenants to change their landlords to a housing assocation or even a private landlord, and for parents to opt their schools out of local authority control, are both included in current (1988) legislation – although it remains unclear to what extent they will be activated. The marginalization of some services in the 1980s has clearly undermined previously important welfare rights – notably in the current use of 'bed and breakfast' hotels as quasi-permanent accommodation for thousands of homeless people, supposedly guaranteed the right to rehousing by 1977 legislation. Incremental but significant declines in the public legitimacy of even the National Health Service and state education have also taken place. Under-funding of pay awards and a relentless search for 'efficiency' improvements under the Thatcher government by 1987 contributed to the public perception of a major crisis in the financing and staffing of the NHS as a whole. The Conservatives are likely to propose significant changes in public health care arrangements at or before the 1991–2 general election. And a whole series of decremental social security 'reforms' have progressively increased the selectivity of and restrictions upon access to welfare entitlements. All these erosions have been pushed through against a background of sweeping reductions in higher income tax rates and mounting statistics of significantly increasing social inequality. The evidence thus strongly suggests that the British welfare apparatus now is less securely based in popular or elite support than is the case in other West European countries (Ashford, 1986).

Continuities in UK policy-making

Underlying these significant differences between the 1980s and the statism of the early post-war period, however, there appear to be some key continuities in UK policy behaviour. The continuing strength of the right and the shallow penetration of the labour movement scarcely need underlining for the 1980s. The main changes were the SDP's split from Labour in 1981 and the revival of the centre voting tradition. Inside the Conservative party there is some evidence of finance capital's growing political influence (Ross, 1983). Thatcher's accession to the Conservative leadership both reflected and accentuated a considerable movement by people working in financial firms and professions into the party organization. Such people even began turning up with increasing frequency in this period in administrative positions such as leading Conservative councils, from which the managers and businessmen of manufacturing companies broadly withdrew over half a century earlier (Clements, 1969).

In macroeconomic terms the change of government in 1979 brought new shocks into the system, as the first Thatcher government pursued a simple version of monetarism designed to ensure no repetition of the 1976 sterling crisis. In practice, extreme monetary caution plus the impact of North Sea oil revenues produced such high interest rates and financial market enthusiasm that the exchange rate was allowed to rise to an exaggerated level (touching $2.40 to the pound). From the autumn of 1979 until late 1982, high interest rates and the gross over-valuation of sterling hammered the competitiveness of British manufacturing industry, producing a major fall in capital investment and a shake-out of labour which doubled unemployment totals in three years, squeezing the fiscal space available for other public programmes (Riddel, 1983; Jay, 1985, pp. 164–229). Eventually by the mid 1980s the Conservative government was able to stabilize its monetary policies considerably, albeit by maintaining historically high real interest rates. Its achievement in sustaining a degree of predictability for investment decisions has been rewarded by a modest regrowth of manufacturing investment. But its task has been greatly simplified by the paring down of economic policy-makers' objectives to very minimal levels. By 1983 only the rate of price inflation really figures as an influence in econometric models of policy-making behaviour (Moseley, 1984). Unemployment was dropped as an influential policy variable even before 1979, while the Thatcher government's first term obsession with money supply figures as a proxy indicator of future inflation rates did not last long into the Conservatives' second term.

At the macroeconomic level the Thatcher government publicly renounced all forms of corporatist practices. But at a microeconomic level a few government initiatives have remained corporatist in form, although it is a bipartite, government-industry relationship which rigorously excludes policy influence for trade unions. Both the second and third Thatcher terms have been characterized by a partial recognition of the impossibility of pursuing 'market liberalism in one country' in a world where virtually every other advanced industrial state is integrally involved in subsidizing and trying to direct its contemporary industrial development. For example, in information technology the government belatedly began funding along corporatist lines when the UK's international position in key sunrise industries seemed to be slipping badly in 1982 (Keliher, 1987). However, what remains rather distinctive about the British case is the lack of any broad political consensus underlying virtually all the interventions undertaken.

Conclusions

British policy for the mixed economy and welfare state in the early post-war period (and in a lesser way up to the mid 1970s) seems distinctive for several reasons. It involved a relatively heavy institutionalization of direct government and public sector controls and responsibilities and relied less than most other liberal democracies on intermediate public/private forms of provision. Government provision of goods in kind has been greater and use of transfer payments less than in comparable countries. The British norm for intervention for thirty years stressed government ownership of industries and direct provision of welfare services. This pattern is additionally problematic because it has coincided with levels of substantive government intervention which seem unexceptional by cross-national standards.

The statism of British public policy-making has not been grounded in some commonplace foundations – such as the weakness or fragmentation of the right, the strength of the left parties, the prevalence of corporatism, or the strength of a pro-welfare national consensus. The Conservatives remain the most securely based UK political party with a strong record in government throughout this period. By comparison the Labour party never completely substituted for the Liberals in competition with the Conservatives. Corporatism has remained controversial and weakly developed at either the macro-economic or sectoral policy levels. Public opinion has broadly accepted a system which guarantees only a low level of earnings replacement to the state dependent population. And macroeconomic policy, far from providing a stable basis for the development of statist patterns of intervention, has been erratic in purpose, with periodic crises fracturing the development of government policies for both the mixed economy and the welfare state. This 'ungrounded' character of British statism has been dramatically underlined in the 1980s by the relative ease with which the Thatcher government has inaugurated apparently far-reaching changes in industrial policy by privatizing public corporations. In social policy too the 1980s has been a period in which central government has disengaged from concern for welfare provision, and vigorously promoted the development of mixed public/private systems of intervention substituting for or bypassing traditionally statist forms of policy-making – such as local government provision.

The key factors explaining these paradoxes of ungrounded statism in the early post-war period seem to be twofold. The first group of causes involves the long-term cultural weakness of industrial capital in the UK, plus the cleavage between large-scale companies orientated to external markets and medium and small firms too small to undertake much of an active role in influencing government policy-making. In addition the growth of finance capital to a position of some dominance within the UK economy has reduced the stake of British capital in productive industry and welfare state intervention. The influence of finance capital reinforced strong tendencies in macroeconomic policy-making towards short-termism, and exposed UK companies to searching stock market scrutiny. These effects powerfully contributed to the reluctance of industrial capital to remain in low profitability/high investment areas of production, and stimulated a general business withdrawal from 'public' responsibilities unrelated to their immediate profitability, such as social insurance, socialized consumption provision, and education and research.

Second, the experience of extraordinary wartime mobilization in the UK had a powerful series of infuences on post-war statism. Previous supply-side barriers to an expansion in the level of government involvement were relaxed. But more importantly, public attitudes to the efficacy of state control shifted dramatically, reflecting the positive evaluation of wartime planning and public administration. Finally, the dismantling of the British colonial empire and overseas military commitments created a considerable amount of free policy space in central administration and finances which facilitated the expansion of the domestic welfare state and of quasi-government agencies in the industrial policy area.

The changing form of government intervention in the 1980s reflects the decay of the wartime experience and the progressive crowding of this previously free policy space. The collapse of Labour's challenge to the Conservatives and revival of centrist voting in the 1980s has contributed to the progressive widening of Tory ambitions to remodel the public sector. The direction of most of the 1980s changes has so far been towards the diversification and 'Europeanization' of state intervention, rather than towards major quantum reductions in its scope. A more fragmented welfare state, with far greater mixed public/private provision, more use of quasi-voluntary organizations for service delivery, and a considerably increased reliance on transfers to individuals rather than direct provision of services seems likely to result. In industrial policy the Thatcher government's determination to renounce ownership control of public corporations has entailed some compensating expansion of regulatory controls over public utilities. In intermediate policy areas new patterns of intervention have involved public/private collaboration, such as government franchising of new infrastructure projects. These lines of development towards a post-statist configuration of policy-making closer to those found in other liberal democracies seem set to continue.

References

Abramovitz, M. and Eliasberg, V. 1957: *The Growth of Public Employment in Great Britain*. Princeton: Princeton University Press.
Ascher, K. 1987: *The Politics of Privatization: Conracting Out in the Public Services*. London: Macmillan.
Ashford, D. 1986: *The Emergence of the Welfare States*. Oxford: Blackwell.
Bacon, R. and Eltis, W. 1978: *Britain's Economic Problem: Too Few Producers*. 2nd edn London: Macmillan.
Banting, K. 1979: *Poverty, Politics and Policy: Britain in the 1960s*. London: Macmillan.
Barnett, C. 1986: *The Audit of War*. London: Macmillan.
Barry, N. 1987: *The New Right*. London: Croom Helm.
Blank, S. 1977: Britain: the politics of foreign economic policy, the domestic economy, and the problem of pluralistic stagnation. *International Organization*, 31 (4), 674–721.
Buchanan, J. (ed.) 1978: *The Economics of Politics*. London: Institute of Economic Affairs.
Butler, D. and Sloman, A. 1980: *British Political Facts, 1900–1979*. London: Macmillan.
Castles, F.G. 1978: *The Social Democratic Image of Society*. London: Routledge and Kegan Paul.
Castles, F.G. (ed.) 1982: *The Impact of Parties*. Beverley Hills, CA: Sage.
Catt, H. 1988: Tactical voters: was there an anti-Conservative majority? (Paper to the Political Studies Association annual conference, Plymouth Polytechnic, 12 April).
CDP 1975: *Whatever Happened to Council Housing?* London: Community Development Project.
Clements, R. 1969: *Local Notables and the City Council*. London: Macmillan.
Coates, K. and Topham, T. 1980: *Trade Unions in British Politics*. Nottingham: Spokesman Books.
Cowling, M. (ed.) 1978: *Conservative Essays*. London: Cassell.
Crosland, A. 1956: *The Future of Socialism*. London: Cape.

Douglas, J.E. 1976: Review article: the overloaded crown. *British Journal of Political Science*, 6 (4), 483–505.

Dryzek, J. and Goodin, R. 1986: Risk-sharing and social justice: the motivational foundations of the post-war welfare state. *British Journal of Political Science* 16 (1), pp. 1–34.

Dunleavy, P.J. 1980: The political implications of sectoral cleavages and the growth of state employment: Part I, Alternative approaches to production cleavages, *and* Part 2, Cleavage structures and political alignments. *Political Studies*, 28 (3), 364–83, and 4, 527–49.

Dunleavy, P.J. 1981: The professions and policy change: notes towards a model of ideological corporatism. *Public Administration Bulletin*, 36 (2), 3–16.

Dunleavy, P.J. 1983: Socialized consumption, economic development and political change. Unpublished paper (available from the author), London: LSE.

Dunleavy, P.J. 1984: The limits to local government. In M. Boddy and C. Fudge (eds) *Local Socialism*, London: Macmillan.

Dunleavy, P.J. and Husbands, C. T. 1985: *British Democracy at the Crossroads: Voting and Party Competition in the 1980s*. London: George Allen and Unwin.

Dunleavy, P.J. and O'Leary, D.B. 1987: *Theories of the State: the Politics of Liberal Democracy*. London: Macmillan.

Dunleavy, P.J. and Rhodes, R.A.W. 1988: Government beyond Whitehall. In H. Drucker, P. Dunleavy, A. Gamble, and G. Peele (eds) *Developments in British Politics 2*, (revised edn), London: Macmillan.

Emsley, I. 1987: *The Voluntary Housing Movement in Britain*. New York: Garland.

Finer, S.E. (ed.) 1975: *Adversary Politics and Electoral Reform*. London: Wigram.

Finer, S.E. 1980: *The Changing British Party System, 1945–79*. Washington, DC: American Enterprise Institute.

Foster, C., Jackman, R. and Perlman, M. 1980: *Local Government in the Unitary State*. London: George Allen and Unwin.

Fraser, D. 1973: *The Evolution of the British Welfare State*. London: Macmillan.

Gamble, A. 1980: *Britain in Decline*. London: Macmillan.

Gamble, A. and Walkland, S.A. 1986: *The British Party System and Economic Policy, 1945–85*. Oxford: Clarendon Press.

George, V. and Wilding, P. 1976: *Ideology and Social Welfare*. London: Routledge and Kegan Paul.

Gilmour, I. 1978: *Inside Right: A Study of Conservatism*. London: Quartet.

Goodin, R. and LeGrand, J. (with others) 1987: *Not Only the Poor*. London: George Allen and Unwin.

Gough, I. 1979: *The Political Economy of the Welfare State*. London: Macmillan.

Grant, W. and Marsh, D. 1977: *The CBI*. London: Hodder and Stoughton.

Green, D. 1982: *The Welfare State: For Rich or For Poor?* London: Institute of Economic Affairs.

Green, D. 1987: *The New Right*. Brighton: Wheatsheaf.

Heald, D. 1982: *Public Expenditure*. Oxford: Martin Robertson.

Hibbs, D. 1977: Political parties and macroeconomic policy. *American Political Science Review*, 71, 1467–87.

Hill, M. 1976: *The State, Administration and the Individual*. London: Fontana.

Hogwood, B. and Peters, B.G. 1983: *Policy Dynamics*. Brighton: Wheatsheaf.

Hood, C. 1983: *The Tools of Government*. London: Macmillan.

Jay, D. 1985: *Sterling: Its Use and Misuse – A Plea for Moderation*. Oxford: Oxford University Press.

Johnson, P.S. 1985: *British Industry: An Economic Introduction*. Oxford: Blackwell.

Jones, G.W. 1987: *Privatization: Reflections on the British Experience*. Institute of Policy Studies, Victoria University, Wellington, NZ.

Katzenstein, P. 1985: *Small States in World Markets*. Ithaca, NY: Cornell University Press.

Keegan, W. and Pennant-Rea, R. 1979: *Who Runs the Economy?* London: Temple Smith.

Keliher, L. 1987: *Policy-making on Information Technology: A Decisional Analysis of the Alvey Programme*. Unpublished doctoral thesis. London: London School of Economics and Political Science.

King, A. 1975: Overload: problems of governing in the 1970s. *Political Studies*, 23 (2), 284–96.

King, D. 1987: *The New Right*. London: Macmillan.

Lawson, N. 1981: *The New Conservatism*. London: Conservative Political Centre.

LeGrand, J. 1982: *The Strategy of Equality*. London: George Allen and Unwin.

Lindblom, C.E. 1977: *Politics and Markets*. New York: Basic Books.

Lindsay, T.F. and Harrington, M. 1979: *The Conservative Party, 1918–79*. London: Macmillan.

Mackenzie, W. and Grove, J. 1957: *Central Administration in Britain*. London: Longmans, Greene.

Marmor, T. 1987: Crisis-mongering. *London Review of Books*, 21 May 1987, 12–15.

Marquand, D. 1988: *The Unprincipled Society: New Demands and Old Politics*. London: Cape.

Marshall, T. 1950: *Citizenship and Social Class, and other essays*. London: Cambridge University Press.

Marwick, A. 1973: *The Deluge: British Society and the First World War* (new edn). London: Macmillan.

Marwick, A. 1974: *War and Social Change in the Twentieth Century: A Comparative Study of Britian, France, Germany, Russia, and the United States*. London: Macmillan.

Marwick, A. 1980: *Class: Image and Reality in Britain, France and the USA Since 1930*. London: Collins.

Mather, G. 1988: Britain's post-war industrial decline. *Contemporary Record*, 1, (4), 35.

Merret, S. 1979: *State Housing in Britain*. London: Routledge and Kegan Paul.

Middlemas, K. 1979: *Politics in Industrial Society*. London: André Deutsch.

Moseley, P. 1984: *The Making of Economic Policy: Theory and Evidence from Britain and the USA since 1945*. Brighton: Harvester.

Mosteller, F. and Tukey, J. 1977: *Data Analysis and Regression: A Second Course in Statistics*. Reading, Mass.: Addison-Wesley.

Niskanen, W. 1971: *Bureaucracy and Representative Government*. New York: Aldine Atherton.

Niskanen, W. 1973: *Bureaucracy: Servant or Master*. London: Institute of Economic Affairs.

Nutter, G.W. 1978: *Growth of Government in the West*. Washington, DC: American Enterprise Institute.

Oakeshott, M. 1962: *Rationalism in Politics and Other Essays*. London: Methuen.

OECD 1985: *Social Expenditure, 1960–1990*. Paris: OECD.

Offe, C. 1975: The theory of the capitalist state and the problem of policy formation. In L. Lindberg, R. Alford, C. Crouch and C. Offe (eds) *Stress and Contradiction in Modern Capitalism*, Lexington, Mass.: Lexington Books.

Ovendon, K. 1978: *The Politics of Steel*. London: Macmillan.

Panitch, L.V. 1979: *Social Democracy and Industrial Militancy*. Cambridge: Cambridge University Press.

Parry, R. 1985: Britain: Stable aggregates, changing composition. In Rose et al., *Public employment in Western Nations*.

Parry, R. 1986: United Kingdom. In P. Flora (ed.), *Growth to Limits: The West European Welfare States Since World War II*. Berlin: De Gruyter.

Peacock, A. and Wiseman, J. 1968: *The Growth of Public Expenditure in the United Kingdom*. Princeton, NJ: Princeton University Press.

Peden, G.C. 1979: *British Rearmament and the Treasury, 1932–39*. Edinburgh: Scottish Academic Press.

Power, A. 1987: *Property Before People: The Management of Twentieth-Century Council Housing*. London: George Allen and Unwin.

Rees, M. 1973: *The Public Sector in the Mixed Economy*. London: Batsford.

Riddel, P. 1983: *The Thatcher Government*. Oxford: Martin Robertson.

Rose, R. 1981: *Do Parties Make a Difference?* London: Macmillan.

Rose, R., Page, E., Parry, R., Guy Peters, B., Pignatelli, and Schmidt, A. 1985: *Public Employment in Western Nations*. Cambridge: Cambridge University Press.

Ross, J. 1983: *Thatcher and Friends: The Anatomy of the Tory Party*. London: Pluto Press.

Savas, E.S. 1987: *Privatization: The Key to Better Government*. Chatham House, New Jersey: Chatham House.

Scruton, R. 1981: *The Meaning of Conservatism*. London: Macmillan.

Social Trends 1974: London: HMSO.

Stokey, E. and Zeckhauser, R. 1978: *A Primer for Policy Analysis*. New York: Norton.

Strange, S. 1971: *Sterling and British Policy*. Oxford: Oxford University Press.

Tarn, J. 1973: *Five Per Cent Philanthropy*. Cambridge: Cambridge University Press.

Tawney, R.H. 1937: *Equality*. London: George Allen and Unwin.

Tivey, L. 1973: *Nationalization in British Industry*. London: Cape.

Tullock, G. 1976: *The Vote Motive: An Essay in the Economics of Politics, with Applications to the British Economy*. London: Institute of Economic Affairs.

Veljanovski, C. 1987: *Selling the State*. London: Weidenfeld and Nicolson.

Watkin, B. 1978: *The National Health Service: The First Phase, 1948–74 and After*. London: George Allen and Unwin.

Weiner, M. 1981: *English Culture and the Decline of the Industrial Spirit, 1850–1980*. Cambridge: Cambridge University Press.

Westergaard, J. and Resler, H. 1976: *Class in a Capitalist Society: A Study of Contemporary Britain*. Harmondsworth: Penguin.

Whiteley, P. 1983: *The Labour Party in Crisis*. London: Methuen.

Woolf, C. 1979: A theory of non-market failures. *Journal of Law and Economics*, 22, 107–40.,

Young, H. and Sloman, A. 1984: *But, Chancellor: An Inquiry into the Treasury*. London: BBC.

8

Taking Exception

Explaining the Distinctiveness of American Public Policies in the Last Century

Edwin Amenta and Theda Skocpol

Introduction: The Stereotyping of American Exceptionalism

A chapter on the distinctiveness of public policy in a particular country presents a task that is difficult, but straightforward. One must show what makes the country's profile of public policies stand out from those of other countries, convince the reader that the differences matter, and offer an explanation for them. A chapter on the distinctiveness of American public policies has to do the same things, but with different emphases. There is no trouble in convincing the reader that American policies are different from others, for public policy in America is often considered the quintessential case of exceptionalism. To show what stands out and to advance an explanation – these constitute trickier problems. One must first shatter stereotypes, because readers tend to have their own answers to what makes American policies different and why they are different.

When speaking of US public policies, by exceptionalism people usually mean underdeveloped. The standard case might run as follows. American policies were slow in getting started, little of importance happened until the Great Depression, and low levels of spending and taxation persist to this day. To home in on finer distinctions, it might be pointed out that America has an incomplete system of social insurance which includes neither health insurance nor family allowances. To complete the case, there is the American position securely on the low-inflation-high-unemployment segment of the Phillips curve. Like many stereotypes, this one is not entirely false. American social insurance was minimal until the 1930s, and today Americans do not benefit from a complete system of social insurance. Moreover, American social spending as a percentage of income amounts to less than most of the other rich countries. In 1981, American social spending amounted to 20.8 per cent of GDP (OECD, 1985, p. 21), and in 1980 American tax receipts 30.7 per cent (OECD, 1981, p. 11), in both cases ranking 14th of the 18 long-standing OECD countries. Finally, there are the high rates of unemployment. From 1950 to 1984 American unemployment averaged 5.3 per cent, higher than all but 5 of 18 OECD countries (OECD, 1984).

The problem is not that this stereotype has no elements of truth. The problem is that it takes too narrow a view of public policy, a view that includes only the major social spending programmes, only the crudest indicators of economic or employment policies, and only the post-Second World War period. To understand American public policies, in the sense of public lines of social spending, taxing, employment, and economic strategies that influence people's chances in life, one must go beyond the discussion of recent history and consider American developments in the light of recent theoretical advances. In examining the last century of American public policies in this wider sense, one can discern two paradoxes.

The first paradox is the erratic pattern of the history of American public policies. According to one influential model of Western European history, the development of social insurance policies advanced haltingly, but in a unilinear direction (Flora and Alber, 1981). From the late nineteenth century through the early twentieth century there was a period of experimentation, as different schemes were tested. The next phase, occurring between the wars, saw the consolidation of the social insurance experiments of the previous period. Immediately after the Second World War most countries completed a profile of social insurance policies, enacting insurance against the four main types of risk. In the post-war period, there was steady growth in coverage and expenditures. Although the model includes only social insurance and does not describe the pattern of every Western European polity, one can use if for purposes of comparison because the history of US public policies departs dramatically from it.

American public policies did not merely lag behind European innovations while following the same pattern, however arrested and thwarted, as perhaps was the case with Japan. Instead, the history of American public policies exhibited a pattern of zigzags that can be divided into four somewhat different periods. In the late nineteenth century, the United States was a leader in activist public policies. These policies included a primitive old age pensions system, a public employment programme and a macroeconomic policy on tariffs. These policies, however, were seen by middle-class American reformers as corruption and as obstacles to placing policies on a modern basis, as defined by European innovations. In the second phase, running from the turn of the century to 1930, many of these initial policies were undermined, but were not replaced as the United States fell behind other rich nations in the development of modern public policies. The period from 1930 to 1950 witnessed the heroic period of American public policies, as America was once again briefly a leader, constructing innovative public policies and planning even more progressive ones. Needless to say, this phase was mainly a failure. America fell behind again in the post-war period, with only a brief period of innovation in the 1960s and early 1970s.

Great as the influence of twentieth-century policy innovations have been, American public policies of the late twentieth century closely resemble the policies of the late nineteenth century. This is the second paradox. The following five characteristics are common to both centuries: (1) an emphasis on spending programmes with divisible rather than collective benefits, and ephemeral rather than permanent benefits; (2) a system of taxation that was largely a product of wartime, but afterwards used for peacetime revenue purposes and overburdened with distributive and economic goals; (3) the reliance on nationalistic macroeconomic policies, avoiding both classical market liberalism and more detailed and selective economic interventions; (4) an extensive, but ambiguous public employment system not legitimated in political discourse; (5) a selectivist social spending policy with a division between two types of programmes: generous programmes, usually administered by the national government, whose recipients, including certain groups of veterans, the aged, and widows, have been considered deserving; meagre programmes, usually administered by lower units of government, whose recipients have been considered undeserving and have been subject to surveillance.

To explain the distinctiveness of American public policies is to resolve these paradoxes.Why did American public policies follow the zigzagging historical pattern that they did? Why do American public policies of the late twentieth century resemble the policies of the nineteenth century? Although the political class-struggle model helps to explain post-Second World War developments in spending and innovations, the model as usually constructed cannot explain the developments in the nineteenth century or many of the characteristics of public policies. One needs a model including the roles of the state, political parties, and crises. Briefly, we argue that American state political institutions made it likely that public policies would be early in appearance and pre-modern in form. Changes in the political party system and the wrenching influence of crises made it possible to overcome these predispositions and account for the pace of change and many of the characteristics of the policies. In the end, the influence of the parties and crises only partly overcame the mediating influence of state political institutions, and nineteenth-century policies were reasserted. Before these riddles can be solved, a history of the four phases of American public policies is needed – to reveal their peculiarities and to flesh out their manifestations in current policies.

The Beginning and the End of Pre-modern Public Policies

The public policies of late nineteenth-century America were notable for their comparatively high levels of spending and for their distributive or patronage character. The most expensive experiment in patronage-based social policy was the Civil war pension system. In this context, patronage is not corruption, or breaking laws for personal or political gain, although corruption was rampant. By definition, patronage benefits can be divided amongst constituents or timed with political discretion, or both; they are defined in opposition to automatic and collective benefits accruing to large categorical groups. The more discretion involved in the benefit, the greater the element of patronage.[1] The pension system of the Civil War period (1861–5) was established as a categorical scheme of payments to soldiers injured in battle and to widows of soldiers killed in action, but by the end of the century this programme had been transmuted into a sort of discretionary old age and survivors' pension. A second aspect of nineteenth-century public policy constituted a primitive public employment programme: federal government jobs for those with suitable political connections. Pensions and positions were funded mainly with revenues generated by a system of tariffs strengthened greatly during the Civil War. The tariff system was also a source of distributive benefits, and protection constituted the main economic policy. On the state and local levels of government, innovations were made in mass public education, a form of early American social spending that stood apart from the national programmes.

The next period, from 1900 to 1930, reversed many of these trends. These three decades include the two periods known in American historiography as the Progressive Era and the Twenties and were notable for the rise of attempts at bureaucratic reform and state building. A middle-class reform movement with adherents in both political parties, as well as a short-lived political party, the Progressive movement sought to attack party machines by way of altering electoral rules and creating bureaucratic executive institutions at all levels of government. This movement helped to end Civil War pensions as selective old age insurance and numbered the days of using the government bureaucracy as an employment programme. The national political dominance of the Republicans in the 1920s ensured that tariff protection would remain the main economic policy, although tariffs declined as a source of revenue.

Instead, it was at the state and local levels that experiments in modern social spending policies began.

The late nineteenth century: premature public policies

The military origins of the Civil War pension system have usually prevented it from being considered a form, however primitive, of public social provision. But, before the end of its peculiar career, it grew to a system of greater size than early social insurance programmes elsewhere. As the system was originally devised by the Republican party, it benefited only war widows and injured veterans, and by the middle of the 1870s the number of claimants had started to drop. In 1879, however, the so-called Arrears Act became law; it gave incentives to press equivocal and sometimes false claims on the government, for it authorized the payment of all the benefits an injured or widowed party was due from the time of the alleged injury or death. Claims soared, and so too did the new numbers of recipients, for it was difficult to determine who was eligible. For one thing, claimants provided their own evidence. For another, the primitive bureaucracy and its political operatives could not have checked the stories even if they had desired to do so. A political coalition based on Republican congressmen with some northern Democratic support, spurred on by a newly activated soldiers' interest group, increased the coverage and then the benefits of the programme. In 1890, the so-called Dependent Pensions Act legislated benefits to almost anyone who served and could not perform manual labour, for whatever reason. In 1904, the pension bureau considered old age a disability in itself, and other acts increased benefits. Benefits for widows tended to follow in the wake of legislation for disabled men, but with less money and more disqualifications based on style of life.[2]

Categorical as these bursts of legislation seemed, the benefits were nothing like automatic. There was always a waiting list of applicants, and politicians decided who would be pensioned, when, and at what rate. This aspect of the programme was more significant than the fact that some people received pensions illegally. The overall numbers of recipients grew regularly. In 1873, at the system's apparent peak, there were about a quarter of a million pension recipients. Due to the act of 1879, this number had more than doubled by 1889, approaching half a million. Under the influence of the 1890 legislation, the numbers of recipients reached a peak of nearly a million by the end of the century. Legislated increases in benefits continued after almost everyone who could possibly qualify was receiving a pension. To gain access to legislated increases in benefits required a similar process of applying and waiting. Pension expenditures constituted more than 40 per cent of government spending and more than one per cent of GNP by the middle of the 1890s (US Census, 1975, pp. 1104, 1114).

By the standards of modern social insurance, this performance was perhaps unimpressive. The programme did not select according to need or, as in the case of German social insurance, according to work record. It provided benefits to those (northerners) who had made a mildly plausible case for their importance in preserving the Union, and it helped to have a connection to a political organization, preferably Republican. For the late nineteenth century, however, the performance was notable. A sizeable proportion of the American aged received a pension. The more than half a million elderly men on the rolls translated to approximately 29 per cent of American men 65 years old and older in 1910. And the amount of benefits compared favourably to those given in Germany or Britain. The average pension for the disabled soldier in 1910 amounted to about 30 per cent of average earnings, for widows, 25 per cent; in Britain, an old age pension came to 22 per cent of average annual earnings, and in Germany, about 17 per cent (Skocpol et al., 1987).

A second kind of national public policy concerned the creation of jobs for people not in the middle class and without professional credentials. This policy was tied more closely to political activity: governmental positions went to party supporters, whose form of repayment usually included political work and a taxing of salaries. On the national level, blatant use was made of the post office and the customs houses. Unlike the Civil War pension system, this policy was not used by professional politicians to make rhetorical appeals to the electorate. Although civil service reform made some headway with the Pendleton Act of 1878, the number of federal government positions available was substantial (Keller, 1977; White, 1958).[3] For the late nineteenth century and early twentieth century, there were more than 100,000 federal government jobs available. For instance, in 1891, of the 157,442 civilian employees of the federal government, more than 60 per cent worked in the post office. All told, less than 22 per cent of federal civilian employees were classified as part of the competitive civil service (US Census, 1975, p. 1103). There were many more at other levels of government, especially in cities, not to mention jobs with businesses allied to local party machines or public works (Bridges, 1984). Although the numbers of such jobs were inadequate and the choice of recipients biased (Keyssar, 1986), in comparative perspective this ambiguous public employment programme stands out.

A complex tariff system paid for these programmes. From immediately after the Civil War until the First World War, the tariff system generated about half of the revenues of the national government, a relatively high figure. In 1890, for instance, customs provided 57 per cent of national revenue, compared to about 21 per cent in Great Britain (Keller, 1977, p. 307). The system was boosted during the Civil War and, unlike the primitive wartime income tax and other emergency internal taxes, tariffs were not rolled back after the war. Whenever the government began to run a deficit, upward adjustments in tariff schedules were passed. Eventually the system became the focus of partisan politics, with the resurgent Democratic party proposing to use the income tax to eclipse the tariff. In 1890, the same year that a Republican Congress transformed Civil War disability benefits into old age pensions, a tariff-stiffening bill was also passed. Tariffs were strengthened again when the realigning election of 1896 brought renewed Republican dominance.[4]

Fiscally lucrative as it was, the tariff system was much more than a means of revenue generation. In the tariff, the issues of revenue generation, distributive benefits and economic policy were bound together, and these other characteristics were at least as important as the first. Tariff protection constituted American macroeconomic policy even before the economic crisis of the late nineteenth century when many other countries turned to protection (Gourevitch, 1986). Like the turn-of-the-century Australian system, tariffs were used to defend established industries as well as to protect infant industries (Castles, 1985). Tariffs were used rhetorically to merge the interests of capitalists and industrial workers. Unlike the Australian system, American tariffs were not negotiated by representatives of organized capital and labour. The American tariff system was devised within congressional committees and party caucuses; attempts to rationalize tariff formation through tariff commissions failed. Moreover, the system was not combined with compulsory wage arbitration which was rejected at the turn of the century by the organized working class. As they would do for most of the next century, industrial workers and capitalists fought wage battles more or less privately, except for the use of the courts by capitalists to stop strikes. The Republican party portrayed itself as the party of prosperity and the tariff as the means to prosperity and, with the aid of the depression of 1893, won over many industrial workers in their capacity as voters.

Tariffs were also distributive benefits dominated by specific duties, not *ad valorem* schedules. Various interest groups turned congressional tariff-making into a political balancing act in party caucuses. This sometimes led to conflicts over the system. For instance, to keep together the political coalition for tariffs, in 1877 Republican party legislators successfully fought an attempt by industrialists to lower the schedules for raw materials used in industry and other attempts to remove tariffs from congressional control. The multifaceted nature of the tariffs underlined the long-term political weakness of the taxation system. In an economy as competitive as the American one became, tariffs could not forever remain the main economic policy. More important, they eventually stopped generating great amounts of revenue and politicians were forced to devise new types of taxes. These taxes were harsher, politically speaking, for they could not be portrayed simultaneously as benefits to important groups.

The final element of public policy, the expansion of American education, ran outside this national system and ultimately did not suffer its fate. The early rise of American education was well under way by the middle of the nineteenth century. By the Civil War, the dominance of public primary schools over private schools had been established. American education in the nineteenth century was notable in comparative perspective for its high level of enrolments and its lack of formal stratification (Heidenheimer, 1981). Moreover, American public education flourished throughout the nineteenth century when it had begun to falter in other places such as Germany. The movement to institutionalize public education was led by local Republican parties and professional educators, emerging first in rural areas (Meyer et al., 1979; Rubinson, 1986). This movement won its battles mainly in the localities, with enabling laws and subsidies from higher levels of government, and throughout American history education policy has been characterized by state and local control of the primary and secondary schooling. This lack of connection with the national distributive system of politics worked to the advantage of education policies. When national public spending policies were attacked, programmes at the lower levels of government survived. This was also the case for twentieth-century spending policies developed at the state and local levels.

The Progressive era and the Twenties: rolling back the nineteenth-century system 1900–1930

The reforms of the Progressive Era, 1900–20, were not sweeping; local political machines mainly survived and state-building was only partial. But the pre-modern public policies of the nineteenth century were gradually defeated. Civil War pensions were opposed by Progressive reformers who considered them corrupt. The passing of the aged pensioners made their job easier as new legislation was required to provide similar benefits to later veterans. No national social insurance programme replaced pensions, partly because reformers feared that any national programme would repeat the performance of Civil War pensions. In any case, the dying-off of Civil War pensioners brought no fiscal dividend because pensions paid to First World War veterans with service-related disabilities kept the total spent on military pensions at nearly a constant level (Dillingham, 1952, ch. 5; Ross, 1969, ch. 1). And reformers prevented the growth of the backdoor system of public employment through governmental jobs. By 1916, the number of federal civilian employees had reached approximately 400,000, or about two-and-a-half times the number in 1891, but nearly three-quarters of appointments were on a merit basis (US Census, 1975, p. 1102).

If spending policies no longer gave advantages to aged veterans and gave fewer advantages to party workers, the selectivist policies grew to include additional widowed mothers, not only those formerly married to Civil War veterans. The first state-level public spending programme concerning one of the major risks was mothers' pensions legislation, a primitive form of family allowances. Enabling legislation was passed in 39 states between 1911 and 1919. The typical law allowed localities to provide means-tested pensions for widowed mothers, and later in some places to deserted mothers, to keep their children at home. These systems were staffed mainly by middle-class women and most programmes included strict rules of eligibility (Leff, 1973). In addition, state-level programmes for infants and expectant mothers were encouraged by federal grants-in-aid mandated by the Sheppard-Towner Act of 1921, an act that was repealed before the Great Depression. Like Civil War pensioners, these recipients were portrayed as exceptionally worthy of assistance. Other lasting state-level reforms did not upset this pattern. One sort of reform came in what was known as labour legislation, but which was not typically initiated by organized labour. Child labour and women's hours legislation were promoted by reformers and supported to some extent by organized labour because of the competitive threat posed by women and children. In addition, various health and safety laws were established and enforced by state industrial commissions (Brandeis, 1935). One major risk, industrial accidents, was covered by a species of state-level regulatory policy. Workmen's compensation was passed in 42 of the 48 states between 1911 and 1921 and required businesses to insure, not necessarily through the state, their workers against industrial accidents. Moreover, many things were lacking from workmen's compensation that one would expect in social insurance: elements of public spending and national controls or incentives (Asher, 1971). In the 1910s, state-level movements for health and unemployment insurance and old age pensions often made it to the study-commission stage of the state politics, but foundered after that (Nelson, 1969; Brandeis, 1935; Starr, 1982). Although health insurance was removed from the political agenda in the 1910s, in the 1920s the movement for means-tested old age pensions made advances near the end of the decade. Before Hoover was sent from office, 12 states had passed compulsory old age pensions. In early 1932, the first unemployment compensation programme was passed.

The tariff system lost its pre-eminence in generating revenue. In 1913, the assumption of national political power by the Democrats, with their southern and western bases of support, led to the establishment of individual and corporate income taxes. The individual income tax tapped the income of the rich, for the vast majority of people making less than $4000 per year were exempted. The tax was boosted by the need to pay for the war and by continued Democratic rule. Both corporation and individual income taxes were made much stiffer and more progressive with the individual income tax retaining its class basis. Only about 13 per cent of the labour force filed returns in 1920 (Witte, 1985, chs. 4 and 5). The rise of the Republicans in the 1920s put the weakening of income taxes at the top of the political agenda, and the Treasury Department of Andrew Mellon claimed that lowered income taxes would promote investment, a forerunner of so-called supply-side economics (Stein, 1969, ch. 1). Despite tax cuts, by 1929 a combination of corporate and individual income taxes was providing the bulk of national government revenue. In comparison, the tariff system constituted less than 16 per cent of federal revenues (US Census, 1975, p. 1102).

Yet tariff protection continued to be the key economic policy. The system was still controlled congressionally, mainly by the Republican party. The ascension of the Democratic party to national power lowered the levels of protection somewhat, but, as in 1894, it did not undermine the basic policy. Even these minor changes were reversed in 1922 by the Republican Fordney-McCumber Tariff Act which was designed to defend established industries as well as protect the wartime infant industries, such as chemicals and metallurgy, and to appease agricultural interests by increasing rates on wheat, sugar, wool and butter, amongst other things; no doubt the influence was largely symbolic, as the United States was an agricultural exporter (Ratner, 1972, ch. 3). The last hurrah of tariff protection was the 1930 Hawley-Smoot Tariff Act, an agricultural relief measure which was amended to please the gamut of industrial interests (Schatschneider, 1963). The act engendered an international reaction; trade barriers were soon established elsewhere. The making of tariffs was removed from congressional control only after being eclipsed by the Roosevelt administration's more interventionist economic policies.

Modern Public Policies and the Return of the Nineteenth Century

For any number of reasons, one might have expected the rise of a coherent, nationalized and modern scheme of public policies during the Great Depression and the Second World War. These two great international crises coincided with the political dominance of a president, Roosevelt, and a political party, the Democrats, that had become committed to these goals. The party allied itself with a rising labour movement which threw its support behind social spending. State-building accelerated. Accordingly, the administration attempted to put under the control of the national executive social spending, taxation, economic and employment policies. By the end of the 1930s, these initiatives ended, temporarily, America's status as a laggard in interventionist public policies. By the end of the 1940s, the bid to create an almost social democratic scheme of public policies had failed. Instead, a hybrid system took hold. It included some innovations, such as old age and survivors' insurance, a revamped income taxation system, and greater control by the executive branch over macroeconomic policy-making. However, these modern initiatives became enmeshed in a framework of policies similar to the nineteenth-century system, a system mainly at the discretion of congressional actors. Like that system, it included similarly selectivist social spending policies, a distributive, quasi-public employment policy, this time relying on military contracting, and an overburdened taxation system. Innovations in post-war public policies have followed the lines established immediately after the war.

US public policies during depression and war: an attempt to construct modern public policies

Roosevelt took action on many policy fronts when he assumed office in 1933. But it was not until the end of 1934 that national committees and administrative bodies started to plan sweeping changes in national public policies. Such planning began with the Committee on Economic Security, a cabinet-level group which drafted the bill that became the 1935 Social Security Act, the centrepiece of the so-called Second New Deal. Planning was continued by the Social Security Board, the administrative body in control of the national aspects of the act, and the National Resources Planning Board, part of the (1939) Executive Office of the President. These organizations proposed a nationalized system of social insurance, supported both by payroll taxes and strongly progressive and broad-based income taxes, nationally controlled employment relying on direct employment and public works, and a left wing Keynesianism which envisaged macroeconomic deficit spending combined with an industrial policy.[5]

Although gains were made, nationalized and comprehensive social insurance policies were not enacted. The Social Security Act created only one national social insurance programme, old age insurance, which had its own payroll tax, or social security contribution. Even this programme, as a result of congressional changes in the bill, excluded blacks by excluding agricultural and domestic workers. The greater part of the 1935 Act was devoted to national incentives for the states to legislate their own social spending programmes. For one thing, it provided taxation incentives for states to create a second social insurance programme, against unemployment. All states had programmes by 1938. For another, the Act provided grants-in-aid for states to establish old age assistance programmes, which many states had already passed, and for mothers' pensions, whose new name became aid to dependent children. Because of the wide variety of standards, these state-level programmes were regarded as mere experiments by the New Deal planners who wanted them to be superseded by national ones and to be augmented by national health and sickness insurance. In 1939, administration forces passed important amendments to the Social Security Act, adding benefits for the survivors of qualifying workers, but the programme was not safe until the amendments of 1950. Unlike Britain, which completed a national system of social insurance soon after the war, the United States entered the 1950s with only one national programme.

The United States also gained one national spending programme that fitted neither the plans of the New Dealers nor cross-national trends in social insurance programmes. By the end of the war, a comprehensive system of veterans' benefits was enacted. These benefits included a type of unemployment compensation, educational benefits, free medical care, and incentives to help able-bodied veterans to purchase homes. This group of benefits came in addition to the ones granted to disabled veterans who automatically benefited from the categorical legislation enacted after previous wars. Faced with a choice between long-term spending policies for all Americans and ephemeral spending policies for veterans, Congress did not hesitate.

As a result, social spending programmes were incomplete, for the risk of illness was left uncovered, and ran along two tracks. Old age and survivors' insurance was separated programmatically and fiscally from the other programmes. In this system, which pre-empted the name social security, national controls were combined with national payroll taxation and bureaucratic distribution with minimal surveillance of the recipient population. In the other system, which became known as welfare, benefits and eligibility were controlled by the states which applied means tests and a local system of surveillance. The planners imagined these programmes would disappear with the growth of social insurance and the assurance of full employment. Neither happened.

Employment policies were the strongest of all national New Deal pro-grammes. The American approach to fighting the effects of the Depression was the provision of public employment. In 1935 the administration called for the creation of the Works Progress Administration. Under this programme, Congress appropriated money, state and local governments sponsored projects, and the WPA decided which ones to fund and then ran them. This was a departure from previous employment programmes:

the creation of jobs was the explicit goal and the executive branch exerted control over the system. In 1939, when the programme was formally institutionalized under executive reorganization, the WPA (renamed the Work Projects Administration) and other public employment programmes employed more than three million people and accounted for about 20 per cent of national government expenditures. When the war brought temporary full employment and when the 1942 elections brought a strongly conservative coalition into Congress, however, these programmes died. Unlike in Sweden, which also fought the Depression with employment strategies, the main American antidepression device did not outlive the war.

Economic policy was closely related to employment policy. Here, too, interventionist solutions were attempted and then abandoned. The Roosevelt administration followed the lead of Britain in abandoning the gold standard, and the administration attempted intrusive recovery policies, notably the quasi-corporatism of the National Recovery Administration which allowed the capitalists of industries to organize themselves to fix production levels and, for a while, prices. When that scheme mainly failed and was ruled unconstitutional in 1935, the administration began to emphasize the promotion of competition and the fight against monopoly, a fight which included the guarantees of labour organization enshrined in the 1935 National Labour Relations Act (Hawley, 1966).

By 1938, after the start of Roosevelt's own recession, the administration added a peculiar Keynesian logic to its initiatives. The American version of Keynesianism was not a hands-off manipulation of aggregate spending; it called for redistribution, the creation of large social spending policies, and direct intervention in what was considered a permanently stagnant economy. The administration and its followers had to settle for purposely running deficits. Deficits had characterized earlier Roosevelt policy, but after 1938 the administration stopped trying to balance the budget and, in any case, the war made such a task impossible (May, 1981; Stein, 1969). Immediately after the war, an attempt was made to legislate the principle of deficit spending to achieve full employment, but this unworkable policy was deleted by Congress in its passage of the weak Employment Act of 1946 (Bailey, 1950). Because of failures in social spending policies and the destruction of public employment policies, there were no programmatic means to implement an interventionist Keynesian policy.

National taxation initiatives had somewhat greater long-term success than did most New Deal public policies. The planners hoped to break the national dependence on regressive excise taxes, which had funded the early New Deal, with more progressive measures. Later New Deal taxation policies included innovative business taxes, which were intended in part to promote competition. These taxes did not bear the main burden of economic policy-making, however, and had more symbolic than fiscal or policy significance (Leff, 1984). The breakthroughs came in the shadow of war, during 1941 and 1942. The individual income tax was transformed from a tax on upper incomes to a tax on almost everyone and became more progressive and productive of revenues. National revenues jumped from 7.4 per cent of GNP in 1939 to 18.7 per cent in 1946 (US Council of Economic Advisors, 1980, pp. 203, 288). These gains were made secure during the early 1950s. Impressive as they were, the taxation increases were not as complete as they might have been for there was a failure of taxation explicitly for social spending. Social security contributions were not only not increased; Congress rejected scheduled increases legislated before the war. State-level taxation systems innovated during the 1930s and 1940s limiting the process of fiscal centralization often promoted by depression and war.

The post-war period: the return of nineteenth-century policies but without party control and corruption

The innovations of the New Deal and the Second World War were ultimately incorporated into a policy framework which resembles that of the nineteenth century. Congress has regained the control over the details of policies, but without the corruption and the party control of the nineteenth century. The one national social insurance programme, for the retired, has become part of a selectivist social spending scheme that does not veer too far from the groups covered by Civil War pensions. Military spending, like the earlier use of the national bureaucracy, has been used as an inefficient, backdoor public employment policy. Taxation policy, forged during war, has become burdened with economic and distributive goals. One difference is that the national executive gained more control over economic policies. Like tariff protection, however, these policies are macroeconomic, relying on few direct controls, and attempt, however unsuccessfully, to merge the interests of industrial capital and labour.

As for social spending policy, veterans of the Second World War and retired veterans of wage-earning employment and their survivors have become relatively advantaged. Numerous legislated increases in coverage and benefits have created a sort of welfare state for the qualified aged – contrary to the stereotyped view of American social policy. The augmentation of old age and survivors' insurance has been promoted, usually during election years, by Democratic congresses throughout the post-war period (Derthick, 1979). New risks were insured. The insurance of permanent and total disability was introduced in 1956, and the Democratic administration of President Lyndon Johnson (1964–9) oversaw the adoption in 1965 of Medicare, social insurance for the hospitalization costs and doctors' fees of the elderly. Perhaps more important, coverage for old age and survivors' insurance became almost universal and the benefits were increased, especially from the late 1960s to 1972. As a result, there was a rise in the replacement rate, the degree to which benefits allow continuity in earnings, to levels not as high as in Sweden and Germany but higher than those in Canada and the UK (Myles, 1988). These public insurance programmes have been augmented by many private benefits in pensions and insurance. These private programmes chiefly have covered the white-collar and unionized work force and are under the control of large corporations. This post-war private welfare state now accounts for most consumer spending on health and about a quarter of all welfare spending (Stevens, 1988).

The separation between the programmes known as social security and those known as welfare has widened. Welfare or means-tested programmes have made gains, but have not fared as well as the insurance programmes and have been damaged by the Reagan administration. Old age pensions, the state-level, means-tested programme, were, as expected, eventually eclipsed by old age insurance. The renamed Aid to Families with Dependent Children (AFDC), the means-tested American answer to universal family allowances, however, continued to grow to much greater levels than the programme executives of social security initially expected. Innovations came in the wake of Johnson's War on Poverty and the civil rights movement in the 1950s and 1960s (Haveman, 1977). One of these was Medicaid, the less generous part of the American answer to national health insurance. Like AFDC, Medicaid is a national subsidy programme to states for means-tested assistance, but for medical care. In addition, spending for AFDC exploded in the late 1960s and early 1970s. These programmes for poor people have had narrow political support and they were the main victims of the Reagan administration's attack on social welfare policy (Schwarz, 1983). The inadequacy of these programmes largely accounts for America's poor social spending performance.

Post-war economic policy has been concerned with the manipulation of aggregate spending and taxing, relying on fiscal stimulation rather than classical liberalism. There has been an American comparative advantage in deficit spending. American fiscal policies have tended to be expansionary, with relatively large deficits being run during the late 1960s and the 1980s. These policies have been run chiefly by presidents, with the assistance of the Council of Economic Advisors, a body created in 1946. Fiscal policy has amounted to a limited type of Keynesianism. One technique, if taking no action can be called technique, has been the use of so-called automatic stabilisers: taxes have not been raised during recessions, while spending has increased because of the increased numbers of people who qualify for programmes such as unemployment insurance. A second form has been the stimulative tax cut or the increase in military spending not covered by new taxes. Post-war Democratic administrations have proposed tax cuts to increase consumption. Similarly, the Reagan administration has claimed that its so-called supply-side tax cuts, motivated at least partly by a conservative dislike of progressive income taxes, were designed to stimulate the economy (Stein, 1984). Both Democratic and Republican administrations have increased military spending without tax increases.

Other types of Keynesianism, understood as the manipulation of aggregate spending, have been politically unworkable. First, it has been impossible to increase social spending strictly for the stimulation of the economy. Second, it has been impossible to pursue restrictive Keynesianism on the British model in which tax increases are adopted solely to slow inflation. The one-sidedness of the policy is due to the difficulties in forming a political coalition to increase social spending or to raise taxes. Cutting taxes has proved less than flexible; Congress has frequently used the occasion of an administration-sponsored tax bill to add many provisions of its own.

To fight inflation, for recent presidents, has meant to provoke recessions, which at once slow demand and reduce labour militancy. Although the Federal Reserve Board, which influences interest rates and the supply of money, is nominally independent, it has been susceptible to presidential pressure. As a result, managed recessions have been instigated by Republicans and Democrats alike – by Republicans in 1969 and in 1981, both at the beginning of presidential terms, and by Democratic President Carter in 1979, oddly, near the end of his one term in office. The Federal Reserve Board has pursued nothing approaching a monetarist policy in which the money supply follows automatic decision rules relating to economic growth. Favourable as the American performance on inflation has been, it has not been due to an independent bureaucratic guardian of price stability, as in the German case. Partly for this reason, the inflation rate of Germany remained low during the recessionary 1974–84 period, while the inflation rate of the United States approached the OECD average (Schmidt, ch. 3 this volume; OECD, 1984).

So far as the processes of wage determination have been concerned, the post-war United States has mainly followed its historical path – with little direct state control, but with administrative influence over the process. Collective bargaining was sanctioned in 1935 by the so-called Wagner Act, was put into action during the war, and has continued thereafter. Wage and price controls were ended soon after the war and were experimented with only briefly afterwards, during the early 1970s. In the post-war period, legislation has been somewhat less favourable to labour than in the late 1930s, beginning with the 1947 Taft-Hartley Act which nullified some of labour's advantages at the bargaining table. Unsurprisingly, the system had produced relatively high levels of industrial conflict (Korpi and Shalev, 1980). In recent years, however, labour's bargaining power has been undercut by induced recessions and by Republican administrations, diminishing labour's militancy.

In addition to Keynesianism, there has existed a sort of direct employment policy only partly connected to economic conditions and the rhetoric of employment. The provision of jobs through military contracts has been the counterpart to the provision of federal jobs in the nineteenth century. Since the Second World War, the United States has spent more than any OECD country on the military, with little change in the rankings since 1950 (Keman, 1982). Military 'investment', a category dominated by weaponry, has constituted about half the military budget in any given year, and more than half during the 1979–85 build-up, and the vast majority of weaponry is domestically produced. The policy has lent itself to congressional log-rolling; military appropriations bills often have included expenditures throughout many areas of the country (Russett, 1970). This is not to say that American international policy has been motivated by domestic concerns over unemployment. It is not to say that the economy requires such spending or that contracting for weapons is an efficient employment strategy. All the same, specific sectors of the economy, and their workers, have been underwritten, and these purchases have been probably somewhat greater than they otherwise would have been. The number of workers making weapons rose to 2.8 million during the Vietnam War. In 1977, before the recent build-up, the number had dropped only to approximately 2 million or about 2 per cent of the labour force, and had risen in 1986 to 3.4 million (Griffin, 1984; *New York Times*, 1987). Military employment and aggregate demand stimulation has been no substitute for a flexible Keynesianism, a targeted public employment system and labour-market interventions. However, the policies probably have kept American unemployment lower than otherwise might be expected. Specifically, these policies have perhaps kept unemployment from rising to relatively high levels during world-wide declines in economic growth. In the 1950s, a period of relatively low economic activity for the Western world, the American average unemployment rate approximated the average of 18 OECD countries. In the 1960s, a period of higher growth, the American unemployment rate was almost twice as high as the average of the other OECD countries. Similarly, from 1974 to the middle of the 1980s, the US rate of unemployment has risen, but has become closer to the average of the long-standing OECD nations and is not, in the late 1980s, amongst the countries with the highest unemployment, such as Britain (OECD, 1984).

Of all major public policies, the late twentieth-century American taxation system most closely resembles its nineteenth-century counterpart. In both cases American taxes were forged in war and put to different uses during peacetime. Since the Second World War, the income tax has become a tool of economic policy and a distributive benefit system. Under the influence of Keynesian advisers, Democrats have promoted the permanent lowering of income tax rates to gain short-term economic benefits, notably in 1964 with the so-called Kennedy tax cut. Using a somewhat different 'supply-side' logic, the Reagan administration has permanently lowered taxes, also partly in order to promote economic growth. Both types of administrations have allowed recessions to pass without making attempts to augment tax revenues.

Distributing benefits through the tax system has been achieved through selective forgiveness. 'Tax expenditures' are usually measured as deviations from the revenues that would have been generated under the so-called structural provisions of the tax. Congress has attached tax forgiveness provisions especially to administration bills that modified the structure of tax codes for reasons of economic policy. This modern congressional patronage has been the cost of securing programmatic changes in schedules. From 1970 to 1981 there have been 105 modifications in the direction of increasing such provisions and only 43 modifications decreasing them (Witte, 1985, ch. 12). The most generous dispensations under the individual income tax have been deductions for mortgage interest payments for home owners. Tax expenditures grew from 4.4 per cent of GNP in 1967 to 8.4 per cent in 1982. Strong presidential lobbying for the 'revenue-neutral' 1986 Tax Reform Act and the spectre of enormous deficits eliminated some of these expenditures. Many remained, however, and congressional leaders devised numerous exceptions to the reforms.

In short, patronage, meaning divisibility in benefits and the use of discretion, has run throughout American social spending, employment and taxation policies in the post-war period. In this way the post-war policies resemble those of the nineteenth century. It perhaps seems obvious that patronage has characterized government contracts for military procurement and construction. Similarly the term tax expenditures implies that small constituencies have been the beneficiaries. But patronage has also been evident to some extent in the most programmatic of spending policies, old age and survivors' insurance. For that programme, the timing of increases in benefits has frequently corresponded to elections (Derthick, 1979).[6]

Explaining the Distinctiveness of American Public Policies

Not only do people have their own ideas of what constitutes American exceptionalism in public policy. They also tend to have stereotyped views of why American exceptionalism exists. Sometimes these arguments are based on political or social characteristics deemed to be uniquely American. The most helpful of recent explanations of differences in post-war public policies focus on class struggles. Yet this perspective tends to shunt American politics into a residual category: America is a place where the political strength of labour has been decidedly inferior to the strength of capital.

The limits of the class struggle approach

The features of the social democratic model, the dominant political class struggle perspective, are well known (see Shalev, 1983). The model holds that the earlier and more extensively industrial workers become organized in centralized unions and in social democratic parties, and the more frequently that these parties hold office, the sooner and more extensive the development of the welfare state. How American conditions correspond to the model is also well known. American labour organization has been minimal compared to most capitalist democracies, with divisions between craft and industrial workers. The typical indicators of the strength of organized labour give the United States the lowest score on centralization and a low score on union density. In addition, America has had no real socialist party. In cross-national research, the United States typically scores zero on the number of years ruled by a social democratic party. For the American case, the implications of the model are generally negative: this gap in American political organization has made strong public policies impossible. The only positive statements to be made are counterfactual. Undoubtedly, the argument is true as far as it goes.

It does not go far, however, in answering the questions posed by this chapter. It cannot explain the trajectory of US public policies. Policies comparatively favourable to workers and to the disadvantaged were achieved in the late nineteenth century and in the 1930s. Yet the United States would score low on social democratic strength in both periods. The early rise of education and Civil War pensions owed little to organized labour movements and less to social democratic parties. This failure to explain initial developments is not limited to the United States. The origins of European social insurance programmes have been attributed to conservative monarchs and liberal politicians (Flora and Alber, 1981). More important, in its standard form, the model cannot explain why a supposedly bourgeois polity made an abortive bid in the 1930s to establish public policies of a social democratic kind. Similarly, even though the model works best in the post-war period, it does not explain well the characteristics of post-war American public policies. The model would expect strict market liberalism, for instance, rather than demand stimulus as an economic policy. Moreover, the model cannot explain why American provision for the retired is in some ways more favourable than such provision in Britain, where a social democratic party has frequently held office. Furthermore, the model cannot explain the character of the innovations of the 1960s during which many programmes were tailored specifically to appeal to blacks.

A major shortcoming of the model is its assumption that state capacities in the realm of public policies are well developed. According to the logic of the model, once a social democratic party gains power it has few obstacles in the way of creating a comprehensive set of public policies. It is implicit that the instruments of the state are developed well enough to implement the social policies of a transnational consensus amongst socialists. In the American case, however, state capacities have been underdeveloped. Such capacities have had to be built, else policies were pursued with the inadequate means at hand. Additionally, in its standard form, the model also plays down the fact that a labour movement can be, and occasionally has been, politically strong even in the absence of a social democratic party. American labour has frequently allied itself with political parties, especially the Democratic party since the 1930s, and when these parties have achieved power legislation favourable to workers, sometimes bordering on the social democratic, can be passed. Generally speaking, the model plays down the role of strategy within the labour movement. Labour movements make different choices at different times, the push for social policy improvements being only one possible strategy. In the American case, organized labour has often been only in the background of movements for public policy innovations and sometimes labour has opposed them.

A second political class-struggle hypothesis holds that deficiencies in American public policies have been due to the existence of a unified right-wing political party (Castles, 1982). Various categories of post-war social spending have been shown to be significantly lower in places where the right-wing parties have controlled the government. In the United States, the right-wing party is the Republican party, which has alternated in office with the centrist Democrats. This line of explanation has some explanatory advantages. It does not cordon off America from other countries whose public policies are similarly stingy. It makes sense of the fact that the twentieth-century Republican party has tended to oppose social spending policy innovations and has defined itself on the national level with its opposition to the income tax. It is helpful in explaining when waves of reform are possible; the reforms and innovations of the 1930s and 1960s came when the Republican party was not in power. And it underscores the importance of understanding historically whether and how the major constituents of the political right coalesced around political parties and how early decisions about trade and economic development influence the formation of the party system. Like the social democratic model, however, the right wing parties model has difficulty in explaining many of the specifics in the historical pattern and character of American public policies. It not only cannot account for the nineteenth-century policy developments; it is contradicted by the fact that in the nineteenth century Republicans initiated spending policies, including Civil War pensions and education. Similarly, because the argument is negative, it has trouble in explaining the character of public policies. To explain the trajectory and characteristics of American public policies, one needs to incorporate the insights of political class-struggle approach into a wider view of political parties, as well as to pay greater attention to other political institutions and processes.

A wider approach

To explain the two aspects of distinctiveness in American public policies is to answer a number of smaller questions. As far as the historical pattern of public policies is concerned, first, one must explain the rise of the public policies of the late nineteenth century. Why did they occur when they did? Second, why was this system undermined to some extent in the early twentieth century and to a greater extent during the 1930s? Third, one must account for the attempt and the failure of the new approach of the 1930s and the re-emergence of policies reminiscent of the late nineteenth century. So far as the characteristics of public policies are concerned, one must first explain why the policies of the nineteenth century took the forms that they did. Notable here is the distributive or patronage nature of policies. Second, one should account for the often racial and gender bases of policies. Third, one needs to explain why certain policies of the late twentieth century differ from their counterparts in the late nineteenth century.

Our framework emphasizes the mediating effect of state political institutions. These institutions predisposed American public policies to form certain patterns. American political institutions were characterized early on by a strong separation of powers, a lack of state executive bureaucracies and widespread manhood suffrage. These characteristics combined to lead to the early provision of patronage-based benefits geared to white men. The district representation system of Congress also encouraged, and continues to encourage, patronage policies. In addition, state institutions influenced the forms of mobilization of political groups and their strategies, as well as the mobilization of other political groups and the form and nature of the party system.

Next, the model incorporates political parties and the political party system. Political parties could overcome these predispositions; a sustained period of rule of a political party often results in the building of new state capacities and the institutionalization of new policies. At first, political parties were oriented more towards patronage than collective programmes and became more programmatic over time. And sustained party rule occurred only rarely in America. All the same, the rhythms of party politics account for much of the change in public policies, including the bid to create a social democratic scheme of policies in the 1930s and the innovations of the 1960s. An urban Democratic coalition, an American functional approximation to a social democratic party, came into power in the 1930s. This coalition accounted for programmatic policy breakthroughs. The coalition failed to be sustained, however, and its failure ensured that national policies would be replaced mainly by patronage ones; individual congressmen rather than a programmatic faction of a party took charge of policy-making. This coalition briefly rose to power again in the 1960s with similar effects.

Additionally, the extensiveness and patterns of crises have had an impact on public policies. The American experience of geopolitical crises differed substantially from most other countries. The most severe war in US history came in the middle of the nineteenth century. This created additional pressure for early public social benefits, pressure that was transformed into policy by democratic institutions. Otherwise, geopolitical crises were not as severe in the United States as they were in most large Western nations and had the effect of reinforcing previous policies. Yet the US geopolitical trajectory brought world political and economic hegemony. This situation has helped to return Congress to a position of dominance on domestic policies generally, but has given the executive an extra degree of freedom in the running of aggregate economic policies. Although for ease of presentation the following sections discuss individually the state, parties, and crises, the interaction of these theoretical components is important.

State Political Institutions

It has been frequently noted that America began with no strong and centralized bureaucracy. Executive institutions began weak. The under-development of the American bureaucratic state meant that state capacities in specific public policy areas would be relatively meagre. When the autonomy of the state in the policy-making of liberal democracies is discussed, scholars point to the contributions of bureaucrats and civil servants in the creation or reworking of public policies. Unsurprisingly, these actors were less prevalent in America than elsewhere. The processes of state-building relied to some extent on crises such as war and depression to bring power to the national state. State-building also relied on the success of reform movements, such as Progressivism, to forge new areas of bureaucratic authority. These movements were only modestly successful, and frequently prospective state-builders wanted first to overturn previous developments in public policies, including the Civil War pension system, which combined patronage and corruption. However, where state capacities were created, in which particular policy areas, often influenced the later development of public policies. The chequered growth of executive state capacities across policy areas and across levels of government had a strong impact on the pattern of American public policies.

Nevertheless, it was not so much the weakness of the state as the overall character of political institutions that influenced public policy-making. These political institutions are part of the state as it is usually defined: as a set of organizations that extract resources and extend coercive control and political authority over territories and their inhabitants. State political institutions can be more or less democratic, including or not including representative institutions with varying degrees of suffrage. Moreover, these political institutions can be structured in different ways, with powers and functions focused or separated.

Representation, voting rights and public policies

A second key concerned the history of representative democracy and voting rights. America was a leader in granting suffrage on a wide basis, and suffrage mattered. Electoral results were not merely symbolic for they decided who would man the many political offices. White male suffrage was secured by the 1830s. Yet the winning of the vote for other groups was more difficult. Black men gained the franchise in the post-Civil War reforms of the radical Republicans, but enfranchisement soon led to disenfranchisement in the South, where most blacks resided. The losing of the vote began at the end of Reconstruction (1865–76) and was largely completed by the beginning of the twentieth century (Kousser, 1974). It was not until the 1960s that the civil rights movement helped to secure voting rights for southern blacks (Morris, 1984). Women also mobilized for the suffrage in the nineteenth century. Although this movement was not completely successful until 1919, its success was permanent.

The early adoption of the vote for white males made it more likely that benefits for lower classes would be publicly provided. As has been shown in cross-national research, the granting of the vote generally leads to the extension of public benefits (Schneider, 1982; Flora and Alber, 1981). But the democratization of the electorate did not proceed smoothly, and the mobilization of groups also varied – with consequences for public policies. Early public policies reflected the lack of influence of blacks and women. Civil War pensions for women were less generous and had more restrictions, including restrictions not only for widows but for women who served in wartime non-combat roles. Similarly, blacks were excluded from most New Deal social policies. Both of these groups, unlike white males or workers, fought for the suffrage as members of distinctive groups, and public policies reflected this fact. The political empowerment of women resulted in early twentieth-century spending programmes for women which were staffed by women. In the wake of the civil rights movement, the public policy innovations of the Johnson regime explicitly appealed to blacks. These policies were partly designed to bring this group into the Democratic electoral fold.

Two aspects of American electoral institutions influenced the shape of the party system. First, technical characteristics of representation helped to ensure that only two major parties emerged. Winner-take-all electoral systems, such as that for Congress, discourage third parties; the Electoral College, the means by which presidents are elected, has frequently led third parties to ally with larger parties in order to influence the outcome (McCormick, 1986, ch. 4). As a result, third parties have been rare, and successful ones rarer. Second, the fact that the democratization of politics mainly preceded the development of national bureaucratic institutions affected the type of party system, and through it public policies. For these two processes partly determined whether political parties were geared toward providing patronage, granting divisible and discretionary benefits to constituencies, or toward programmes appealing to established groups with collective goods. Where democracy appeared much sooner than bureaucracy, as it did in the United States and Italy, political parties were disposed towards patronage policies. In places such as Germany, the opposite occurred and parties appealed to the electorate with collective programmes (Shefter, 1977). In the American case, the decentralization of government ensured that these patronage-oriented parties would be organized locally, with a network of local parties coalescing to take control of the many governments and to use them to distribute benefits and keep up the strength of the party organization.

The separation of powers

A third key initial characteristic of these state political institutions was the separation of powers in government. Legislatures and courts have exercised great authority to make governmental decisions. The powers of these institutions dwarfed the powers of bureaucracies, national or subnational (see, for example, Huntington, 1968, ch. 2). American legislatures are based on geographic units of representation; under this system the representative usually must reside in the district. Legislatures have mattered not only on the national level, but also in the subnational governments which have overlapped with the national government in their functions and hence have competed with the national government for power. Although American courts were not initially granted judicial review, the power to overturn laws, the Supreme Court appropriated this power and has used it and other powers, as have lower courts, in influencing public policy, especially in the realm of labour law. The struggle to enact modern public policies can be seen partly as bids by the executive to create central bureaucratic authority and to wrest authority from the national and state legislatures, as well as from the courts – with these other governmental actors struggling for power amongst themselves.

The nature of American legislative institutions and their strength relative to the executive and its bureaucracies promoted divisible and discretionary benefits in policies. To the extent that legislatures, with their geographical system of representation, made policies, these policies took on a distributive or patronage character rather than a programmatic one. Representatives represent their local interests. Only the strongest system of political parties can keep coalitions of individual legislators from distributing benefits amongst their constituents. Only the dominance of a party with strong programmatic tendencies, a requirement not often met in American history, has been able to induce such a system to provide the collective benefits characteristic of modern public policies. Under typical conditions, this legislative system of control helped Civil War pensions and tariffs to take a brokered character, as did many post-Second World War public policies. The set-up of Congress assumed more importance as the nineteenth-century patronage parties declined in the twentieth century.

The many overlapping legislative institutions ensured that there would be conflict over the control of public policies. This situation has impeded national control of public policies. And to the extent that nationalization has meant more generous and less intrusive ones, the system of legislative institutions has worked against that. Most state and local policies, from education onward, that have passed with the support of professional groups have been difficult to nationalize. The clearest example of this came in the 1930s. The Social Security Act mainly gave national financial support to state-level programmes (Skocpol and Amenta, 1985). Roosevelt's later attempts to nationalize social policies conflicted with previous state developments in social spending (Amenta and Skocpol, 1988). Similarly, in that period the national state did not monopolize key sources of taxation. State level innovations were advanced in both income taxation and sales taxation. Thus the overlapping powers of legislative institutions have contributed to the two-track nature of American social spending policies.

State political institutions and capitalist industrialization

The interaction between these processes of state institutionalization and the process of capitalist industrialization also had important implications for public policies. Whereas the processes of democratization, industrialization and bureaucratization were world-wide in their impact, they differed from country to country in their timing and sequence. In America, the democratization of the polity came somewhat before the industrialization of the economy, which had made great strides before the bureaucratization of the state. The fact that industrialization preceded bureaucratization no doubt had influence on the *locus* of control of early public policies. To the extent that nineteenth-century industrialization led to problems of national economic development, the devising of solutions fell to the national legislature. This is not to say that Congress was likely to solve the problems, but at least it devised policies and wrapped them in the symbolism of economic policy, regardless of their effect. The nineteenth-century tariff schedules were nothing like a rationally devised economic policy. Yet protection could not be granted by local governments and hence the national legislature and its political party managers attempted to fill the void. The early congressional control of economic policy no doubt stems from this situation.

More important, the fact that electoral democracy came before industrialization led to a bifircated form of political mobilization for workers. Locally based political parties came into being before the rise of labour and agrarian movements. Because of many centres of power, political parties organized locally to control the spoils of office. These parties mobilized the electorate according to the most salient group boundaries, ethnic and religious ones. The rise of workers' movements led to a separate form of organization. When labour movements began, they organized labour into trade unions rather than political parties (Katznelson, 1981). Partly because of this form of mobilization, these unions have been concerned chiefly with issues of organization and pay. The early rise of locally based political parties ensured that capital also would organize itself in a fragmented manner; organized capital would not be able to control policy outcomes (Vogel, 1978).

In short, the initial structure of state political institutions explains certain tendencies in American public policies. The early rise of democracy helped to bring the early achievement of generous public policies. The overlapping of legislative authority meant that national-level public policies would have to compete with policies devised at lower levels of government. The underdevelopment of bureaucracies, at the centre and the state level, and the idiosyncracies of state building ensured that autonomous policy developments would form an uneven pattern. Early manhood suffrage in the context of a weak bureaucracy assisted political parties devoted to patronage. The dominance of these parties within a certain type of legislature meant that policies would frequently take a distributive character. If American state political institutions help to explain the early rise and the patronage character of early American public policies, other aspects of the trajectory of public policies and their characteristics are left unexplained. Why was there an attempt to undo the nineteenth-century public policies? Why was there an attempt to create a nationalized scheme of public policies along social democratic lines? Why did congressional policy-making re-emerge in the post-war period? The structure of state political institutions made it seem unlikely that bids to upset the system would succeed. But they succeeded partially, and the attempt and the partial successes require explanation. To help answer these questions, one must address political parties in a wider sense than taken by the social democratic and the right-wing parties models. Our approach includes organizational characteristics of the party system and the nature of party competition, as well as the class and group nature of party support.

A Second Look at Political Parties

The place to start a discussion of American parties is with their initial organizational characteristics and the nature of inter-party conflict. In the middle of the nineteenth century, parties were locally based and oriented towards patronage benefits rather than collective programmes, although sectional and religious divisions existed. As the twentieth century progressed, parties were weakened as institutions. The organizational basis of parties was attacked throughout the twentieth century by middle-class reformers, who opposed their often illegal methods, and by party leaders concerned with more programmatic issues (Schiesl, 1977). Thus parties simultaneously became more programmatic and weaker.

The making of programmatic parties was not without obstacles. What became the right-wing party of the twentieth century, the Republican party, was a state-building and centrist party in the nineteenth century, and the Democratic party performed a similar turnaround. In the nineteenth century, the Democratic party was the main source of opposition for national spending programmes and public education. The conflicts of the formative years of the parties continued to have influence later, preventing the Democrats from making a complete transition from right to left. The dominance of one party over another has influenced the historical trajectory of American public policies. State-building and policy-making have often been effected by a political party with a sure grasp of political power (Skowronek, 1982, pp. 165–9). In the twentieth century, to pass programmatic changes in public policy required not merely that the government be controlled by the Democratic party. Instead they required a Democratic president and a Congress dominated by Democrats from areas, usually cities, where organized labour was strong. Although this coalition gained power only briefly, mainly during the 1930s, it brought major changes in public policies.

The lack of sustained party dominance has had an even greater impact on public policies. In the late nineteenth and late twentieth centuries, the absence of party dominance has been the rule. The fragmentation of American governmental powers has meant that frequently no political party or programmatic political coalition has been able to control the government. When one party or major faction within a party has controlled the national government, it has been followed by a longer period in which neither major party nor programmatic factions within major parties were able to do so. This lack of control promoted the provision of divisible benefits in both the late nineteenth and late twentieth centuries.

American parties and public policies in the nineteenth century

In Europe, the crystallization of party systems took place in the early twentieth century, with the extension of voting rights to lower orders (Lipset and Rokkan, 1967). In America, the party system, or the 'third party system' as it is known in American political science literature, had largely been set by the middle of the nineteenth century. Afterwards, no other parties were able to join the system.[7] The process of building national parties was a matter of forming coalitions of parties rooted in local politics. The national Democratic party, for instance, was little more than the concerted efforts of state and local parties to win national elections. The national party had little control over the local parties. Near the end of the century, the parties were in their heyday as vote-getting institutions. In the 1876–92 period as a whole, 77 per cent of the eligible electorate voted in presidential elections, 82 per cent outside the South (Kleppner, 1987, p. 43). Aside from characteristics of the electoral system and the caution of trade union leaders – who avoided close connections to political parties, including nascent farmer-labour parties, for fear of losing membership – the sheer strength of the two major parties helped to prevent third parties of any kind from becoming permanent contenders (Shefter, 1983; 1986).

The nineteenth-century parties were polarized along two lines. First, they were divided according to section. In the middle and late nineteenth century when the Republican party won national power, it was because of its strength in the industrial North and the Midwest, the main sources of opposition of the extension of the system of slavery. Although the Democratic party was competitive in these areas, it was strongest in the South. After the end of the Reconstruction, Republican influence there was increasingly diminished, partly because of the sectional split and especially because of the restriction of the suffrage, which resulted in a one-party South by the end of the century. Second, the party system was divided along ethnic and religious lines. People subscribing to ritualistic religions, such as Catholicism and German Lutheranism, tended to vote Democratic, and those subscribing to pietistic religions, including most strands of Protestantism, tended to vote Republican (Kleppner, 1979). This separated the two parties on questions of personal liberty, with the Republicans frequently supporting temperance legislation and the Democrats opposing all such restrictions.

Business and labour, like other organized groups, had to work within this system to gain leverage over public policies. The two major parties appealed to both upper and lower classes, drawing contributions mainly from the former and votes from the latter. Party divisions split the upper classes: the industrial elites of the North stayed Republican and the landed elites of the South became Democratic. The parties also split industrial workers along ethnic and religious lines. At the end of the nineteenth century, in the wake of the depression of 1893, industrialists and industrial workers had thrown their electoral support mainly behind the Republicans, and the party system continued to be polarized along sectional lines (Bensel, 1984; Kleppner, 1987). As parties declined in strength they became divided in different ways. Industrial workers left the Republican party in large numbers at the end of the 1920s and the beginning of the 1930s. Its nativism and the failure of its economic policies pushed industrial workers into the Democratic fold, and Democrats mobilized many working-class immigrant voters and their wives who had not previously voted (Anderson, 1979). Similarly, the Republicans, with their historical opposition to the national income tax, drew heavier support from right wing forces such as organized business groups. The Democrats, however, were still a sectional party and therefore an unlikely vehicle for policy reform and state-building. There was always a southern delegation devoted to thwarting national power and redistributive policies.

An absence of party dominance characterized the second half of the nineteenth century. The Republican party was able to control the national government only from 1861 to 1875. During this period a number of issues were settled, notably, the end of slavery, but also the tariff and the so-called money question, how to retire 'greenbacks', and the return to the gold standard (Sharkey, 1959; Unger, 1964). This was followed by a period of two-party competition lasting until 1896. During this time, the Republicans and Democrats each controlled about half of the national electorate (Kleppner, 1979). What mattered more was that only rarely did one party control both the presidency and Congress. In this sense, the Republicans ran the government only for four years, and the Democrats for two. This period of party competition, or this lack of dominance by one party, corresponded with the rise of distributive public policies, such as Civil War pensions, as the Republicans bid for support to break the electoral stalemate.

American parties and public policies in the twentieth century

The election of 1896 brought 34 years of Republican hegemony, with brief, if significant, interruptions (Burnham, 1970). The Republicans controlled the national government from 1877 to 1911 and again from 1921 until the end of the decade. For four years in the 1910s the Democrats controlled the presidency and Congress. This control was due, however, to a split within the Republicans. The Progressive party, an urban middle-class movement concerned chiefly with the reform of political parties and governmental practice, attracted enough votes to elect Democrats and to influence policies, although not enough to win a permanent place in American politics. Republican dominance meant that industrial protection remained the main economic strategy and that income taxes were kept to minimal levels. Partly as a result of these taxation policies, national spending programmes were negligible and confined to the state level, where more favourable political coalitions might conspire to enact them.

The Depression ended this period of rule and completed the process of turning the voters of large cities into Democrats. Democrats dominated the presidency and Congress for most of the next two decades. It was during this period that the break with past public policies was most thorough. The Depression and, more important, a large Democratic majority in Congress gave the administration powers to build state institutions and enact new policies. Urban and labour Democrats dominated in Congress from 1935 to 1939 and to a lesser extent from 1939 to 1943. As mentioned previously, the new economic policies involved direct controls, national employment policies were pursued, and modern, collective social spending policies were begun. By the end of the 1930s, many new programmes of public employment and social spending had been set in motion; administration planning bodies had gained sufficient tenure to devise a social democratic political agenda.

The dominance of the Democrats and their new sources of urban support eventually led to an alliance with organized labour. One obstacle to the quick cementing of an alliance was the weakness of labour. In

1933 there was little organization of labour to speak of, about 11 per cent of the non-agricultural labour force. Labour's upsurge came mainly as a result of Democratic policies to promote it. Despite the dampening effect of low economic activity on labour organization, workers streamed into the industrial unions, especially after 1935. That year saw the passage of the so-called Wagner Act, protecting union organization and authorizing collective bargaining. The process accelerated during the Second World War when labour mainly traded wage restraint for organizational gains (Brody, 1981, ch. 3). As labour organized, the connection between it and the administration and urban Democrats in Congress became closer. Yet Democratic dominance did not bring to power a cross-class coalition of workers and farmers. Partly this failure had to do with Roosevelt's initial reluctance and later inability to purge conservative Democrats, especially in the South; in that region the dominant planter class and the state Democratic parties opposed generous social spending policies as a threat to the system of labour control (Quadagno, 1988). The South was riddled with rotten boroughs where poor blacks and whites were denied the vote and political representation.

In the absence of such a cross-class coalition, to pass elements of the quasi-social-democratic agenda required the congressional presence of a labour-supported president and a coalition of *urban* Democrats in Congress.[8] Although Roosevelt was elected four consecutive times and Truman was elected in 1948, Congress met these strict standards only from 1935 to 1939, the period of greatest reform. It was close to achieving this standard from 1939 to 1943, and again from 1949 to 1951. These periods witnessed the greatest gains in collective social spending policies. With this sort of political coalition, the administration and its supporters could overcome the opposition of Republicans and rural Democrats. Needless to say, the requirements for forming such a coalition were daunting and were made more formidable by the rural bias of political institutions. For this coalition to control the 435-seat House of Representatives in the 1940s, for example, it was necessary to win almost all of the approximately 240 districts where labour had a strong electoral presence.

One can go too far in comparing the Democrats to social democratic parties. Although the two were connected electorally, neither the Democratic party nor organized labour was bound by the policies of the other, unlike most social democratic parties. The looseness of the connection between labour and party made it possible for labour to win social welfare battles in its dealings with capital and lose them in the political arena. In the immediate post-war period, labour reached the peak of its organized power. In 1945, union members accounted for 35.5 per cent of the non-agricultural labour force – eight percentage points higher than the 1938 level (US Census, 1975, p. 178). During the war,

American organized labour grew at a faster pace and was on the offensive so far as strikes were concerned, much more so than British labour (Amenta and Skocpol, 1988). Yet, unlike in Britain, American organized labour's strength with respect to capital outran the strength of its allies in the national government. Although labour pushed for strong pension and health policies in its dealings with the state and with capital in the immediate post-war period, it achieved more success with capital. This combination of public failure and private success eventually resulted in a greater selectivity in the provision of pensions and health benefits; organized industrial workers were able to add a private tier of benefits to pre-existing public ones.

In the post-Second World War period, competition between partisan factions has resembled the type of party competition prevalent in the late nineteenth century, with similar effects on public policies. For the most part, neither left-wing nor right-wing political factions have been able to achieve a sustained dominance of governmental institutions. Although Congress has mainly been dominated by the Democratic party, the presidency has shifted back and forth between the parties. The sort of overwhelming Democratic dominance of Congress characteristic of the late 1930s occurred only during the middle of the 1960s. Similarly, the right has gained complete political power only during the early 1980s.

The post-war lack of partisan control has inhibited the construction of programmatic and comprehensive policies devised by the executive and has reinforced congressional control over the making of most public spending policies. Although various local political parties, with their emphasis on patronage, have been weakened throughout the twentieth century, the patronage character of American public policies was reasserted by way of congressional control. And although some have attacked this sort of patronage as corruption, strictly speaking it is not illegal and is thus more securely founded. The breakthroughs in partisan control have accounted for the innovations and cutbacks of public policies during the period. Finally, the expansion of one spending policy, old age and survivors' insurance, was due partly to its establishment in a period of urban Democratic control and its adaptability to congressional electoral needs in a more competitive period.

The mediating influence of state political institutions and the direct influence of political parties go far in answering questions about the historical pattern and characteristics of American public policies. The character of American state political institutions has predisposed American policies to take particular directions, and American political parties have reinforced some predispositions and opposed others. Parties have influenced the pace of change and have determined many characteristics of policies. Although the American experience of crises has mainly reinforced these patterns and characteristics, crises have also exerted an independent influence on policies.

The Crises of Depression and War

Crises can bring changes in public policies in two main ways. Crises often promote state-building and hence might augur later changes in public policies. During major crises political power shifts to the centre of the system, with national authorities gaining at the expense of others. The second way is more indirect. A crisis often implies political failure, which in turn augurs changes in public policies. Previous policies and institutions are often discredited and new approaches attempted, frequently by new political regimes. Most major shifts in American electoral behaviour have come in the wake of depressions or wars, but the crisis itself is not as important as the direction of the political changes. When crises are viewed in this way and when American crises are placed in comparative perspective, it is the peculiar pattern of American geopolitical crises and their outcomes that have influenced the trajectory and character of public policies. Depressions have had less influence. Although crises have had to some extent independent effects, they have had a greater impact when working in tandem with developments in state political institutions and political parties. And the initial weakness of the national American state and the initial dispersion of power in the American system has magnified the importance of crises.

To some extent the influence of geopolitical crises on American public policies has been negative. American geopolitical crises have not been as severe as those experienced by other large countries. America started from a favourable, if isolated, geopolitical position; no major opponent faced it on the North American continent. It took relatively little effort to subdue and expropriate the native peoples and, aside from the Civil War, the largest nineteenth-century war was against a militarily feeble former Spanish colony, Mexico. The weakness of early opponents had a mildly expansive effect on early public spending policies. A great deal of territory and other land-based resources came under the control of the national state. But this occurred without building up state military and bureaucratic institutions. The resources at the disposal of the state gave the United States a comparative advantage in the early development of distributive public policies; the lack of opponents gave state-builders few opportunities to build national executive institutions.

Similarly, the world wars of the twentieth century made less of an impact in the United States than in other places. In both wars, the United States entered later, with a lesser degree of economic mobiliza-tion and, like Britain, on the winning side of both world wars. Unlike

Germany and Japan, the United States has never lost a major war and has never been conquered or, leaving aside Pearl Harbor, invaded. As was the case in the nineteenth century, the comparatively minor influence of the world wars did not stimulate the sharpening of the instruments of the American executive state. That America ended up on the winning side of most wars reaffirmed American state political institutions. Having passed the test of war, regardless of the reasons for passing, the institutions were perceived as working and therefore requiring no major changes (see Marwick, 1974). Also, no conquerors came to rebuild them.

This geopolitical story might lead one to believe that war has had a similar, though somewhat less severe, impact on America as it has had on Britain. This has not been the case. In Britain, modern wars came in an ascending pattern of severity, from the Boer War to the Second World War. In America the influence of war and its aftermath has taken a pattern that contrasts with the British pattern. So far as civilian casualties were concerned, America's greatest war came earlier – in the middle of the nineteenth century. The Civil War claimed about 1.71 per cent of the American population; this figure compares to the 0.13 per cent and 0.31 per cent killed in the First and Second World Wars respectively (Singer and Small, 1972). On the other hand, the smaller American wars, in Korea and Vietnam, which were analogous to the Boer War, have come in the late twentieth century. As a result, the greatest pressure for compensatory public policies came earlier in America, before the world had gained much experience with modern public policies. This pressure was translated through a state with democratic representation and a party system that dictated the form and the timing of adoption of such benefits.

Finally, the outcomes of wars have pushed the US and Britain in opposite geopolitical directions. At the end of the Second World War, the United States was the major world economic and military power. Having accepted world leadership, a role it eschewed after the First World War, the United States built executive institutions devoted to geopolitical purposes. The executive branch, dominated as it was by the Democrats during the Second World War and immediately afterwards, had to pay closer attention to international events. In its battles with Congress, it used its influence to gain foreign economic and military aid as well as expanded military programmes and, relatively speaking, turned its attention away from the making of domestic public policies. Domestic policies attracted the most executive attention in the 1930s, and thus Congress was given more leeway in the making of such policies. So, in addition to the post-war difficulties in achieving political coalitions in favour of expanded and programmatic domestic public policies, geopolitical developments helped to return power over domestic policy-making to Congress.

The mobilization for and the geopolitical impact of the Second World War had its greatest independent effect on American employment and economic policies. The effects were twofold and worked in opposite directions. On the one hand, the short-term full employment brought by war helped to undermine the direct public employment programmes of the Depression period. These were no longer immediately necessary and were eliminated when a conservative Congress was elected. The post-war resurgence of Congress doubtless would have restricted these executively controlled programmes had they survived the war.

On the other hand, the results of the war brought American political and economic predominance, and the international economic institutions of the post-war period were devised in the interest of the United States. These arrangements have made it easier to run stimulative fiscal policies. For instance, the gold standard was abandoned when it came into conflict with deficit spending. In addition, the new American geopolitical role has required permanently higher levels of military spending.[9] These programmes have meshed neatly with the needs and constituencies of Congress.

Analysts of American public policies often make the connection between depression and changes in public policy (Leman, 1977), claiming that the Great Depression stirred the American system into action. No doubt this is partly true, as crises often sanction state-building. And many of Roosevelt's reforms were aimed partly at recovery. However, it is difficult to separate the direct effects of the Depression on policy from the political formation that accompanied it. It helped to bring Roosevelt and the urban Democrats to power. Moreover, the Depression was a worldwide phenomenon and was severe in all industrial countries. Therefore depression in itself cannot explain why some countries, such as Germany, Sweden and the United States, broke with orthodox economic and fiscal policies and why others, such as France and Britain, did not (Gourevitch, 1986; Weir and Skocpol, 1985). A similar logic applies to the economic crises of the late nineteenth and late twentieth centuries.

Conclusion

The resemblance of current American public policies to nineteenth-century ones suggests questions about the prospects of change. Will the current policies be undermined? Will they be augmented by other modern innovations such as health insurance? Will they continue indefinitely? These questions can be approached from two directions. One can look at the internal logic of the policies to determine whether they are stable. One can ask whether the conditions of party politics and geopolitical crises that promote change in public policies are likely to occur. Both directions indicate that slight modifications of current policies are in order, but no fundamental changes.

The logic of the policies suggests the continuation of distributive policies, but of a less lucrative nature. On the one hand, the current system of congressional patronage is more stable on two counts than the nineteenth-century system of party patronage. First, the most flagrant corruption has been removed. Despite the often repeated claims about unscrupulous welfare beneficiaries, the fraudulence of Civil War pensions has not been matched by current policies. Accordingly, although there have been complaints about the financing of congressional campaigns, there has been no sustained movement to end congressional patronage procedures. Second, political parties and fractions of political parties are no longer in control of distributive programmes. In the nineteenth century, the party caucus was a key mechanism for making decisions about distributive policies. In the recent period the system has responded to coalitions of individual congressmen. There is nothing to attack – except Congress, an unlikely target.

On the other hand, unlike the case in the late nineteenth century, the many functions of the tax code have weakened rather than reinforced the system. The weakness of the US tax state argues against the profusion of greater distributive spending and against the augmentation of collective benefits. With respect to total tax receipts as percentage of GDP, the United States ranked 11th amongst the OECD nations in 1950 and dropped to 14th in 1980 – before the large tax cuts of the current administration. The American tax state grew at a slower rate than all but four OECD countries from 1950 to 1980. American taxes, excluding social security contributions, have grown little since 1950 (OECD, 1981, pp. 11, 13). The American revenue workhorse, the social security contribution, which has grown at a rate higher than the average OECD country, is not likely to make up the gap in the future. The greatest increases in social security taxes have come only after new benefits have been legislated. The last major increase in benefits was legislated in 1972. To pay for this series of benefit increases, tax increases were passed in 1977 and again after the elections of 1982.

One source of change seems unlikely to upset the system. The advantages of geopolitical crises have disappeared with the possibility of the recurrence of such crises. World wars like those of the first half of the twentieth century cannot be repeated, and the small wars of the superpower tend to drain resources rather than to generate new ones (Wilensky, 1975, ch. 4). There will be no innovations of the tax system due to war if the Vietnam War and the 1980s military build-up indicate the future. Although military spending will probably not grow, it will remain at a high level. If the impact of world politics suggests anything, it is that the United States will probably lose its comparative advantage in running deficits as its economic power continues to decline and other countries, such as Germany and Japan, begin to gain a voice in world economic affairs commensurate with their economic strength. Although the future may hold additional economic decline, a depression of the order of the 1930s is unlikely.

The final source of change, the rise of pro-social policy political coalition, is less unlikely. On the one hand, the strength of organized labour has slumped to its lowest point in the post-war period. Job security and arresting the slide in union organization have become more important to the labour movement than improvements in public policies.. Moreover, urban areas have declined relatively in population and congressional representation. Furthermore, the reforms in the last two decades in the process of nominating presidential candidates do not ensure a Democratic candidate will form a strong alliance with labour. On the other hand, the victory of democracy in the South has meant more black representatives and Congressmen relying on the votes of blacks who generally favour generous and activist public policies. Constructing a left-wing political coalition will not be impossible, but will undoubtedly be difficult and will depend partly on the appearance of fortuitous disasters that the electorate attributes to the policies and rule of Republicans and the right. Even if a left-wing coalition comes to power, unless it rules for a long period of time the public policies of the United States will continue to have one foot in the nineteenth century.

Notes

For helpful comments and criticisms on a previous draft, the authors thank Bruce G. Carruthers, Larry J. Griffin, Sunita Parikh, the members of the Workshop on Comparative Politics at the University of Chicago, and the members of the Workshop on the Comparative History of Public Policies.

1   The definition of patronage is drawn from Shefter (1983).
2   The following paragraphs on the history of pension legislation draw on Glasson (1918) and Oliver (1917).,
3   Even when civil service reform succeeded, it usually specified that those previously holding positions would keep them.
4   The following paragraphs on tariffs draw on Ratner (1972), Terill (1973), Rothman (1966, ch. 3), Poulshock (1962), Summers (1953) and Taussig (1905).
5   This section relies heavily on Amenta and Skocpol (1988).
6   It is no surprise that the literature on the so-called Tufte hypothesis, including Tufte's own work, concerning the influence of elections on spending has concentrated so heavily on the post-Second World War United States.

7 During the 1850s, the Republicans were established and permanently joined the Democrats to constitute the American party system. Of course these parties changed considerably and American political science has characterized these changes as the creation of (five) different party systems. Although the four periods of public policy correspond to some extent with these party systems, they do not overlap completely. The characterizations here are motivated only partly by electoral conditions.

8 For an extended discussion of this point, see Amenta and Skocpol (1988).

9 Compare the argument of Russett (1970). He claims that higher American military spending in the post-war period is due to the 'ratchet effect', that is, to a political inability to decrease military spending after a war, not to an expanded American geopolitical role.

References

Amenta, E. and Skocpol, T. 1988: Redefining the New Deal: World War II and the Development of Social Provision in the United States. In M. Weir, A.S. Orloff, and T. Skocpol (eds) *The Politics of Social Policy in the United States.* Princeton, NJ: Princeton University Press, ch. 3.

Anderson, K. 1979: *The Creation of a Democratic Majority 1928–1936.* Chicago: University of Chicago Press.

Asher, R. 1971: Workmen's Compensation in the United States, 1880–1935. Ph.D. dissertation, University of Minnesota.

Bailey, S.K. 1950: *Congress Makes A Law: The Story Behind the Employment Act of 1946.* New York: Columbia University Press.

Bensel, R. 1984: *Sectionalism and American Political Development, 1880–1980.* Madison, Wis.: University of Wisconsin Press.

Brandeis, E. 1935: Labor Legislation. In J.R. Commons (ed.) *History of Labor in the United States, 1896–1932.* vol. 3. New York: Macmillan, 399–700.

Bridges, A. 1984: *A City in the Republic: Antebellum New York and the Origins of Machine Politics.* New York: Cambridge University Press.

Brody, D. 1981: *Workers in Industrial America: Essays on the Twentieth Century Struggle.* New York: Oxford University Press.

Burnham, W.D. 1970: *Critical Elections and the Mainsprings of American Politics.* New York: W.W. Norton.

Castles, F.G. 1982: The Impact of Parties on Public Expenditure. In F.G. Castles (ed.) *The Impact of Parties.* Beverly Hills, CA: Sage, 21–96.

Castles, F.G . 1985: *The Working Class and Welfare: Reflection on the Political Development of the Welfare State in Australia and New Zealand, 1890–1980.* Wellington: Port Nicholson Press.

Derthick, M. 1979: *Policymaking For Social Security.* Washington DC: The Brookings Institution.

Dillingham, W.P. 1952: *Federal Aid to Veterans, 1917–1941.* Gainesville, Fl: University of Florida Press.

Flora, P. and Alber, J. 1981: Modernization, Democratization, and the Development of Welfare States in Western Europe. In P. Flora and A.J.

Heidenheimer (eds) *The Development of the Welfare State in Europe and America*. New Brunswick, NJ: Transaction Books, 37–81.

Glasson, W.H. 1918: *Federal Military Pensions in the United States*. New York: Oxford University Press.

Griffin, L.J. 1984: USECON84, Machine Readable Data File. Indiana University.

Gourevitch, P. 1986: *Politics in Hard Times: Comparative Responses to International Economic Crises*. Ithaca, NY: Cornell University Press.

Haveman, R.H. (ed.) 1977: *A Decade of Federal Anti-Poverty Programs: Achievements, Failures, Lessons*. New York: Academic Press.

Hawley, E. 1966: *The New Deal and the Problem of Monopoly*. Princeton, NJ: Princeton University Press.

Heidenheimer, A.J. 1981: Education and Social Security Entitlements in Europe and America. In P. Flora and A.J. Heidenheimer (eds) *The Development of the Welfare State in Europe and America*. New Brunswick, NJ: Transaction Books, 269–304.

Huntington, S.P. 1968: *Political Order in Changing Societies*. New Haven, Conn.: Yale University Press.

Katznelson, I. 1981: *City Trenches: Urban Politics and the Patterning of Class in the United States*. New York: Pantheon.

Keller, M. 1977: *Affairs of State: Public Life in Late Nineteenth-Century America*. Cambridge, Mass.: Harvard University Press.

Keman, H. 1982: Securing the Safety of the Nation State. In F.G. Castles (ed.) *The Impact of Parties*. Beverly Hills, CA: Sage, 177–224.

Keyssar, A. 1986: *Out of Work: The First Century of Unemployment in Massachusetts*. Cambridge and New York: Cambridge University Press.

Kleppner, P. 1979: *The Third Electoral System, 1853–1892*. Chapel Hill, NC: University of North Carolina Press.

Kleppner, P. 1987: *Continuity and Change in Electoral Politics, 1893–1928*. New York: Greenwood Press.

Korpi, W. and Shalev, M. 1980: Strikes, Power, and Politics, in the Western Nations, 1900–1976. *Political Power and Social Theory*, 1, 301–34.

Kousser, J.M. 1974: *The Shaping of Southern Politics: Suffrage Restriction and the Establishment of the One-Party South 1880–1910*. New Haven, Conn. and London: Yale University Press.

Leff, M.H. 1973: Consensus for Reform: The Mothers' Pension Movement in the Progressive Era. *Social Service Review*, 47, 397–417.

Leff, M.H. 1984: *The Limits of Symbolic Reform: The New Deal and Taxation, 1933–1939*. Cambridge: Cambridge University Press.

Leman, C. 1977: Patterns of Policy Development: Social Security in the United States and Canada. *Public Policy*, 25, 261–91.

Lipset, S.M. and Rokkan, S. 1967: Cleavage Structures, Party Systems, and Voter Alignments. In S.M. Lipset and S. Rokkan (eds) *Party Systems and Voter Alignments*. New York: The Free Press.

McCormick, R.C. 1986: Political Parties in American History. In R.C. McCormick, *The Party Period and Public Policy: American Politics From the Age of Jackson to the Progressive Era*, New York: Oxford University Press, ch. 4.

Marwick, A. 1974: *War and Social Change in the Twentieth Century: A Comparative*

Study of Britain, France, Germany, Russia, and the United States. London: Macmillan.

May, D.L. 1981: *From New Deal to New Economics: The American Liberal Response to the Recession of 1937.* New York: Garland Publishing.

Meyer, J.W., Tyack, D., Nagel, J. and Gordon, A. 1979: Public Education as Nation-Building in America: Enrolments and Bureaucratization in the American States, 1870–1930. *American Journal of Sociology*, 85 (3), 591–613.

Morris, A.D. 1984: *The Origins of the Civil Rights Movement: Black Communities Organizing for Change.* New York: The Free Press.

Myles, J. 1988: The Politics of the Retirement Wage: Understanding America's Modern Welfare State. In M. Weir, A.S. Orloff, and T. Skocpol (eds) *The Politics of Social Policy in the United States*, Princeton, NJ: Princeton University Press.

Nelson, D. 1969: *Unemployment Insurance: The American Experience, 1915–1935.* Madison, Wis.: University of Wisconsin Press.

The New York Times 1987: Economic Expansion in U.S. Continues Into a 59th Month. 1 October, 1, 32.

Oliver, J.W. 1917: History of Civil War Military Pensions, 1861–1885, *Bulletin of the University of Wisconsin*, 844, History Series, 1.

OECD 1981: *Long-Term Trends in Tax Revenues of OECD Member Countries, 1955–1980.* Paris: OECD.

OECD 1984: *Historical Statistics, 1960–1983.* Paris: OECD.

OECD 1985: *Social Expenditure, 1960–1990: Problems of Growth and Control.* Paris: OECD.

Peacock, A. T. and Wiseman, J. 1961: *The Growth of Public Expenditure in the United Kingdom.* Princeton, NJ: Princeton University Press.

Poulshock, S.W. 1962: Pennsylvania and the Politics of the Tariff, 1880–1888. *Pennsylvania History*, 29 (July), 291–305.

Quadagno, J.S. 1988: From Old-Age Assistance to Supplemental Security Income. In M. Weir, A.S. Orloff and T. Skocpol (eds) *The Politics of Social Policy in the United States*, Princeton, NJ: Princeton University Press, ch. 8.

Ratner, S. 1972: *The Tariff in American History.* New York: Van Nostrand.

Ross, D.R.B. 1969: *Preparing For Ulysses: Politics and Veterans During World War II.* New York: Columbia University Press.

Rothman, D.J. 1966: *Politics and Power: The United States Senate, 1869–1901.* Cambridge, Mass.: Harvard University Press.

Rubinson, R. 1986: Class Formation, Politics, and Institutions: Schooling in the United States. *American Journal of Sociology*, 92 (3), 519–58.

Russett, B.M. 1970: *What Price Vigilance? The Burdens of National Defense.* New Haven, Conn.: Yale University Press.

Schatschneider, E.E. 1963: *Politics, Pressures, Tariffs.* Hamden, Conn.: Archon Books.

Schiesl, M.J. 1977: *The Politics of Efficiency: Municipal Administration and Reform in America, 1880–1920.* Berkeley, CA: University of California Press.

Schmidt, M.G. 1989: West Germany: The Politics of the Middle Way. In this volume, ch. 3.

Schneider, S.K. 1982: The Sequential Development of Social Programs in Eighteen Welfare States. *Comparative Social Research*, 5, 195–220.

Schwarz, J.E. 1983: *America's Hidden Success: A Reassessment of Twenty Years of Public Policy*. New York: W. W. Norton.

Shalev, M. 1983: The Social Democratic Model and Beyond. *Comparative Social Research*, 6, 315–51.

Sharkey, R.P., 1959: *Money, Class, and Party: An Economic Study of Civil War and Reconstruction*. Baltimore, Md: The Johns Hopkins Press.

Shefter, M. 1977: Party and Patronage: Germany, Italy, and England. *Politics & Society*, 7, 404–51.

Shefter, M. 1983: Regional Receptivity to Reform: the Legacy of the Progressive Era. *Political Science Quarterly*, 98, 459–83.

Shefter, M. 1986: Trade Unions and Political Machines: The Organization and Disorganization of the American Working Class in the Late Nineteenth Century. In I. Katznelson and A. Zolberg (eds) *Working-Class Formation: Nineteenth-Century Patterns in Western Europe and the United States*, Princeton, NJ: Princeton University Press, ch. 6.

Singer, J.D. and Small, M. 1972: *The Wages of War: 1816–1965: A Statistical Handbook*. New York: Wiley.

Skocpol, T. and Finegold, K. 1982: State Capacity and Economic Intervention in the Early New Deal. *Political Science Quarterly*, 97, 255–78.

Skocpol, T. and Amenta, E. 1985: Did Capitalists Shape Social Security? *American Sociological Review*, 50.

Skocpol, T., Sutton, J.R., Orloff, A.S., Amenta, E. and Carruthers, B.G. 1987: A Precocious Welfare State? Civil War Benefits in the United States, 1870s–1920s. Presented at the Annual Meeting of the American Sociological Association. Chicago.

Skowronek, S. 1982: *Building a New American State: The Expansion of National Administrative Capacities, 1877–1920*. Cambridge: Cambridge University Press.

Starr, P. 1982: *The Social Transformation of American Medicine*. New York: Basic.

Stein, H. 1969: *The Fiscal Revolution in America*. Chicago: University of Chicago Press.

Stein, H. 1984: *Presidential Economics: The Making of Economic Policy From Roosevelt to Reagan and Beyond*. New York: Simon & Schuster.

Stevens, B. 1988: Blurring the Boundaries: How Federal Social Policy Has Shaped Private Sector Welfare Benefits. In M. Weir, A.S. Orloff, and T. Skocpol (eds), *The Politics of Social Policy in the United States*, Princeton, NJ: Princeton University Press, ch. 4.

Summers, F.P. 1953: *William L. Wilson and Tariff Reform*. New Brunswick, NJ: Rutgers University Press.

Taussig, F.W. 1905: *The Tariff History of the United States*. New York: Putnam.

Terill, T.E. 1973: *The Tariff, Politics, and American Foreign Policy, 1874–1901*. Westport, Conn.: Greenwood Press.

Unger, I. 1964: *The Greenback Era: A Social and Political History of American Finance, 1865–1879*. Princeton, NJ: Princeton University Press.

US Bureau of the Census 1975: *Historical Statistics of the United States, Colonial Times to 1970*. Washington DC: US Government Printing Office.

US Council of Economic Advisors 1980: *The Economic Report of the President, January 1980*. Washington DC: US Government Printing Office.

Vogel, D. 1978: Why Businessmen Distrust Their State: The Political Consciousness of American Corporate Executives. *British Journal of Political Science*, 8, 45–78.

Weir, M. and Skocpol, T. 1985: State Structures and the Possibilities for 'Keynesian' Responses to the Great Depression in Sweden, Britain, and the United States. In P.B. Evans, D. Rueschemeyer, and T. Skocpol (eds) *Bringing the State Back In*, Cambridge and New York: Cambridge University Press, 107–63.

White, L. 1958: *The Republican Era, 1869–1901: A Study in Administrative History*. New York: Macmillan.

Wilensky, H.L. 1975: *The Welfare State and Equality: Structural and Ideological Roots of Public Expenditures*. Berkeley and Los Angeles: University of California Press.

Witte, J.F. 1985: *The Politics and Development of the Federal Income Tax*. Madison, Wis.: University of Wisconsin Press.

Index

Index by Geraldine Beare